THE GRAND JIHAD

Praise for *The Grand Jihad*

"Our freedom is under assault as never before. For years, we've known about the Left's campaign to undermine our constitutional liberties and about radical Islam's campaign to destroy our way of life. What we now see, thanks to Andy McCarthy's piercing eye and gripping narrative, is that these campaigns work together, seamlessly. *The Grand Jihad* tells a story America needs to hear."

—Rush Limbaugh

"Andy McCarthy has written one of the most important exposés of the dangers from and deception perpetrated by Islamist groups in the United States in a diabolical alliance with the left wing of American politics. McCarthy brilliantly recounts and dissects the origins of the growing Islamist threat in the United States, abetted by many in the media and government. Once I opened the first page, I could not put it down. This book is mesmerizing and deeply shocking—written in a brilliant narrative that won't let you stop reading until you finish the book. It is one of the most important books written in the last 20 years. McCarthy has produced an unparalleled masterpiece that every American must read. His book finally provides the American public with the first truthful narrative of Islamic threat that government officials have minimized for years, and he exposes Islamic ideological overlaps with the current Administration. This book is critical to the safety of our country. The American public owes McCarthy an invaluable debt of gratitude for writing the definitive book on the history and threat of Islamism in the US. His devastating analysis of the ulterior agenda secretly promoted by Islamic groups, in collaboration with and encouraged by the Obama Administration, should be required reading by every American citizen."

—Steven Emerson
Bestselling author of *American Jihad: The Terrorists Living Among Us*, and five other books; Executive Director of the Investigative Project on Terrorism

THE GRAND JIHAD

How Islam and the Left Sabotage America

Andrew C. McCarthy

Encounter Books   New York • London

First American edition published in 2010 by Encounter Books,
an activity of Encounter for Culture and Education, Inc.,
a nonprofit, tax exempt corporation.
Encounter Books website address: www.encounterbooks.com

Manufactured in the United States and printed on
acid-free paper. The paper used in this publication meets
the minimum requirements of ANSI/NISO Z39.48-1992
(R 1997) (*Permanence of Paper*).

FIRST AMERICAN EDITION

LIBRARY OF CONGRESS CATALOGING-IN-PUBLICATION DATA

McCarthy, Andrew C.
The grand Jihad : how Islam and the left sabotage America / by Andrew C.
McCarthy.
p. cm.
Includes bibliographical references and index.
ISBN-13: 978-1-59403-377-3 (hardcover : alk. paper)
ISBN-10: 1-59403-377-3 (hardcover : alk. paper) 1. Terrorism—United States.
2. Jihad. 3. Revolutionaries—United States. 4. Socialism—United States. 5.
Obama, Barack. I. Title.
HV6432.M33 2010
322.4'20973—dc22
2010003842

10 9 8 7 6 5 4 3 2 1

For Alexandra

CONTENTS

1. With Willing Submission 1
2. Islamism: A Triumph of Hope over Experience? 19
3. Jihad Is Our Way 43
4. Eliminating and Destroying the Western Civilization from Within. 57
5. We Will Conquer America through *Dawa* 83
6. Faustian Bargain 105
7. E Pluribus Umma 121
8. The American Doesn't Know Anything. 133
9. Not Such Strange Bedfellows 157
10. Islam and the Revolutionary Left 171
11. The Ties That Bind 187
12. Muslim World Traveler 201
13. Islam, the Left, and Apocalypse in Kenya. 213
14. Social Justice, Obama Style 221
15. The "Mountain" Goes to Mohammed 239
16. Rigging the Numbers 255
17. Stars of State and Screen 265
18. Flying Imams: The Sabotage Campaign in Action. 277
19. No Stronger Retrograde Force Exists in the World 299
20. On Language 313
21. The Enclave of Minnesota 331
22. Back in the Fold 347
23. Isolated Extremists 357
Epilogue 367
Notes 377
Index 437

Fight those who believe not
In Allah nor the Last Day,
Nor hold that forbidden
Which hath been forbidden
By Allah and His Messenger,
Nor acknowledge the Religion
Of Truth, from among
The People of the Book,
Until they pay the Jizya*
With willing submission,
And feel themselves subdued.

—The Koran, Sura 9:29 (The "Verse of the Sword")

---

* The *jizya* is a tribute (or poll-tax) appropriated by Muslim authorities from *dhimmis*—
i.e., non-Muslims permitted to live in Islamic lands—to provide for the *dhimmis*' mainte-
nance and remind them of their inferior status.

chapter one

WITH WILLING SUBMISSION

A nd so he bowed.

Barack Hussein Obama swept into the royal reception hall. With the election won and power assumed, it was suddenly all right to hype "Hussein" again, and the new president had adjusted accordingly. All successful politicians are manipulators of language, of course, but even masters of the game had to marvel at Obama's prowess. This wasn't just the routine squaring of "equal protection" with "affirmative action" or transforming "abortion" into "choice." This guy had actually managed to morph his own name from calling card to epithet and back in nothing flat, as if it were the most natural thing in the world. Which, for him, it was. No wonder that even here, in Buckingham Palace, he was the

center of rapt attention, as he had been for each of the seventy-two days since his inauguration. In fact, it had been this way ever since his improbable run caught fire two years before.
Suddenly, his purposeful strut came to a halt. Then it happened, for all to see.

The 44th President of the United States of America bowed deeply, reverentially, before King Abdullah bin Abdul Azziz, Keeper of the Two Holy Mosques, the absolute monarch of the Kingdom of Saudi Arabia.

The prostration was all the more shocking beneath these vaulted ceilings. The leaders of the world's richest nations—mostly Western democracies along with Abdullah's police state—were in London for the G-20 Summit. They were hobnobbing cordially but, unlike America's president, with their amour-propre very much intact along the gilded walls, bedecked by portraits of Britain's heroes.

What could Obama have been thinking instead? That there was an American presidency owed to sheer defiance of this majestic setting. That there was a United States owed to America's exceptionalism—the historically unique determination, forged in the blood of patriots, to refuse submission to a tyrannical power. This history is the steel in America's backbone. It is why United States presidents look foreign royalty straight in the eye, with a dignity befitting leadership of the world's most powerful, most munificent, most freedom-loving nation. They don't bow.

Obama had seemed to grasp that . . . at least when it came to the United Kingdom, that bastion of Western imperialism so reviled by his Kenyan Marxist forebears. At their first encounter the day before, the president had appropriately greeted Queen Elizabeth II with a steady handshake, while his wife pressed self-regard to the point of impropriety, presuming a huggy familiarity with the sovereign. Michelle's faux pas, endured with characteristic grace by the queen, might have faded unnoticed if not for Obama's other flashes of indifference—no, of hostility—to the sensibilities of America's staunchest ally. For this president, it was plainly not a priority to reaffirm the special Anglo-American relationship, long the linchpin of global security. That was the old order under Western leadership, the order this herald of "change" had come to dismantle.

In his first days in office, the new president expelled from the White House a bronze bust of Winston Churchill, lent to the United States by the former Prime Minister Tony Blair in the wake of the 9/11 attacks. Stunned British diplomats implored the new administration to keep this symbol of trans-Atlantic solidarity—as British soldiers continued fighting side-by-side with their American allies in the war on terror. Curtly, Obama staffers told them there was no room in the White House's 55,000 square feet for it.

Shortly afterwards, Obama hosted Prime Minister Gordon Brown in Washington with a jarring lack of ceremony. Brown, like Obama, is a committed man of the Left, and one whose Labour government then teetered on the brink. No matter: no state dinner, no customary joint press conference, and no show of support. The president, moreover, was downright bizarre in the exchange of gifts between heads of state. He bestowed on the prime minister a set of American movie DVDs that were not formatted to play on British machines. And what would a new president—veteran of less than four years in the Senate (most of which were spent campaigning for higher office)—give Elizabeth II, queen for over a half-century of the United Kingdom and what are now fifteen sovereign states? Why, an iPod loaded with recordings of some of Obama's favorite speeches . . . by Obama, of course.

It was different—very different—with Abdullah.

As the French President Nicolas Sarkozy and a cluster of diplomats looked on, agog, Obama prostrated himself waist-deep before the grinning, eighty-four-year-old Saudi despot with an ostentation that rendered even more laughable than usual the evasions of Robert Gibbs, the White House press-secretary, who dutifully accused the videotape of lying.

Didn't the "post-racial" new president know that Saudia Arabia was still officially in the slave trade when Obama had been born in 1961 (and that the practice has been unofficially indulged ever since)? Through a series of post-World War I routs, Abd al-Aziz ibn Saud, then the family dynast, cobbled the "Kingdom" together from former British protectorates and the last vestiges of what had been Ottoman domination of the Arabian Peninsula. Still ruled today by the House of Saud, it is one of the world's most repressive, discriminatory, anti-Semitic regimes. It is, furthermore, a regime that, since the 1960s, has spent tens of billions of dollars on a sedulous campaign to undermine American constitutional democracy.

The place is a money-machine rather than a forgotten desert wasteland due to the discovery of vast oil reserves, finally developed in the 1950s by the U.S. and the U.K.—the Saudis having been too backwards to do the job themselves, then too narrow-minded to build a diverse, productive economy once they'd appropriated the American and British handiwork. Oil is America's economic lifeblood, and as the United States shifted over the decades from net producer to net importer, American presidents had taken to blandishing Saudi royals with red-carpet attentions. That's distasteful, but it neither explains nor is on a par with Obama's subservient display: The new president's supplication occurred with oil prices in free-fall during a global recession.

So, of all the planet's potentates, why would an American president demean his station in homage to *this* one? Because

Saudi Arabia is the cradle of Islam. More specifically, it is the bottomless purse and symbolic crown of a movement which aims at nothing less than supplanting Western political, economic, and cultural values. The subversion of those values is Obama's fondest wish: the work of his presidency, the Hope behind the Change. The president was bowing to a shared dream.

Supremacism and Dhimmitude

The cities of Mecca and Medina are Abdullah's trust. They are Islam's most sacred sites, the "Two Holy Mosques": respectively, the birthplace of Mohammed in 571 A.D. and the sanctuary where converts to the prophet's new religion—Allah's *deen*—fled under siege nearly fifty years later, hardening both their resolve and their scriptures in preparation for an eventual violent return and conquest. Mecca is the locus of the Kaaba, toward which all Muslims, wherever on earth they may be, turn to recite their daily prayers. It is the place to which all able-bodied Muslims are required, at least once in their lives, to make the Hajj pilgrimage—as millions do each year.

Non-Muslim tourists, however, are barred from both cities. Only believers are deemed worthy of entering. To most people, that might seem downright immoderate. It might even make the most engagement-obsessed president rethink that whole bowing business. After all, imagine the howls from our elite "Religion of Peace" cheering section if Muslims were banned from, say, Rome or Washington.

Americans, however, are not supposed to see it that way. Sure, your religion may be mocked with abandon—the Christmas crèche cast as a threat to the Constitution, the Jewish state equated with racism. Not Islam, though. This is their faith, Americans are told, and we're simply expected to accept its, er, eccentricities. And by the way, it is the Islamic faith we are talking about here, not some purported perversion of it. The supremacist edict that bans non-Muslims from Islam's core territories was not, after all, al Qaeda's idea. It comes, undeniably, from Islam itself: "The pagans are unclean," instructs the Koran's Sura 9:28, "so let them not . . . approach the Sacred Mosque." Our "moderate" friends, the Saudis, enforce this injunction without a hint of apology, in the same way they insist that a just resolution of the Israeli/Palestinian dispute must include a purging of Israeli settlements from enlarged Palestinian territories while the heretofore Jewish state is coerced into granting a suicidal "right of return" to millions of Palestinians—the "one-state solution" to be implemented, without firing a shot, by democratic means.

Grand Ayatollah Ali al-Sistani, Islam's most influential Shiite cleric, makes even more explicit the dehumanizing leitmotif of Muslim scripture. Relying on centuries of Shia scholarship, he teaches that non-Muslims should not be touched, much less associated with. They are considered in the same category as "urine, feces, semen, dead bodies, blood, dogs, pigs, alcoholic liquors, and 'the sweat of an animal who persistently eats filth.'"[1] You don't like that? You'll love this: The United States government deems Sistani to be our key "moderate" ally in the new Iraq.

In the Sunni tradition, more preponderant by far than Shiism among the world's 1.4 billion Muslims, the Saudi monarchy is Islam's physical, financial, and moral guardian. Islam is the irreducible core of what King Abdullah represents to the world. The House of Saud was built on a mid-eighteenth-century alliance between its patriarch, Muhammad ibn Saud, and the Muslim scholar Muhammad ibn Abd al-Wahhab, founder of Wahhabism. This creed hearkens back to the practices of Islam's founding generations. To this day, Wahhabism remains Saudi Arabia's official

religion, and the Kingdom claims the Koran as its only constitu-
tion.² Thus, the tenets of Islam are strictly enforced.

In cracking the whip, the regime gets enthusiastic support
from the *Mutaween*, the Commission for Promotion of Virtue
and Prevention of Vice. It is an Islamic police force, several thousand strong, that monitors the various niceties of sharia, Islam's
divinely ordained law—including dress codes, prayer observance,
and restrictions on women's travel and even driving. Interestingly,
the basis for the driving prohibition is a fatwa—or Islamic religious edict—issued by the late Abd al-Aziz bin Abdullah bin Baz,
who was appointed Grand Mufti of Saudi Arabia by Abdullah's
predecessor, King Fahd. Bin Baz is best known to Saudis for his
1966 fatwa declaring the world flat.³ The rest of his oeuvre—in
particular, numerous pronouncements against Christians, Jews,
and "infidel" Westerners—is too Islamically mundane to be very
memorable, though these edicts are still regarded as authoritative
in the Kingdom.⁴

Atop the Mutaween priority list is keeping the sexes seg-
regated—on pain of six months' imprisonment and 200 lashes
with a rattan cane, as a nineteen-year-old woman learned in 2007
when she was sentenced after being gang-raped by seven Saudi
men. But the Kingdom is clearly evolving: In 2009, a seventy-
five-year-old woman who allowed the bread delivery man to enter
her home got only forty lashes to go along with four months in
the slammer.⁵

George W. Bush, Obama's predecessor, had nauseated Amer-
icans in 2005 by holding hands with Abdullah (then the Crown
Prince) on a stroll through the president's ranch in Crawford,
Texas. But Bush's adoption of this Arabic custom was merely a
demonstration of friendship—a gesture of the sort not atypical of
Bush's cloying "compassionate conservatism," however ill-suited

it may have seemed to the "cowboy" president of popular caricature. In real-world terms, it was a nod to the de facto chairman
of an international oil cartel by a chief executive then getting
domestic political heat for spiking gas prices. But a chummy nod
or holding hands is not a bow. Obama moved matters to a new
low.

The target audience for his submissiveness was the world's
Muslims. Ironically, from their perspective, and even from the
perspective of Abdullah himself, a bow would ordinarily be
thought unseemly. In many interpretations of Islam, including
Wahhabism, overt subservience is the equivalent of worship.
Muslims reserve worship for Allah and no other. In fact, many of
al Qaeda's most devoted terrorists, including Mohammed Daoud
al-`Owhali, who killed over 200 people when he bombed the U.S.
embassy in Nairobi in 1998, decline to swear allegiance to Osama
bin Laden, the organization's emir. Like subservient bowing, they
see pledges of fealty (or making *bayat*) to another human being as
a violation of Islamic tenets.

There is, however, a telling exception. The Koran endorses
the prostration of an infidel before his Muslim better—or, writ
large, the subordination of the West before the might of Islam.
Such a gesture amounts to a "willing submission" as Sura 9:29,
the "verse of the sword," puts it. It signifies that *dhimmis*, non-
Muslim subjects, have not only surrendered but "feel themselves
subdued."

The Messenger

Long before humbling himself to Abdullah, Barack Obama had
signaled his intention to steer the United States toward submission
and appeasement. This was back in October 2007, the heady days
before the Democrats' nomination battle intensified and invo-

cations of Obama's middle name by political adversaries ignited fusillades of media indignation. The candidate grew downright whimsical when he told PBS,

> Well, I think if you've got a guy named Barack Hussein Obama, that's a pretty good contrast to George W. Bush. . . . If you believe that we've got to heal America and we've got to repair our standing in the world, then I think my supporters believe that I am the messenger who can deliver that message.[6]

Such beliefs were indeed shared by Obama's acolytes, to whose ears the incantation "Barack *Hussein* Obama" was music. This progressive vanguard ached for the antidote to "Bushitler" and his "war on Islam"—a.k.a. the "war on terror" or what, in Obama parlance, is now called the "overseas contingency operation." For these suddenly ascendant leftists, the United States is the permanent culprit in tensions between America and Islam. The United States, in fact, is the permanent culprit, period. The left has thus made common cause with Islam—or, at the very least, with Islamism, Islam's large fascistic subset that is driven by the religion's dehumanizing supremacism. Contrary to popular belief, this supremacist ideology, because it is rooted in doctrine, is entirely mainstream in the Muslim world. Leftists see America—not the fascistic, supremacist ideology but *America*—as the trigger of jihadist terror's rampage. And in grand enemy-of-my-enemy tradition, that arrangement suits the Islamists just fine.

Obama cements the arrangement. He was elected president because he knew how to speak to these forces annealed in resentment. He could give voice to the words and the symbols that ring their chimes while seemingly standing above, rather than among, them. This was more than a first-term senator of sparse record and thinner accomplishment. This was Obama the Saul

Alinsky-schooled "community organizer," a master of the art of harnessing grievance, of appropriating popular language and values in the service of radical ends.

"I am *the messenger* who can deliver that message," the candidate had told PBS. Would anyone seriously believe that Obama, a deft communicator and no stranger to celestial imagery, was not intentionally evoking images of Islam's Prophet in remarks fashioned for Islamic consumption? For Muslims, after all, Mohammed is the "excellent model of conduct" who ceaselessly announced himself as "the messenger"—the last in a line of "messengers," including Moses and Jesus, sent by Allah to call mankind to the one true faith.[7] For argument's sake, though, let's pretend this thought never crossed Obama's mind. There can still be no denying that the candidate was seeking to highlight the incandescent power of his middle name, "Hussein." It is, after all, a name straight out of Islam's glorious lore. Hussein, Mohammed's grandson, was a central figure in the triumphant campaigns of Islam's original "rightly-guided" caliphs. His is among the most common names in the Muslim world.

As Obama deployed it, Hussein was not merely a name. It was a cipher. The sleepy American press would not break the code, but antiwar leftists in America and their Islamist allies worldwide instantly got the message. For those dreaming jointly and hungrily for the anti-Bush, Obama was offering an overture of empathy, of like-mindedness. They would seize on Obama's ties to Islam, and the "hope" those ties portended for undermining the last remaining superpower, the object of their mutual disdain.

As the 2008 campaign wore on, candidate Obama saw fit to deny his Islamic heritage, vehemently at times. He came to fear it as the most potent threat to his electability in post-9/11 America—certainly more potent than the competing candidates. For Obama, power trumps all. It is vital to bear in mind that the president is an Alinskyite, so steeped in the ideology of the seminal community organizer that he became a top instructor in Alinskyite tactics for other up-and-coming radicals. Alinksyites are fifth-columnists. They have, in substance, the same goals as open revolutionaries: overthrowing the existing free-market republic and replacing it with a radical's utopia. That is why Obama could befriend such unrepentant former terrorists as Bill Ayers and Bernardine Dohrn and take inspiration from Jeremiah Wright, a black-liberation theologist.

Alinskyites, though, are more sophisticated, patient, and practical. They bore in, hollowing out the system from within, taking on the appearance and argot of the heartland. Their single, animating goal is to overthrow the capitalist social order, which they claim to see as racist, corrupt, exploitative, imperialist, etc. Everything else—including the cultivation of like-minded Islamists—is negotiable: They reserve the right to take any position on any matter, to say anything at any time, based on the ebb and flow of popular opinion. That keeps them politically viable while they radically transform society. Transform it into what, they haven't worked out in great detail . . . except that it will be perfect, communal, equal, and just.[8]

The Neocommunist and the Islamist

This shallow nihilism makes alliances easy to strike . . . and, when necessary, to shove allies under the bus. If Islam needed pushing aside for a time to secure power, Islam would be pushed aside. Yet the president's Islamic heritage is deeply rooted. As we shall see, to the extent Obama had a religious faith in his formative years, it was Islam. That doesn't make him a Muslim, much less the Muslim "Manchurian Candidate" of anti-Obama paranoia. There is no record of his ever having professed Islam as an adult (profession of the faith being the first pillar of Islam). While much about Obama remains a mystery—despite the 850 pages' worth of autobiography and policy prescriptions he had published by the age of forty-five—the religion he publicly professes is Christianity, and there is no reason to doubt him on that score.

No reason because his formal religion is nearly irrelevant. The faith to which Obama actually clings is neocommunism. It is a leftism of the most insidious kind: secular and uncompromising in its rejection of bourgeois values, but feverishly spiritual in its zeal to tear down the existing order, under the banner of its all-purpose rally-cry: "social justice."

Neocommunists need not adhere to a formal religion. Instead, they tend to infuse causes like environmentalism, privacy, and secularism with religious fervor. For most leftists, though, religion is a useful tool. It is never a straitjacket because neocommunists consider themselves no more bound by the strictures of creed than by the constraints of tradition.

Thus is Obama the Christian the most uncompromisingly pro-abortion president ever to hold the office, just as he was the senate's most vigorous supporter of abortion rights—and, before that, while serving in the Illinois legislature, an apologist for infanticide as the remedy for botched abortions in which the baby inconveniently survived. In America, where it has become déclassé to question, much less examine, a person's fidelity to his avowed religious creed, formal religion is endlessly malleable. This is a tremendous asset for the neocommunist. Formal religion lends a patina of transcendence to his attack on the existing order. And any religion will do if its principles can be marshaled—however faithlessly—into a rationale for dissolving American constitutional democracy.

This explains how Obama can purport to have found Christ through the baleful Jeremiah Wright. It explains how he could sit comfortably for twenty years in Rev. Wright's Trinity Church in Chicago, soaking up the fiery pastor's Black Liberation Theology, a pseudo-Christian Marxism colored in anti-Semitic hues, defined most clearly by its anti-Americanism. Sure, when Wright became an electoral issue for Obama, the candidate cast him aside, much as he had cast his Islamic heritage aside, pretending to have been absent or wearing earplugs during the Rev's more bombastic Sundays. But the truth was always there for anyone willing to see it: The grievance-mongering, race-obsessed Obama had imbibed enough to find in Wright the inspiration for his second bestselling me-book, *The Audacity of Hope*, and to parrot such standard Wright tropes as: "White folks' greed runs a world in need." It should have surprised no one when Obama staffed his White House with race-bating Marxists, including "Green Jobs Czar" Van Jones, an admitted communist who, when not claiming 9/11 was somehow both America's just desert and an inside job, brooded about "white polluters" conspiring to "steer poison into the people of color communities."

Neocommunism is leftism liberated by the collapse of the Soviet Union. Many naively believed the Soviet demise would be a cautionary tale for the left, a warning against the hubris of big-government schemes to perfect man and society. The opposite, instead, is the case. David Horowitz, today's most eloquent and incisive observer of the revolutionary left, the movement in which he was raised and on which he turned so fiercely, offers a perfect diagnosis:

> Far from instilling humility in progressives . . . , the collapse
> of socialism has revived their self-righteousness and reener-
> gized their assault on the democratic West. The disappearance
> of the Soviet bloc has had only one consequence of note. It
> has lifted the burden of having to defend . . . an indefensible

regime. Because the utopian vision is no longer anchored in the reality of an actually existing socialist state, the left can now indulge its nihilistic agendas without restraint.[9]

Nihilism is the key. Today's hard left is defined by what it is against: the United States, free-market capitalism, and any foreign policy premised on defending American interests or promoting individual liberty. Only this part of the agenda is concrete, leaving neocommunism elastic enough to strike alliances with any movement that shares it. What neocommunists are for, by contrast, is a set of abstractions—"social justice," "equality," "redistributive rights," the "rule of law," and, of course, "our values." The details of those can be worked out later, once the more pressing imperative of undoing the existing order has been realized.

This explains Obama's ruinous spending, the *trillions* in debt, far surpassing in just a few months the total debt accumulated since the nation's founding. Not content with that accomplishment, the president is rushing headlong to bankrupt the treasury permanently with additional trillions for nationalized healthcare and crushing tax increases—which experience assures us will *reduce* total revenues available for redistribution—including a "cap and trade" energy scheme that will nullify industry's capacity to generate value. Critics from the right and what used to be the mainstream left are dumbfounded, wondering aloud whether the new administration is in over its head. This drastically underestimates Obama. Quite the opposite of overwhelmed, he has methodically done exactly what was predicted by those who took the time, during the 2008 campaign, to study his radical background: exploiting the new administration's wind-at-its-back period to crush the capitalist system under an enormous commitment of future dollars, a commitment that will be nigh impossible to roll back once the public is finally roused from its slumbers.

This "change" is not designed to create a new system. Its purpose is to destroy the old one. What comes next is negotiable.

That is why neocommunism aligns so seamlessly with revolutionary movements catalyzed by religious fervor. What comes next for a millenarian movement may not be negotiable, but before the new can be imposed the old must be swept aside. That calls for collaboration among all factions that need to depose the established order, even if their ultimate designs don't perfectly mesh.

Well before the demise of Soviet Communism and its doctrinaire atheism, religious revolutionaries—particularly but not exclusively Islamic revolutionaries—joined in marriages of convenience with the hard left. The Bolsheviks tolerated Islamist elements before the Stalinist purge. Iranian Communists backed Khomeini against the Shah, the Muslim Brotherhood aligned with Nasserite socialists against the Egyptian monarchy, and so on. The marriages tend to last only as long as it takes to ring out the old. But that's for tomorrow. For today, there is nothing novel in this latest alliance between political socialists and religious extremists, except perhaps its foresight in co-opting the modern mechanisms of law.

Just as the Soviet collapse has been a boon for the left, the ferocity and overreach of Muslim terrorists has been a dual boon for Islamism. So atrocious has been the bloodbath wrought by al Qaeda, its affiliates, and its imitators that it has enabled more methodical Muslim extremists to operate under the radar. Repeated terror strikes, culminating in the death of nearly 3000 innocents and the surreal demolition of the seemingly impregnable Twin Towers, shocked Americans and their government into a myopic determination to prevent additional mass-murder attacks. In this climate of fear, the calculating but apparently nonviolent Islamist compares favorably with the uncompromising,

15

blood-soaked Islamist terrorist. He is thus regarded as cause for hope—indeed, as a moderate—by government and opinion elites. This, despite the fact that his agenda is essentially the same as the terrorist's: only their methods differ, and even those differences are shades of gray.

The Islamist rides on the terrorist's back even as he intentionally beclouds their relationship, coy about whether he and the terrorist are friends or foes, impressing you with his comparative calm and cool. The Islamist will occasionally condemn "terrorism" while endorsing "resistance." The outrage he expresses at attacks that claim Muslim lives is oblique: he won't be pinned down on whether his objection is to the wanton killing or to the wanton killing *of Muslims*. He will feign disgust at the terrorist's invocation of scripture to justify barbarity, but never quite explain how the terrorist got it wrong. And all the while, he calls for terrorist organizations to be formally recognized as political parties, effectively legitimizing their brutality. Abdullah's kingdom has posed indignantly as America's staunch counterterrorism ally even as it has thwarted the FBI's investigation into Iran's bombing of the Khobar Towers (nineteen members of the U.S. Air Force killed), bred three-quarters of the 9/11 suicide hijackers, and exported the ideology that spawns terrorism.

In all these ways, the Islamist extorts his way into our public consciousness and policy-making. He is the polite collector you pay in the hope that the leg-breaker won't be next at your doorstep. And even as he sneers in his nice suit at the leg-breaker's crudity, you somehow know all your money is going to the same place.

Like the neocommunist, the Islamist works to impose his version of "social justice." It is a very specific Islamic prescription, and elements of it diverge markedly from the neocommunist's more amorphous utopia. But the essentials of their visions

16

coalesce: They are totalitarian, collectivist, and antithetical to the core conceit of American constitutional democracy, individual liberty. Today's left-leaning, Islamophilic Obamedia consciously ignores the convergence, but America's 44th president and America's enemies have a common dream.

The president's bow to the Saudi king should have surprised no one. It was a submission to their mutual aspiration: a symbolic moment in the transformation from the America that was to the America of Barack Obama's fancy, a vision that would mark a giant leap forward for the global Islamist project.

chapter two

ISLAMISM

A Triumph of Hope over Experience?

The "global Islamist project"? Yes, there most certainly is one. There has been for a long time. Its purpose is to supplant American constitutional democracy with sharia law, just as it would establish sharia throughout the world. What's more, Islamists have a sympathetic ear in President Obama. Already, his administration has dramatically furthered their cause—to the detriment of American national security. But we're getting ahead of ourselves. Preliminarily, it is necessary to pause over our hopelessly confused public discourse on Islam and to consider some key terms, such as "Islamist," since so much of the campaign to control our lives hinges on controlling our language.

The question before the house is: What should we call the challenge that confronts the West? The most straightforward approach—and candor is usually the key to undoing confusion— would be to call it "Islam." This, however, we resist at all costs. There are good and bad reasons, or at least motives, for that posture. While they surely warrant exploring, it is remarkable how much energy is expended on a quest for just the right adjective, prefix, or suffix—anything to deflect the foreboding sense that Islam and the West, distinct civilizations, can neither assimilate nor co-exist harmoniously.

Despite our best efforts, this stubborn reality abounds in life's mundane details as much as in weighty matters of national security. A baby boy born in London today is more apt to be called Mohammed than Jack, Thomas, or Daniel. The prophet's name is the most popular for baby boys born in the British capital, and fares no worse than a close second if the whole of England is counted. It's difficult to say for sure because the British Office of National Statistics intentionally obscures its record-keeping, separately counting, as if they were different names, the fourteen transliterated spelling variants of "Mohammed"—a practice also followed by other European governments fearful of alarming their shrinking non-Muslim majorities. Britain's swelling Islamic community now stands at roughly two million, or 3 percent of total population, though it is difficult to get an accurate fix on that, too, illegal immigration being rampant in the U.K. The number of Muslims will double by 2015 because the Muslim birthrate is at least three times higher than that of non-Muslims. Indeed, so meteoric is Islamic growth that it is driving an English population explosion: The number of Britons may eclipse the 77 million mark in the next half-century, a one-third increase that would vault it ahead of Germany, notwithstanding that, today, Germans outnumber Brits by over 20 million. The surging and, for now, insular Islamic community does not give its children recognizably British names (which is to say, Christian names). Nor is it adopting the Western culture whose torch Old Blighty was once proud to carry but now douses in contempt. Islam is not adapting to England. Islam is transforming England.[1]

If we are unwilling to make the obvious explicit and say "Islam" is the tide that seeks to wash away our civilization, how shall we describe it? "Radical" is probably the qualifier most frequently invoked. Yet, the phrase "radical Islam," like its obverse, "moderate Islam," confounds.

In common parlance, someone is a "radical" Muslim only if he is a practitioner of jihadist terrorism, as if it were perfectly normal to want exactly the sharia state the terrorist wants as long as one refrains from terrorist methods in seeking it. The U.S. government, as well as our states and municipalities, clings to this connotation. At all levels—administrations of both political parties, intelligence agencies, law-enforcement, members of Congress, the federal bench, state and local authorities—officials would rather stick pins in their eyes than grapple with the incontrovertible nexus between Islamic doctrine and the savagery committed by Muslims throughout the world for decades. We are led to believe that the only real "radicals" are the terrorists. Any other Muslim, no matter how supportive of terrorist goals, is deemed a "moderate" so long as he doesn't seem, right this minute, to be plotting the next Armageddon.

This is sheer lunacy. Of Islam's approximately 1.4 billion adherents worldwide, there are, to estimate *very* modestly, hundreds of thousands of Muslims in the United States, and tens of millions globally, who desire the adoption of policies sensible people would find quite radical. The moderate masquerade enables them to make common cause with the radical Left in one big, "progressive" campaign for "social justice."

The pervasiveness of Islamic antipathy for Western norms can easily be seen even if we play by government's politically correct rules—that is, even if we strictly limit our consideration to Muslim attitudes about terrorist *violence*, which conventional wisdom assures us Muslims find deplorable. That is, let's put aside for the moment the inconvenient matter of Muslim support for terrorist *goals* (which happens to be robust).

If we focus only on terrorism *in the West*, sure, the percentage of sympathetic Muslims is relatively small, but it is hardly insignificant. For instance, a 2007 poll by the Pew Research Center found that 13 percent of Muslims in America believe "the use of suicide bombing against civilian targets to defend Islam from its enemies" is justifiable.[2] As we shall see, there is considerable debate about just how many Muslims there are in the United States, but assuming for argument's sake that the number is about 3 million, that would mean this view is held by close to *half a million people*. Similarly, one year after fifty-two Britons were murdered in the terrorist bombings of July 7, 2005, a London *Times* poll found 7 percent of Britain's Muslims endorsed such strikes against civilian targets. The figure spiked to 16 percent for "military" targets (i.e., armed forces and police facilities), while 13 percent regarded the four terrorists who carried out the 7/7 attacks as "martyrs."[3] With a Muslim population as large, and growing, as the U.K.'s, this "relatively small" percentage computes to over *a quarter-million people*. Need we be reminded that it took only nineteen to pull off 9/11?

The "Religion of Peace" Fantasy

Still considering only attitudes about terrorism, notice what happens when we refocus our lens on terrorism (a) *in Israel* and (b) against Westerners *in Islamic countries*: The approval figures skyrocket. The reasons for this, though rarely uttered, are obvious. It is a commonplace among Muslims to describe such terrorism as "resistance" to perceived sieges against Islam. They regard it as a religious duty—as jihad. Its perpetrators are hailed as heroes and, if they are suicide terrorists, as martyrs.

In 1979, Smadar Kaiser, her husband Danny, and their two small daughters, four-year-old Einat and two-year-old Yael, were awakened in their northern Israel apartment at midnight by gunfire and exploding grenades. A team of terrorists sent by Abu Abbas's Palestine Liberation Front was in the neighborhood. While a trembling Smadar hid with Yael in the dark, suffocating crawl space, the terrorists grabbed Danny and Einat and marched them down to a nearby beach. There, one of the four shot Danny in front of his daughter so that his death would be the last sight she'd ever see. Then the ruthless ringleader, Lebanese-born Samir Kuntar, bashed in the four-year-old's skull against a rock with the butt of his rifle. Hours later, upon finally being "rescued" from the crawl space, two-year-old Yael, too, was dead—accidentally smothered by her petrified mother in the effort to keep her quiet as the terrorists searched for more Jews to kill.

The Israelis captured Kuntar, who was sentenced to life in prison. For years, however, Palestinian leaders and masses agitated for his release, lionizing this monster as a "brave leader" and "model warrior." In 2007, the government of Prime Minister Ehud Olmert finally capitulated, exchanging Kuntar and other imprisoned terrorists for the remains of two deceased Israeli soldiers. Kuntar was welcomed to the West Bank as a conquering hero. The Palestinian Authority granted him and another released terrorist honorary citizenship "as an act of dedication to their struggle and their heroic suffering in the occupation's prisons."[4]

Such blood-curdling stories—and this one is hardly singular—do not stop us from living a "Religion of Peace" fantasy. In an astounding interview shortly before Kuntar's release, Secretary of State Condoleezza Rice told the columnist Cal Thomas, "You can look at any opinion poll in the Palestinian territories and 70 percent of the people will say they're perfectly ready to live side by side with Israel because they just want to live in peace."

It doesn't do justice to the ludicrousness of Rice's claim to say the opposite is true. It's much worse than that. Reliable polling at the time showed that *93 percent* of young Palestinian adults (aged eighteen to twenty-five) deny Israel's right to exist—as compared with "only" *75 percent* when the total population is factored in. How could it be otherwise? The cause of destroying the "Zionist entity" is seen as a core religious obligation. It is an explicit constitutional command of both Hamas and Fatah, the factions that control, respectively, Gaza and the West Bank. It is the soundtrack of Palestinian life, the leitmotif of the media and Islamic schools controlled by the authorities.[5]

Israel serves as the commentariat's unified field theory for explaining all Islamic hostility. The theory is fatuous. The most influential Muslim jurisprudential authorities endorse the principle that killing American and allied military personnel in order to induce them to leave Iraq and Afghanistan is a duty. It was the American military presence in Saudi Arabia and Kuwait during the first Gulf War that inspired al Qaeda to take its jihad global. That Westerners in Islamic countries believe they are sacrificing to defend Muslims and provide them with a chance for a better life is irrelevant. In the eyes of the "umma," the world's Muslims, they are occupiers. They must be expelled or slaughtered.

It is true enough that fewer Muslims actively incite terrorism than passively endorse it. Fewer yet materially support terrorist plots, and the subset that would actually carry them out is smaller still. That is cold comfort, though. The unmistakable reality for those willing to see it is that Muslim approval of terrorism increases dramatically when Muslims perceive a place as Islamic territory, or associate a target with a Western government seen as occupying or interloping in Islamic territory. Furthermore, if we broaden the scope from attitudes about terrorism to attitudes about the imposition of sharia—i.e., about the regulation of all life's aspects by Islamic law, and the consequent evisceration of the line dividing the secular from the spiritual—Muslim support goes through the roof.

You'd never know that. Islam's apologist legions counter-factually assure you that Muslims overwhelmingly reject terror. They intimate that violence is the only issue and that nothing "radical" is afoot as long as terrorism is not in the mix. Abdurrahman Wahid, a globally renowned Muslim moderate whom we'll discuss momentarily, estimates—without offering any supporting data—that radicalism, or what he calls the "virulent ideology," holds sway over only 10 to 15 percent of Muslims. He cheerily posits that the remaining "85% to 90%" is comprised of the "traditional and Sufi leadership and masses, who are not yet radicalized" (and notice the word *yet*, which tells you everything you need to know about which way even he knows the wind is blowing).[6] Even if he were right about the comparatively paltry "radical" population, we'd still be talking about nearly *200 million* people. But the problem is that Wahid is not right. As bracing as that huge number may be, he is low-balling. The actual numbers are closer to the opposite of the lopsided preponderance of ur-tolerant moderates he portrays.

In 2007, the University of Maryland joined with the pollster World Public Opinion to survey Islamic views. The poll included Muslims from the Middle East and North Africa to Southeast Asia, Arab and non-Arab. The results were jarring. Nearly two-thirds, 65.5 percent, said they would endorse the requirement of "a strict application of sharia law in every Islamic country." In fact, they said they would like to see all Muslim countries unified under a single caliphate, a position shared even by half of Indonesian Muslims.[7] As we shall see, Islam in Indonesia is thought, with justification, to be among the moderate brands on the planet. Yet even there fundamentalism is on the rise, particularly in Aceh, where sharia rules and where the provincial parliament last year enacted the time-honored penalty of stoning to death for adultery. As the intrepid writer Sadanand Dhume observed, homosexuals and those who engage in premarital sex "drew a lighter rebuke . . . 100 strokes of a rattan cane."[8]

The 2007 poll figures match up with what related global polling suggests. In 2008, for example, 40 percent of *British* Muslims (i.e., close to a million people, including many British-born converts to Islam) favored the implementation of sharia in Britain—with 32 percent holding that killing in the name of religion is at least sometimes justifiable, 40 percent favoring a prohibition against mingling between the sexes, and 33 percent endorsing a global Islamic caliphate.[9] In Pakistan, a plenary Muslim country of 175 million people, four in five favor strict enforcement of sharia (over half "strongly" so). Not surprisingly, in a 2007 poll, Pakistanis by a five-to-one margin preferred Osama bin Laden (at 46 percent approval) to then-President George W. Bush (9 percent)—bin Laden also easily topped Pakistan's then president Pervez Musharraf (38 percent).[10]

It boggles the mind that, eight years after 9/11, there remains widespread ignorance of what Muslims believe. Were this not the case, Muslim attitudes about the imperative of Islamic domination would be assumed in an era such as ours, when Islam is ascendant. After all, those attitudes remained ingrained even in Islam's darkest modern hours, during World War I, as the Ottoman empire was being vanquished. As the scholar Andrew Bostom observes, C. Snouck Hurgronje, the leading Dutch Orientalist of the time, marveled in 1916 at the grip the concept of Islamic hegemony held on the Muslim masses:

It would be a gross mistake to imagine that the idea of universal conquest may be considered as obliterated. . . . The canonists and the vulgar still live in the illusion of the days of Islam's greatness. The legists continue to ground their appreciation of every actual political condition on the law of the holy war, which war ought never be allowed to cease entirely until all mankind is reduced to the authority of Islam—the heathen by conversion, the adherents of acknowledged Scripture [i.e., Jews and Christians] by submission.

Muslims, of course, understood the implausibility of achieving such dominance in the near term. Still, Hurgronje elaborated, the faithful were "comforted and encouraged by the recollection of the lengthy period of humiliation that the Prophet himself had to suffer before Allah bestowed victory upon his arms." So even as the caliphate lay in ruins, the conviction that it would rise again remained a "fascinating influence" and "a central point of union against the unfaithful."[11] Their time, Muslims were sure, would come once again.

The Moderate Delusion

Perhaps their time is here. It's fair to say we are confronted by a horrifyingly large pool of potential terrorists. But the terrorist threat pales beside a lurking reality: the massive fundamentalist pool is churning out legions of activists who wish to end our way of life and who believe that there are plenty of avenues besides mass-murder for pursuing that goal. In fact, after three generations, the fundamentalist movement has matured and metastasized, to the point that its many non-terrorist members insist the terrorists are retarding their progress. That's debatable to say the least: without the climate of intimidation created by the terrorists,

27

the non-terrorists would be ignored, not appeased. Yet, the fact that it's a debate at all should trouble us.

It is delusional to regard as "moderate" people whose designs are radical. If the threat to freedom is geometrically broader than the threat of mass-murder attacks, it is national suicide for a free, self-determining people to pretend that our problems are limited to Muslim terrorists. Moreover, if one accepts that Islamic scripture is plausibly interpreted to endorse violent jihad as a method of creating or preserving Islamic societies—a proposition that should be undeniable—then there isn't anything very radical about "radical Islam."

A fashionable alternative to the term "radical Islam" is "extremism." Gaggles of policy-makers and pundits prefer this moniker because it omits any mention of Islam whatsoever. In their telling, the "international community" (not just the West) is locked in a "struggle" (not a "war") against "*violent* extremism"— not mere "extremism," lest anyone doubt that we're fine with any insane belief system anyone comes up with so long as things are not going boom.

Let's assume, though, that we can at least agree we are grappling with *Islamic* extremism. One could certainly make a case for that label. After all, even if seeking conquest in the name of a doctrine that commands conquest is not especially *radical*, it is *extreme*. It calls for the application of seventh-century ordinances, as conclusively defined by the jurisprudence of ninth-century Islamic scholars, to a very different twenty-first-century world. To be sure, the justification for that position is chillingly rational when one considers Islam's scriptures and history of conquest. But the position is still extreme, no matter how many people take it.

There are other semantic difficulties, though, with using the word "extremist." It can be unintentionally offensive. To be *extreme* is not to be faithless but faithful-on-steroids. Thus labeling terrorists "extremists" implies that pure Islam—as in a hardcore, originalist, "true-believer" variety—compels violence. There is a powerful, albeit immensely unpopular, argument that this is true. It may be that courageous apostates like Ibn Warraq and Ayaan Hirsi Ali are correct when they contend that a "reformed" Islam would no longer be Islam. But such a conclusion, even if it has exegetical merit, would defy rather than describe our everyday experience.

Plainly, there is too much Islamic terrorism. As we look around us, however, it is clear that most Muslims resist violence— however much one wishes more Muslims would also openly and convincingly condemn it. Similarly, while a disquieting number of Muslims agree that sharia always and everywhere should be the law, a significant number do not agree. Maybe the latter are ignoring the dictates of their faith. Maybe they sincerely believe Islam does not mandate adherence to Allah's law. Or maybe they honestly construe the most harrowing elements of sharia to have been superseded by changing modern circumstances. Regardless of the explanation, the fact is that there are millions of such Muslims.

Relative to the garden-variety bookmaker, one might call a mafia hitman an "extreme" criminal. You wouldn't, however, say a daily communicant was an "extreme" Catholic; you'd call her "devout." There is no upside in suggesting that the only devout Muslims are the terrorists. Clarity is essential, but we can strive for it without needlessly antagonizing millions of peaceable Muslims who consider themselves devout—Muslims who should be our allies.

The runnels of discord through the Muslim world should illustrate something else for us: It is a gross oversimplification to speak of "Islam" as if there were only one Muslim belief system. Our Manichean public discourse does exactly this; and we compound the problem by blathering about a single "true" Islam, about which we are clueless . . . except for our supreme self-assurance that this "true" Islam simply must be different from the "false" Islam of the terrorists. American officials gush about a monolithic "religion of peace" (former Secretary Rice even promoted Islam to "a religion of *love* and peace"). Jacqui Smith, Britain's former Home Secretary, mindlessly branded terrorism "un-Islamic activity": just by dint of its being terrorism it somehow couldn't possibly have anything to do with Islam—in fact, it was inherently hostile to Islam.

There's no denying the good intentions of these doctrinal dabblers. They are sincerely trying to impress on the umma that the West doesn't have it in for them—freeing tens of millions of Muslims from tyranny having evidently failed to do the trick. Of course, common sense ought to tell such well-meaning officials, and us, that their influence in the umma pales beside the drumbeat of fundamentalist clerics and scholars who've spent their lives studying Islamic law, who speak the language in Muslim countries beset by illiteracy, and who despise the West.

There is not one single Islam, let alone one "true" Islam. There are many. They have a common core, but numerous interpretations of the faith are legitimately identifiable as "Islam." To give just a small demonstration of this, putatively moderate Indonesia was riven in April 2008 when fundamentalists screaming, "Burn, burn!" and "Kill, kill!" torched and stoned a mosque belonging to a sect known as the Ahmadi. The latter consider themselves Muslims but are deemed heretics by the former because they neither accept Mohammed as the final prophet nor violent jihad as a divine injunction.[12] If we could find the story any longer (it's been purged from the Associate Press's archives), we could no doubt figure out a way to attribute this regrettable immoderation to Israel—or perhaps Guantanamo Bay. The salient point for present purposes is that there are numerous contrasting forms of Muslim faith. When we thoughtlessly invoke "Islam" as if there were only one, we are being unclear and inaccurate. When we speak of a "true" or "false" Islam, we are speaking nonsense. This shortchanges our understanding of the Muslim world and our influence on it.

The terrorists and those who share their aspirations for an Islamicized world typically draw on the Muslim *Sunna*: an agglomeration of the Koran (taken by believers to be the verbatim word of Allah, dictated to Mohammed in Arabic by the angel Gabriel), the *tafsir* (authoritative Koranic commentary), the *hadith* (the words and traditions of Muhammad recorded in six different voluminous collections that date from the eighth and ninth centuries), and the *sira* (authoritative biographies of the Prophet, including the remnants of a hagiographic account written by Ibn Ishaq in the eighth century, about 150 years after Muhammad's death).[13] Within this corpus, there is abundant scriptural compulsion toward, and approbation of, terrorism, beheadings, limb-severing, stoning, slavery, etc. When the "radicals" cite it accurately to justify their atrocities, and we respond by harrumphing about "false" Islam and "un-Islamic activity," we sound like idiots to the audience we're trying to reach.

Western elites are not the only ones undermining their credibility in a futile effort to show how sophisticated and well-meaning they are. Four years ago, the *Wall Street Journal* published an op-ed by the aforementioned Abdurrahman Wahid, the former president of Indonesia, 88 percent of whose nearly quarter-billion citizens are Muslim, making it the most populous Islamic nation. Wahid, furthermore, once led the world's largest Muslim organization, *Nahdlatul Ulama*. By any estimation, he is an authentic moderate who urges interfaith tolerance. His essay,

"Right Islam, Wrong Islam," was about the "global struggle for the soul of Islam": the battle between two opposing camps he described, respectively, as the "moderates" and believers in the "Wahhabi/Salafi ideology—a minority fundamentalist religious cult fueled by petrodollars," that, he added in case we hadn't gotten the point, is "extreme and perverse." This description would probably have surprised, for example, the twenty-four million Saudis for whom this extreme, perverse minority cult is the state religion.

To be fair, there was much to admire in Wahid's analysis. Especially apt was his admonition that, "to neutralize the virulent ideology," both Muslims and non-Muslims must "identify its advocates, understand their goals and strategies, evaluate their strengths and weaknesses, and effectively counter their every move." Still, his description of this "virulent ideology" was disheartening. Wahid asserted that Wahhabi-Salafism "rests upon a simplistic, literal and highly selective reading of the Koran and the Sunna. That is an enormous concession. He may just have been admitting the irrefutable but, in so doing, Wahid acknowledged that those who pursue violent jihad and seek to impose sharia are *literally* accurate when they cite various scriptures. And while it's all well and good that Wahid, a man of great learning, finds the "radical" construction of Islam to be "simplistic" and "selective," that critique is likely to impress only Western audiences, not Muslim ones. In Western intellectual circles, is it considered fashionable, erudite, and admirable to complicate something that may actually be simple. In most of the world, including most of America, this is deemed pedantic, boorish, and off-putting.

In the West, moreover, our religious scriptures are understood to have been authored by men under divine inspiration.

We are also steeped in an Enlightenment tradition of reason. The controversy that erupted after Pope Benedict's 2006 speech at Regensburg stemmed from his emphasis on the galvanizing role of reason in faith. The pontiff was taken to be comparing Roman Catholicism with Islam (though Benedict later denied this was his intention) because, in making his point, he expressly relied on a fourteenth-century Byzantine emperor who castigated Mohammed for spreading Islam by the sword rather than by reasoned persuasion. The pope's point was an effective one because Westerners are predisposed to embrace arguments that trumpet reason. We are open to the notion that there is license for a religious doctrine to evolve and that, as we apply our reason to modernity's ever-changing circumstances, it does so.

This is a much harder sell in Islam. The Koran is taken by Muslims to be the verbatim, immutable word of God. Scripture is not thought to be mediated by imperfect men. It does not readily lend itself to reinterpretation if it seems questionable or unsuited to evolving circumstances. It's one thing to say an Evangelist erred; it's quite another to urge that Allah got it wrong or failed to anticipate the future. And Islamic thinkers have often regarded human reason with suspicion: the means by which men try to justify deviating from what God has commanded.

Whatever its validity, Wahid's rebuke of the Wahhabi-Salafists for being "simplistic" undoubtedly had very little impact on the audience that needs convincing, regardless of how it may have titillated Westerners to hear a prominent Muslim say such things. Further, to claim, as Wahid did, that radicals "selectively" quote scripture might have been persuasive if he had given even a single example of terrorists distorting scriptural meaning by taking verses out of context or failing to include mitigating verses that soften the harsh ones. But he gave none.

In truth, it is at least as common for Islam's apologists to bleach away the ferocity of Muslim scripture as it is for terrorists to overstate it. We shall see this bowdlerization tactic in President Obama's ballyhooed speech on Islam and the West. Wahid, too, used it in declaring that the "essence of Islam" is set forth in the Koran's instruction, "For you, your religion; for me, my religion."

This verse, from Sura 109, is drawn from Mohammed's early Meccan phase, when he was trying to entice converts to the new faith. By contrast, Sura 9's verse of the sword, like numerous other scriptural commands to war and conquest, is from the later Medinan phase, when Islam was spread by force of arms. As Robert Spencer countered in a critique of Wahid's essay, "Traditional Islamic theology has held for centuries that on points of disagreement the later Medinan suras take precedence over the early Meccan ones." And that rule of construction was not dreamed up by al Qaeda or rabid Wahhabis. As Spencer demonstrates, it traces back to medieval times through numerous scholars revered in the Muslim world.[14] Those who claim terrorists rip scriptures out of context can't consistently portray Sura 109's ecumenical message as if it arose in a vacuum; it, too, must be considered in context—in this case, with later scriptural commands to intolerance.

Again, there is not just one Islam, and our passionate desire for terrorists, radicals, and extremists to be wrong does not make it so, nor does it make the Gospel of Tolerance resonate through the umma. Spencer adds that believers in what Wahid paints as a wayward Islam have "a coherent, developed, and traditionally-based theology explaining why they take sura 9 over 109." If Wahid has a competing doctrinal theory for why Muslims should adopt the tolerant scriptures that have been abrogated by the later intolerant ones, he did not share it with *Wall Street Journal* readers.

George Cardinal Pell, the Catholic archbishop of Sydney, writes that Islam in Wahid's neighboring Indonesia "has been tempered significantly both by indigenous Animism and by earlier Hinduism and Buddhism," as well as by pacific Sufism (to say nothing of the poor Ahmadi, whose plight is mentioned above). The resulting brand is unique: "syncretistic, moderate and with a strong mystical leaning." The brand thrives because it is reinforced in schools established by Wahid's Nahdlatul Ulama.[15] It may be the Islam we wish were universally taken as "true," but it is surely not the Islam of hundreds of millions of Muslims in Pakistan, Afghanistan, Iran, Turkey, and the Arab world—Muslims who themselves adhere to variegated interpretations that, generally speaking, are more militant than the Islam of Indonesia (which, as we've seen, is itself under siege by the country's militant Islamic elements).

Our challenge here is two-fold. First, we must come to grips, at last, with the nature of the threat. Second, on the much overrated "war of ideas" front, we must formulate arguments that will be persuasive to hundreds of millions of Muslims—the one-third, or hopefully more, of the Muslim world that could potentially ally with us on counterterrorism, tolerance, and individual liberty. The first task is essential. The second depends on the first, and we must be open to the possibility that it may be impossible.

Wahid worries that the virulent Muslim ideology "threatens the very foundations of civilization." He is right, of course, but Samuel Huntington reminded us that "civilization" has two different meanings. There is the singular sense, the one Wahid uses, in which civilization is what separates us from the barbarians. And then there is the plural sense: the idea that there are several distinct civilizations, and that no one of them has a monopoly on the ideal human life. The former, Huntington observed, has "lost some of its cachet" because "a civilization in the plural sense could in fact be quite uncivilized in the singular sense." The cachet deprecia-tion has been steep in the multi-culti West, where the academy has spent decades teaching students—students who have come of age and are now running the U.S. government—that their ancestors were nothing more than rapacious, murderous, slave-holding, racist imperialists who turned to the colonial exploita-tion of oil-rich Muslim lands once they had stolen the Southwest from Mexico and run out of Indians to kill.

It is simply a fact that Islam and the West are different civiliza-tions. When an influential Muslim moderate like Abdrurrahman Wahid speaks of a threat "to the very foundations of civilization" as if there were only one real civilization founded on Western values, he is getting nowhere with many, if not most, Muslims. They believe Allah prescribed the perfect civilization, and that Western reason, with its resulting corrosive immorality, is what threatens that civilization's very foundations. If Wahid is not going to dem-onstrate in a convincing way that these "radical" Muslims have misinterpreted Islam, if he is merely going to stamp his feet and say the virulent ideology must be wrong because it is inimical to Western values, his message will fall on deaf ears where it counts, no matter how much we remaining defenders of Western values may draw false comfort from it.

Yes, we are infatuated with the "war of ideas." It is easier than fighting real wars. Hopelessly abstract, and without real met-rics for determining whether we're actually making headway, it is seductive. We can delude ourselves into believing that other people are just like we are, that it is within our power to change their implacability if we just say or do the right thing, and that they will be influenced by the arguments we find so thoroughly persuasive. Therefore, we tell ourselves, it is unnecessary to deal with the more grisly sort of war or to concentrate on that which we actually can control: our self-defense. All the while, as all those British Mohammeds might tell us, the other civilization in the mix is under no illusions about easy co-existence—they think the war of ideas is already over and Allah won.

The challenge here is a daunting one, calling for one of two very difficult possibilities. On the one hand, reformers could try to place the jihadist scriptural citations in a broader doctrinal context that *convincingly* undermines them as support for terrorism, conquest, and the imposition of sharia. That is problematic because these citations are supported by extremely learned scholars. The fact that these reformers or scholars may be wrong hardly means that the millions who believe they are right will be won over to the reformist side. On the other hand, reformers could try to demonstrate (as in *compellingly show*, not monotonously natter) that the jihadist scriptural commands really were intended to apply only to the unique circumstances of the seventh century. This, too, is an uphill climb. Again, the scriptural commands are deemed to be the exact words of Allah, who transcends time and was providing comprehensive guidelines for the life of His creation. They also involve the words and deeds of Mohammed, Islam's "excellent model of conduct" (Sura 33:21). We should not underestimate how hard it will be for reformers to convince Muslims that a doctrine presented as an enduring ideal for the conduct of human life was obsessed (in a way God did not realize would be confusing) with a relative nanosecond in human history. And even if you get over that hurdle, there remains the challenge of developing a cogent rationale for why the violent scriptural directives are obsolete but the nice, tolerant scriptures we like better are for all time. This being the age of feelings, we may feel our pieties are transcendant, but that is hardly a convincing argument that they are.

37

It may be that convincing arguments can be developed. There is a very good chance, however, that they cannot. In the latter eventuality, our security task becomes figuring out not how to coexist with the Islamic world but how to have as little to do with it as possible until such time, if ever, as it undertakes radical change. But in either event, by burying our heads in the sand, by not confronting the undeniable nexus between scripture and what we like to think of as radicalism, we have abandoned the field to our enemies. That can only have bolstered their credibility in the eyes of the umma.

Choosing "Islamist" over "Islam"

The terms "radical Islam" and "Islamic extremism" will not serve our purpose of clarity. Furthermore, our understanding of "jihad" is very incomplete. And here I refer to the true jihad: the often but not always military mission to establish an Islamic order. I am not talking about the familiar, fatuous wrangling over whether "jihad" must mean a violent struggle or can instead be Oprahfied into feel-good pabulum, like "the internal struggle to become a better person"—or into the equivalent of a "literacy campaign" or the "fight against AIDS," as Yasser Arafat's call for jihad against Israel was once described by Professor John Esposito, Georgetown University's apologist-in-chief (and, you'll be shocked to learn, a key State Department adviser on Islamic movements during the Clinton years).[16]

"Islamist" is the most apt descriptor for the belief system which holds that Islam is the complete, obligatory guide to human existence, governing all matters political, social, cultural, and religious, from cradle to grave (and, of course, beyond). "Islamist" is the term invoked over three-quarters of a century ago by the Muslim Brotherhood founder Hassan al-Banna.[17] It refers not just to terrorists but to the hundreds of millions of believers who share the terrorist goal of installing sharia societies though they do not actively encourage brutality. For clarity's sake, the Islamist *terrorists* should be referred to as exactly that: "Islamist terrorists."

Admittedly, this may be a triumph of hope over experience. To be sure, when Banna spoke about "Islamists," he was not drawing the distinction I am trying to draw. For Banna, an Islamist was one who sought to live in complete accordance with the tenets of Islam. Banna was not designating believers who accepted sharia *in toto* and rejected the separation of political life from spiritual life; for Banna, *that is Islam.* The term "political Islam"—which is favored by some commentators to distinguish what I am calling Islamists from so-called moderate Muslims who do not seek the imposition of Muslim law—would have made no sense to Banna. He saw Islam as innately political, and I think he was right.

Further, it is indisputable, as Andrew Bostom contends, that as late as the mid-nineteenth century, "'Islam' and 'Islamism' were synonymous, meant to be equivalent to 'Catholicism,' 'Protestantism,' and 'Judaism'—not to radical or fundamentalist sects of any of these religions." And when the term "Islamist" first came into vogue, it denoted a scholar of Islamic doctrine, not a subset of Islamic believers. Indeed, as Bostom recounts, many Muslims (most prominently, those I would call Islamists) are offended by designations such as "Islamist" and "moderate Muslim" that suggest Islam is infinitely malleable. "These descriptions are very ugly," decried Turkey's Islamist Prime Minister Recep Tayyip Erdogan in 2007. "It is offensive and an insult to our religion. There is no moderate or immoderate Islam. Islam is Islam, and that's it."[18]

So is it wrong, then, to shrink from the conclusion that the real problem is Islam? Have I rationalized my way into a less egregious

39

but still counterproductive form of the very political correctness I condemned in *Willful Blindness* and, again, throughout this book? I am not a Muslim, and I appreciate that there is a plethora of Islamic forms. But I also believe Banna was right: what he referred to as "Islamism" is what Islam essentially calls for. Hair-splitting between "Islamism" and "Islam" runs the risk of doing exactly what we must avoid doing: minimizing the challenge confronting us and suggesting that there is a vibrant, preponderant "Islam," markedly different from purportedly aberrant "Islamism," that somehow does not see sharia-imposition as obligatory. In my heart of hearts, I don't believe that is true.

But here's the problem: It's not my call to make. The stubborn fact remains that there are hundreds of millions of Muslims who either do not wish to live under the tyranny of sharia or are so indifferent that, even if they would abide by sharia in a Muslim country where it applies, they do not support converting non-Muslim societies into sharia enclaves. What are we to do about them? Are we to tell them they are wrong, that their only alternative is to renounce Islam—even those who live in fundamentalist societies where the penalty for apostasy is death? Are we to give those people no place to go? If our desire—as human beings, as Americans concerned about our security, as Westerners faithful to the imperatives of reason and tolerance—is that Islam should reform, then what sense does it make to alienate the only Muslims who might reform it by telling them they're not true Muslims?

By denominating the challenge "Islamism," we reserve the mantel of Islam for the millions who reject intolerance. Of course we must do so with our eyes open. We must recognize that the Islamists are faithful Muslims, that they are hostile to our civilization, and that they may substantially outnumber our potential allies in the umma. Our primary objectives must be to defeat militant Islamists who attack us at home and abroad, and to shield ourselves from other Islamists who seek to undermine our freedoms in more sophisticated ways. We should reserve the designation "Islam" in the hope that tolerant voices can redeem it, but our defense must never be hostage to that hope, which may, after all, be futile.

Defending ourselves will require flushing out the Islamists: identifying them and imposing on them the burden of defending their totalitarian ideology against the positive case for liberty and human reason. Doing so will undeniably burden true moderate Muslims as well: Given the prevalence of anti-Constitutional beliefs in Islam, foreign Muslims should not be permitted to reside in America unless they can demonstrate their acceptance of American constitutional principles. But those who satisfy this burden should be welcomed, encouraged, and given the space necessary to seek reform.

Allah is our objective.
The Prophet is our leader.
The Koran is our law.
Jihad is our way.
Dying in the way of Allah is our highest hope.
Allahu-Akbar! Allahu-Akbar! *

* *"Allahu-Akbar!"* means "Allah is the greatest!" It is a common Muslim expression, but it has become the signature cry of defiance against the West by Islamists and Islamist terrorists.

chapter three

JIHAD IS OUR WAY

This is the notorious battle cry of *Hizb al-Ikhwan al-Mus-limin*, the Muslim Brotherhood (or "the Ikhwan"), the font of Islamist thought for nearly a century.[1] In marked contrast to terror networks like al Qaeda and Hezbollah, the Brotherhood purports to forswear violence. Still, its slogan remains unchanged to this day. That fact tells you most everything you need to know about where two decades of consciously avoiding inquiry into our enemies' ideology has gotten us.

Do you know what *dawa* is? It happens to be the Islamists' primary method of undermining Western values and American constitutional society. Have you even heard of it?

How about *siyash*? Thanks to our modern infatuation with democratic processes—as opposed to democratic principles—it has become the Islamists' most promising avenue for imposing their sharia-based prescriptions for daily life. Have you ever heard anyone in the Western press or the United States government so much as utter the word? Have you even a clue what it means?

What about *Wassatiyya*? And no, it's not *"What's it to you?"*— as a journalist to whom I once mentioned the term took me as saying. The word is *Wassatiyya*. It is nothing less than the ideology that dominates today's global Islamist movement. Indeed, Fahad bin Abdul Aziz al Saud adopted *Wassatiyya* as his own personal brand of Islam.[2] You probably have heard of him: he was better known as King Fahd, the late Keeper of the Two Holy Mosques and the predecessor of Abdullah, another *Wassatiyya* adherent and the happy recipient of President Obama's reverent bow at Buckingham Palace.

Not that "What's it to you?" has no part in this conversation. That question concisely states the thinking of opinion elites in and out of government when it comes to Islamist ideology. After all, they'd have you understand, this is America and we don't do ideology. We only care about stopping terrorists, not inquiring into what motivates them, much less what motivates their ideological allies. In fact, in the telling, those ideological allies are portrayed as the terrorists' ideological *adversaries* even though, in their different but related ways, the two camps are struggling for precisely the same thing: sharia societies.

If *What's it to you?* is the question, I suppose the answer is: Nothing . . . other than our survival as a liberty culture—as America.

No, no, say our government officials and our commentariat's foreign-policy gurus. They spend a lot of their energy these days urging open U.S. diplomatic engagement with the Brotherhood and other Islamists—and carrying out that engagement behind the scenes. The chorus includes such heavyweights as the Brookings Institution scholar and former Clinton National Security Council official Kenneth Pollack, who contends that Islamists are largely benign and thus that we should be working with them.[3] The Brotherhood, such experts insist, is mainstream and moderate. Why, in Egypt, where the Ikhwan was founded, they point out that it is the Brothers and not the repressive Mubarak regime that dons the mantle of democracy, pining for free elections. This is a trend Pollack says we must encourage, drawing Islamists into the electoral process in nations where we have influence . . . despite what he grudgingly concedes is the danger that, once in power, they might well undermine the political process that got them there. That, inconveniently, is where *siyash* comes in: the political process—riding on terrorism's back, but not getting its hands dirty with explosives—is the Brotherhood's chosen path for achieving its ends.

The Ikhwan's American fan club confounds the Brothers' political ingenuity with political virtue, all the while studiously ignoring the decidedly immoderate, unenlightened ends the Brothers seek to achieve through ordinary politics. Thus, the enormity of the motto: The Brotherhood has never forsworn jihad, even if you believe it has abandoned terrorism—a dubious claim, propped on such chicanery as a definition of "terrorism" that excludes "resistance," and a phony distinction between encouraging violence and directly executing it. The Brothers have not changed the motto because the Brothers have not changed, period. For them, jihad is still "our way," and "dying in the way of Allah," the martyrdom glorified by Islam's prophet, remains "our highest hope."

To speak of jihad without brutality seems contradictory. It is not, but the explanation for this differs markedly from the cheery rationale offered by Muslim apologists and revisionists. They claim the Islamic obligation of jihad (which literally means

45

"struggle") is not about violence or "holy war." In their fable, the "greater" jihad has always been a Muslim's struggle to live a virtuous life, and the term's bellicose connotation is no more meaningful than commonplace calls to metaphorical "war"—against drugs, poverty, tobacco, and the like. They acknowledge a "lesser jihad," a vestige of Islam's violent, tribal history, but claim it is relevant in modern times only when Muslims are under siege.[4]

This smiley-face jihad remains unconvincing. Bernard Lewis, the West's preeminent scholar of Islam, points out that "the overwhelming majority of early authorities, . . . citing relevant passages in the Koran and in the tradition, discuss *jihad* in military terms."[5] The encyclopedic *Dictionary of Islam*, first published by the British missionary Thomas Patrick Hughes in 1886, defines jihad as "a religious war with those who are unbelievers in the mission of Muhammad." So entrenched is jihad's nexus with violence that forthright Islamophiles concede it. In *The Age of Sacred Terror*, for example, the former Clinton officials Daniel Benjamin and Steven Simon claim that a "domestication of jihad" has transformed it into an "internal battle" for personal betterment waged through "acts of charity, good works in society, and education." Still, they ruefully attest that jihad grew up as "exclusively actual, physical warfare," and that the "domestication" they perceive is a "modern-day" contrivance.[6]

Jihad and Sharia

So if jihad and violence are joined at the hip, how can the Brotherhood, self-proclaimed jihadists, abandon violence? The same way a fierce army captures territory without firing a single shot, or the Mafia collects usurious loans while busting only the occasional kneecap. The answer, very simply, is extortion, combined

with a shrewd sense of the ground a timid, multi-culti West is
only too willing to cede.

We're not so shrewd. It has been thirty-one years since the
Khomeinist revolution in Iran and seventeen years since jihadists declared all-out war on the United States by bombing the
World Trade Center. Yet we still understand precious little about
Islamism and the threat it portends. It is a conscious avoidance.
My book *Willful Blindness* undertook to expose this suicide ethos
as it pertained to maintaining our security against the terrorist
threat. Yet, the broader Islamist threat—the wolf that comes, if
not quite in sheep's clothing, as nothing more dangerous than a
sheepdog—is the more insidious one. Knowledge is power, but
only if knowledge is coupled with the fortitude to confront the
dangers of which one becomes aware.

Very simply, the purpose of jihad is not violence for its own
sake. It is to pave the way for the imposition of sharia, the Muslim
legal code and the necessary precondition for erecting an Islamic
state and society. That is a peril we simply don't want to deal with.
Doing so would require confronting the brute fact that such a
state would be antithetical to American democracy. If we wanted
to safeguard American democracy and the principles—the individual liberties—it stands for, we would need to fight not only
terrorists but Islamists. We would need to reject not only savagery but sharia. For that, we appear to have no stomach.

Thus, we avert our eyes from our enemies' goal and fail to recognize both who our enemies are and why the accommodations
they demand, some of which seems harmless enough on the surface, must be opposed. Our national-security policy obsesses over
means—in particular one tactic, terrorism—while ignoring the
end the means seek to accomplish. Because America is a beacon of
religious freedom, we've limited our focus to operatives who plot

and execute acts of terror. The ideology fueling this brutality, we rationalize, is not our concern. Otherwise, our first principles are betrayed and every Muslim is smeared as a terrorist.

The disposition that we must not critically examine Islam is both unnecessary and self-defeating. It is unnecessary because the Framers gave us a Constitution that guarantees freedom of conscience, not freedom from examination. You can believe whatever you wish to believe, but you do not foreclose your beliefs from inspection by labeling them "religion"—even if the label is accurate.

If a revelation of a lunar god made out of blue cheese comes to you, worship the full, gooey moon if you'd like. But you have no claim on our respect for such beliefs, let alone our approval. What you get is our indulgence of your right to hold even absurd views, nothing more. And you most certainly do not have an unqualified right to exercise your faith however you see fit—whether that entails, say, participating in violent jihad, or giving "alms" to a "charity" that you know is part of a terrorist organization. In America, where Judeo-Christian morality and rationality inform our individual liberty, we respect religion, but religion is not given an unqualified berth. Our jurisprudence has long held that neutral laws of general applicability—i.e., laws that do not discriminate against particular religions and that make the same literal demands on every person—must be obeyed by everyone. Your faith may call for the ritual use of peyote, but the narcotics laws render peyote use illegal and there is no religion exemption.

Judeo-Christian ethics are fundamental to American democracy—they are inherent in the American character, even though we are protected against the establishment of a state religion, a protection that people must have if they are to be authentically free.[7] Nevertheless, various strains of Protestant Christianity, evangelism, Catholicism, and Judaism—in short, the deeply rooted religious traditions of the West—are subjected to scathing censure on a daily basis in the American public square. Meanwhile, in the Muslim world, Islamic sects still fight religious wars against each other, abuse each other (as we saw with the Ahmadi), attack each other's mosques, and accuse each other of apostasy, a capital offense under sharia. Even if we were not threatened by forces who draw their motivation from Islamic doctrine, it would be ridiculous to suggest that Islamic doctrine should be afforded a sacrosanct status that no other religion enjoys in America and that Muslims do not extend to each other in Islamic countries.

Not Merely a Religion

The self-defeating nature of our aversion to critical examination is easy to see, if we allow ourselves to do so. To begin with, Islam is not merely a religion. It is a comprehensive socio-economic and political system, which believers take to be ordained by Allah. To be sure, its elements include tenets we in the West would regard as religious creed—e.g., the fundamental monotheistic belief that there is no God but Allah, the conceit that Mohammed is Allah's final prophet, the obligations of daily prayer and pilgrimage to Mecca, the rejection of such Christian concepts as "original sin" and God's divisibility into a trinity, etc. Such tenets, however, constitute only a fraction of the overarching Islamic project.

What we thoughtlessly call the "religion" of Islam also includes an all-encompassing corpus of law: not just religious canons but civil and criminal rules and procedures. Moreover, Islam entails voluminous guidelines for social interaction, including sexual conduct, other relations between men and women, and relations between Muslims and non-Muslims. It prescribes guidelines for the foundation of government; for property ownership, use, development, and inheritance; for the conduct of commercial transactions; and for the use of force, the striking of treaties, and the circumstances under which seemingly solemn agreements may be abrogated.

Though ostensibly part of what Westerners see as the secular realm, these elements of Islam are deemed to have been dictated by God Himself every bit as much as Muslim teachings that are, for Westerners, recognizably spiritual. They are considered every bit as compulsory and non-negotiable. And crucially, Islam does not separate mosque and state—it rejects the animating premise of secular democracy. When we blinker ourselves to Islamic ideology, in well-meaning deference to the Judeo-Christian principle of rendering unto God what is God's, we are unilaterally surrendering far more than the space society owes to religion—the space that, in America, guarantees only (but crucially) freedom of conscience and reasonably uninhibited religious practices. Islam, especially as interpreted by the Islamists, is totalitarian in its designs. It would usurp almost all of what, in American society, is the secular space controlled by free people governing themselves in accordance with their own desires, under no obligation to heed any creed.

Furthermore, as we've already seen, it grossly distorts reality to speak of "Islam" as if there were only one Muslim belief system, a definitive "true" Islam in relation to the assertedly "false" Islam of Islamists. This is the common fallacy of construing phenomena as one wishes them to be, or through the prism of one's own pieties, rather than as they are understood on their own terms and in their own milieu.

Manifestly, a counterterrorism strategy premised on delegitimizing violent jihadism as "anti-Islamic" is doomed to fail. (And let's not forget, the threat confronting us is much broader than violent jihadism.) Though *we* find fundamentalist strains that urge violent jihad unsavory, they boast a rich pedigree, lie squarely within the tradition of Mohammed, and are supported by centuries of scholarship rooted in the literal commands of scripture. As we've already seen, their adherents number in at least the tens of millions when we account for both the small percentage of Muslims willing to take up arms and the far larger number who support forcible action though they would not commit terrorist acts themselves. Pretending they represent a bare fringe has left us blind and vulnerable.

In addition, means can't be separated from ends without confusing both. Perhaps on a gut level our policymakers grasp that jihad is not an end unto itself. Alas, they obdurately refuse to grapple with jihad's actual end, namely, to establish a Muslim state. They treat the violence as if it is the endgame—as if al Qaeda blew up buildings for no better reason than to blow up buildings. Because policymakers won't come to grips with what Islamists are trying to accomplish, they can't even see that there are far more Islamists than terrorists. Focused myopically on only one of the jihadist's means, violence, they mistakenly assume that ending the violence would perforce end Islamism's threat to our way of life. The *Wall Street Journal's* Ian Johnson put it well in an essay for the Hudson Institute's invaluable Center on Islam, Democracy, and the Future of the Modern World: "The 9/11 attacks have focused attention on Islamist links to terrorism—a natural development but one that overlooks the real achievement of [Islamist] activists: the creation of a robust legal framework for the Islamist cause despite years of setbacks."[8]

Compared to U.S. policymakers who won't look at the thinking behind jihad at all, Islam's other apologists are an interesting contrast. They actually *do* appreciate that jihad is not the objective, that it is a means to something transcendent. But they shy away from the actual "something." Because they refuse to accept jihad's palpably violent roots, they overlook its corporate nature. Some are secularlists mired in what Judge Robert Bork describes as modern liberalism's radical individualism;[9] others are revisionists enraptured by the counterfactual insistence of leading moderates that Islam has always been "a personal faith" not "an authoritarian political system."[10] In either case, they miss—or refuse to see— that for hundreds of millions of Muslims, Islam is not principally about the individual. It is about the umma, the Muslim nation. It is at least as focused on dominance in this world as on salvation in the next. It is about the communal obligation to establish and spread Allah's law on earth, to create Islamic societies, to recreate and expand the Caliphate. Yes, Islam is intensely concerned about the individual. It wants to dictate every facet of the individual's life. Primarily, though, that is because the individual is a cog in the Muslim weal.

Jihad, then, is not about becoming a better *person* by doing good deeds, but becoming a better *Muslim* by submitting to this divine cause—"submission" being the meaning of the word *Islam*. Jihad is shorthand for *jihad fi sabil Allah*: to struggle in the path of Allah. The cause of Allah is not to consume fewer calories or brush after every meal. The *Dictionary of Islam* elaborates that jihad was established as "a divine institution" for the specific "purpose of advancing Islam." *That* is the end to which the jihadist dedicates himself: to advance Islam. Jihad is about promoting the Islamic state, not the individual Muslim. It unquestionably has a military connotation. Regardless of the rose-tinted glasses donned by Islam's Western admirers, Islam's established jurisprudential schools construe *fi sabil Allah* as a reference to those fighting for

God's cause.[11] Nevertheless, the purpose of jihad is not to kill
infidels. The purpose is to institute sharia.

Annihilation Is Fine, but Surrenders Are Gladly Accepted

Here, it is necessary, again, to address some sleight-of-hand. The
Koran croons many an ode to tolerance. Most, like the afore-
described verse about interfaith tolerance quoted by Abdurrahman
Wahid, are from Mohammed's early Meccan period, when he
was seeking to recruit converts to the new religion. Again, Islam's
established schools hold that these benign injunctions were
superseded by the contrary, brutalizing verses of the later Medinan period. As Robert Spencer points out, Sura 9—home to Sura
9:29, the verse of the sword—is taken by most authorities to be
the very last Koranic chapter revealed.[12] That is, it is thought to
be Allah's last word on the subjects it addresses. That uncongenial
fact is ignored by the "religion of peace" crowd. Their unparalleled favorite scripture is Sura 2:256, the Meccan instruction that
there shall be "no compulsion in religion." Thus they argue, à la
Jacqui Smith, that jihadist violence simply must be anti-Islamic,
and that jihad itself simply must be a salubrious obligation along
the lines of giving up candy for Lent.

No, the objective of jihad is to induce the adoption of sharia,
by armed combat if necessary. Though it doesn't pass my personal straight-face test, imposing sharia is said to be consistent
with the injunction against compulsion in religion because sharia
does not force non-believers to convert—it "merely" sets up a
caste system in which Muslims are favored and non-Muslims are
told their subordinate status can be modified only by conversion
or death. Still, while Islamist terrorists would surely be delighted
if, say, the destruction of the Twin Towers induced everyone

to convert, conversion is not the direct goal of jihadist activity, violent or not. The goal is sharia. Sayyid Qutb, a luminary in the Muslim Brotherhood, explained that jihad proceeds whenever Islam is obstructed by "the political system of the state, the socio-economic system based on races and classes, and behind all these, the military power of the government." This system is then supplanted by Islamic law. *At that point,* Islam can be "addressed to peoples' hearts and minds," purportedly without compulsion, "and they are free to accept or reject it with an open mind."[13]

Jihad is not trying to convert you—not directly. It is seeking the imposition of Allah's law, which, so the story goes, will lead us all to become Muslims but not force us to do so. Allah's law happens to be antithetical to bedrock American principles: It establishes a state religion, rejects the freedom of citizens to govern themselves irrespective of a religious code, proscribes freedom of conscience, nullifies economic freedom, destroys the principle of equality under the law, subjugates non-Muslims in the humiliation of dhimmitude, and calls for the execution of homosexuals and apostates. Nevertheless, its adoption produces what Islamists risibly portray as the "non-coercive" environment in which people then "freely" embrace Islam.

That environment is achieved by violence *only if violence is necessary.* On that score, of greater significance than actual violence is the *effect* of violence, not terrorism but *terror.* The pump is primed by an omnipresent message: the religious duty of jihad makes the Islamist willing to resort to savagery, or at least to encourage and defend resort to savagery, whenever that may be necessary to advance his cause. The effective communication of this message enables the Islamist to achieve his ends without resorting to violence—to exploit the atmosphere of intimidation created by the terrorist without having to engage in more than saber-rattling himself.

In his seminal 1960 study, *The Society of Muslim Brothers*, the late Arabist Robert P. Mitchell explained the thinking of Ikhwan founder Hassan al-Banna (my italics):

> The certainty that *jihad* had this physical connotation is evidenced by *the relationship always implied between it and the possibility, even the necessity, of death and martyrdom.* Death, as an important end of *jihad*, was extolled by Banna in a phrase which came to be a famous part of his legacy: "the art of death." "Death is art." The Koran has commanded people to love death more than life. Unless "the philosophy of the Koran on death" replaces "the love of life" which has consumed Muslims, then they will reach naught. Victory can only come with the mastery of "the art of death." . . . The movement cannot succeed, Banna insists, without this dedicated and unqualified kind of *jihad*.[14]

It is only natural, then, that the term *jihad* is drenched in historical gore: Sharia authoritarianism is not a very attractive proposition. Those seeking to foist it on the unwilling understood—how could they not?—that violence would often be necessary. It is not so much death, though, as the *art of death*, the searing demonstration of purpose and commitment, that is required.

In a book he called *Jihad*, Banna maintained:

> *Jihad* is an obligation from Allah on every Muslim and cannot be ignored nor [*sic*] evaded. Allah has ascribed great importance to *jihad* and has made the reward of the martyrs and fighters in His way a splendid one. Only those who have acted similarly and who have modeled themselves upon the martyrs in their performance of *jihad* can join them in this reward.[15]

To support this proposition, Banna relied on scripture. Included, as one would expect, was Sura 9:29, which makes clear that willing submissions are welcome. Jihad enthusiastically endorses war. War, though, is about much more than violence. It is about defeating the enemy's will by resort to any and all means, including combat, that one is willing to use. "Fighting the unbelievers," Banna urged, "involves all possible efforts that are necessary to dismantle the power of the enemies of Islam including beating them, plundering their wealth, destroying their places of worship, and smashing their idols."[16]

The jihadist needn't savage his targets if Islam can be advanced without a fight. An invading army does not go home if the locals surrender. It pushes forward, adding to its domains until it finally meets real resistance. At that point, it promptly deems itself under siege and gets back to all that "lesser" jihad.

chapter four

ELIMINATING AND DESTROYING THE WESTERN CIVILIZATION FROM WITHIN

It is not every day that, even as the game is being played, the opposition's playbook falls into your hands, telling you, chapter and verse, exactly how he intends to beat your brains in. Yet the United States has long been in possession of the Muslim Brotherhood's playbook—in multiple iterations, as a matter of fact.

Those of us who follow such things could perhaps be forgiven for wondering, at least for a moment, if that's really much of a coup. True, the Brothers are a slippery lot, their positions often couched in ambiguity to keep critics off-balance. Yet, through the years, many Brothers have graduated to terrorist activity, and many others have been just as blunt in speaking their minds as our solons have been reliable in ignoring and suppressing what they say. Plus, "Jihad is our way. Dying in the way of Allah is our highest hope," etc., is not exactly subtle.

Still, by any standard, the Brotherhood memorandum obtained by the FBI and presented in Texas at the *Holy Land Foundation* terrorism-financing trial in 2007 was an eye-opener. The document, called "An Explanatory Memorandum on the General Strategic Goal for the Group In North America," and dated May 22, 1991,[1] had been prepared by Mohamed Akram (a/k/a "Mohammed Adlouni"), an intimate associate of Sheikh Yusuf al-Qaradawi, currently Ikhwan's chief theoretician. At the time, Akram was the organization's top leader in America. Writing for what he obviously thought would be Brotherhood eyes only, he didn't mince words:

> The Ikhwan must understand that their work in America is a kind of grand jihad in eliminating and destroying the Western civilization from within and "sabotaging" its miserable house by their hands and the hands of the believers so that it is eliminated and God's religion is made victorious over all other religions.

In fact, this grand jihad-by-sabotage has been underway for nearly half a century. Its bottom-up elements have stressed Islamist domination of Muslim education, community centers, and mosques. That means it is now raising, in our midst, its third generation of operatives and sympathizers.

The methodical campaign and its resulting infrastructure have been made possible by untold billions in funding from the Kingdom of Saudi Arabia, which has been the Brotherhood's lifeline since the 1950s. We hear constant clamor over alleged Saudi financial contributions to *terrorism*, allegations the Kingdom indignantly denies, at least insofar as they pertain to the *regime*— the evidence of terrorism underwriting by individual Saudi *citizens* and *institutions*, like the evidence of terrorist acts by individual Saudis, is too overwhelming to be denied. Comparatively little is said, however, about Saudi underwriting of *Islamism*. That's not so easy to deny: the Saudis, after all, *are Islamists*. So they're hoping you'll continue not to notice while the Brotherhood continues "eliminating and destroying the Western civilization from within." That is, taking their lead from the U.S. government, the Saudis figure all will be well as long as they continue keeping their fingerprints off the bombs the ideology they export makes inevitable.

As the startling 1991 Brotherhood memo elucidates, the Islamists fittingly describe themselves as engaged in a "civilizational jihad." The United States has been an express target of this jihad since the 1970s. The memo is far from the only smoking gun to that effect.

In 1977, Youssef Nada, a master organizer who has been a Brotherhood member since the 1940s, convened a meeting of Islamist luminaries, including Sheikh Qaradawi, in Lugano, Switzerland. Its purpose, the journalist Ian Johnson reports, was to "set up a structure to guide the growth of political Islam in Europe and the United States."[2] Nada was the director of the al-Taqwa Bank of Lugano, and for years he has been suspected by Swiss and American authorities of laundering money for al Qaeda, Hamas and various other terrorist groups. As a result, he has been specially designated as a global terrorist under both American and United Nations legal procedures for the past nine years.[3] Within weeks after the 9/11 atrocities, Swiss authorities raided Nada's posh Campione villa. As Patrick Poole recounts,

Included in the documents seized during the raid . . . was a
14-page plan written in Arabic and dated December 1, 1982,
which outlines a 12-point strategy to *"establish an Islamic
government on earth"*—identified as *The Project*. According to
testimony given to Swiss authorities by Nada, the unsigned
document was prepared by "Islamic researchers" associated
with the Muslim Brotherhood.

What makes *The Project* so different from the standard
"Death of America! Death to Israel!" and "Establish the global
caliphate!" Islamist rhetoric is that it represents a flexible,
multi-phased, long-term approach to the "cultural invasion"
of the West. Calling for the utilization of various tactics, rang-
ing from immigration, infiltration, surveillance, propaganda,
protest, deception, political legitimacy and terrorism, *The
Project* has served for more than two decades as the Muslim
Brotherhood "master plan." . . . Rather than focusing on terrorism as the sole method of group action, as is the case with
Al-Qaeda, in perfect postmodern fashion the use of terror
falls into a multiplicity of options available to progressively
infiltrate, confront, and eventually establish Islamic domination over the West.[4]

The seizures of the Brotherhood's gameplan leave no doubt
about its intentions. As aptly described by the former U.S. intelligence analyst Joseph Myers, these Islamists seek nothing less
than "the usurpation and replacement" of America's foundations—Judeo-Christianity and Western liberalism—by Islam.[5]
Given that reality, and the equally indisputable fact that the sabotage strategy relies on leveraging American liberties and democratic processes to Islamist advantage, the current U.S. strategic
response of embracing the Brotherhood is akin to confronting an

epidemic by increasing one's unprotected exposures to the contagion. Like a pathogen or a predator, the Ikhwan won't be dissuaded upon seeing what nice people we are.

The Brotherhood's Islam of the Founders

What the Brotherhood is and how it operates can be elusive. Its founder, Hassan al-Banna, once called it "a Salafiyya message, a Sunni way, a Sufi truth, a political organization, an athletic group, a cultural-educational union, an economic company, and a social idea"[6]—and that was decades before it diffused into an alphabet soup of global tentacles. Nonetheless, we need to grasp what we're up against.

Banna, a charismatic, Cairo-trained educator known to his acolytes as "the Guide," established the Brotherhood in 1928, in the Egyptian town of Isma'iliyaa. The movement was virulently anti-colonial, but not because Banna was a nationalist or an Egyptian patriot—he was neither. Banna's loyalty was to the Muslim umma and the ideal that Islam must dominate across national lines. He was anti-colonial because he abhorred the West. In his mind, as the French feminist Caroline Fourest perceptively writes, "the worst feature of colonialism was not the occupation itself, but the fact that the occupation went hand in hand with an acceptance of Christianity and, above all, with the liberalization of moral standards."[7] Banna thus harbored deep resentment of the presence and influence Britain retained long after formally granting its Egyptian protectorate independence in 1922.

The Brotherhood's development was also spurred by Turkey's rigorous campaign of secularization. Following the final defeat of the Ottoman Empire in World War I, Kemal Ataturk had spearheaded a successful independence movement, expelling occupiers and establishing an independent state. Determined to turn westward, Ataturk drove Islam out of the public square and marginalized it in the classroom. In 1924, he abolished the Caliphate, a symbolically shattering event for Muslims even though the institution had withered by then into a ceremonial office.[8]

The horrified Banna had drawn precisely the opposite conclusion about the sorry state of the Muslim world. For him, Islam was the solution. The problem had been too little of it, not too much. And not just any Islam. Banna had in mind a very particular brand: Salafism.

The term *Salafiyyah* comes from the phrase *al-Salaf al-Salih*, the "Righteous Ancestors," referring to Mohammed and his companions.[9] Banna, a scholar of Salafism's original nineteenth-century theorists, reasoned that by degrading the unalloyed Islam of the first Islamic community with countless accommodations to modernity, Muslims had strayed from the prophet's teaching and example. Banna, moreover, was a student of Rashid Rida, an intensely anti-Western "reformer" who reaffirmed the inseparability of Islam as a religion and as a political entity, arguing that "Islam is not fully in being as long as there does not exist a strong and independent Muslim state that is able to put into operation the laws of Islam."[10] Rida decried rationalism and sought to steer Salafism away from modernizing influences. Like Rida, Banna championed what Fourest describes as an "archaic fundamentalism": a "version of Islamism violently opposed to any form of rationalism that bore the slightest resemblance to Western ways," in particular, the separation of the secular and spiritual realms.[11]

Only by returning to the Islam of the founders could the umma reverse its political, economic, and social torpor. This would require faithfully implementing the divine law, sharia. With sharia's injunctions firmly in place, the Muslim Nation would inevitably rise to the hegemony that was Allah's due. "It is the nature of Islam to dominate, not to be dominated," Banna taught. The mission of Islam is "to impose its law on all nations and to extend its power to the entire planet."[12]

Today, ignorance about Islamist ideology is widespread, even after decades of attacks have made terrorism the top U.S. security challenge. Salafism, in particular, remains a mystery to most Americans, though it is the enemy's animating ideology. Many have heard the word, but few grasp what it denotes. Reasonably, but not apodictically, even knowledgeable Muslims use "Salafism" interchangeably with "Wahhabism," the aforementioned fundamentalist Islam of Muhammad ibn Abd al-Wahhab that is Saudi Arabia's state religion.[13] To mention either one in our public discourse is usually to hurl an epithet, not to convey any actual understanding of what the terms mean. Islamists have used our ignorance to great effect. Most Americans who have some passing acquaintance with the term "Salafist" assume it is a label for terrorists. Therefore, in the public mind, Salafists (and Wahhabists) are the real bad guys, to be sharply distinguished from the ubiquitous Muslim "moderates"—who are "moderate" because they allegedly "reject terrorism," not because their views are actually benign.

This is a hopelessly ill-conceived way of looking at the world, but leftists—who dominate policy circles, the academy, and the media—are delighted to have us see it that way. With Americans in the dark, Islamists freely pass themselves off as moderates. That makes it politically palatable for the left to collaborate with them in undermining the American establishment. There's no reason, however, why the rest of us should abide an arrangement, steeped in fiction, that is progressively (pardon the pun) eroding our liberty and security.

To be clear: Salafism, the original inspiration of the Muslim Brotherhood, is the guiding ideology of all Islamists, the Islamist terrorists *as well as those Islamists who purport to reject terrorism.* Both types of Islamists want the same thing, the Islamicization of society. Both reject Western rationalism and the Christian unity of faith and reason. Both favor sharia determinism. Both support the development of fundamentalist Muslim enclaves and the ultimate supplanting of American constitutional democracy by Islamic law. Non-terrorist Islamists want to overthrow the United States government every bit as much as the terrorists do. They are not moderates. Their differences with the terrorists are over means and methods, not goals.

It is freely conceded that some of these differences are intense and each side fires invective, and worse, at the other. Furthermore, occasional efforts to refine Salafism by nuance or doctrinal innovation prompt raging protest from terrorists and spark controversy between other Islamists.[14] But we should not be fooled by any of this. For all their infighting, the Islamists and the terrorists start and hope to end in the same place. They are the flip sides of the same revolution, playing a good-cop/bad-cop routine—which is really bad-cop/worse-cop. The differences between the two camps are overwhelmingly a matter of tactics, not goals. They have a lot more in common with each other than they do with West—starting with brute fact that they both see America as their enemy.

Banna's ultimate ambition was the re-establishment of the Caliphate, not as a vestige of bygone glory but as the vibrant seat of Muslim empire, in the Arab world and beyond. He wanted to restore it to the centrality it held under Abu Bakr, Umar, and Uthman, Islam's original "rightly guided" caliphs.[15] Banna's plan, however, was not dreamy. It was practical, patient, and thoroughgoing, from the ground up—civilizational, not transiently political.

Revolution from the Ground Up

Just as any great journey must begin with a single step, the pursuit of universal dominion had to begin by sculpting the individual Muslim. The seven-step plan of Banna, the teacher, began with the education and "forming" of the Muslim person. From there it built out progressively to the "forming" of the Muslim family, "the active fulfillment of the meaning of Islam among the Brothers, and the most fundamental of its 'educational' instruments."[16] The family was the foundation for building the Muslim society, a process that included an emphasis on training and preparation for martyrdom. The Muslim society would lead to Muslim government.

Having grabbed the reins of power through this process (called "grassroots Islamicization" by Gilles Kepel), the Brotherhood would move on to transforming Muslim countries into sharia states.[17] Then, upon consolidating power over the Islamic world, the umma could set its sights on expansion. First, Islam's one-time European holdings would be recaptured, for as Banna wrote:

> We want the Islamic flag to be hoisted once again on high,
> fluttering in the wind, in all those lands that have had the
> good fortune to harbor Islam for a certain period of time and
> where the muzzein's call sounded in the *takbirs* and the *tahlis*.
> Then fate decreed that the light of Islam be extinguished in
> these lands that returned to unbelief. Thus Andalusia, Sic-
> ily, the Balkans, the Italian coast, as well as the islands of the

Mediterranean, are all of them Muslim Mediterranean colonies and they must return to the Islamic fold. The Mediterranean Sea and the Red Sea must once again become Muslim seas, as they once were.[18]

The plan was that eventually the growing Muslim Nation would achieve global dominance. Banna anticipated his seven steps would unfold in three stages, beginning with "the first stage through which all movements must pass, the stage of 'propaganda, communication, and information.'" Above all, that meant controlling the classroom, "pedagogy as propaganda."[19] This was the surest means for the Brotherhood to "recruit and indoctrinate core activists," notes Steven Emerson, America's leading expert on Islamism. The Brotherhood put a high priority on establishing press outlets to spread the Islamist message and refute its adversaries; it developed lessons and trained lecturers to carry its doctrines into schools, mosques, and meeting halls; Banna himself, a spellbinding speaker, personally taught classes in preaching and guidance, with the goal of exporting Brotherhood ideology.[20]

The second stage would involve "formation, selection, and preparation," with the Brothers "endearing themselves to the population by creating charities, clinics, schools, and other services." It would also stress military preparedness: formation into "rovers," "battalions," and a "secret apparatus" to spearhead the eventual revolution. As Professor Mitchell observed in regard to "the tone of the training which gave the Society its distinctive qualities":

If the Muslim Brothers were more effectively violent than other groups on the Egyptian scene, it was because *militancy* and *martyrdom* had been elevated to central virtues in the

Society's ethos. Its literature and speeches were permeated with references identifying it and its purposes in military terms. Banna told members again and again that they were "the army of liberation, carrying on your shoulders the message of liberation; you are the battalions of salvation for this nation afflicted by calamity." They were "the troops of God" whose "armament" was their "Islamic morality." (Emphasis in original).[21]

This holistic indoctrination would anneal the Brothers for the final stage of "execution": the point at which the Muslim communities, having formed countless "battalions" that were fully prepared intellectually, physically, and spiritually would "conquer . . . every obstinate tyrant."[22]

It's worth mulling over the fact that Banna is still required reading in the indoctrination of would-be Brothers in all those "moderate" Ikhwan branches said to be foreswearing terrorism throughout the world. A couple of things are especially noteworthy about his trailblazing Islamist blueprint. First, while the plan is revolutionary in all its aspects, and has pervasive overtones of violence and martyrdom—Banna's "art of death"—comparatively little of it involves combat. Most of the headway is to be made by controlling the education system, influencing the media, and ingratiating the movement with an unsuspecting population. This is the very program being implemented today, before our very eyes, in America and the West.

Secondly, even though Banna never forswore terrorism, as some of his progeny claim to have done, we nevertheless find in his roadmap the seeds of modern Islamism's internecine turbulence. Western opinion elites would like you to believe that the Ikhwan and other "nonviolent" Islamists are worth cultivating because, by rejecting at least some jihadist savagery, they have purportedly broken with the terrorists. Yet Banna's blueprint illustrates that Islamists who stress nonviolent jihadist strategies *are not opposed to violence in principle*. Indeed, they spend much of their energy preparing for the possibility—many "nonviolent" Brotherhood branches maintain paramilitary training camps. The Brothers simply want violence, when employed, to be productive. They want it to be sprung only at mature point of readiness, when it actually stands a chance of defeating the enemy.

The Islamist's problem with the terrorist is not that the latter acts forcibly but that he acts *prematurely*. Jonathan Dahoah Halevi, an Israeli military reserves officer who studies Islamism at the Jerusalem Center for Public Affairs, puts it well: the Brotherhood fears "that an al Qaeda attack against the West at this time might hamper the Islamic movement's buildup and focus the West on the threat implicit in Muslim communities."[23] If forcible jihad operations wear the enemy down and render him ripe for the taking, however, all to the good. In fact, when it comes to terror strikes against Western forces stationed in Muslim countries, the Brotherhood not only approves but actively encourages violent jihad.

At its highest level, the Ikhwan acknowledges that it is on the same team as al Qaeda. Asked in a 2008 interview, for example, whether he considered Osama bin Laden to be a terrorist, Mohammed Mahdi Akef, the Brotherhood's current Supreme Guide, was adamant that he did not. "In all certainty," he proclaimed, bin Laden should be considered a "mujahid"—a term of honor for a raider or warrior participating in jihad for Allah's cause.[24] Akef added that he had "no doubt" about bin Laden's "sincerity in resisting the occupation," a point on which bin Laden was "close to Allah on high." Though the Supreme Guide said he objected to al Qaeda's killing of civilians, he stressed, "I support its activities against the occupiers."[25]

Targeting America: Violence Overseas, Sabotage at Home

It is indeed a core Ikhwan principle that violent jihad is a duty against infidels who occupy any territory Islamists deem to be Muslim land. It makes no difference that the infidels are in the Muslim land for the purpose of freeing Muslims from tyranny. So it should have come as no surprise, even to the Brotherhood's "2–4–6–8, who could be more moderate?" pep squad, when the Brotherhood publicly issued an August 2004 global appeal exhorting the umma to support Muslims fighting against coalition forces in Iraq.[26] Nor should any eyebrows have arched when Sheikh Qaradawi followed up that appeal with a fatwa declaring it a religious duty for Muslims to fight the United States in Iraq— just as al Qaeda and others were then doing, to horrific effect.[27]

Remarkably, even after this edict, Qaradawi's admirers in and out of the U.S. government continue to swoon over his "condemnation" of the 9/11 attacks. For anyone not desperate to be convinced that night is day and Brothers are moderates, the sheikh's objection to the suicide-hijackings was transparently tactical. Not so, Ikhwan apologists counter, Qaradawi clearly stated that his objection centered on al Qaeda's targeting of civilians.

Well, of course he did. The Brotherhood's jihad strategy, as they've told us again and again if we'd only listen, is sabotage. Devastating as 9/11 was, Qaradawi knew it was not going to destroy the United States and would surely provoke a blistering American military, intelligence, and law-enforcement response. That was certain to make the lives of all Islamists highly unpleasant for a while—to be precise, until around mid-2004, when the pendulum began swinging back in the Brotherhood's favor thanks to the U.S. government's obstinate avoidance of Islamic scripture's nexus to Islamist terror, coupled with the traction the Left's war against the war finally got from the Abu Ghraib prisoner-abuse scandal.

Taken at face value, Qaradawi's claimed opposition to attacks on civilians was not just prudent public-relations but consistent Brotherhood ideology. Civilians are potential converts to Islam and a source of financial support to the Muslim state. As the verse of the sword reminds us, if they don't convert, they must pay the *jizya*.

There is, however, no reason to take Qaradawi merely at face value. Once the 9/11 heat was off in 2004, he not only issued his fatwa but took pains to clarify his stand on "civilians":

> I said that I forbid the killing of civilians. I said that it is
> permitted to kill only those who fight. Islam forbids killing
> women, youth, and so on. I said so openly, but I asked, "Who
> is a civilian?" When engineers, laborers, and technicians
> enter [Iraq] with the American army, are they considered
> civilians? Is a fighter only the one inside the tank or also the
> one servicing it? I am speaking of the interpretation of the
> word "civilian."

By this logic, Emerson points out, "anyone providing support to a military force in a Muslim country" would be fair game for violent jihad: from the mechanic who services the tank, to the defense factory worker who builds it, to the American taxpayer who pays for it.[28] Qaradawi subsequently reaffirmed that this was exactly his position on American civilians in Iraq, telling the Arabic press, "One who abets the occupiers—his status is identical to theirs. The occupation is fighting against Muslims and anyone who helps the occupation has the same status as the military."[29]

Underscoring the influence of Qaradawi and the Brotherhood, scholars at storied al-Azhar rallied to defend his position. Abd Al-Mu'ti Bayyoumi, a former dean of the "Faculty of Religious Fundamentals," echoed that "civilians who take part in military operations, whether it be supplying food or giving medical treatment to the fighters, their legal status is that of fighters who are attacking land, honor, and property, and therefore there is no prohibition in Islam against killing them." Mansur Al-Rifa'i Ubeid, once the Undersecretary of the Department of Religious Endowments, added that it was "illogical" to believe that "the U.S. is sending its civilians to Iraq in the state of war without their having a role in the military operations. Therefore, they are not civilians, but fighters whose status is identical to that of the military combatants." A prominent al-Azhar lecturer, Dr. Salih Zaydan, was blunt: "Whoever cooperates with the fighters who attack the land of Muslims, like the American civilians who are aiding the military in Iraq, becomes through his actions a fighter himself. Muslims are permitted to fight against such people and to kill them so as to defend land, honor, and property, and thus there is no prohibition against killing them."[30]

On this point there is no meaningful difference between the reasoning of Qaradawi and the Islamist scholars, on the one hand, and al Qaeda, on the other. Bin Laden rationalized in late 1998, after bombing the U.S. embassies in Kenya and Tanzania, that "every American man is an enemy—whether he fights us directly or pays his taxes." He hit the same notes shortly after 9/11:

The American people should remember that they pay taxes to their government, they elect their president, their government

manufactures arms and gives them to Israel and Israel uses
them to massacre Palestinians. The American Congress endorses all government measures, and this proves that all of America
is responsible for the atrocities committed against Muslims. All
of America, because they elect the Congress.[31]

Qaradawi and bin Laden obviously differ on when killing
Americans is helpful to the cause, but they are both all for killing
Americans. The Islamist differs from the Islamist terrorist in his
calculation that terrorism is sometimes counterproductive, that
poorly chosen targets can set the movement back. Terrorism is
not recommended if its likely net effect is to stiffen the enemy's
resolve and provoke a retaliation that reverses gains hard won
by other jihad strategies: propaganda, education, indoctrination,
communication, ingratiation, and infiltration. But terrorism is
fully supported and encouraged in many instances. In fact, Qaradawi has pointedly said, "I hope my life will end with a virtuous
death, like [the death] sought by warriors fighting Jihad for the
sake of Allah"—a "virtuous death" by "martyrdom" while fighting
"the enemies of Islam," he vividly added, in which he hoped his
"head would be severed from [his] body," like the suicide bombers
he has glorified.[32]

And as between al Qaeda and America, there's no doubt about
where the Brotherhood's sympathies lie.

A Civilizational Movement

The movement created by Banna has gone through tumult and
transition throughout its eighty-two-year history, but it has survived and now thrives because it combines ideological rigidity
with tactical flexibility. In an important research monograph

on the Brotherhood, the Hudson Institute's Israel Elad Altman observes that this combination is compatible with "an inclusive mass movement rather than an exclusive, elitist, vanguard organization," indicating that the Brotherhood "looks at itself not as one more socio-political force among others, but as the real Muslim community."[33]

This fact is underscored by Banna's choice of the organization's name. He instructed his underlings, "Leave aside appearances and officialdom. Let the principle and priority of our union be thought, morality, and action. We are brothers in the service of Islam, so we are the Muslim Brotherhood."[34] As Fourest observes, "Banna understood that a movement that could not be pinned down would be indestructible." The name "Muslim Brotherhood" reflects the ambiguity strategically built into Ikhwan positions: It makes for a serviceable title, but "brother" is also a monotonous mode of address among Muslims. "Muslim Brotherhood" was thus "an official movement and a school of thought that one could claim to belong to, or deny being part of, according to circumstances."[35]

The scam has clearly had its intended effect on Western diplomats and intelligence agencies. They resist accepting the role of ideology and culture in Islamist militancy, and consequently delude themselves that Brotherhood franchises—and even such unabashedly terrorist organizations as Hamas (a Brotherhood creation) and Hezbollah (Shiite Iran's forward militia)—are akin to political parties. Unlike al Qaeda, which even the most optimistic big-thinkers generally concede is global and incorrigible, our experts see these other Islamists as motivated by local grievances of a political nature; they can be refined into reason and normalcy, so the theory goes, by the alchemy of "participatory democracy."

This egregious fantasy misconstrues both the nature of Islamism and the Ikhwan's self-conception. The Muslim Brotherhood is a transnational, civilizational movement with hegemonic aspirations and what Altman rightly calls a "universal message" that is contemptuous of individual liberty. It is committed to spreading Islam, in Qaradawi's description, as

> a creed, a way of worship, a set of behaviors and ethics, as a law and as an ideal civilization that connects the earth to the heavens, finds a place between the heart and mind, balances between rights and obligations and between individual rights and communal interests.[36]

The movement transcends ordinary, parochial politics. When expedient, the Brotherhood will gladly use politics just like it will use any other tool at its disposal. In the early days, Banna himself even accepted financial help from the British government and its perceived cat's paw, the Egyptian monarchy—which, much like today's sages, embraced the hallucination that the Brotherhood might be a useful lever against other opponents—even as the Brotherhood proclaimed its hatred of colonialism, the West, and democratic politics.[37] (When called on it, Banna tried to explain his acceptance of enemy largesse; when that didn't fly with his dismayed followers, the Guide, in the best Brotherhood tradition, simply denied the whole thing ever happened.)[38] But the Brotherhood has never been political in the sense that, say, the Republican Party is. Islamism does not participate in politics; it *uses* politics. And when it does, we overlook at our peril that it is doctrinally and incorrigibly anti-democratic. For Islamists, democracy is a tool for acquiring power, not a culture of governance.

The Brotherhood's Western apologists are profoundly impressed, and expect you to be too, by the fact that Islamist terrorists "look with contempt and derision" on the Brotherhood's apparent acceptance of "the rules of the game set by 'apostate rulers,'" as Fawaz Gerges puts it.[39] But this willingness to engage in politics—whether in democratic or authoritarian societies—is not a concession. It is a jihad strategy, called *siyash*, and it is fully consistent with sabotage.

Yet government experts natter endlessly about condemnations of the Ikhwan by the likes of bin Laden's deputy, Ayman al-Zawahiri, and Omar Abdel Rahman, the "Blind Sheikh" who instigated the 1993 World Trade Center bombing (and is the central figure in my *Willful Blindness*). These terrorists, though once close Ikhwan allies, reason that by interacting with secular governments—particularly the ones that fail to enforce sharia in Muslim countries—the Brotherhood legitimizes those regimes. Further, it breaks faith with Sayyid Qutb, its martyred hero who even in death remains, alongside Banna, the Brotherhood's most influential theorist. Qutb was long imprisoned and finally executed by Nasser in 1966, when Zawahiri and Abdel Rahman were just coming of age. Heavily influenced by his scholarship, they have spent their lifetimes trying to overthrow the secular Egyptian government of Nasser's successors.[40] Patience not being a notable virtue of mass-murderers, the Brotherhood's sleeping-with-the-enemy strategy enrages them. By their lights, it indicates a lackluster commitment to jihad. Seizing on this point of fierce contention, our big thinkers deduce that if the terrorists figure the Brothers are soft, they obviously must be moderates— so *we can work with these guys!*

It's preposterous. The journalist Lawrence Wright accurately observes that "Banna completely rejected the Western model of secular, democratic government, which was opposed to his notion of universal Islamic rule."[41] The Brotherhood has never wavered from its original "insistence on (1) Islam as a total system, complete unto itself, and the final arbiter of life in all its categories; (2) an Islam formulated from and based on its two primary sources, the revelation in the Koran and the wisdom of the Prophet in the Sunna; and (3) an Islam applicable to all times and to all places."[42] Even as Banna consorted by day with governments, his organization worked relentlessly by night to overturn them. He did not embrace politics for the sake of compromise or because he believed in the give-and-take of everyday governing; his assessment was that engaging government and infiltrating governmental institutions was the most promising route to radically transforming them. He dealt with terrorist backbiting from the start, warning that the mountain to be climbed was steep and rashness would only set the movement back; but he did so while readying his charges for violent jihad and assuring them he knew that only "action, not speech, and preparation, not slogans, would guarantee victory."[43] His differences with "the anxious and the hasty" were over the timing of force, not its use. Banna was no more a democrat than is Zawahiri or Abdel Rahman, and, much like them, he would have preferred an authoritarian government that was at least nominally Muslim to a democracy based on the consent of the governed.

In that regard, what could be said of Banna can also be said of Sheikh Qaradawi, who, like his mentor, has also dilated on the differences between Islamists and Islamist terrorists. Like many of Islamism's most noxious instigators, the eighty-three-year-old Egyptian was a prodigy; he had memorized the Koran by the age of ten and went on to scholarly renown at al-Azhar University, earning a doctorate in Muslim jurisprudence. His life has spanned the life of the Brotherhood: He became a Banna disciple in his youth, was imprisoned during the persecution of Qutb, and has at least twice been offered the position of Supreme Guide—a distinction he has turned down in favor of spreading Islamism's tentacles in the West and evolving its mass-communications potential. Among other institutions, the sheikh sits on the board of the Oxford Centre for Islamic Studies and heads the Dublin-based European Council for Fatwa and Research. He has also developed a huge international following through his pioneering exploitation of the Internet and his weekly television program, "Sharia and Life," broadcast by al-Jezeera in Qatar, where he has been based since 1961.[44]

Qaradawi has remained the Brotherhood's leading light, its acknowledged intellectual powerhouse. In our upside-down world, that makes him the recipient of lavish praise from the U.S. State Department. It was in 2005, a year after Qaradawi's fatwa calling for the killing of American troops in Iraq, that Alberto Fernandez, then-Director for Public Diplomacy at State's Bureau of Near Eastern Affairs, gushed that the sheikh was an "intelligent and thoughtful voice from the region, . . . an important figure that deserves our attention."[45] Naturally, Fernandez shared these pearls of wisdom in a guest-appearance on IslamOnline.net, Qaradawi's project for promoting Islamism via the web. America's top public diplomat in the region, whose accomplishments in that post also included taking to al-Jezeera's airwaves to rip the "arrogance and . . . stupidity from the United States in Iraq,"[46] was Qaradawi's perfect foil: As he lavished praise on the sheikh and bragged about the incorporation of sharia law in the new constitutions State had helped write for Afghanistan and Iraq (for Fernandez, that's evidently not where our "stupidity" comes in), he mentioned neither Qaradawi's fatwas authorizing the murder of Americans nor the fact that Qaradawi had been banned from entering the United States since 1999 for promoting terrorism.

The nauseating Fernandez did have one thing right, though. Qaradawi deserves our attention.

A Practical Man in a Practical Jihad

As the sheikh has framed the Brotherhood's contretemps with al Qaeda and other terrorists, those who "wish to hurry to establish an Islamic state with an Islamic rule seek clashes with the existing regimes in the Arab states despite the fact that they [i.e., the terrorists] don't have sufficient strength; they don't have military strength and not even the mental strength to establish an Islamic rule." At the same time, Qaradawi ruefully observes, "there are great forces" in Muslim societies that support the existing regimes—a fact he blames on the enemy West:

> [Muslim] elites . . . especially among the intellectuals who are described, unfortunately, as "the elites" . . . have westernized, and the westernization of their thought and culture corrupted the Arab regimes. The cultural invasion, the cultural colonialism, the westernization—call it what you want—reshaped the way these elites are thinking, and turned them into foreign elements amongst their own people. We must change them, and this is why the campaign continues and it must continue on different levels—on cultural, educational, social, traditional, and political levels, on the level of constitutional reforms, political reforms, and the granting of freedoms to peoples, including freedom for jihad.[47]

Qaradawi and the Brotherhood are not opposed to terrorism as a matter of principle, far from it. They simply think, given cur-

78

rent conditions in Muslim countries with secular governments, that terrorism is not the best tool in the jihad kit for the job at hand. In point of fact, Qaradawi has great enthusiasm for violent jihad where it is most likely to work. For example, in Israel (known in Islamist parlance as "Palestine"), he not only supports suicide bombings but has issued a fatwa approving female participation in them. Yes, for the Muslim woman, driving her own car to the local market may raise major sharia issues, but "martyrdom operations" are quite another matter. Qaradawi reminds us, with the usual reliance on scripture, that such operations are

> the greatest of all sorts of jihad in the cause of Allah. A martyrdom operation is carried out by a person who sacrifices himself, deeming his life of less value than striving in the cause of Allah, in the cause of restoring the land and preserving the dignity. To such a valorous attitude applies the following Koranic verse: "And of mankind is he who would sell himself, seeking the pleasure of Allah; and Allah hath compassion on (His) bondmen [Sura 2:207]." But a clear distinction has to be made here between martyrdom and suicide. Suicide is an act or instance of killing oneself intentionally out of despair, and finding no outlet except putting an end to one's life. On the other hand, martyrdom is a heroic act of choosing to suffer death in the cause of Allah, and that's why it's considered by most Muslim scholars as one of the greatest forms of jihad.

When jihad becomes an individual duty, as when the enemy seizes the Muslim territory, a woman becomes entitled to take part in it alongside men. Jurists maintained that when the enemy assaults a given Muslim territory, it becomes incumbent upon all its residents to fight against them to the extent that a woman should go out even without the consent of her husband, a son can go too without the permission of his parent, a slave without the approval of his master, and the employee without the leave of his employer. . . . I believe a woman can participate in this form of jihad according to her own means and condition. Also, the organizers of these martyr operations can benefit from some believing women as they may do, in some cases, what is impossible for men to do.[48]

Tough to argue with him on that last observation—a man is apt to have a tough time passing off the telltale swell of explosives under his tunic as the natural effects of pregnancy.

And that's the point: Qaradawi is a practical man in a practical jihad, where goals are clear but methods are negotiable. Consequently, the participation of Islamists in the political system, and even their maintaining cordial relations with regimes that fail to abide by Allah's law, are deemed proper and prudent when options are limited. As Qaradawi puts it, again pointing to Israel:

It is incumbent upon us to maintain some kind of contact with the present rulers so we can act. How could we strengthen the Intifada [i.e., the Palestinian terrorist uprisings unleashed by PLO strongman Yassir Arafat]? We are unable to do anything [without those rulers]. At the very least, the Intifada must go on, intensify, become more sophisticated, and broaden its base. And we must take whatever we can from the current rulers who are incapable of fighting. We must act within the parameters of the current restrictions.[49]

Such political understandings with infidels are, of course, not forever. Qaradawi is quick to point out that compacts with hostiles are expedient only as long as Islamists are in a position of weakness. Once the military and mental strength are up to the task of conquest, Qaradawi, like Banna, like Qutb, is all in. Thus,

Qaradawi reminds his flock that while the prophet Mohammed was in Mecca, his friends urged him "to shatter idols" on display there in order to provoke their enemies. However, "the Prophet ruled that the time was yet to come, and he even signed the al-Hudaybiya agreement with [his adversary] the Quraysh tribe." Only two years later, though, when Mohammed judged that his forces were ready "to conquer Mecca," Mohammed ignored the agreement and "picked up a lance" to strike the idols.

That is jihad by politics for the Muslim Brotherhood. The Islamists of Qaradawi's day, like the Islamists of Banna's day, are working on all fronts toward the goal of sharia societies. Because they have not been seriously confronted, because they have been allowed to slipstream behind their terrorist allies, they enjoy broader acceptance than ever. Qaradawi—he of the edicts approving the murders of American soldiers and Jews in the Middle East—is the acknowledged intellectual dynamo behind a global mass-movement. As he reassured his followers that the time for violent revolt would come, it's worth noting that he was then head of the Islamic law faculty at Qatar University. The emirate of Qatar, the headquarters of the rabidly anti-American al-Jezeera television network, is an absolute Islamic monarchy. The same State Department that lauds Qaradawi as an "intelligent and thoughtful voice from the region" also deems Qatar a key American ally in the "War against Terror." Or is that the "Overseas Contingency Operation against Man-Caused Disasters"?

chapter five

WE WILL CONQUER AMERICA THROUGH *DAWA*

It is called jihad by *dawa*. Of all the elements of Hassan al-Banna's blueprint for achieving universal Islamic hegemony, it is the most vital—the catalyst. It is thus the torch that Sheikh Yusuf al-Qaradawi most prominently carries forward in today's Muslim Brotherhood. *Dawa* is the missionary work by which Islam is spread. But don't be fooled by the term "missionary." *Dawa* no more resembles the Western connotation of "missionary work" than Islam resembles the Western notion of religion. Just as Islamism aspires to domination rather than a place at our ecumenical table, *dawa* is not mere proselytism but, as Qaradawi proclaims, the key to "victory."

On that point, he could not be more straightforward: "Conquest through *dawa*, that is what we hope for."[1] Notice the striking candor. Its stark difference from the Brotherhood's coy approach to public discussions of forcible jihad is easily explained: Islamists have shrewdly adapted to the enemy's—to America's, to the West's—incoherent posture of obsessing over terrorism while turning a blind eye to terrorism's animating ideology. U.S. experts stubbornly maintain, regardless of the evidence, that Muslim hostility to the West is a result of poverty, Israel, resentment, Israel, misinformation, Israel, or whatever other excuse we are using this week. Meantime, the Brotherhood methodically proceeds with its grand jihad-by-sabotage, and the unabashed Qaradawi openly proclaims, "We will conquer Europe, we will conquer America, not through the sword but through *dawa*."[2]

Qaradawi is a true *dawa* visionary. He leads a "broad intellectual movement" that the Hudson Institute's Eric Brown fittingly brands the "New Islamists" because its thinkers represent a Tony Blairesque "middle way" between accommodating Western societies and waging a crude terrorist campaign against them.[3] In fact, Qaradawi calls the doctrine *Wassatiyya*—derived from the Arab word for "middle."

The concept is simple. In Islamist theory, Western nations and, indeed, all non-Islamic lands have always been regarded as *Dar al-harb*. Tellingly, that means the realm of war, as distinguished from *Dar al-Islam*, the Muslim world. The mission of Islam, and thus the purpose of jihad, is to induce all of *Dar al-harb* to submit to Allah's religion, to make it part of *Dar al-Islam*. But as Qaradawi has explained, there are several ways to skin that cat.

In making the point, the sheikh relies, as Muslims are enjoined to rely, on the example of the prophet. Mohammed, he recounts, did not launch an armed jihad until after he arrived in Medina. During the pre-Hijra years in Mecca, when the original

Muslims were outnumbered and out-muscled by infidel powers, Mohammed instead "supported unarmed jihad," often against the wishes of his devoted but hot-headed companions—just as today's more prudent Islamists must manage a variegated jihad in tension with the demands of devout but rash Islamist terrorists.[4]

Is that really so hard to understand? It's actually common sense, if you allow your eyes to see it. At the start of the 1991 Gulf War, the U.S.-led Coalition spent months massing forces, a half-million strong, preparing for just the right time to launch their overwhelming attack. Let's say an impatient commander, without clearing it with his chain-of-command, attacked during the build-up's infancy and got routed by the more numerous, better prepared Iraqis, setting the whole mission back. We would not say that, because his superiors angrily disagreed with the commander's rashness, they were therefore "opposed to violence," much less that they were "moderates." To the contrary, we'd say the chain-of-command was made up of careful warriors—focused on the goal and working to ensure that its achievement was not undermined by recklessness, however well-intentioned.

As Islamists see it, modern Muslims in America are surrounded by their enemies, vastly outnumbered, and incapable of mounting a realistic armed attack—the same daunting straits faced by seventh-century Muslims in Mecca. Nevertheless, Qaradawi sagely reasons that Muslims in America, just like their forebears, can advance their mission by regarding the infidel country where they reside as *Dar al-Dawa*. The aim remains exactly the same as when Islamists viewed infidel territories strictly as the realm of war: namely, to induce America to submit. But the *dawa* strategy adjusts to the reality on the ground, just as Banna's original "from the ground up" blueprint counseled. It recognizes that a full frontal assault on the American system would simply be crushed, but that the missionary work—jihad by sabotage—will gradually eat away from within, abrading both the system and the will to preserve it.

Here again, Western chattering classes engage in deep self-delusion. Our experts are desperate to believe the Islamist threat is not profound. They insist that it is political rather than civilizational in nature and thus susceptible to their business-as-usual political charms. In their puerile analysis, Qaradawi's middle way—the middle way he candidly describes as a plan to "conquer America"—somehow becomes a hopeful sign of moderation. By extension, the Brothers morph into modernizing liberals.

To be sure, it helps that Qaradawi describes his doctrine in vaporous prose only an academic or a bureaucrat—or an Alinskyite—could love. *Wassatiyya*, says he, "lies between spirituality and materialism, between idealism and realism, between rationalism and sentimentalism, between individualism and collectivism, between permanence and evolution."[5] That is, it means everything and nothing, depending on Qaradawi's—or the State Department's, or the academy's—sense of what the circumstances require. No surprise, then, that Qaradawi frequently gives Western audiences what is music to their ears, a concession that the Israeli/Palestinian conflict is strictly about land and politics, not religion;[6] yet, feeding red meat to his al-Jezeera audience in 2009, he brayed that the Holocaust was "divine punishment" for the Jews and that, "Allah willing, the next time will be at the hand of the believers"—believers like himself, who would "shoot Allah's enemies, the Jews."[7]

Compounding the "moderate reformer" hallucination, apologists are enraptured by Qaradawi's resort to *ijtihad*. This is the Islamic principle of free and independent inquiry to discern Allah's will. Its employment results in toleration for some variances from the literal commands of scripture. As Brown puts it, *Wassatiyya's* somewhat "modernist orientation . . . has allowed its adherents to adopt a more pragmatic approach to the task of assimilating to the realities of life in Western democracies."[8] The trend gives Brotherhood admirers goosebumps because terrorists and many other Islamists reject it—making the Brothers look comparatively enlightened. A glowing 2007 profile of Qaradawi by Barbara Stowasser, the director of Georgetown University's Center for Contemporary Arabic Studies, is typical:

> Qaradawi strips many traditions (Hadith) and old fatwas of
> their normative significance by affirming that their meaning
> was historical. Similarly he contextualizes some Koranic rules
> in historical terms. For example, when a revelation addressed a
> specific situation in the Prophet's household or community, it
> is not necessarily applicable to all Muslims for all times. He is
> focused on the "spirit" and overall purpose of the revelation and
> the law, rather than on the predominant opinions of the schol-
> ars of the law even though he knows those opinions very well.[9]

It is not for nothing that Georgetown, awash in millions of dollars from the same Saudi regime that has long backed the Brotherhood, has been dubbed "the most Wahhabi-friendly university in America."[10] Stowasser's effusion was prompted by her discovery that Qaradawi supports the rights of women to vote and hold elective office. Of course, she neglected to mention that he also supports female circumcision, sharia rules that limit female inheritance to half of a man's share, the right of men to have multiple wives, the right of men to beat their wives, and the punishment of female rape victims ("For her to be absolved from guilt," the sheikh has explained, "a raped woman must have shown good conduct"; if she is dressed immodestly, she is deemed to have brought the sexual assault on herself).[11]

To be fair, Qaradawi is more enlightened on women's rights than the average Salafist cleric—but that's not a very high bar. He is an enthusiastic supporter of women's education, duly proud of the doctorates earned by three of his daughters.[12] Still, the sheikh's conceit that women should take their places in politics and the academy springs from the same rationale as his support—blithely skipped over by Stowasser—for women's becoming suicide bombers. It is not a matter of personal enrichment of the woman but corporate defense of the umma: If Muslim women are not active in the education and politics, those arenas will be left to secular women and their corrosive Western influences. Moreover, Qaradawi's nuanced view of women in politics (tempered by confidence that female office-holders will be "few in number" and thus pose no "danger" of acquiring what Stowasser gently calls "general guardianship over men") must be seen in the context of his general disdain for Western democracy and human liberty. It is safe to allow women to serve in parliament, he reasons, because neither men nor women may make law for themselves in any event: "Legislation belongs to God," he says, "and we only fill in the blanks."[13]

These Are the Great Modernizers?

If it weren't clear enough that Qaradawi is less the reformer than meets the guileless Western eye, common sense ought to factor in, even if supplies are short. Islam has always made some realistic compromises to assuage the plight of Muslims living in non-Muslim lands. How could it not? It is Islam's aim eventually to rule over those lands, so it must have a presence in them. And given that Islam is not a mere religion but a comprehensive legal and socio-political framework, allowances have to be made if Muslims are to inhabit jurisdictions that have not (yet) adopted that framework. The point of those allowances is not, as Western intellectuals naively hope, to forge a reformation of Islam. Islamism has the opposite in mind. At work is a strategy to make it easier for more Muslims to relocate to non-Muslim lands. As they gain in numbers and influence, the plan is not for Islam to evolve and assimilate to their new circumstances; it is for them to push the non-Muslim society toward embracing fundamentalist Islam.

Moreover, it is noteworthy that as discussions about Islamic doctrine shift from narrow questions about scriptural justifications for terrorism to more general questions about how life should be lived, it becomes ever more specious to pretend that Islamists are a fringe. Islamist *terrorists* are a fringe. By contrast, Islamists—Muslims who reject individual liberty, freedom of conscience, secular democracy, and equality of opportunity—are preponderant among believers who regard themselves as religious (as opposed to lapsed or merely cultural Muslims). They count among their number both profoundly influential, globally renowned Muslim scholars and Islamic regimes, such as the Saudi royal family, which command millions of believers. Even believers who do not walk the walk revere Islamist prescriptions in theory. The majority of Muslims accept as a given the conclusion of Islam's four major jurisprudential schools that the so-called Gates of *Ijtihad* have been closed for more than a millennium—i.e., that by about 900 A.D., all essential questions of doctrine had been settled with finality. Qaradawi and *Wassatiyya* adherents are not trying to upend that deeply rooted conviction in a radical way. They are merely saying that there remains limited room for "the explanation, application, and . . . interpretation of the doctrine as it had been laid down once and for all."[14]

This conviction is as old as Salafism's nineteenth-century origins and, in reality, does not come close to signaling the reformation of liberal fantasy—and isn't it amazing how Western intellectuals spend half their time assuring us that Islam is just splendid as is, and the other half musing about a reformation? Jamal al-Din al-Afghani, the founder of Salafism who was studied deeply by Qaradawi, Qutb, Banna, and Rida, among others, was hostile to modernity and the West. His objective in reaching beyond Islam's orthodox schools of jurisprudence was quite the opposite of evolving the faith so it would be congenial to contemporary sensibilities. He was a retro-reformer, hearkening back three centuries before the Gates of *Ijtihad* were closed. He wanted to return to the formative Islam of the seventh-century founders.[15]

In point of fact, there is little daylight between *Wassatiyya* and traditional Salafism. *Wassatiyya* is not moving to open the Gates of *Ijtihad* more than a crack, and its purpose is not necessarily to embrace reason or take Islam in what Western liberals (as opposed to Leftists) would see as an enlightened direction. Indeed, as Brown observes, Qaradawi's ascension to the leadership of the prestigious International Association of Muslim Scholars actually marks a trend toward "greater ideological radicalization," not liberalization.[16]

Wassatiyya is plainly grounded in Banna's Salafist philosophy. Putting aside Qaradawi for a moment, its most influential theorist was another al-Azhar–educated Egyptian scholar, the late Mohammed al-Ghazali. Sheikh Ghazali's last notable "accomplishment" was to testify on behalf of the Islamist militants who killed Farag Fouda, an authentic moderate reformer. As the *New York Times* reported, Ghazali told an Egyptian court at the 1993 trial that "anyone who openly resisted the full imposition of Islamic law was an apostate who should be killed either by the government or by devout individuals."

Like Qaradawi, Ghazali held the West, and in particular the
United States, in utter contempt. In a 1953 tirade against American democracy, he warned Muslims against "spreading American ways," condemning U.S. domestic life and foreign policy as
"actually a systematic violation of every virtue humanity has ever
known."[17] He also adhered to the Brotherhood strategy of maintaining cordial ties with secular regimes, once even attempting
to persuade the Mubarak government to appoint a committee to
instruct Egyptians on Islamic piety. As usual, that *sounds* harmless enough, perhaps even virtuous in a predominantly Muslim
society . . . except when one considers Ghazali's caveat: Those
who failed to repent after receiving the committee's instructions
on piety should be killed, in accordance with sharia.[18]

When he died in 1996 at age seventy-eight, Sheikh Ghaz-
ali's remains were flown to Saudi Arabia for burial in Medina.
The plane for the Ghazali family was provided by Crown Prince
Abdullah—now the Saudi king and revered ally of President
Obama.

And then there is Qaradawi. When we talk about "modernist
orientation" with Qaradawi as our barometer, we must bear in
mind that we are talking about a Salafist cleric who approves
suicide terrorism; who says it is a Muslim duty to kill American
troops and their civilian support personnel in Islamic countries;
who fomented the murderous global Islamist rioting that claimed
200 lives in 2005, when an obscure Danish newspaper published
unflattering cartoon images of the prophet; and who boasts that
Islamists will "conquer" America and Europe—which seems to
hint that he doesn't see co-existence as much of a possibility.

The sheikh's admirers are quick to point out that he does not
call for the death of all apostates, as terrorists and many other
Islamists commonly do. And it's true: for *private* apostates who
quietly go their separate way, Qaradawi holds that ostracism is

a sufficient penalty, with God left to impose the punishment of eternal damnation at the time of His choosing. Qaradawi draws a sharp distinction, however, on *public* apostasy, in which the renouncing Muslim seeks to infect and divide the umma with his disbelief. For this "offense"—commonly committed by Muslim intellectuals and reformers—Qaradawi decrees that "the punishment . . . is execution."[19] That is why Qaradawi enthusiastically agreed with Ghazali's condemnation of Farag Fouda. In Islam, the umma is all—it cannot be divided, depleted, or watered down; it wants a toe-hold, then an enclave, then the whole enchilada.

Need more? Okay, here's the great modernizer justifying sharia's condemnation of homosexuality as a crime warranting death:

> The spread of this depraved practice in a society disrupts its natural life pattern and makes those who practice it slaves to their lusts, depriving them of decent taste, decent morals, and a decent manner of living. The story of the people of Prophet Lut [Lot], peace be upon him, as narrated in the Koran should be sufficient for us. Prophet Lut's people were addicted to this shameless depravity, abandoning natural, pure, lawful relations with women in the pursuit of this unnatural, foul and illicit practice. That is why their Prophet Lut, peace be on him, told them, "What! Of all creatures, do you approach males and leave the spouses whom your Lord has created for you? Indeed, you are people transgressing (all limits)!" [Koran, 26:165–166] . . .
>
> Muslim jurists have held differing opinions concerning the punishment for this abominable practice. Should it be the same as the punishment for fornication, or should both the active and passive participants be put to death? While such punishments may seem cruel, they have been suggested to

maintain the purity of the Islamic society and to keep it clean of perverted elements.

Manifestly, Qaradawi's *Wassatiyya* Islam is nothing more than Salafist-Wahhabist Islam with a few nuances. That is why the Saudis so admire it. The Ikhwan's Western fans seize on these nuances because they provoke infighting between Qaradawi's *dawa* jihadists and bin Laden's violent jihadists. But this is strictly an intramural scrimmage. Everyone in each camp is an Islamist. To be sure, their doctrinal hair-splitting is cause for tendentious internal bickering.[20] But for us, the non-Muslims and non-Islamist Muslims targeted for conquest by both sides, they are fighting over trifles.

To get a sense of how trifling, a recent controversy is instructive. In 2005, the Swiss Islamist Tariq Ramadan (grandson of Banna and son of the important Brotherhood theorist Said Ramadan), proposed a moratorium on sharia's execrable *hudud* laws. These prescribe, for example, death by stoning for apostates and adulterers, amputation of the hand for thieves, and so on. The Western commentariat goes up in a balloon at the slightest hint of Islamic enlightenment, so naturally there were rose petals for Ramadan. The rest of us might note, however, that he was not calling for a repeal of *hudud*, just a moratorium. In his view, these draconian measures remained mandatory and immutable. His contention was that until countries *fully* adopted sharia, the conditions were not in place to assure that *hudud* would be justly imposed. And of course, he wants sharia fully adopted.

The truly interesting aspect of the controversy, though, was the reaction of Qaradawi and his conglomerate of academic and media acolytes. There were blistering diatribes condemning Ramadan. His proposal was belittled as an "unfounded innovation" that was "juristically baseless" and that threatened the well-being of the umma. That last, by the way, is an extremely serious charge. It is substantially the same as public apostasy because sowing discord divides the umma, which is then derailed from its animating purpose of conquering unbelief—highlighting, yet again, that tolerant coexistence is not part of the program.[21]

This flaying of Ramadan should come as no surprise. *Dawa* jihadists are not reformers. In carrying out their war against the West, they are more sophisticated than the mass-murderer jihadists whom they alternatively align with, distance themselves from, or capitalize on as dictated by the needs of the moment. What's more, the Fabian method of *dawa* jihadists is to entwine the West in sharia: first legitimize Islamic law in Western eyes; then establish the principle that, where applicable, Islamic law can override existing secular law; and finally, work to increase the areas of Western life in which Islamic law is deemed applicable.

By contrast, if Ramadan's theory were to take hold, various sharia provisions would be suspended until the society first became Islamicized. For the Brotherhood, that would put the cart before the horse. In that sense, this impasse between *dawa* jihadists (i.e. Islamists) is reminiscent of the tactical debate between violent jihadists (i.e., Islamist terrorists). The Blind Sheikh, Omar Abdel Rahman, used to complain about those who wanted to table violent jihad "until the establishment of an Islamic army." He reasoned that Muslims were too far from the point of having an imposing military capability—one that could win, straight up, on a traditional battlefield. "If it is an army which should do the jihad," he warned, "then there will never be jihad." That was unacceptable: Allah's injunction would go unfulfilled. Thus, Abdel Rahman surmised, the better plan was to proceed on two tracks. Small cells ("battalions of Islam") would proceed in the here and now with terrorist strikes. Over time, the success of these operations (i.e., the demonstration that they intimidated the West, and therefore that Islam's enemies were weak) would encourage Muslims. That, in turn, would forge recruitment for the greater Islamic army, which would eventually conquer all remaining enemies.

Analogously, the Brotherhood, in the here and now, wants every concession to sharia that it can get from the West—building on the small victories to the eventual conquest. If it waited for societies to be fully open to Islamicization before imposing elements of sharia, sharia might never take root. And it is worth repeating: the purpose of jihad is to implement sharia.

Sharia Creep

This is not to say Islamists are failing to prioritize the Islamicization of Western society. Like Abdel Rahman's theory, under which violent jihad proceeds on two tracks, Sheikh Qaradawi has a plan for Islamicizing Western societies on a macro level while the micro-work of gradual sharia implementation proceeds. That plan is the establishment of autonomous Muslim enclaves, parallel societies adherent to sharia law. It is a gambit analysts have aptly labeled "voluntary apartheid."[22]

That it is a Trojan-horse cannot be seriously doubted. Qaradawi is candid: "Were we to convince Western leaders and decision-makers of our right to live according to our faith—ideologically, legislatively, and ethically—without imposing our views or inflicting harm upon them, we would have traversed an immense barrier in our quest for an Islamic state."[23] Notice, again, the mindset: *without inflicting harm upon them*. One might think it difficult to fathom anything more harmful to individual liberty than the establishment of an Islamic state. Yet, that's not how we think. Qaradawi adroitly reads the West's temperament: We're tunnel-focused on terrorism, concerned only about forcible damage to life, limb, and property. As long as we're told there will be no *harm*, he rightly figures we'll assume he means no *terrorism*. If terrorism is not in the equation, we go back to sleep—amenable to all manner of accommodation, even to sowing the seeds of our own destruction at the behest of people who tell us, flat-out, that their goal is conquest. In our suicidal disposition, "democracy" somehow requires this of us.

The enclave strategy has already been implemented to great effect in Europe. Qaradawi made it sound unthreatening enough. In early 2005, at a session of his European Council for Fatwa and Research, he encouraged the continent's sizable Muslim population—which is still a minority, for now—to integrate into European society. There was just one caveat: the integration must be done "without violating the rules of sharia." There is only one way such an integration can happen on Qaradawi's terms: Muslims must capitalize on their unity and growing strength to pressure Europe into adopting sharia, bit by bit.[24]

Obviously, the strategy is working. The eminent Bernard Lewis stunned Western readers when he predicted that Europe will be Islamic by the end of the twenty-first century,[25] but, judging from the whirlwind pace of things, he may be several decades behind the curve. Already, the landscape in Europe, as well as Australia, is dotted by "no-go" zones: Muslim neighborhoods where police no longer patrol, sovereignty having been effectively surrendered to the local imams, shura councils, and Muslim gangs. In France, for example, police estimate that some eight million people (12 percent of the population—and climbing) live in the country's 751 *zones urbaines sensibles*, sensitive urban areas.

And when French police do make arrests, an ever greater percentage of the offenders is Islamic, with Muslims now constituting 60 percent of the national prison population.[26] In 2005, an effort to arrest two Muslim teenagers, who electrocuted themselves trying to hide in a power station, touched off three weeks of mass rioting, arson, and vandalism. Over 8000 cars were torched and nearly 3000 people arrested. Rioting has broken out sporadically ever since. Press coverage, though, is muted: The authorities have encouraged the media to suppress the story for fear of reigniting the rampages of what journalists euphemistically call "youths" of "South Asian" heritage.

The United Kingdom may be in even greater crisis. There, the Islamic ascendancy dovetails with the Labour government's transnational progressivism in a campaign against cultural Britishness. As the columnist Leo McKinstry observes: "England is in the middle of a profoundly disturbing social experiment. For the first time in a mature democracy, a Government is waging a campaign of aggressive discrimination against its indigenous population."[27] Sharia has become a key element of that campaign.

Exploiting the feature of British law that permits parties, on consent, to bring their legal disputes to "voluntary arbitration tribunals" rather than law courts, a Muslim commercial-law barrister named Faisal Aqtab Siddiqi shrewdly established a sharia court as the "Muslim Arbitration Council." Quipping that "these are early days," the brilliant writer John O'Sullivan notes that the British sharia court "so far only handles civil cases such as divorces and inheritance disputes, since British society isn't ready for such innovations as public floggings and hand-choppings."[28]

Still, the present caseload is plenty alarming. English police officers are enforcing sharia judgments on domestic violence complaints—meaning there have been instances of investigations dropped after the Islamic authority sides with accused husbands, in deference to the Koranic endorsement of spousal abuse. There has also been at least one decision awarding an estate's male heirs twice as much as the female heir.[29] And by granting extra welfare benefits to men with multiple families, England, like much of Europe, is giving tacit approval to Islamic polygamy (Muslim men may marry up to four women; women, you'll no doubt be stunned to hear, are restricted to one husband). Similarly, thanks to Muslim activists and feckless bureaucrats, the British welfare state—honoring a decree from the European Court of Human Rights—forces taxpayers to subsidize suspected foreign terrorists whom the government seeks to monitor under anti-terror laws but cannot deport because of Britain's alien-coddling immigration laws.[30]

Simultaneously, "hate speech" laws have been interpreted by police and bureaucrats in Britain's immigrant Muslim hubs to bar such exhibitions of "racism" as the raising of the Union Jack (or wearing clothes that bear its likeness)—a stigma also being attached to national flags in the Netherlands, Sweden, France, and other European countries.[31] Meanwhile, writing in the *Brussels Journal*, the commentator Fjordman recounts instances of Britons being banned from swimming at a popular sports club in London during "Muslim men only" sessions; assaults on Christian clerics in London; and a police threat to Christian preachers in Birmingham: Desist handing out gospel leaflets lest you be arrested for committing a "hate crime"—or, worse, beaten by local Muslims without intervention by the police (after all, you've been warned).[32]

Then there is the matter of violent crime, particularly rape, by Muslim immigrants. Rape, the unspoken epidemic of Western Europe, is as much and more about psychological domination as it is about physical gratification. As a violent jihadist tactic, it has long been an infamous weapon in the Sudanese Islamist regime's genocidal arsenal, used first against Christians and Animists in the south in the early Nineties and, more recently, in western Sudan against the Muslims of Darfur, whom Islamists judge to be insufficiently Islamic. Now, with the tide of immigration, jihad by rape has been imported to Europe, where indignation by the politically correct press is predictably reserved not for the perpetrators but for the few journalists willing to report on it.

Consistent with Sheikh Qaradawi's aforementioned view that the rape victim is to blame for her plight if she has failed to adhere to fundamentalist protocols for women's attire, Shahid Mehdi, a top Islamic cleric in Denmark, has explained that women who fail to don a headscarf are asking to be raped (an admonition also given voice by Sheik Faiz Mohammed, a prominent Lebanese cleric, during a lecture he delivered in Australia).[33] Not surprisingly given such encouragement, Fjordman painstakingly documents that it has become a commonplace for young Muslim men to participate in sexual assaults and absolve themselves from culpability.[34] As a psychologist working in the prison system, the incomparable Theodore Dalrymple witnessed the six-fold spike in Britain's Muslim inmate population between 1990 and 2005. He bluntly notes that "thanks to their cultural inheritance, [the Muslims'] abuse of women is systematic rather than unsystematic as it is with" white and black inmates.[35] Robert Spencer elaborates:

The Islamic legal manual 'Umdat al-Salik, which carries the endorsement of Al-Azhar University, the most respected authority in Sunni Islam, stipulates: "When a child or a woman is taken captive, they become slaves by the fact of capture, and the woman's previous marriage is immediately annulled." Why? So that they are free to become the concubines of their captors. The Qur'an permits Muslim men to have intercourse with their wives and their slave girls: "Forbidden to you are . . . married women, except those whom you own as slaves" (Sura 4:23–24).

As atrocious as rape is on its own, the Sudanese experience demonstrates that it is even more harrowing as a component in a broader intimidation campaign. Writing in *Frontpage Magazine*, the former Australian army officer Sharon Lapkin has recounted (my italics):

> Retired Australian detective Tim Priest warned in 2004 that the Lebanese gangs, which emerged in Sydney in the 1990s—when the police were asleep—had morphed out of control. "The Lebanese groups," he said, "were ruthless, extremely violent, and they intimidated not only innocent witnesses, but even the police that attempted to arrest them." Priest describes how in 2001, in a Muslim dominated area of Sydney two policemen stopped a car containing three well-known Middle Eastern men to search for stolen property. *As the police carried out their search they were physically threatened and the three men claimed they were going to track them down, kill them and then rape their girlfriends.* . . . As the Sydney police called for backup the three men used their mobile phones to call their associates, and within minutes, 20 Middle Eastern men arrived on the scene. They punched and pushed the police and damaged state vehicles. The police retreated and the gang followed them to the police station where they intimidated staff, damaged property and held the police station hostage. Eventually the gang left, the police licked their wounds, and not one of them took action against the Middle Eastern men. Priest claims, "In the minds of the local population, the police are cowards and the message was, 'Lebanese [Muslim gangs] rule the streets.'"[36]

The situation, Lapkin learned, was the same in Malmo, Sweden's third largest city, where police concede that they are no longer in control. Muslim immigrant gangs rule the streets. To make their dominion emphatic, even ambulance personnel are routinely attacked and abused. They won't go into many neighborhoods without police protection, and the police, in turn, will not enter without additional back-up.

Islamists are taking the measure of the West and finding it to be a shallow, self-loathing husk. When Muslims riot over mere cartoons, the intelligentsia's first impulse is to condemn the publisher. After an Islamist terrorist's brutal murder of Theo van Gogh, who directed Ayaan Hirsi Ali's screenplay "Submission," about the treatment of women in Islam, the first impulse of the Netherlands was to encourage Ms. Hirsi Ali to leave the country. In Birmingham, a conservative group called the "English Defense League" has demonstrated in opposition to what it is careful to call *militant* Islam, stressing that it has no quarrel with Islam or with Muslims who do not wish to change British law or life. Predictably, Muslim groups reacted violently, exhorted by imams at the Birmingham Central Mosque to show the umma's "solidarity." The first impulse of the British media? To side with the rampaging Muslims, whom they portrayed as heroic "anti-fascists"—fighting side-by-side with their socialist allies, to challenge the "anti-Islamic" activists of the right-wing."[37]

These are but a surface scratch of the mosaic that gives Sheikh Qaradawi such confidence that Islam will "conquer" Europe—that Islam is *this minute* conquering Europe—and that it will eventually bring America to heel as well. Consider too that European leaders have chosen this time, the moment Islamists are engulfing their continent, to float the idea of a joint European/Islamic confederation. In late 2007, British Foreign Secretary David Miliband took center stage at the College of Europe in Bruges, Belgium, to propose an expansion of the European Union—a "model power," as he put it, that would embrace not only Islamicizing Turkey but also the Muslim Middle East and North Africa. "As a club that countries want to join," Miliband envisioned, the expanded union would "persuade countries to play by the rules, and set global standards."[38] But whose rules and standards? When the principles of liberty and reason meet those of totalitarianism—shrouded beneath such cheery euphemisms as "diversity," "cooperation," and "social cohesion"—it is liberty and reason that are compromised. The expanded EU, and such schemes as French President Nicolas Sarkozy's "Club Med" (a union of EU countries with Islamic nations bordering the Mediterranean Sea), can only hasten, by the force of law, the suffocation of freedom that is now proceeding by sheer Islamist will.[39] Even Qaradawi at his most hubristic—which is saying something—would not be audacious enough to suppose Europe would simply hand Islamists what he is urging them, gradually, to take.

Sharia creep, moreover, does not stop at the Atlantic's eastern shores—far from it. Witness, for example, a 2005 proposal by Ontario's former attorney general to incorporate sharia in the Canadian legal code. Like emerging British sharia, the scheme would have approved the use of Muslim law to settle such domestic relations matters as divorce and child custody involving the province's estimated 600,000 Muslims. It was defeated, barely, with the help of non-Islamist Muslims, especially women fearful of losing the equality and protection they enjoy under Canadian law.[40] Undoubtedly, Muslim activists will be back for a second bite at the apple, but in the meantime they've already won a substantial victory.

Though their sharia initiative failed, it induced Canada, a few months later, to repeal its traditional embrace of Judeo-Christian religious tribunals for the voluntary settling of family law matters. This remedy, of course, was said to be mandated by the principle of equality. It made no difference that there is no greater iniquity than treating fundamentally different things as though they were identical. Thus the irony: equality, a Judeo-Christian concept rooted in the parity of all human beings in God's sight, is twisted into a command that Judeo-Christianity be suppressed for the purpose of placing it on a par with an inherently discriminatory, supremacist doctrine.

In the event, it counted for nothing that Judaism and Christianity, the dominant religious traditions of North America, promote harmony and tolerance within Canadian society. It counted for nothing that they are the antithesis of Qaradawi's enclave strategy, the apartheid scheme that fueled this aggressive promotion of sharia. Thus the skirmish turned into a significant victory for *dawa* jihadists: Even if Islamists were not yet strong enough to have sharia officially installed, and even though they constitute but a tiny minority of Canada's population, they still managed to delegitimize Western institutions in Western eyes.

As for the American *dawa* front, Zeyno Baran offers this assessment:

Qaradawi . . . has repeatedly advised Muslims living in the West to create their own "Muslim ghettos" to avoid cultural assimilation. If American Muslims start forming parallel societies, it will be much easier for the Ikhwan to push for the introduction of sharia in these societies. While this may seem far-fetched, it cannot be so easily dismissed given how close the Islamists came to introducing sharia for Canadian Muslims. And since most of the American Muslim organizations are in the hands of Islamists, who enjoy seemingly unlimited money, media attention, and political influence, few non-Islamists would be able to fight back.[41]

She's right. As we shall see, the enclave strategy is taking hold in the United States. Seeds sown over a half-century ago are bearing fruit as never before.

chapter six

FAUSTIAN BARGAIN

On the surface, no greater catastrophe could have befallen the Muslim Brotherhood than Gamal Abdel Nasser's rise. For two decades after their fleeting alliance dissolved in jihadist violence, the Ikhwan felt the dictator's fury. Islamists were persecuted. Their guiding light, Sayyid Qutb, was imprisoned and finally executed. Muslim Brothers not killed or imprisoned fled Egypt with abandon.

History, though, is not a matter of the surface, but of the deep currents. Nasser quelled Egyptian jihadists as a prerequisite for his own ambitious totalitarian project, pan-Arabism. Quite unintentionally, he became the global Islamist project's greatest catalyst, pushing his enemies—Brotherhood Salafists and Saudi

Wahhabists—into each other's combustible arms. To this day, Americans are imperiled by the aftershocks.

The Brothers and the Saudis needed each other. For the Ikhwan, it was a straightforward matter of survival. They were driven out of their own country and needed a hospitable place to start over. From the Kingdom's perspective, it was a natural fit. On a very basic level, the Brothers were competent. "To put it bluntly," Gilles Kepel observes, "they could read and write. While the Wahhabi ulama were ill at ease in dealing with the modern world, the Brothers were well traveled and relatively sophisticated." Ikhwan leaders, in the mold of Banna and Qutb, were academics. They were everything the Saudis weren't: educated, urbane, politically savvy, and attuned to the ways of the West. Saudis also admired their valor in standing firm, often in the face of brutal repression, against Nasser and the Left's secularism.[1]

With Wahhabism as its compass, Saudi Arabia was inward, tribal, and hardwired to reject foreign innovations. One novel concept it had no interest in engaging was pan-Arabism. The House of Saud perceived Nasser's vision as a predominantly secular socialism, the road to permanent satellite status in the emphatically atheistic Soviet orbit. More to the point, Nasser's conception of pan-Arabism would make Cairo—as opposed to the Keeper of the Two Holy Mosques—the center of the Islamic world.

Egyptian Salafists were not as developmentally arrested as Saudi Wahhabists. They did not reject modernity; they sought to dominate it. They did not want to return to the seventh century. Within the stultifying limitations of sharia, Qutb expressed enthusiasm for scientific inquiry and economic productivity.[2] What the Salafists yearned for was a reconciliation of modernity with the unadulterated, centralized, expansionist principles of seventh-century Islam.

Yet, even with Egypt's al-Azhar scholars looking down their
noses at the comparative backwardness of Saudi Muslims, the
commonalities of Salafism and Wahhabism were more weighty
than their differences, and that made accommodation easy when
the mutuality of other interests was accounted for. Like Wahhabism, Salafism was fundamentalist in its outlook. Where Islamic
dictates and contemporary sensibilities collided, it was modern
life that had to yield. Reason was not rejected entirely, but its
limited role was to determine which Islamic principles applied in
a given situation, not to evolve the principles or justify ignoring
them.

It is often said that the Saudis have lavishly bankrolled and
promoted the global proselytism of their Wahhabist ideology.
That's not quite accurate. They were importers before they
became exporters. What they have exported so aggressively for
the last half-century is not, strictly speaking, Wahhabism. It is
"pan-Islamic Salafism," a melding of Wahhabism and Muslim
Brotherhood Islamism, which is to say, Banna's interpretation
of Salafism.[3] There was, Kepel recounts, "a cross-fertilization of
ideas . . . between the exiled Brotherhood and the austere teachings of what might be described as the Wahhabi rank and file."
Transnational Islamist organizations were established and they
were headquartered in the Kingdom to ensure continuing Saudi
control. The intellectual and operational forces behind these
entities, though, were leading Brotherhood figures.[4]

Plainly, the desire to propagate Islam was a strong motivator
for the Saudis. The central imperative of Islam is the propagation of its doctrine and law. The Saudis not only wanted to be
perceived as sentries of the faith. They want to *be* the sentries, for
reality to match the perception. Nonetheless, the Saudis were also
actors in a geopolitical world, and they saw the Islamist project as
a national interest every bit as much as an ideological injunction.

Pan-Islamic Salafism was not merely an ideology but a political strategy designed to compete with Nasserite pan-Arabism. In 1962, when the Kingdom founded the Muslim World League in Mecca, it dutifully disseminated, throughout the Islamic world and beyond, the works of Banna, Qutb, and other prominent Salafist thinkers. But a central point of the exercise, as far as the founders were concerned, was to discredit Nasser in Muslim eyes—homing in on the Egyptian's contention that socialism and Islam were compatible, as well as his attempt to dilute al-Azhar University's fundamentalist construction of Islam.[5]

This raises a larger point about the trysts we see, again and again, between Islamism and government. These relationships are coldly utilitarian and eventually doomed. How could they not be? Over the long haul, Islamists are essentially asking the powerful to cooperate in their own demise. Banna was all for cultivating and co-opting authoritarian governments, but always with the understanding that, as soon as the time was right, the authority would become sharia.

Marriages Doomed to Fail

When Sheikh Qaradawi was asked how he could abide the concept of a woman taking on the role of government legislator, he scoffed that, in Islam, legislators don't really *do* anything anyway; they are merely vessels for implementing the divine law, which is known and inalterable. Muslim rulers may nod piously in the face of such assertions by their influential co-religionists . . . but it is not what they want to hear. Rulers want to rule. They want to exercise their discretion, their authority. They want to survive. The Saudis routinely posture that their government functions "in total adherence to the Islamic religion"[6] . . . but then they beg the infidel Americans to come protect them from Saddam Hussein. To put it mildly, Islamists do not have a worldly tolerance for such hypocrisies.

Unless a regime is willing to submit, to subordinate itself wholesale to the Islamist interpretation of the faith, it cannot go the distance with Islamism. An ideologically sympathetic regime like the Saudi government can make such a partnership work better and longer than, say, a Nasser—who needed the Muslim Brotherhood for only as long as it took to overthrow the Egyptian monarchy, after which the Islamists became a net liability. As night follows day, though, the Saudis, like every other government that can't resist playing this game, eventually felt the lash.

It has to be this way. The goal of Islamism is fixed and supremacist while the agendas of governments—even a government run by Wahhabist autocrats—are transitory and bound up in concerns about self-preservation. Sure, as a matter of principle, the Saudis believed Soviet communism was antithetical to Islam in certain significant particulars. Undoubtedly, they were offended by moves to alter the character of al-Azhar. What they mostly opposed, however, was Nasser.

To the contrary, Brotherhood Salafists were more animated by the mission of spreading fundamentalist Islam—before, during, and after Nasser. By attaching themselves at the hip to the Ikhwan, the Saudis were taking on a like-minded partner, but one whose priorities would not always match theirs. Worse, they were inextricably tying themselves to a complex partner whose internal factions were (and are) often at odds on crucial tactical questions: Whether to work within existing political systems in order to achieve the ideal Islamic society (what we might call the Banna/Qaradawi position), or whether to overthrow those systems in order to impose Islamic law and mores (the Qutb refinement of Banna favored by al Qaeda).

As we've seen, there are many shades of gray and intense debates between these two poles. Intramural alliances and enmities among Islamists are complicated and shifting. By marrying themselves to the Brotherhood, the Saudis dove headlong into the cross-currents—finding themselves, to this day, trapped in a complex drama where Osama bin Laden emerges as Islam's avenging angel one minute and its ruinous villain the next.

Sayyid Qutb's brother and fellow academic, Mohammed, was among the Brotherhood majordomos enthusiastically welcomed by the regime, becoming a prominent Islamic studies professor at the University of Medina and King Abdulaziz University in Jeddah. But what did the regime suppose he was teaching in those classrooms, where one of his students was an up-and-comer named Osama bin Laden? How surprising is it that, when he decided the time was right, the Saudi lifeline he'd been given meant nothing to Qutb. Eventually, he became a formative leader of "the Awakening," a cleric-driven movement that urges rebellion against the Saudi monarchy—a movement whose modern leaders, such as Safer al-Awali and Salman al-Auda, have inspired bin Laden and the 9/11 hijackers.[7] Islamists will always accept your help . . . right until the moment they decide you're dispensable.

For decades, the Saudis have rationalized that, because they were the most Islamist regime, they had the least to fear. There was, they figured, a plethora of targets more deserving of jihadist wrath. Yet, having been scorched repeatedly by the terrorists they help sustain, the Saudis have lately taken more care to condemn violent jihadists. Now, they promote *dawa* Islamists, operatives of the Brotherhood stripe, who say they want to work within the system to Islamicize societies. The shift hardly undoes the damage wrought by support the Saudi government recklessly provided for years—and looked the other way as its citizens provided—to the most violent jihadist elements.

More to the point of the Grand Jihad, the new approach does not change the fact that the Saudis are still assiduously working to destroy the West. By encouraging and underwriting Islamist factions that are less overtly terrorist, including the modern Ikhwan, they're just being smarter about it.

Financing the Infrastructure of Sabotage

Since the Saudi government struck its partnership with the Ikhwan and founded the Muslim World League in 1962, it has underwritten *dawa* jihadists to the tune of about $100 billion. The propagation of their totalitarian brand of Islam has been accomplished, day in and day out for a half-century, through the worldwide establishment of Muslim institutions, neighborhood Islamic centers, and mosques.[8] The United States has been a focal point of their attention.

The true amount of Saudi financing for Islamism could actually be much higher. It is a question rarely explored given our myopic concentration on *terror* financing, to the exclusion of the more significant challenge, the underwriting of Islamist ideology. After all, even the subset category of terror-support defies reliable measure. The Kingdom's financial system is opaque and mysterious, making transactions difficult to trace. Saudi tax laws do not require personal income records to be kept. The population prefers to transact in cash.

More significantly, because Saudi Arabia is a sharia society, its twenty-four million citizens are obliged to perform *zakat*, one of

Islam's five "pillars." Islam's cheerleaders in our government, the academy, and the media, usually translate this divine injunction as "charity"—as in: "Isn't Islam wonderful? It calls on Muslims to tend to the less fortunate by donating a percentage of their annual incomes to charity (usually about 2.5 percent)." In fact, *zakat* is a far more insidious and insular enterprise than this fairy tale suggests.

In January 2010, Haiti was rocked by a devastating earthquake, followed by several aftershocks. Tens of thousands of people have been killed; even more are homeless, ravaged by crushing injuries, disease, and roving bands of brigands. The Western world, led as always by the Great Satan, instantly opened its hearts and pocketbooks. Within days, the nonpareil investigative journalist Claudia Rosett found, the U.S. government had pledged $90 million in public funds (44 percent of the total forked up by governments worldwide). That, moreover, was just a fraction of the true American contribution. Private citizens, in a time of skyrocketing unemployment, gave tens of millions from their own pockets (i.e., beyond what Uncle Sam had confiscated). The U.S. armed forces mobilized to provide food, medical treatment, and other humanitarian aid. In addition, untold additional millions in American taxpayer contributions were disguised as relief efforts by the United Nations, the International Committee of the Red Cross (ICRC), and the World Bank, all of which are propped up by substantial U.S. support. Further, despite the global recession, governments in Europe, Canada, Japan, and even South America also donated millions.[9]

What of the Islamic world? Over the same period of time, it accounted for a whopping 0.1 percent of the total donations committed by governments. Roughly speaking, that's a rounding error for a Saudi sheikh's weekend in Vegas. Indeed, drawing a telling contrast, Claudia Rosett notes that the House of Saud's annual contribution to ICRC operations in 2008 came to a grand total of $216,460 (less than a penny per Saudi), and Iran's 66 million citizens kicked in a grand total of $50,000, while the U.S. gave $237.8 *million.*

How could this be? How could that oil-drenched realm of mandatory benevolence lag so embarrassingly behind Dar al-Greed? Very simple: *Zakat* is not "charity" as we understand that term. It is the underwriting of Muslims by Muslims, for the single purpose of fortifying and extending the umma. Indeed, Sayyid Qutb, the Brotherhood's chief theoretician, rejected the portrayal of *zakat* as "charity" because it is commanded by sharia: "As for the proceeds of *zakat*, this is the law: It is to be received as a right, not given as a charity." And because its paramount purpose is to ensure "social solidarity in Islam," it is to be given only to Muslims. *Zakat*, Qutb dilated, is the "share taken by the state and spent on *the welfare of Muslims* to supply their bodily needs, to preserve their dignity, and to protect their power of conscience" (emphasis added).[10] We grubby capitalists may think the Haitians are suffering beyond calculation, but for Muslims there *is* a calculation. The Haitians are infidels. The families of Palestinian suicide bombers and imprisoned al Qaeda terrorists rate a brotherly helping hand, but the Haitians don't.

It is fashionable to dismiss Qutb out of hand because he is the leading light for Islamist terrorists. But in this, as in most things, he speaks for mainstream Islam. Can *zakat* properly be given to non-Muslims? That precise question was put to Shaykh Faraz Rabbani at "Sunni Path," the "Islamic Academy" popular among Muslim web-surfers. The answer was a blunt "no." In all four major Sunni schools of Islamic jurisprudence, Rabbani instructed, "There is consensus of all those whose positions we know from the people of knowledge that a non-Muslim (dhimmi) cannot be given any *zakat*."[11] As Raymond Ibrahim observes, the tireless portrayal of Islamic charities as akin to "say, the Salvation Army, a Christian charity organization whose 'ministry extends to all, regardless of ages, sex, color, or creed,'" is flatly false. In Islam, it's all about creed.[12] *Zakat*, like all Islamic tenets, serves the overarching cause of promoting Islam to the exclusion and at the expense of nonbelievers.

Zakat is mischief cloaked in piety. As the analyst Matthew Levitt notes, Pakistani scholars count among "charity" recipients: "orphans" with living parents, "impoverished women" bedecked in jewels, and "old people" who have long since died.[13] But fraud is the least of the problem. Besides stipends for the families of suicide bombers and imprisoned terrorists, qualifying humanitarian causes are known to include the social welfare wings maintained by such terrorist organizations as Hamas and Hezbollah—apparatuses designed to make these organizations more attractive to Muslims, thus functioning as a gateway to recruitment for violent jihad.

Don't be fooled into thinking this makes *zakat* yet another of those countless Religion of Peace virtues that have supposedly been warped by those rascally al Qaeda types. In truth, there can be no meaningful *zakat* line between beneficence and belligerence. Islam quite intentionally chooses not to distinguish real humanitarian giving from material support to terror. Oh, *individual Muslims* surely draw such lines in their own minds. But *Islam* does not. As Raymond Ibrahim explains, "Most schools of Muslim jurisprudence are agreed to eight possible categories of recipients—one of these being those fighting 'in the path of Allah,' that is, jihadis, also known as 'terrorists.' In fact, financially supporting jihadis is a recognized form of jihad."[14]

Ibrahim is entirely correct. The issue is not just that "charities" often operate in conflict zones, a setting that would make
any authentically humanitarian endeavor vulnerable to terrorist
infiltration—to be exploited either as straight funding sources or
as laundering devices to conceal money transfers and the movement of munitions. (Witness those Red Crescent trucks that seem
to spend as much time ferrying Hamas jihadis as ministering to
Hamas families). The stark fact is that the Islamic conception of
alms, as rendered by its influential clerics, its storied institutions
like al-Azhar, and its sharia-based regimes, unabashedly embraces
what Ibrahim describes as "the money jihad" (*jihad al-mal*). A
canonical hadith quotes the prophet Mohammed's sentiment on
the matter: "He who equips a raider [i.e., mujahid] so he can wage
jihad in Allah's path . . . is himself a raider [i.e., achieves the same
status of mujahid]."[15]

Indeed, the Saudis' incorrigible support for violent jihadists
is more easily understood once one grasps that, in various places,
the Koran actually prioritizes the need to fund violent jihad over
the need to fight it. Sura 9:41 declares: "Go forth, light-armed
and heavy-armed, and *strive with your wealth* and your lives in
the way of Allah! That is best for you if you but knew" (emphasis
added). Ibrahim elaborates that, according to authoritative
Muslim jurists, several other verses "make the same assertion and,
more importantly, in the same order: striving with one's *wealth*
almost always precedes striving with one's *life*, thereby priori-
tizing the former over the latter."[16] The imperatives of funding
jihadism and denying the humanity of non-Muslims, the blueprint for spreading Islam, also explain the Koran's encouragement of slavery. As Ibrahim puts it, the Islamic term for spoil
(*ghanima*) applies to not only to property but to persons seized by
force from non-Muslims. Men are generally held as prisoners and

killed or exchanged for ransom. Women and children are kept as slaves—with the masters of enslaved women doctrinally encouraged to keep them as concubines.[17]

A Strong Ally to the United States?

Financial jihad is a staple of Islamist theory. For instance, our favorite Brotherhood "moderate," Sheikh Qaradawi, has decreed that Muslims must donate money to "support Palestinians fighting occupation and other struggles of Muslim populations, such as in Bosnia." "If we can't carry out acts of jihad ourselves," he says, "we at least should support and prop up the mujahideen financially and morally."[18] That admonition is echoed by Sheikh Hassan Nasrallah, the emir of Shiite Hezbollah:

> All the institutions, committees, parties, private and collective initiatives throughout the Muslim world must be spurred on to collect money, everywhere in the world, and to bring that money to Palestine. With it they will buy bread and rebuild their houses. The money will bandage their wounds. With that money they are assured of the ability to buy weapons, for the men and women of Palestine will not be weakened. The [challenge] of our era is found today in Palestine. If we cannot give them arms, we can give them the money to buy them.[19]

The Saudi government, for all its anti-terror pretensions, sings the same tune, under the murky cover of *dawa*. Their collaboration with the Muslim Brotherhood has given the Saudis a hammer-lock on American mosques, the very places where worshippers are routinely encouraged to send money to foreign terrorists. In his important book *Hamas: Politics, Charity, and Terrorism in the Service of Jihad*, Matthew Levitt recounts the communication of a fatwa promoting financial jihad to Muslims at the Islamic Center of Washington—site of the treacly mosque visit President George W. Bush somehow thought it necessary to make while rescue workers picked through the carnage of 9/11. Drawing on Freedom House's 2005 report on Saudi propagation of Islamist hate ideology, Levitt writes:

> Prepared by the Saudi government's so-called Permanent Committee for Scientific Research and the Issuing of Fatwas, the decree was in response to an inquiry as to whether the transfer of charitable donations (*zakat*) from the United States to Islamic countries is permissible. The Saudi Committee wrote: "Transfer of *zakat* from country to country is allowed when legitimate, such as when those to whom it is transferred are in greater need *or in legitimate jihad*." In another document, in which a senior Saudi cleric ruled that Muslims should not, as a general rule, use banks that offer interest on their accounts, the scholar ruled that "there is an exception if the banks offer interest without prior agreement or knowledge on the Muslim depositors' part, it is proper to take the money provided it is spent on helping the poor *or those engaged in Jihad against the infidels*." (Emphasis added.) [20]

Quite apart from the multitudinous purposes alms-giving can satisfy, Saudi contributions are also difficult to quantify because they are often made anonymously. They are also frequently diverted—wittingly or not—from one charitable entity to another. And charities can't (or won't) keep straight which donations are private and which come from governmental sources: The huge royal family and its extensive supporting bureaucracy give overlapping in their personal and public capacities. As the Congressional Research Service so charitably puts it, these practices "complicate efforts to estimate the amounts involved and to identify the sources and end recipients of these donations."[21]

What is not complicated is the essence of the propaganda campaign purchased by all this Saudi largesse. It is Islamist supremacism, reeking with anti-Americanism. Yet, American officials persistently describe the Saudis as "a strong ally to the United States" in combating terrorism financing.[22]

The cognitive dissonance is easily explained—except, of course, if you don't want to understand it. The official position of the U.S. government is: Our only concern is terrorism; there is no nexus between terrorism committed by Muslims and Islamic doctrine; Islam must in fact be twisted and perverted to justify terrorism; and, therefore, the propagation of Islam has utterly nothing to do with the promotion of terrorism. So what if Islamic schools, conventions, and institutions inculcate in Muslims a rabidly anti-Semitic, anti-Christian, anti-Western ideology that rejects core American precepts? After all, that is what First Amendment religious freedom is all about, right?

Well, no, wrong. Indeed, that suggestion would have been astounding to our founders. In the late eighteenth century, as American vessels were besieged by the Barbary Pirates in the Strait of Gibraltar, U.S. emissaries Thomas Jefferson and John Adams paid a visit to Sidi Haji Abdrahaman, Tripoli's envoy in London. Christopher Hitchens relates that "they asked him by what right he extorted money and took slaves in this way." He replied (as Jefferson later reported to Secretary of State John Jay, and to the Congress) that this right

> was founded on the Laws of the Prophet, that it was written
> in their Koran, that all nations who should not have answered
> their authority were sinners, that it was their right and duty
> to make war upon them wherever they could be found, and to

118

make slaves of all they could take as prisoners, and that every Mussulman who should be slain in battle was sure to go to Paradise.[23]

In point of fact, things were even worse than His Excellency suggested. He might also have told Jefferson and Adams that Islam holds pirates in special esteem. "The seafaring jihadist," Raymond Ibrahim explicates, "is forgiven all sins upon setting foot in a boat to wage war upon infidels; he receives double the reward of his terrestrial counterpart—which is saying much considering that the martyred mujahid is, of all Muslims, guaranteed the highest celestial rewards."[24] In any event, Islamic doctrine hasn't changed any in the ensuing centuries, just as it hadn't changed in the millennium-plus before Ambassador Abdrahaman was good enough to edify our founders. But *we* have clearly changed.

In the early nineteenth century Jefferson went to war with the Islamic states of North Africa, giving birth in the process to the United States Marine Corps. Our third president, the author of the Declaration of Independence, was not dissuaded from acting decisively, and without apology, against the first Muslim terrorists to torment Americans. He was not moved by the "religious" airs they put on their predations. He saw them for what they were: a vulgar, socio-political imperialism dressed up in religious finery. Alas, Jefferson's clarity of mind is woefully absent from early twenty-first-century America. Now, it's the Muslim Brotherhood looking for a few good men, with an eye toward destroying what Jefferson has bequeathed us.

chapter seven

E PLURIBUS UMMA

Faithful to Banna's bottom-up model, the Saudi/Brotherhood proselytism enterprise has always emphasized indoctrination through the education system. With the loosening of immigration restrictions in the 1960s, Muslim aliens flocked to the United States, particularly students anxious to study in American universities. This wave was concentrated in the Midwest. Brotherhood acolytes thus incorporated the Muslim Students Association in Indiana and founded its first chapter at the University of Illinois Urbana-Champaign in January 1963.[1] Additional MSA chapters soon began popping up at various universities. They provided young Muslims with English versions of Islamist works, particularly the writings of Qutb and Banna. This created a rich recruiting pool for the Ikhwan: young Arab Muslims schooled in, and now adherent to, its ideology. Today, the MSA has nearly 600 chapters in the United States and Canada, "nurturing Islamist ideas among next-generation American Muslims," as Zeyno Baran puts it so well.

In 1972, the same Brotherhood operatives who had forged the MSA helped create the World Assembly of Muslim Youth in Riyadh. The express purpose of WAMY was to "arm the Muslim youth with full confidence in the supremacy of the Islamic system over other systems." It grew into the world's largest Muslim youth organization, operating in over sixty countries.[2] Despite their occasional lip-service to peaceful coexistence mouthed for the ears of credulous Westerners, WAMY is intolerant of non-Muslims, supportive—financially and otherwise—of violent jihad, boldly anti-Semitic, and intimately connected to the Saudi regime. For example, the Kingdom's current Minister of Islamic Affairs, Endowment and Dawa once served as WAMY's president.

Typical of the literature the organization disseminates to young Muslims is *Islamic Views*, which just happens to be published by the Saudi government's Armed Forces Printing Press. This short Arabic language book helpfully teaches that "the Prophet Mohammad fought against the infidels and the Jews 'til he triumphed over them, conducted himself about twenty invasions, and sent tens of regiments led by his companions for jihad." Lest you miss the point, *Islamic Views* expands on it: Islam "is a religion of jihad," and jihad is "an answer for the Jews, the liars." Fellow Muslims are beseeched to "teach our children to love taking revenge on the Jews and the oppressors, and teach them that our youngsters will liberate Palestine and al-Quds [Jerusalem] when they go back to Islam and make jihad for the sake of Allah."[3]

WAMY's education programs are not limited to theory. As my friend Steve Emerson explained to the 9/11 Commission,

Ahmed Ajaj provides a window into how practical they can be. In 1992, Ajaj was arrested trying to enter the U.S. in order to bomb the World Trade Center—a feat his traveling companion, Ramzi Yousef (who was briefly detained but released), pulled off a few months later. At the time, Ajaj was carrying an official WAMY envelope, printed with the organization's return address in Saudi Arabia. It contained a handy manual, "Military Lessons in the Jihad Against the Tyrants."

The booklet details how to establish and maintain clandestine terror cells, stressing the role of Muslim "youth" in waging jihad to establish Allah's law. It also offers concrete instruction in such essentials as forging identification documents, finding housing, obtaining and storing weapons, conducting reconnaissance, planning and carrying out attacks, countering surveillance, kidnapping enemy soldiers, assassinating foreign tourists, sabotaging civilian targets, and so on.

Reading as if Qutb were channeling Mao, the manual is emphatic that the only thing infidel regimes really understand is "the dialogue of bullets, the ideals of assassination, explosion and destruction, and the politics of the machine gun." WAMY's lesson has obviously made the rounds: Six years later, investigators seized the same booklet in the London flat of Khalid al-Fawwaz. The United States is still trying to extradite him for the 1998 bombings of American embassies in Kenya and Tanzania that killed over 200 people.[4]

WAMY's American branch was founded in Virginia by Osama bin Laden's nephew, Abdullah Awad bin Laden.[*] The Saudi government is extraordinarily protective of the bin Laden clan, one of the Kingdom's most prominent. The regime insists that the

---

[*] Abdullah Awad bin Laden should not be confused with Abdullah bin Laden, Osama's brother and the bin Laden family's sometime spokesman.

family, like the House of Saud itself, has disowned Osama and is repulsed by terrorism. If that's the case, nephew Abdullah, like the Saudi regime, sure seems oddly enthusiastic about the ideology that spawns the likes of Uncle Osama.

No doubt owing to Saudi pressure, neither WAMY's headquarters nor its U.S. hub in Falls Church, Virginia, has ever been designated as a terror facilitator. The organization, however, has been banned in Pakistan, where it shared office space with the Benevolence International Foundation, an al Qaeda charitable front founded by Osama bin Laden's brother-in-law, Mohammed Jamal Khalifa. WAMY has also been accused by the governments of India and the Philippines of abetting terrorism. WAMY ties have been relied on by the U.S. military as part of the basis for continuing to detain enemy combatants held at Guantanamo Bay. And WAMY's Virginia office was raided by the FBI in 2004 (no charges have been filed).[5] Yet, Abdullah Awad bin Laden and his brother Omar, who shared a Falls Church home, were somehow among the prominent Saudis (including several other bin Laden family members) permitted by our government to be whisked out of the United States in the hectic days immediately following 9/11—while the skies were closed to American travelers, and before anything resembling a competent investigation of potential terror ties could have been carried out.[6]

That was curious, to say the least. Hani Hanjour and Nawaf Alhazmi, two of the fifteen Saudi nationals who carried out the 9/11 attacks, lived on the same street just three blocks away from WAMY's U.S. office. On the day before the attacks, Hanjour, Alhazmi, and their fellow 9/11 hijacker Khaled al-Midhar checked into a Marriott Residence Inn near Dulles Airport. That same day, Saleh Hussayen—a Saudi government official then touring the U.S. offices of WAMY, the Muslim World League, and other

Saudi concerns—left his nearby hotel and checked into the very same Residence Inn.[7]

Coincidence? Well, after the three hijackers plowed Flight 77 into the Pentagon, the FBI tried to interview Hussayen. But, as an FBI agent later testified, Hussayen "feigned a seizure, prompting the agents to take him to a hospital, where the attending physicians found nothing wrong with him." Though the agent wanted Hussayen to be barred from fleeing the U.S. until she could conduct the interview, higher-ups rebuffed her recommendation. Hussayen was allowed to return to Saudi Arabia on September 19, 2001. That is to say, he flew the coop the moment air travel resumed.

A few months later, our friends the Saudis promoted Hussayen. He is now the minister in charge of overseeing the palatial mosques in Mecca and Medina. Shortly after that, Hussayen's nephew, a computer scientist named Sami Omar Hussayen, was indicted for material support to terrorism based on his administration of a website that expressly advocated suicide bombing and the use of planes as weapons. Sami Hussayen was acquitted—not because he didn't lend his skills to the Islamist cyber endeavor but because a jury elected not to hold him responsible for the posted content.

The site Sami ran was tied to the Islamic Assembly of North America. Based in Michigan and stridently anti-American, the IANA publicly broadcasts the fatwas of Safer al-Awali and Salman al-Auda—the aforementioned Saudi "Awakening" clerics who give al Qaeda attacks the sheen of Islamic legitimacy. The organization has disseminated publications calling for suicide bombings against the United States. It has hosted senior al Qaeda recruiter Abdelrahman Dosari at several of its conferences. It condemns Western equality between the sexes and defends such despicable practices as female circumcision. Several IANA operatives, moreover, have been convicted on federal fraud and money laundering charges.[8]

Consistent with its pattern, the once smitten Saudi regime has become less enamored of IANA as its Islamism has become more openly anti-regime. But it is important to remind ourselves—as it is almost every time the Saudis tell us they are "cracking down"—that the only reason the IANA exists is Saudi support. Historically, the organization got about half of its funding from the government. Lo and behold, its biggest financial backers have included none other than Saleh Hussayen. The *Washington Post* reports that the Saudi mosque minister has chipped in $100,000, and that he is acknowledged to be a deep IANA pocket by both the FBI and his nephew Omar. In fact, Hussayen even made time to visit the IANA's Michigan offices on the U.S. tour that led him to stay in the same hotel as the hijackers on the eve of 9/11.[9]

You can easily see why our government would let him avoid interrogation and race back to the safety of the Kingdom, can't you?

The Islamist "Nucleus"

In 1973, the Saudis backed their Brotherhood partners at the Muslim Students Association in the creation of the North American Islamic Trust, which, like the MSA, was incorporated in Indiana.[10] Flush with funding and exempt from U.S. taxation, the NAIT has effectively seized control of three-quarters of the approximately 2,300 mosques now operating in the United States.[11]

With WAMY, the MSA, and the NAIT in place, the table was set for 1981, a banner year for the global Islamist project. By then, it had become clear that many of the Muslim immigrants who had been flooding the U.S. for a generation, including MSA graduates, were not returning home. In tandem with the rising number of Muslims settling in America came the jolt of the 1979 Iranian Revolution. That Khomeini was a Shiite was beside the point. Young Islamists swelled with confident pride over the smashing success of a fundamentalist upheaval—one in which university students played a vital part. It could happen, they told themselves, even in the late twentieth century, even in a nation heavily influenced by America and the West. Maybe it could even happen here.

The Brotherhood perceived the need for an overarching structure to husband this growing energy. Thus in 1981, the NAIT and the MSA gave birth to the Islamic Society of North America, headquartered in Indiana (indeed, incorporated at the same address as the MSA and the NAIT).[12] ISNA was conceived, in its own words, as an umbrella organization "to advance the cause of Islam and service Muslims in North America so as to enable them to adopt Islam as a complete way of life." It was to be like a post-graduate extension of the MSA. In fact, ISNA and the MSA consider themselves to be one organization, sharing a single, common history. On its website, ISNA claims to have been created in 1963—actually the year MSA was created—and ISNA labeled its 2009 annual convention as its "46th."[13] As internal Ikhwan documents put it, the MSA "was developed into the Islamic Society of North America (ISNA) to include all Muslim congregations from immigrants and citizens, and to be a nucleus for the Islamic movement in North America." To underscore the Siamese connectedness of these ventures, NAIT has stated that it "provides protection and safeguarding for the assets of ISNA/MSA and other communities by holding their assets and real estate in 'waqf' [Islamic charitable endowments]."[14]

ISNA/MSA has become exactly the nucleus the Brotherhood hoped for: It exercises dominant control of the ideological content at the hundreds of U.S. mosques controlled by the NAIT.[15] Its aforementioned annual convention now draws tens of thousands of Muslims—which, of course, means the federal government can't keep itself away. The 2009 convention keynoter was none other than Valerie Jarrett, one of President Barack Obama's closest aides. She managed not to mention that the Justice Department had named ISNA as an unindicted coconspirator in the most significant terrorism finance case in U.S. history—a designation the trial evidence proved to be well-founded.

One of the students involved in ISNA's 1981 founding was a then twenty-two-year-old Muslim Brotherhood member named Sami al-Arian.[16] Born to Palestinian refugees in Kuwait, al-Arian graduated with an engineering degree at Southern Illinois University. He would go on to obtain a computer engineering doctorate at North Carolina State University before being awarded a prominent teaching post at the University of South Florida. The United States does a remarkable job of educating its enemies, and the Islamophilic academy continues the service, securing comfortable employment for them.

In any event, it was during 1981 that al-Arian teamed up with two other students, Mousa Abu Marzook and Khalid al-Mishal, both of whom were Muslim Brotherhood operatives. Marzook, born to Yemeni parents in Gaza, was then thirty. Ostensibly, he was in the United States to pursue a doctorate in industrial engineering at Columbia State University in Louisiana. He had, however, become a Muslim Brotherhood activist while living in Abu Dhabi in the Seventies. Mishal, then twenty-five, had been born in the West Bank district of Ramallah while it was under Jordanian rule. While growing up in Kuwait, where he eventually earned a physics degree and pursued an academic career, he was so enraptured by the Muslim Brotherhood that he joined in 1971, when he was only fifteen.[17]

In Chicago, the trio established the Islamic Association of Palestine. The IAP made no bones about being a Brotherhood satellite—its declared purpose, Zeyno Baran recounts, was "to communicate the Ikhwan's point of view" and "to serve the cause of Palestine on the political and media fronts." The IAP became the platform from which Marzook spent his next fourteen years: orchestrating terrorist operations against Israel, raising funds to execute them, and working toward the Islamicization of American society. In fact, while in the U.S., Marzook became the head of Hamas. Upon his subsequent arrest, Mishal succeeded him.

For his part, al-Arian became a major player in Palestinian Islamic Jihad, a murderous organization begun in the Gaza Strip in 1979 by three Palesinians (Fathi Shikaki, Abdul Azziz Odeh, and Bashir Moussa) who found the Muslim Brotherhood insufficiently militant to suit them. PIJ, like the Brotherhood, is dedicated to the elimination of Western influences; for instance, it would like to converge all Muslim lands into a single Islamic caliphate. Today, forty years after its founding, PIJ continues to target Jews for terrorist strikes, both in Israel and in the Palestinian territories. In typical Brotherhood fashion, al-Arian denied being a PIJ leader for years—even as he was recorded urging Muslims to contribute money for jihadist attacks, and even as he turned the campus on which he taught into a hub for PIJ and the Islamist cause. He was convicted in 2006 for conspiring to provide material support to a terrorist organization.

Transforming Middle America

In 1981, the Brotherhood enjoyed yet another middle American coup, using the NAIT to wrest the Bridgeview Mosque in

Chicago from its moderate founders. The mosque became an anchor for the Brotherhood's voluntary apartheid strategy. As the *Chicago Tribune* reported in 2004, the mosque's leaders "are men who have condemned Western culture, praised Palestinian suicide bombers and encouraged members to view society in stark terms: Muslims against the world." Those leaders drove out moderates, they enforced Islamic dress codes and strict separation of the sexes, and they imported Salafist clerics, whose salaries were paid by Saudi Arabia. The mosque's communiqués reeked of Brotherhood doctrine: one brochure, for example, warned that Chicago Muslims were at risk of "melting in the American society, culture and lifestyle"; a plea to a Saudi charity sought funding "before it becomes too late and we may lose our children because they are living in an unIslamic society."

Most apparently, a swath of one of America's largest cities was radically transformed. As the *Tribune* recounted:

> A whole new community sprang up. The area became an upscale enclave, featuring new houses with Arabic script over the doors and sparkling chandeliers. Mosque leaders built two schools and started a youth center for basketball and religious classes. New clothing stores, groceries and restaurants opened in Bridgeview. A floor-covering store turned into a Middle Eastern restaurant. A music store became an Islamic hair salon.
>
> Men who attended the mosque grew their beards and traded their T-shirts for long tunics. Women draped themselves in loose, ankle-length robes.
>
> Cook County was fast becoming home to more Palestinians than any other part of the nation. And the mosque was now one of the area's largest Islamic centers. . . .
>
> Most non-Muslims moved away from the mosque neighborhood, frustrated by traffic jams on Fridays and the call

to prayer that rang out over mosque loudspeakers. Muslims were happy to take their places. . . . Some immigrants moved there to be near relatives. Some felt persecuted by the backlash against Muslims during the first gulf war. Others wanted to protect their families from what they saw as the increasing immorality of American culture.

[One woman] came to the mosque because of her oldest daughter. [She] worried about the 3rd grader's fitting in at a public school and enrolled her in one of the mosque Islamic schools. [The woman], who had only prayed at home before, started attending the mosque and covering her hair.

"I started to understand that this was a way of life," she recalled. "For me, this mosque became a place of tranquility." Still others joined the mosque because they liked the pro-Palestinian politics, sermons in Arabic and what they saw as its authentic interpretations of the Koran, the Muslim holy book. "The community was serious about Islam," [one] worshiper recalled. "It was easier to practice the faith here."[18]

It was also easier to join the Muslim Brotherhood there. After his arrest in Gaza for helping finance Hamas operations, Mohammad Salah, a Chicago academic (what else?), told Israeli authorities that he'd been recruited into the Brotherhood by Jamal Said, an imam at the Bridgeview Mosque whose salary was subsidized by the Saudi regime. Salah eventually became a top aide to Marzook, who incorporated him into the "Palestine Organization," a precursor of Hamas. He confessed to the Israelis that Marzook had sent him to the Palestinian territories four times between 1989 and 1993 to fund the terrorist group's military operations.[19]

Finally, 1981 also saw the establishment of the International Institute of Islamic Thought, formed, as usual, by Saudi money and Brotherhood know-how. The IIIT is a think-tank based in Herndon, Virginia, with branch offices throughout the world, dedicated to what it describes as "the Islamicization of knowledge." That is a "euphemism," Baran surmises, "for the rewriting of history to support Islamist narratives," such as the claim that Spain, having once been conquered by Islamic forces (and renamed "al-Andalus"), is the rightful property of Muslims. The IIIT features the familiar web of Brotherhood connections. Its founders included Jamal Barzinji (of WAMY and the MSA) and Sayyid Syeed, who was a member of the original ISNA board of directors and served as ISNA's secretary-general for a dozen years (until 2006). And the IIIT's $50,000 contribution made it the top donor to al-Arian's Florida think-tank, the World Islamic Study Enterprise (or WISE), which IIIT deemed an extension of itself.[20] In fact, after al-Arian's terrorism-support conviction, a federal grand jury filed contempt charges against him for refusing to testify about, among other things, the operations of IIIT.

These and other Islamist institutions laid the groundwork for the Saudi-backed Brotherhood to focus more systematically on *dawa* in America. It would be difficult to imagine a more successful implementation of Banna's grass-roots blueprint.

chapter eight

THE AMERICAN DOESN'T
KNOW ANYTHING

C ompletion of the Islamist infrastructure in America proved
timely. In late 1987, a new injection of energy and urgency
coursed through the Brotherhood movement. The Intifada was
launched, stirring visions of that fondest Islamist wish: annihila-
tion of the "Zionist entity."

The siege was ignited by two unconnected events in the
powder keg of Gaza: the December 6 murder of an Israeli, followed four days later by a tragic car accident, in which four Palestinians lost their lives. Falsely but unrelentingly, the accident
was hyped as a revenge killing. Skirmishes broke out and quickly
spilled into the West Bank and East Jerusalem. The violence, a
roller-coaster of lulls and explosions, lasted over six years.

Yasser Arafat well understood the fervor of Islam, having spent his youth in its milieu of Jew-hatred. As an engineering student in Cairo during World War II, he'd been powerfully influenced by Haj Amin el-Husseini, the Mufti of Jerusalem (and probably a blood relative of Arafat's). Husseini had aligned with Hitler and schemed from Berlin to import the Führer's genocidal program to the Holy Land.

Yet the fully formed Arafat was a Marxist totalitarian in the Nasserite mold. To be sure, he made opportunistic use of jihadist rhetoric and imagery. The constitution of his PLO faction, Fatah, casts the liberation of "Palestine" as a "religious" obligation (at least in part), and requires members to pledge their loyalty before Allah.[1] But Arafat's overall program was, at most, a simulacrum of Islam, bearing more the stamp of Moscow than Mecca. In "Palestine," deemed by Islamists to be Muslim territory and thus an obligatory field of jihad against the infidels, the Saudi-backed Brothers were certain they could do better. Thus, they formed their own faction, Hamas.

HAMAS is a transliteral acronym for "*Harakat al-Muqawamah al-Islamiyya*," meaning the "Islamic Resistance Movement." The invocation of "resistance" is noteworthy. The Saudis, the Ikhwan, and other Islamists often effect condemnations of "terrorism." What they mean, though, is "terrorism" *as they define it*. That definition does not include the "defensive" use of force whenever "Islam is under siege." That brand of savagery is called "resistance." In carrying it out, Islamists reserve the right to decide for themselves what constitutes "defense" and when "Islam is under siege"—an Israeli walking into a coffee shop in Tel Aviv or an American soldier protecting an Islamic school in Kandahar may not realize that, in so doing, they are besieging Islam. Thus, the way this game works, *any* act of terrorism, no matter how offensive and brutal, can be rationalized as "resistance." The condemnation of "terrorism" by poseurs who lionize "resistance" is worse than meaningless. It is strategic deceit in the service of the global Islamist project.

Officially, Hamas came into being in mid-December 1987. As Matthew Levitt relates, however, the Muslim Brotherhood from which Hamas sprang had been boring its roots into Palestinian soil for decades. In Gaza, under Nasser's thumb, the Ikhwan became more secretive and hostile. On the west and east banks of the Jordan River, the Brothers developed "an equivocal relationship" with the Jordanian monarchy.

Two longtime Brotherhood hands, Ahmed Yassin and Abdel Azziz al-Rantisi, are credited with establishing Hamas. Yassin had been rendered blind and paraplegic by a childhood accident. He was thus unable to complete his studies at al-Azhar, but his followers bestowed the honorific "Sheikh" on him nonetheless. Rantisi, a medical doctor, discovered the Ikhwan while attending university in Alexandria. Hence his avocation, the destruction of Israel, became his life's calling.

That avocation has always been Hamas's top priority. Leftists and dreamy internationalists seize on this fact as a rationale for distinguishing Hamas from al Qaeda. Hamas, the French Arabist Olivier Roy maintains, is a local political movement engaged in the mere "political ideologisation of Islam . . . which has nothing to do with terrorism." It must be contrasted with the "pure" terrorism of al Qaeda which, by his lights, is more anarchist than Islamist.[2] While it cannot be appeased, Hamas, he argues, should be cultivated.

Roy couldn't be more wrong. Hamas has been committed to the global Islamist project from the very start. As Khalid al-Mishal has explained, "Hamas is not a local organization but the spearhead of a national project, which has Arab, Islamic, and international ambitions as well."[3] That is, it is very much in the Muslim Brotherhood fold. Yes, it had started in its own backyard, Palestine—just as al Qaeda's Zawahiri started in Egypt and bin Laden still targets his own native Saudi Arabia. But Hamas's ambitions are Islamist, not merely Palestinian. They are hegemonic. Indeed, the Hamas charter, which reads as if it were written by Banna, makes that explicit:

> The Islamic Resistance Movement is one of the wings of the Muslim Brothers in Palestine. The Muslim Brotherhood Movement is a world organization, the largest Islamic Movement in the modern era. It is characterized by a profound understanding, by precise notions and by a complete comprehensiveness of all concepts of Islam in all domains of life: views and beliefs, politics and economics, education and society, jurisprudence and rule, indoctrination and teaching, the arts and publications, the hidden and the evident, and all other domains of life.

The charter, moreover, is blunt in proclaiming its method: "The purpose of HAMAS is to create an Islamic Palestinian state throughout Israel by eliminating the State of Israel *through violent jihad*" (emphasis added). Jihad is the mission of imposing Allah's law across the earth, not across just a few square miles.

Like other Islamist organizations structured in accordance with Brotherhood theory, Hamas is multi-tiered. Atop its hierarchy is a political bureau, which is now led by Mishal and Marzook from their exile in Syria under the protection of the Assad regime, and by Ismail Haniyeh in Gaza.[4] The political bureau coordinates terrorist activities by directing two nominally com-

136

partmentalized entities: military forces, called the *Izz el-Din al-Qassam* Brigades, which carry out attacks against Israel; and a *dawa* wing, which (as the Justice Department's original 2004 indictment in the *Holy Land Foundation* case put it) operates as a "welfare agency, providing food, medical care and education to Palestinians in order to generate loyalty and support for the organization and its overall goals."

The military and social activities, in fact, liberally cross-pollinate. *Dawa* indoctrination starts at the cradle. Palestinian children are reared in Islamic supremacism and a dehumanizing hatred of Jews, whom they are taught to regard as the descendents of filthy animals—lessons that are replete with Koranic citations in which Allah does indeed transmute Islam-resistant Jews into monkeys and pigs.[5] Tykes are also schooled in the glories of *sha-hada*: "martyrdom"—or, to be more precise, suicide terrorism—in the noble struggle against the Zionist entity. Hamas, in fact, sponsors children's summer camps that quite consciously imitate the martial ethos of paramilitary camps run by al Qaeda, Hezbollah, and Hamas itself. As night follows day, these aspects of the *dawa* regimen generate recruitment momentum for the military wing. That they masquerade as public education and "social welfare" cannot obscure that reality—at least if we are open to seeing reality.

Hamas and Fatah (the Arafat party in the PLO now run by Mohammed Abbas) have come to despise each other. That was an inevitability from Hamas's earliest days, when Mishal tirelessly challenged Arafat's aging, debauched grip. Despite their intramural enmity, though, the Palestinian rivals' joint commitment to the obliteration of Israel enabled them to work together in the early days, under Arafat's "Unified Leadership of the Intifada." In the first four years—that is, the period before the ebb that marked the onset of the 1991 Gulf War—Israeli defense forces responded to more than 3,600 Molotov cocktail attacks, 100 hand grenade attacks, and 600 assaults with guns or explosives, all of which killed twenty-seven and wounded over 3000.[6]

Relentlessly stoked by Saudi-propelled Brotherhood theorists, insatiable hatred of the Jewish state remains to this day the glue that holds Palestinian society together. Indeed, when Arafat finally succumbed in 2004, Mishal took pains to attend the funeral . . . in the company of the Saudi royal family. The joint ambition of destroying the Jewish state was a force greater than their deep differences. Recent polling found that up to *93 percent* of young Palestinian adults (aged eighteen to twenty-five) deny Israel's right to exist—as compared with "only" 75 percent when the total population is factored in.[7] Given the bile on which Palestinian children are weaned, how on earth could it be otherwise?

Running Hamas from America

With the formation of Hamas, the Brotherhood now had a formal Palestinian satellite engaged in what Islamists saw as obligatory jihadist violence—just as they see killing Americans in Iraq and Afghanistan as obligatory jihadist violence. Supporting the Intifada became imperative for the Ikhwan's Saudi-sponsored global network. The costs of sustaining a years-long campaign that projects armed force on the scale of a modern nation-state are enormous.[8] Consequently WAMY, to take one example, tapped its worldwide membership for tens of millions of dollars. Hamas luminaries like Mishal were feted at conferences and fundraisers.[9]

Not surprisingly, Hamas's first beachhead in the United States was the Islamic Association for Palestine. As we've seen, the IAP had been formed six years before the launch of Hamas by two of the future terror organization's heavyweights, Marzook and Mishal, in conjunction with al-Arian. Shortly after Hamas was created, the Brotherhood had the energetic Marzook form the Palestine Committee, both as an additional fundraising arm and to impose some order and direction over the various pro-Hamas initiatives that were underway.

Those efforts included another Marzook start-up called the United Association for Studies and Research, established to promote Hamas ideology. In addition, the Occupied Land Fund was begun by Shukri Abu Baker and Ghassan Elashi thanks to a $200,000 infusion from—who else?—Marzook (who is Elashi's brother-in-law). In time, the Occupied Land Fund would morph into the infamous Holy Land Foundation for Relief and Development (HLF) and raise over $36 million for Hamas.[10] The HLF operated from within ISNA/NAIT, which kept an HLF account into which were deposited checks payable to "the Palestinian Mujahideen," the original name of Hamas's military wing. From that account, HLF ultimately sent hundreds of thousands of dollars to Marzook, Elashi, Sheikh Yassin's "Islamic Center of Gaza," and various other Hamas entities.[11] By December 2003, senior members of the Senate Banking Committee had alerted the Internal Revenue Service that ISNA and the HLF were among twenty-five Islamist entities that "finance terrorism and perpetuate violence."[12]

It's worth pausing to remind ourselves that these funds were not for a mere PR program. *They were financing terrorist attacks*.

As Stephen Schwartz has observed, "Ordinary Americans should be shocked and outraged to learn that Hamas was running its terror campaign from a sanctuary in the U.S."[13] It was indeed. When Sheikh Yassin was arrested by Israeli authorities in 1989, Marzook took over Hamas. He was named head of the political bureau and ran the terrorist organization from his home in Virginia for the next five years. Levitt elaborates that, by the early Nineties, Marzook had set up a Hamas-feeding paramilitary group, the "Palestine Organization." Through that vehicle, not only did he orchestrate terror attacks by the Qassam Brigades and oversee fundraising operations, he also recruited and trained Hamas operatives on U.S. soil. That training was overseen by Muslim instructors from America and Lebanon, and it involved the preparation of explosive charges. When these operatives were sent to Israel and the Palestinian territories, they were ready for jihad.[14]

Marzook, Mishal, and al-Arian were building Hamas's Islamist support network under Brotherhood direction. That is irrefutable. Marzook was the front man, but as an internal "status report" prepared for the Ikhwan's leadership (i.e., its "Shura Council") related, it was *the Brotherhood* that created IAP and, subsequently, the Palestine Committee

> to serve the cause of Palestine on the political and media
> fronts. . . . The Association's [i.e., the IAP's] work has de-
> veloped a great deal since its inception, particularly with
> the formation of the Palestine Committee, the beginning of
> the Intifada at the end of 1987, and the proclamation of the
> Hamas Movement.[15]

This was the state of play in spring 1991 when Mohamed Akram put pen to paper and produced the Brotherhood's aforementioned American playbook, "An Explanatory Memorandum on the General Strategic Goal for the Group in North America." The memo was written for the benefit of the Brotherhood's Shura Council to supplement the "long-term plan" the council

THE GRAND JIHAD

had "approved and adopted" in 1987—the year, of course, when the Brotherhood had formally established Hamas.

Out of the Shadows

To have any real hope of "eliminating and destroying the Western civilization from within and 'sabotaging' its miserable house," the Brotherhood's "grand jihad" would need to attend to even the smallest details. The goal was to plant and spread Islam from the grass roots, so that it first became part of the soil, and eventually the master of the soil. The Ikhwan and its allies, Akram explained, would have thus to involve themselves in all matters great and small. Only that would yield

> an effective and stable Islamic Movement led by the Muslim Brotherhood which adopts Muslims' causes domestically and globally, and which works to expand the observant Muslim base, aims at unifying and directing Muslims' efforts, presents Islam as a civilization alternative, and supports the global Islamic state, wherever it is.

In the United States, a vast, non-Muslim country with a sparse Islamic presence, such a plan could not be carried out from one central command, and the Muslim Brotherhood could not accomplish it alone. It would be vital to establish an "'Islamic Center' in every city." Islamic centers would become "the 'axis' of our Movement," serving as "the House of Dawa" and providing "the 'base' for our rise . . . to educate us, prepare us and supply our battalions."

It would also be indispensable, Akram surmised, to have in place "firmly-established 'organizations' on which the Islamic structure is built." Some of these organizations would belong to the Brotherhood, but for the most part, "the role of the Ikhwan" would be "the initiative, pioneering, leadership, raising the banner and pushing people" in the right "direction." "We must possess," Akram asserted, "a mastery of the art of 'coalitions,' the art of 'absorption' and the principles of 'cooperation.'"

Fortunately, Akram reported, the Brotherhood had already succeeded in finding partners—some of which the Ikhwan had created. These "organizations of our friends" shared the goals of the Brotherhood's "grand mission." Like the Ikhwan, they saw it as a "civilization jihadist" responsibility. Among these "friends" he expressly listed the now familiar suspects: the MSA, ISNA, the IIIT, the IAP, and the United Association for Studies and Research. And there would be more to come.

For the next two years, though, debate raged within the Brotherhood about the best strategy for achieving its goals in the United States. Should it remain in the shadows, a guiding hand for the web of organizations that it had established and that it heavily influenced? The U.S., after all, was a staunch supporter of Israel and might well decide to crack down on Hamas supporters. Being too public as a Brotherhood member could make one a target.

Still, the immunities America provided for speech and association made it possible to press an anti-American agenda without real penalties. Arguments for more openness were made by such prominent Egyptian Brothers as Mohammed Mahdi Akef and Ahmed Elkadi, the latter a surgeon who had been the personal physician of King Faisal of Saudi Arabia (though the Florida Board of Medicine revoked his license in 1992, concluding he was incompetent). Elkadi had spearheaded the Brotherhood in America for nearly a decade, including a stint as president of the NAIT. Akef, who, in 2003, would assume leadership of the Brotherhood in Egypt, told the *Chicago Tribune* that he had pleaded in debates with his U.S.-based associates: "We have a religion, message, morals and principals that we want to carry to the people as God ordered us, so why should we work in secrecy?" A more public presence could result in more direct Brotherhood control over the direction of Islam in America.[16]

By the end of 1992, after a contentious meeting of over forty Brothers at a Days Inn on the Georgia-Tennessee border, a judgment was made: The Ikhwan would have a more overt American face. In deference to the misgivings that had so freighted this decision, the new entity would not call itself the "Muslim Brotherhood." The conferees opted, instead, to call it the "Muslim American Society."

MAS members would be instructed to dodge questions about their Brotherhood ties by saying they were "independent" and that "Muslim American Society" was "a self-explanatory name." Leaders were further enjoined to claim that, *of course*, they opposed "terrorism"—while also pointing out that "jihad" was one of each Muslim's "divine legal rights," to be used both in self-defense and for the spread of Islam. They would adhere to Brotherhood protocols and obscure their tenets from outsiders, such as their conviction that, even in America, religion and politics cannot be separated—they must be one, and that one must be sharia. They would remain guarded about their ultimate goal, the transformation of the United States into an Islamic country under Islamic law. They would keep under wraps their plan for achieving that goal: The use of democratic processes to elect likeminded Muslims to political office and to seed likeminded Muslims throughout government bureaucracies, while ever more Americans were being converted to Islam, and ever more American Muslims were being born.[17]

The MAS was incorporated in Illinois in 1993. It is now headquartered in Alexandria, Virginia, and has over fifty chapters nationwide. Shaker Elsayed, the former MAS secretary-general who, we shall see, is now the imam at a disturbing Virginia mosque, is faithful to Brotherhood doublespeak: He has denied that MAS is part of the Ikwhan, stressing that it is not run out of Egypt. But quite obviously, the *raison d'être* of MAS is the establishment of an overt Brotherhood presence in the U.S. that *is run in the U.S.* In any event, Elsayed conceded in a 2004 *Chicago Tribune* interview that the MAS was begun by the Brotherhood and continues to operate in accordance with the teachings of Banna. In fact, Elsayed maintained that Banna's ideas represent "the closest reflection of how Islam should be in this life." He also acknowledged that at least 45 percent of the MAS's "active members"—i.e., those who have completed five years of Muslim community service and a course of deep study in the writings of Banna and Qutb—are also members of the Muslim Brotherhood.[18]

Mirroring the Brotherhood, the MAS minces no words in announcing that its mission is to promote "Islam as a total way of life" and to "offer a viable Islamic alternative to many of our society's prevailing problems." Daveed Gartenstein-Ross of the Foundation for Defense of Democracies, who wrote memorably about his own experience being recruited into Islamist ideology,[19] has meticulously documented the MAS's service as an Ikhwan front group. He observes that "the message that all countries should be ruled by Islamic law is echoed throughout MAS's membership curriculum."[20]

Front and center are Banna's cogitations on the importance of infiltrating government. In *The Message of the Teachings*, for example, Banna instructs Muslims to work toward

reforming the government so that it may become a truly
Islamic government, performing as a servant to the nation
in the interest of the people. By Islamic government I mean
a government whose officers are Muslims who perform the
obligatory duties of Islam, who do not make public their disobedience, and who enforce the rules and teachings of Islam.

Consistent with this framework, as well as with Yusuf Qaradawi's
voluntary apartheid gambit, Gartenstein-Ross further notes
Banna's direction that Muslims "completely boycott non-Islamic
courts and judicial systems" and "dissociate [themselves] from
organisations, newspapers, committees, schools, and institutions
which oppose your Islamic ideology." Along these same lines,
aspiring MAS activists are directed to study Fathi Yaktun's *To Be a
Muslim*, which admonishes: "Until the nations of the world have
functionally Islamic governments, every individual who is care-
less or lazy in working for Islam is sinful."

CAIR to Sabotage?

The establishment of the MAS was far from the last momen-
tous development for Islamists in America in 1993. A new, left-
leaning U.S. administration came to power in January, inclined to
be more sympathetic to the Islamist clause. But before he could
bat an eye, President Bill Clinton was confronted by the murder
and depraved mutilation of American soldiers in Somalia. A few
weeks later, on February 26, jihadists bombed the World Trade
Center. The public was angry and appeasing Islamists would have
to wait.

Arafat, however, sensed opportunity. The intifada launched
at the end of 1987 had been an extraordinarily successful gambit

for him. Within a year, even as the body-count mounted, the weak-kneed "international community" was granting the PLO the right to participate (though not to vote) in U.N. General Assembly sessions. And when Arafat made the usual show of renouncing "terrorism"—while he was orchestrating terrorist attacks in conjunction with Hamas, Palestinian Islamic Jihad, and other Islamist factions—the United States recognized him as the Palestinians' legitimate leader, just as the Europeans had done. The PLO chieftain blundered in 1991, throwing in his lot with Saddam Hussein during the Gulf War, and that seemed to bury him with the Bush 41 administration. But Clinton was a new lease on life.

Anxious to chase the holy grail of Middle East peace and suddenly in need of demonstrating toughness against Islamist terror, the new "progressive" president was made to order for the wily Marxist terror master. If Arafat could resell his "I renounce terrorism" carpet yet again, chances were he could cash in. And so he did, purporting to commit the Palestinians to the 1993 Oslo Accord—an empty promise of peaceful coexistence exchanged for hundreds of millions in aid (much of which he pocketed), an open invitation to the Clinton White House (where he became a regular visitor), international recognition (as a statesman, no less), and a ludicrous Nobel Peace Prize (forever degrading a once prestigious honor into a punch-line).

The Muslim Brotherhood, for one, was not amused. Islamists had murdered Egyptian President Anwar Sadat in 1981 for striking a peace pact with Israel. Sure, they knew Arafat and understood what he was up to. But acceptance of the Zionist entity's right to exist was utterly unacceptable, even if done as a ploy, and even if shrouded in sleight of hand. (The PLO, for example, got away with merely promising to amend its charter so that Israel's right to exist would be acknowledged, and with voting to make such amendments . . . but it never quite got around to the actual amending.²¹)

Israel, the Brotherhood also realized, was not be the only thing Arafat would use his new friend Clinton to squeeze. After a shaky start, the president was winning global plaudits for his Orwellian "peace process." That Arafat might be stringing him along was a problem for another day as long as the theater of negotiation and progress kept drawing rave reviews. Yet, the Islamists could spoil the show with their implacable jihad, their blunt insistence that nothing less than Israel's obliteration would satisfy them. They were thus a mortal threat to Clinton's signal political achievement, which gave the fledgling administration a powerful incentive to crack down on them. Arafat had strengthened his hand against his rivals for power.

That was the backdrop when twenty-five Hamas members and supporters gathered at a Marriott Hotel in Philadelphia on October 27, 1993—unaware that the FBI was monitoring their deliberations. The confab was a brainstorming exercise: How best to back Hamas and derail Oslo while concealing these activities from the American government?

The meeting was convened under the auspices of the Palestine Committee. Marzook, as we've seen, had formed several entities to stoke support for Hamas. By 1991, he'd decided a "central committee" was necessary to "work for the Palestinian cause on the American front." So he amended the Palestine Committee's by-laws to assign it that role. That brought under the Committee's umbrella, among other organizations, the IAP, the United Association for Studies and Research, and the Occupied Land Committee (i.e., the soon-to-be Holy Land Foundation). The reorganization would better enable the Palestine Committee to comply with the Muslim Brotherhood's exhortations—documented in an internal Brotherhood memo—to "increase the

147

financial and the moral support for Hamas," to "fight surrendering solutions," and to publicize "the savagery of the Jews."[22]

Significantly, the Islamists anticipated the birth of another organization. In fact, the Palestine Committee's amended by-laws declared that an as yet unnamed entity was already in the larval stage, "operat[ing] through" the IAP. The Palestine Committee "hoped" that this new group would "become an official organization for political work and its headquarters will be in Washington, *insha Allah*." For the IAP—a creation of militants which was then preoccupied with promoting the Hamas charter and its nonnegotiable commitment to Israel's demise—the nature of "political work" was already clear. As the IAP explained in a December 1988 edition of its Arabic magazine, *Ila Filastin*, "The call for jihad in the name of Allah is the only path for liberation of Palestine and all the Muslim lands. We promise Allah, continuing the jihad way and the martyrdom's way."[23]

Blatant summonses to jihad might stir the faithful in an Islamic country stewing in sharia and Jew hatred. But they were not going to fly in America—even less so in an America whose financial heart in lower Manhattan had just been shaken by a jihadist bombing. Those gathered in Philadelphia, including Marzook's brother-in-law, Ghassan Elashi, a co-founder of HLF, realized a new organization was urgently needed. To be sure, the Brotherhood had great ideological depth and its fundraising mechanisms were impressive. Marzook and his confederates had long been concerned, though, that they lacked the media and political savvy needed to advance an agenda in modern America. Now more than ever, they needed what HLF's Shukri Abu Baker called "a media twinkle."[24]

Hamas was now perceived as the principal enemy of the "peace process." Therefore, its known supporters—the Muslim Brotherhood, the Palestine Committee, the IAP, and the others—were tainted in the American mind as terror-abettors, hostile to U.S. interests and the peace process. As one attendee urged in Philadelphia, "We must form a new organization for activism which will be neutral, because we are placed in a corner. . . . It is known who we are. We are marked."[25]

The new entity, by contrast, would have a clean slate. Maybe it could steal a page out of Arafat's book of chicanery. Its Islamism and Hamas promotion would have to be less "conspicuous."[26] It would need to couch its rhetoric in sweet nothings like "social justice," "due process," and "resistance." But if it did those things, it might be more attractive . . . and effective. A Muslim organization posing as a civil rights activist while soft-peddling its jihadist sympathies might be able to snow the American political class, the courts, the media, and the academy. It might make real inroads with the transnational progressives who dominated the Clinton administration.

The IAP, current home of this evolving but still unnamed entity, was well represented in Philadelphia. Omar Ahmad, the IAP's president, was among the surveillance conscious attendees who carefully avoided saying the word "Hamas" out loud, using the inversion "Samah" instead. Ahmed even referred to himself as "Omar Yahya," the better to conceal his true identity from any hidden microphones. The codes apparently wreaked havoc on his memory: Ahmad would later testify that he couldn't recall being in Philadelphia. In fact, the tapes showed he was not only there but called the meeting to order.

Ahmad also gave his confederates thoughtful advice that underscored the extent to which communications strategy was weighing on his mind. It would be better, he counseled, to say, "I want to restore the '48 land" (i.e., return Israel to its original, 1948 boundaries that cannot be defended militarily) than to make crude (i.e., honest) statements like, "I want to destroy Israel." In the same vein, he warned that a new organization in the U.S. could not afford to admit publicly that "We represent Samah [i.e., Hamas]," or to tell a congressman that, say, "I am Omar Yahya . . . and Yasser Arafat doesn't represent me but [Hamas founder] Ahmed Yassin does."

Nihad Awad, then the IAP's public relations director, was also a Philadelphia conferee. Indeed, the same recordings showed him to be an active participant . . . though he, too, later testified to a bout of amnesia about the meeting. No wonder: He had ardently concurred in Ahmad's suggestions about adopting "different but parallel types of address." "When I speak with the American," he elaborated, "I speak with someone who doesn't know anything. As for the Palestinian who has a martyr brother or something, I know how to address him, you see?"[27] Shukri Abu Baker, the head of HLF, concurred in that sentiment. The Islamists were at war, he reminded his confederates, and, as the prophet Mohammed counseled, "War is deception."[28]

In 1994, less than a year after the Philadelphia Hamas fest, the Islamists unleashed their new organization: the Council on American-Islamic Relations. Just as the Palestine Committee by-laws had foretold, CAIR sprang from the womb of IAP and set up shop in the nation's capital.

Actually, CAIR was already in existence and firmly in the Brotherhood fold even before its incorporation was announced. We know that because, in preparing for a scheduled July 30, 1994 meeting, the Palestine Committee prepared a written agenda that was later seized by the FBI. It stated that a top discussion topic would be "suggestions to develop work" for several named "organizations." Included among these was "CAIR," as well as the IAP, HLF, and UASR (i.e., the United Association for Studies and Research). The agenda elucidated that "complete coordination" was sought among the various groups. Critically, it stressed that the effort was under Brotherhood direction: "This is not a separate movement from the mother Group."[29]

The principal aim of that Palestine Committee meeting was the development of a plan to counter efforts by Israel and American Jewish groups to normalize relations between Jews and Muslims. According to the Committee, this would break what Edward Said called the "psychological barrier." Said, Columbia University's now-deceased professor of English and Comparative Literature (and an inveterate Islamist sympathizer), was talking about the mindset that prevents Muslims from accepting Israel's right to exist.

The Committee was determined to fortify this barrier. The meeting agenda explains some of its plans toward that end. It would form "an internal Brotherhood committee to fight the normalization of relations and monitor brotherhood [sic] organizations." It would activate the "MAS" [i.e., the Muslim American Society] to conduct education programs in "all work centers, mosques, and organizations on the necessity of stopping any contacts with the Zionist organizations and the rejection of any future contacts." And, plainly relying on the Brotherhood strategy of using "Islamic Centers in major cities" as the axis of the movement, imams and administrators in these centers would "activate their role in confronting the [Jewish] infiltration of their organizations."

The role of CAIR was already coming into focus: the last element of the Committee's "Confrontation Work Plan" was "activating the role of the Association [IAP] ... to take up its media role in this area." Six weeks later, CAIR was incorporated and began appearing publicly as a new Muslim "civil rights" organization.[30]

CAIR's nominal founders were three IAP leaders, the aforementioned Omar Ahmad and Nihad Awad (who eventually succeeded Ahmad as CAIR's executive director), and Rafeeq Jaber, who had been IAP president before Ahmad. Another former IAP employee and television producer, Douglas Hooper, who became known as "Ibrahim Hooper" after converting to Islam, also come along as CAIR's communications director, and he remains, today, its ubiquitous mouthpiece.[31] Elashi came aboard as the founding director of the Texas chapter.

Marzook, who was still running Hamas at the time of CAIR's formal establishment in 1994, chipped in nearly half a million dollars.[32] As Steve Emerson has shown, another $5000 in seed money came from the HLF—whose assets were finally frozen in 2001 based on the U.S. Treasury Department's conclusion that it provided "millions of dollars annually that is used by HAMAS."[33] Interestingly, in September 2003, by which time he was CAIR's executive director, Awad indignantly denied Emerson's claim of a CAIR/HLF funding connection. He called the seed-money claim an "outright lie" and insisted, "Our organization did not receive any seed money from HLFRD. CAIR raises its own funds and we challenge Mr. Emerson to provide even a shred of evidence to support his ridiculous claim." Emerson promptly produced some pretty good shreds—like the documentation showing a $5,000 wire transfer from HLF to CAIR, and the required IRS form on which HLF disclosed the contribution. Duly shredded, Awad muttered in later Senate testimony that "the amount in question was a donation like any other."

Right. Awad did have one thing right, though: some donations are like others. There being a two-way Islamist street, CAIR helped HLF raise money, too.[34] In fact, after the 9/11 attacks, those perusing CAIR's website found themselves encouraged to "Donate to the NY/DC Disaster Relief Fund"—and when they clicked on the link, they were taken to the HLF website.[35] Small wonder, then, that when HLF was indicted in 2004, in the most significant terrorism support prosecution the Justice Department has ever brought, CAIR was identified by the government as an unindicted coconspirator—along with Hamas, the IAP, ISNA, the NAIT, the United Association for Studies and Research, and others.

Numerous CAIR figures have been convicted of federal felonies, including terrorism offenses. For example, when Elashi, the founder of CAIR's Texas chapter, was found guilty in the HLF case of setting up the lucrative Hamas piggy bank, it marked his third time around the block. He'd been convicted in 2006 for funneling money to Marzook and Hamas, and in 2005 for illegal transactions with Libya and Syria. Randall Royer, a CAIR communications specialist and civil-rights coordinator whose sideline was recruiting would-be jihadists for terrorist training in Pakistan, is now serving a twenty-year prison sentence after his conviction on explosives and firearms charges in the "Virginia Jihad" case. Bassem Khafagi, CAIR's community-affairs director (and a founder of the aforementioned Saudi-subsidized, al Qaeda-promoting Islamic Assembly of North America), also makes this dishonor roll: he was deported to Egypt after convictions for visa and bank fraud. And then there's Rabih Haddad, a fundraiser for CAIR's Ann Arbor chapter who was deported to Lebanon after a "charity" he founded, the Global Relief Foundation, was designated as a terrorist facilitator by the Treasury Department for providing support to al Qaeda.[36]

Even given its Hamas roots and terror ties, the most disturbing aspect of CAIR is its accomplishment of the Muslim Brotherhood's precise aspiration for it. Thanks to its media savvy and the execrable credulousness of government officials and press outlets, which have treated it as the "civil rights" group it purports to be rather than the Islamist spearhead that it is, CAIR has been a constant thorn in the side of American national defense. As Daniel Pipes observes, CAIR's unique role has been well summarized by

153

lawyers for the estate of the former FBI counterterrorism official John P. O'Neill, who was killed on 9/11—shortly after becoming security chief at the World Trade Center. In a class-action civil lawsuit that names CAIR and its Canadian affiliate as members of a criminal conspiracy to promote "radical Islamic terrorism," they state:

> both organizations have actively sought to hamper govern-
> mental anti-terrorism efforts by direct propaganda activities
> aimed at police, first-responders, and intelligence agencies
> through so-called sensitivity training. Their goal is to create
> as much self-doubt, hesitation, fear of name-calling, and liti-
> gation within police departments and intelligence agencies as
> possible so as to render such authorities ineffective in pursu-
> ing international and domestic terrorist entities.[37]

To take just a few examples catalogued by the invaluable Daniel Pipes, CAIR has consistently defended indicted terror-ists, including Osama bin Laden. According to Hooper, the 1998 bombings of U.S. embassies in Kenya and Tanzania were, you see, the unfortunate result of "misunderstandings of both sides"; and CAIR refused to condemn bin Laden for 9/11 until finally embarrassed into it by the al Qaeda emir's public boast that he had directed the attacks. The organization called the convictions of the 1993 World Trade Center bombers "a travesty of justice"; labeled the 1995 extradition of Marzook as "anti-Islamic"; tire-lessly defended al-Arian and slimed his accusers until the pro-fessor finally pled guilty to terror promotion; and squawked relentlessly when the government shuttered the HLF.[38]

Moreover, CAIR vigorously opposes efforts to improve and maintain the capacity of law-enforcement and intelligence agen-cies to prevent and prosecute Islamist terrorism. It was a leading opponent of the Patriot Act—which, for the most part, merely extended to national security agents the same powers prosecutors and police had been using for years in run-of-the-mill criminal investigations. It teamed with the ACLU to sue the National Security Agency over the Bush administration's "Terrorist Surveillance Program"—a successful effort to monitor al Qaeda communications into and out of the United States. And it distributes a "Muslim Community Safety Kit," that advises Muslims to bear in mind, whenever American law-enforcement seeks their cooperation, that "you have no obligation to talk to the FBI, even if you are not a citizen. . . . You do not have to permit them to enter your home. . . . [And] ALWAYS have an attorney present when answering questions."[39]

With flagships like CAIR, ISNA, and the MAS in place, the Muslim Brotherhood has the foundation in America it has always craved. That can't surprise the Ikhwan. After all, they've spent three generations carefully building it. What must be shocking, though, is how well it has worked.

chapter nine

NOT SUCH STRANGE BEDFELLOWS

No question about it, the press release pronounced: Our healthcare system is "broken." To fix it, an enlightened reformer, President Barack Obama, is doing his best to fulfill a solemn promise of Change: A dramatic overhaul to provide guaranteed, irrevocable health insurance coverage for every person in America—while cutting costs! Only by such a commitment might the United States be lifted from its lowly 37th place showing in the World Health Organization's survey of 191 countries—"the only developed nation in the world which does not offer some type of viable healthcare solution to its citizens." This selfless president is being undone, however, by "intimidation" tactics and the "politics of fear," practiced by forces opposed to basic social justice (translation: *conservatives*).

The press release went on: Saddest of all in this spectacle is what has happened to that cherished backbone of participatory democracy: the "congressional town-hall meeting." Historically, you see, this communal coming together has been "a forum . . . for civil discourse between elected officials and their constituents." In recent times, though, such assemblages have been hijacked— "turned into mob style melees where blatantly false accusations and fear inducing tactics have been used to attempt to coerce elected officials." Our beleaguered representatives have even been compared to Nazis! Dazed seniors have been duped "into believing that 'death-panels' are part of a real plan." In fact, at one "presidential town-hall"—evidently, that's a communal gathering of even richer pedigree in the Age of Obama—dissenters were allegedly "brandishing firearms."

Alas, the press release concluded, these "tactics" are not confined to the hot-button of healthcare. They have spread "to public discourse on many critical issues facing our nation. Whether it is healthcare, national security, foreign policy, or immigration, the conversation on these issues is being held hostage by various groups and individuals whose sole purpose is to use fear and misinformation to further their own agenda" (translation: *conservatives*).

If all this sounds like the rote Leftist argument ad hominem with a pastiche of suspect statistics, it should. And the point here is not to digress on healthcare "reform"—its rationing, ruinous redistribution, fast-track to euthanasia, and violations of the Constitution's limitations on federal power and guarantees of economic liberty. Nor is it necessary to retrace how it was the Left (including top Democrats like House Speaker Nancy Pelosi) that first referred to the public as Nazis, not the other way around.[1]

No, for present purposes, the issue is not the message but the messenger. This familiar litany was not put out by the usual Democratic Party operatives or George Soros-funded shock troops of the Left. The champion of Obamacare in this instance is the Muslim Public Affairs Council, which issued the press release in late 2009.

MPAC styles itself a "moderate, inclusive and forward-thinking organization with a history of fostering a strong Muslim American identity, and combating terrorism and extremism."[2] In reality, the organization is yet another Islamist wolf in "social justice" clothing. Its founders include Hassan Hathout, who has described himself as "a close disciple" of Brotherhood trailblazer Hassan al-Banna. Hathout's brother Maher, a senior MPAC adviser, has been lavish in his praise of both Hezbollah's "freedom fighting" and the social justice pioneering of Hassan al-Turabi, the leader of Sudan's National Islamic Front—the genocidal junta that gave safe haven to al Qaeda in the early 1990s. [3]

On September 11, 2001, MPAC executive director Salam al-Marayati was quick to caution against concluding that the suicide hijacking attacks were the work of Muslim terrorists. "If we are going to look at suspects," he told a Los Angeles radio station, "we should look at groups that benefit the most from these kinds of incidents, and I think we should put the State of Israel on the suspect list."[4] Meantime, MPAC hired Edina Lekovic to be its "Communications Director." For years, Ms. Lekovic was the managing editor of *al-Talib*, a Muslim Students Association newspaper at UCLA. On her watch, it published, to take just one example, a "Spirit of the Jihad" issue in July 1999. That is, just a year after al Qaeda bombed the American embassies in Kenya and Tanzania, *al-Talib* was urging Muslims to "defend our brother" Osama bin Laden, who was praised as a "great Mujahid" and "a freedom fighter who has forsaken wealth and power to fight in Allah's cause and speak out against oppressors."[5]

And how about those precious panegyrics about "our" (as in America's, not Islam's) historic commitment to "civil discourse between elected officials and their constituents," declaimed in MPAC's Obamacare press release? That's quite a change in MPAC's tune. In 2007, constituents had a hard time hearing from their elected officials because of MPAC histrionics in front of congressional offices for the purpose of trying to block a sub-committee hearing. The reason? Lawmakers wanted to have a civil discourse about the transfer of U.S. foreign aid dollars to fronts for Islamist terror organizations. They had announced that they would hear testimony from the terrorism expert (and MPAC critic) Steve Emerson.[6] For MPAC, that was apparently enough to spur "blatantly false accusations and fear inducing tactics . . . to attempt to coerce elected officials." There's nothing, I guess, like participatory democracy.

Yet, even with its unsavory background, MPAC has grown in stature—thanks in no small part to the waning gravitas of CAIR, for which the HLF case, lifting the veil on its close ties to Hamas, has proved to be a public relations nightmare. Marayati and other MPAC officials are called upon for congressional testimony on a plethora of issues. They are among the Islamist groups regularly consulted by U.S. law-enforcement and intelligence agencies for the purpose of instructing—which is to say, indoctrinating—our agents in Islamic concepts through "cultural sensitivity" training. They are, moreover, a media fixture, presented as the voice of mainstream Islam.

That voice is now making itself heard not only, or even principally, on matters touching terrorism. MPAC and other Islamist groups are weighing in on public policy matters great and small. After all, Islam—a system for controlling every aspect of human life—has something to say about all of them. And in comparison

to American public opinion, what it has to say is about as mainstream as the voice of the self-proclaimed centrist-pragmatist
now occupying the Oval Office, in whom the Islamist movement
has found a reliable friend.

Like the Muslim Brotherhood, MPAC and other Islamist
organizations have a wide-ranging platform of anti-capitalist
positions on economic issues. M. Zuhdi Jasser, an anti-Islamist
activist, aptly describes these organizations as "collectivist groups"
who fall in line with Brotherhood socialist aims to "increase the
power of government through entitlement programs, increased
taxation, and restricting free markets whenever and wherever
possible."[7] For them, socialized healthcare is a natural. That
explains the MPAC press campaign lionizing President Obama
and lashing his conservative opposition.

The press release was issued by Haris Tarin, MPAC's "national
community development director." Such a title benumbs us.
In the Washington of our first community-organizer-in-chief,
"community development directors" seem like a dime a dozen.
Nonetheless, it would be a mistake to gloss over the term too
quickly in the case of Muslim activists. As we've seen, for hundreds of millions of Muslims, "national community development"
is what it's all about. Islam is not principally about the individual.
Its preoccupation is the "umma," the Muslim Nation. Islam is
at least as focused on dominance in this world as on salvation
in the next. Its central imperative is the communal obligation to
establish and spread sharia, Allah's law, throughout the world, to
build Islamic societies, to recreate and expand the Caliphate. Yes,
Islam is intensely concerned about the individual. It aspires to
dictate every facet of the individual's life. Primarily, though, that
is because the individual must be made to fit the corporate aspirations of the Muslim Nation.

And that is why Islam and the Left are not such strange bedfellows.

Natural Allies in a Fitful Alliance

Historically, Leftist revolutionaries have had complex, sometimes stormy, relations with Islamists. Yet the two camps have never been the enemies they are often presumed to be. The neocommunist Center for Constitutional Rights has long been ensconced as al Qaeda's lawyer. News accounts regularly feature Venezuela's Marxist strongman Hugo Chavez publicly canoodling with Iran's Islamist tyrant Mahmud Ahmadinejad. No matter. Expert analysts furrow their brows, go through their trendy checklists (atheism, abortion, women's rights, and gay rights), and fatuously pronounce that the radical Left and fundamentalist Islam could never make common cause.

That's what the radical Left and the Islamists would like you to believe. It's clever. Leftists and Islamists are well aware that their designs for society—which for both involve drastic transformation—are anathema to most Americans. They have to advance their cause in stealth. Pairing up is mutually beneficial. Since you're told that radicals and jihadists can't co-exist, when you see them together, you figure the radical can't be much of a radical if he's courting Muslims, and that the jihadist can't be much of a jihadist if he's slumming with modern "progressives."

Indeed, shaping conventional wisdom by the same illogic that limns Adolf Hitler and his National *Socialist* Party as a phenomenon of the political Right, Left-leaning journalists unfailingly refer to Islamists—especially Islamist terrorists—as "*conservative* Muslims." It is a mendacious narrative: The Islamists, like the Nazis, are responsible for unspeakable atrocities so they simply must be vulgar, right-wing reactionaries—and, as the Obama

Department of Homeland Security Department says, we'd better keep an eye on those other terrorists waiting to happen, "extremists" agitating for smaller government, the Second Amendment, and the sanctity of life . . . particularly if they are military vets returning home from George Bush's wars of choice.[8]

It's nonsense. With their collectivist philosophy, transnational outlook, totalitarian demands, and revolutionary designs, Islamists are natural allies of the radical Left. That doesn't mean the alliance is naturally enduring. If it were just the two of them, as Churchill might have said, we'd have to make book on which is the crocodile and which the last appeaser to be eaten (not a happy end for the Leftists, I'd wager). But of course, it's not just the two of them, and their ties get quite cozy when there are common enemies to slay—enemies like American constitutional democracy and its bedrock, individual liberty.

A useful snapshot of the fitful marriage between Islamists and Leftists is provided by the early history of modern Egypt. In 1952, when Gamal Abdel Nasser and the "Free Officers" staged the rebellion that overthrew the monarchy, severing colonial ties to Britain and the West, the fledgling Leftist republic immediately re-legitimized the Muslim Brotherhood. After all, they'd been allies. The Ikhwan, too, had openly warred with the monarchy— years of fighting, whose casualties included the killing of Hassan al-Banna in 1948, scattering the Brotherhood into the shadows. With King Farouk as their common enemy, Islamists and Communists melded into the insurgent ranks of Colonel Nasser and General Muhammad Naguib, the titular leader of the Free Officers.[9] In fact, to secure Brotherhood support, the Leftist Nasser personally courted Sayyid Qutb, the Ikwhan's most prominent leader after Banna's death.[10]

The partnership was ill-fated. The Brotherhood was more enamored of Naguib, Nasser's overmatched rival who, fleetingly, was the republic's first president. Upon Nasser's assumption of dictatorial power, it became evident that his pan-Arabism emphasized Egyptian nationalism more than Islamic piety. But these elements of national character are not so easily severable in the Muslim world. In contrast to Ataturk's strategy of vanquishing Islam for the sake of vitalizing the nation, Nasser sought to balance the two. Ostensibly, his platform of "Islamic Socialism" was a declaration of compatibility between Islam and Marxism. To prove his point (or stack the deck, depending on one's perspective), he intervened in the curriculum of the storied al-Azhar University, sponsoring scholars who promoted the view that socialism and Islam could be fused.[11]

Compatibility with *Islamism*, however, proved a harder sell. Qutb and his cohort became increasingly embittered as Nasser's revolutionary council declined even to ban alcohol, let alone install sharia. Nasser's agenda (beyond its promotion of Nasser himself) appeared essentially secular. It would have Islamic trimmings, of course. Nasser knew he needed to pay Islam lip-service in the Arab world's most populous Muslim country—a country in which the Brotherhood's rapid, geometric growth had been triggered in part by outrage over the suppression of Islam in Turkey. Lip-service, though, would not be nearly enough for the Brotherhood. The entente was doomed. Nasser's bullying at al-Azhar provoked Islamist outcry that Communism and socialism "were totally antithetical to Islam."[12]

Matters deteriorated quickly, culminating in Nasser's persecution of the Brotherhood after it attempted to assassinate him in 1954. Though it seemed a catastrophe at the time, we've seen that the purge set the stage for today's global metastasis of Islamist ideology. For purposes of understanding the dynamic between Islam and the Left, however, the point is that Nasser underestimated the ardor of the Islamists and thus overestimated their willingness to play ball with secular socialism. His successor, Anwar al-Sadat, miscalculated from the opposite direction, failing to appreciate the Islamists' political savvy and betting too heavily on their seeming incongruity with the Left.

Nasser had steered Egypt into the Soviet orbit, socializing the economy and nationalizing various industries. After grasping the reins in 1970, Sadat was determined to reverse course, embarking on a "Corrective Revolution."[13] He faced a severe challenge, however. The Left had spent Nasser's reign marching through Egypt's institutions, particularly the academy. Resistance to change would be fierce. Sadat's solution to this quandary was to make Egypt, once again, home base for the Islamist intelligentsia.

This was strictly a power play. Sadat was no fan of the Islamists. He had been vice-president and one of Nasser's closest aides. He was intimately familiar with Islamist abhorrence of the secular regime. He had personally presided over the military trials of Muslim Brotherhood leaders, including Sayyid Qutb, for trying to kill Nasser and topple the government. In truth, Sadat would probably have been the least surprised of all Egyptians by his own murder at Islamist hands on October 6, 1981. Yet, his "enemy of my enemy" calculation was straightforward: For Egypt to thrive, it needed to embrace the West, and that meant marginalizing its pro-Soviet elements.

The Islamists, Sadat intuited, would have more contempt for the Communists than for his regime. After all, he was holding out an olive branch to the Brotherhood and the government in Cairo was at least nominally Islamic, its legal system a blend of sharia and the Napoleonic Code. Sadat anticipated that the Islamists would be vigorous antagonists of the Leftist intellectuals entrenched in the universities and the public square. His program's prospects would improve as the Left diminished.

Alas, Sadat's assumption of implacable antagonism between Islamism and Marxism was flawed. For starters, it oversimplified the Left. Though dominated by the Russians, communism was not monolithic. For instance, Sadat was focused, at least in part, on the chasm between Islamists and Leftists on the matter of atheism. Yes, discouragement of religious belief was a staple of *Soviet* Communism, beginning with Stalin. Nevertheless, it has always been less important to most "small *c*" communists. For example, the fusing of Marxism with spirituality, particularly corruptions of Christianity, was central to the violent radicalism of Frantz Fanon, who powerfully influenced the Black Panthers and the Weather Underground.[14] It was, furthermore, the engine of "Liberation Theology," the revolutionary Marxism that swept Latin America in the Sixties and Seventies, and of its American iteration, the Black Liberation Theology of James H. Cone—the inspiration of Chicago's Reverend Jeremiah Wright, who in turn is an inspiration of Barack Obama.[15]

Even if it were arguably true that religion and Leftism do not easily mix, a perspicacious Leftist would grasp that hostility to Islam is ultimately futile in a Muslim land without the total power to squelch religion and the inexhaustible will to persevere in doing so. Today's Islamist resurgence in Turkey testifies to this, as does Islamism's comeback in Iraq—and it bears noting that even the reputedly secular Saddam Hussein, who pulverized Shiites, was moved to emblazon the Iraqi flag with the Islamic crescent and to make common cause with Sunni Islamists.

Sadat did not account for the potential of alliance between Islamists and Leftists—against his government—on a wide variety of economic and "social justice" issues. More significantly, he failed to factor in the inevitable Islamist reaction to other political developments likely to flow from his turn-West strategy. It was not the *communists*, after all, who shook Menachem Begin's hand in Jimmy Carter's Rose Garden.

In the event, Sadat's gambit of unleashing religious fanatics against communists made his country a friendly clime for Islamism. That made it a bad bet—fatally bad for the president himself. Still, Sadat should get credit for recognizing what we've yet to grapple with in America: You can't expect a governmental system to endure if you cede the universities to its enemies.

In Need of a Common Enemy

Sadat was far from alone in his optimism about the Islamists' anti-communism and his overconfidence in government's capacity to control a partnership with Islamists. He was reflecting the conventional wisdom. We have already seen that their ongoing partnership with Brotherhood-inspired Salafists has proved endlessly complex, and occasionally deadly, for the Saudis. And the Saudis, in cooperation with the American and Pakistani governments, were correct beyond their wildest dreams that Islamist elements from across the globe, if subsidized and armed, would answer the call to jihad against the Red Army after its 1979 invasion of Afghanistan.

In France, officials promoted Islam as a weapon against left-wing radicalism in enclaves teeming with Algerian immigrants.[16] Still in shock over the murders of several members of its team at the Munich Olympiad of 1972—i.e., in the years before the emergence of Palestinian Islamic Jihad, Hezbollah, and Hamas—Israel, too, deluded itself into nurturing a Palestinian religious turn. The government naively imagined this development would be a boon for Israel: a burr in the saddle of the Yasser Arafat, whose Palestine Liberation Organization was robustly backed by the Soviets.

167

Like Nasser, however, Arafat was a shrewd Leftist who appreciated the necessity of accommodating Islam. Though Arafat was a domineering Marxist, the PLO was, and is, an amalgam of entities that always incorporated Islamist elements as well as socialists, secularists, and Arab nationalists. Transparently, the American Left's motive for pinning the purely "secular" label on the PLO and, particularly, on Fatah (Arafat's base within it), is to promote the fiction that Fatah (now the ruling party in the "Palestinian Authority") is "moderate" and worthy of U.S. support. The idea is to draw a flattering contrast to the incorrigible Islamist terrorists of Hamas. As we've seen, though, Fatah is not strictly secular—the claim that it is relies on the savage zealotry of Hamas to overwhelm the facts. Fatah was propelled by jihadist rhetoric and theory, its charter regards the duty to "liberate" Jerusalem as a religious obligation, and it has a decades-long history of rationalizing terror on Islamic scriptural grounds—these are "moderates" who maintain their own terrorist wing, the al-Aqsa Martyrs Brigades.[17]

Similarly astute were Pakistan's Leftists. Zulkifar Ali Bhutto's legacy, the Pakistan People's Party, has always couched its secular-socialist ambitions in Islamic rhetoric. With echoes of the Muslim Brotherhood's slogan, the PPP's motto remains, "Islam is our faith; democracy is our politics; socialism is our economy; all power to the people." And for all her pretensions to Western liberalism, Benazir Bhutto, who followed her father's footsteps to become Prime Minister, was midwife to the Taliban in Afghanistan and stoked jihadist terror in Kashmir—all part of her geopolitical maneuvering against India.[18]

Sadat and both Bhuttos were ultimately killed by Islamists: Sadat slain by the Muslim Brotherhood; Bhutto père executed in the Zia coup d'état, after which Pakistani society underwent a thoroughgoing Islamicization; and daughter Benazir murdered by the Taliban when she reincarnated herself as a crusader for democracy. Fatah, similarly, is holding on for dear life: ousted from the Gaza Strip by Hamas, the Muslim Brotherhood's Palestinian branch, it is hunkered down in the West Bank—hoping that the democracy it purports to champion isn't taken too seriously (notoriously corrupt, Fatah would be likely to lose a true popular election) and praying that Hamas decides jointly annihilating the Zionist entity is a higher priority than crushing an intramural competitor.

There is a moral to these stories. Revolutionaries of Islam and the Left make fast friends when there is a common enemy to besiege. Leftists, however, are essentially nihilists whose hazy vision prioritizes power over what is to be done with power. They are biddable. Islamists, who have very settled convictions about what is to be done with power, are much less so. Even their compromises keep their long-term goals in their sights. Thus do Leftists consistently overrate their ability to control Islamists. Factoring the common denominator, power, out of the equation, something always beats nothing.

In order then that the social compact may not be an empty formula, it tacitly includes the undertaking, which alone can give force to the rest, that whoever refuses to obey the general will shall be compelled to do so by the whole body. This means nothing less than that he will be forced to be free.

—Jean-Jacques Rousseau, *The Social Contract*

Islam began by freeing the human conscience from servitude to anyone except Allah and from submission to any save Him.

—Sayyid Qutb, *Social Justice in Islam*

chapter ten

ISLAM AND THE
REVOLUTIONARY LEFT

That there is no God but Allah and that Mohammed is His
prophet are the bedrock convictions of the Islamic world.
Muslims take these fundamental beliefs to mean Allah, in His
revelations to Mohammed, graced humanity with obligatory
instructions for living the virtuous life. Radical Leftists, by contrast, hew to Karl Marx's nineteenth-century creed.

As commentators stress, Muslims profoundly demur from
some of Marxism's familiar elements, particularly as modern Leftists have evolved them. There is, moreover, the matter of Marx
himself. Sayyid Qutb, the Brotherhood theorist who succeeded
Banna and became the father of modern Islamism, was a stri-
dent anti-Semite. It became for him a constant refrain that "the
atheistic, materialistic doctrine in our world was advocated by a

Jew."[1] That Jew, Marx, had dismissed religion as an invention of man, "the opium of the oppressed."[2] Marx had also made a central imperative of communism the abolition of private property. Islamic law, by contrast, ostensibly ratifies the individual's right to own property, punishes theft severely, and assures (however inequitably) the right to transfer or inherit privately held assets.

But this is a facile analysis. Marx's view of religion was much more sophisticated than the mindless repetition of "opium of the oppressed" suggests. Religion is a matter on which Leftist theory is nuanced, a fact the political Right typically underestimates—a matter of no small importance since, in the service of the Leftist campaign against individual liberty, religion is a potent weapon. Analogously, Qutb's explanation of private property in Islam is similarly multi-layered. In the final analysis, Islam's conception of private ownership resembles leftist doctrine, and it denies the American conception of individual liberty in the acquisition and use of one's assets.

The ties that bind Islamists and the radical Left emerge clearly if we delve briefly into a forebear of Marx. Jean-Jacques Rousseau inspired the Jacobin Terror and became an abiding influence on all totalitarian regimes that followed. He was also an admirer of Mohammed's doctrine.

Rousseau's Civil Religion

Rousseau's enthusiasm for Islam is not hard to fathom. He equated "freedom" with total submission to authority. In the Swiss philosopher's ideal state, that authority was an Orwellian construct he called "the general will"—an "elusive and inscrutable Supreme Authority," as Conor Cruise O'Brien described it, that "became a kind of tutelary deity" for the French Revolution.[3] The general will is the debt Marx owes to Rousseau, "an early adumbration of Lenin's 'democratic centralism.'"[4] In what is (at most) a different pew of this same conceptual church, we also find Ayatollah Ruhollah Khomeini's doctrine of *vilayat-e-faqih* (the guardianship of the Islamic jurist), under which "issues could be debated, even disputed, within the regime—but once the 'Supreme Guide' pronounced the 'final word,' everyone had to fall in line."[5]

The general will is nearly indistinguishable from Islam's notion of "freedom": the "free" choice to surrender oneself totally to Allah. *Liberty*, which is to say *real freedom* as we know (knew?) it in the West, and as Rousseau rejected it, is anathema to the Islamist. In his commendable *Terror and Liberalism*, Paul Berman invoked Qutb and the Baathist theoretician Michal Aflaq to convey the occidental wariness of Western teachings that "invade the Arab mind."[6] Freedom is just such a teaching. Given that both Americans and Islamists are apt to invoke the word "freedom" with regularity, it is critical to remember that when it comes to "freedom," East and West are not talking about the same thing.[7]

Rousseau claimed that man was born free but that eighteenth-century society purportedly put him everywhere in chains—enslaved by an acquisitive and exploitative culture, degrading to both his relations with his fellow man and his innate communal nature. Therefore, Rousseau explained in his seminal political tract, *The Social Contract* (1762), freedom could be achieved only in the enforced equality of the general will. It was to the general will, the central authority, that each citizen, rich or poor, would give himself over and pledge fealty. The general will was "always righteous" because it was perfectly altruistic: the people acting for their collective well-being.

Of course, the riffraff often don't know what is good for them, so they must be steered by leaders. In a "well-intentioned" state, Rousseau's leaders would infallibly interpret the general will to reflect the public interest. The price of freedom was obedience to the general will as expressed by the laws of the state. After all, this "social compact" would not work unless any resister was coerced into submission. In Rousseau's logic, this meant "nothing less than that he will be forced to be free." The philosopher well understood that he was posing an oxymoronic dilemma, but he considered that a trifle, more theoretical than real. The eminent historian Paul Johnson observes that Rousseau figured "obedience would become instinctive and voluntary since the State, by a systematic process of social engineering, would inculcate virtue in all."[8] Qutb made the same calculation. For example, *zakat*, he said, started under the "compulsion of law" but, over time, became ingrained in the "public conscience," such that payment of it became "a natural part of the will."[9]

Elemental to a state based on the general will was what Rousseau called the "civil religion." As articulated by the Presbyterian scholar James H. Smylie, "Civil religion is the way we have identified ourselves as God's people and under his providence, the way we have invoked divine sanction in the use of power and in the support of the civil authority, and the way in which we justify our national actions."[10]

For Rousseau, the perfect state was the state of antiquity, in which authority was indivisible. That is, just as in Islam, the political and theological realms were woven into one: "Each State, having its own cult as well as its own government, made no distinction between its gods and its laws." So things stood through the centuries until Jesus came along and ruined everything. He "set up on earth a spiritual kingdom, which, by separating the theological from the political system, made the State no longer one, and brought about the internal divisions which have never ceased to trouble Christian peoples." Absurdly, in Rousseau's estimation, Christianity subjected people "to contradictory duties, and made it impossible for them to be faithful both to religion and to citizenship." The resulting "conflict of jurisdiction . . . made all good polity impossible."

Though not truly religious himself, Rousseau nodded to what he took to be the religious impulse. Repulsed by the Church of Rome, he nonetheless gushed over the Christian gospel's recognition of our common humanity. But Christianity was fatally indifferent to the affairs of this world. "Having no particular relation to the body politic," no investment in "earthly things," it heeded only the undeniable natural law. Regarding the civil law, the great bond that unites society, it was not merely obtuse; it was traitorous: "If the State is prosperous, [the Christian] hardly dares to share in the public happiness, for fear he may grow proud of his country's glory; if the State is languishing, he blesses the hand of God that is hard upon His people."

Qutb, we've seen, rebuked Marxism for the way materialism became its unified field theory for interpreting all phenomena, to the exclusion of the divine. For Rousseau, Christianity (as he understood it) posed exactly the opposite problem. Such an "entirely spiritual" creed, shunning material concerns, was unnatural: "a society of true Christians would not be a society of men. . . . The flaw that would destroy it would lie in its very perfection." The state would be vulnerable to rogues within and enemies without. Thus "true Christians," Rousseau concluded, were perfect prey for tyrants. In their ethos of "servitude and dependence," they "are made to be slaves, and they know it and do not much mind: this short life counts for too little in their eyes." And here it is worth noting that when Rousseau controversially urged that recalcitrant citizens must be "forced" by the state "to be free," he reasoned that "this is the condition which,

175

by giving each citizen to his country, secures him against all personal dependence." No man is an island. In Rousseau's casuistry, to be free of dependence in civil society mandated forfeiting one's independence—forfeiting his liberty.

Far preferable to Christianity was the "religion of the citizen," which welded the sacred to the secular under a unitary authority. In Rousseau's telling, this civil religion, as in the pagan states of yore, armed the state with

> its gods, its own tutelary patrons; it has its dogmas, its rites, and its external cult prescribed by law; outside the single nation that follows it, all the world is in its sight infidel, foreign and barbarous; the duties and rights of man extend for it only as far as its own altars.

On the upside, such a system united "the divine cult with love of the laws," and made this godly authority "the object of the citizens' adoration." Citizens learned

> that service done to the State is service done to its tutelary god. It is a form of theocracy, in which there can be no pontiff save the prince, and no priests save the magistrates. To die for one's country then becomes martyrdom; violation of its laws, impiety; and to subject one who is guilty to public execration is to condemn him to the anger of the gods.

Potentially, though, there was a terrifying flip-side. Rousseau grasped the possibility that a civil religion, consumed with the events of this world, could be founded not on the general will (as understood by those infallible leaders) but "on lies and error." Such a system "deceives men, makes them credulous and superstitious." Worse, it becomes tyrannous and exclusive, and makes a people bloodthirsty and intolerant, so that it breathes fire and slaughter, and regards as a sacred act the killing of every one who does not believe in its gods. The result is to place such a people in a natural state of war with all others, so that its security is deeply endangered.

A doctrine central to Islamism depicts all who stand outside the realm of the Muslims (*dar al-Islam*) as inhabiting the realm of war (*dar al-harb*). Nevertheless, Rousseau did not see Islam as rife with "lies and error." To the contrary, he lavished praise on the early Muslims, surmising that "Mahomet held very sane views, and linked his political system well together," the civil and the spiritual as one. Anticipating Salafists such as Banna, Rousseau opined: "As long as the form of his government continued under the caliphs who succeeded him, that government was indeed one, and so far good." It was only when "the Arabs" departed from this model—when, "having grown prosperous, lettered, civilised, slack and cowardly," they were "conquered by barbarians"—that Islam fell victim to the Christian pathology: "the division between the two powers" of mosque and state.

Qutb's Civil Religion

The parallels between Rousseau's revolutionary thought and Islamist ideology—even their judgment of where it all went wrong for the *umma*—are startling. Indeed, just as Rousseau perfectly presaged the French Revolution, Qutb observed that "what was theoretically established by human laws during and after the French Revolution was established as a matter of practice by Islam in a profound and elevated form more than fourteen centuries earlier."[11]

And what exactly was established by Mohammed and the Righteous Caliphs? It was what Islamists regard as the essence of their faith, and what, in pitch-perfect harmony, today's revolutionary Left—like the revolutionary Left of the eighteenth century—regards as the solemn obligation of government: social justice. Islam, Qutb wrote, "insists on the guarantee of an absolute social justice under which man shall not suffer from neglect."[12]

In the jihadist onslaught that began in the United States with the 1993 World Trade Center bombing, Americans have been preoccupied by terrorism. Most scrutiny of Sayyid Qutb has naturally focused on his justifications of violent jihad, particularly against non-believers and nominally Muslim rulers who refrained from ruling in accordance with sharia. In the public mind, the image of Qutb—an obscure image given that he was executed nearly half a century ago—blends into that of Osama bin Laden, Ayman Zawahiri, Khalid Sheikh Mohammed, Sheikh Omar Abdel Rahman, and other notorious terrorists. Because our habit is to shun examination of our enemies' beliefs for fear of offending the Muslim community, they are depicted as demented killers— enemies of "the true Islam," whatever that is.

In most cases, we might call this parody: the above Roll-Call of the Infamous lists ruthless men, for sure, but men of considerable learning and accomplishment. In Qutb's case, however, to say "psycho-killer" and move merrily along is downright libelous. His thought is perilous in its implications, but it cannot be dismissed as nutter stuff. It is deep, erudite, and extensive, involving vastly more than the rationale for terror. To ignore that is to miss, and become vulnerable to, the sweep of the Islamist threat. It is to miss what hundreds of millions of Muslims think. It is to miss that Rousseau bequeathed us far more than Robespierre; increasingly, we are living in his world. In Qutb, in Islamism, the specter of jumbo jets ravaging skyscrapers isn't the half of it.

The objective of Rousseau's general will was to secure social justice by stripping the petty, covetous interests of individual human beings from the guidance of human life. The general will allowed no one liberty and reflected no one's self-determination. It was what was best for everyone after all selfish considerations were sublimated to the common good. Islam, too, seeks to impose the common good, but not by concocting a supreme authority through an inductive process. It needs no "general will" or similar human contrivance in order to secure social justice. What is best, what guarantees social justice, has already been prescribed by Allah. It is His law, sharia. And just as in Rousseau's theory, those who resist can be "forced to be free." "Integrating" humanity in "an essential unity" under sharia is, Qutb instructs, "a prerequisite for true and complete human life, *even justifying the use of force against those who deviate from it*, so that those who wander from the true path may be brought back to it." Everything is about the umma—i.e., about "this interdependence and solidarity of mankind"—and "whoever has lost sight of this principle must be brought back to it *by any means*."[13] In Islam, Qutb declared, the "crime" of "unbelief" is "reckoned as equal in punishment" to the "crime of murder."[14]

As Qutb explains, the animating tenet of Islam is that Allah is the Creator of the universe. All that is in it exists to serve Him. His authority is unitary and indivisible: it does not recognize distinctions between the sacred and the secular. Only Allah has the authority to legislate, and the law he gave Mohammed is timeless and comprehensive, intended—commanded—to regulate every aspect of life. There cannot be two ultimate rulers. "The ruler in Islamic law is not to be obeyed because of his own person; he is to be obeyed only by virtue of holding his position through the law of Allah and His Messenger." The function of the Muslim "ruler" on earth is merely to ensure compliance with Allah's ordinances.[15]

179

That alone guarantees human flourishing, in this world as well as the next, because the moral and ethical prerequisites for it will be in place. Man thus has no authority to limit the application of Allah's law, much less to enact provisions that contradict it. Recall Sheikh Qaradawi's rendering of this principle: Legislators don't really legislate, they are merely vessels of sharia.

To narrow the breadth of the divine law—"to confine Islam," as Qutb put it, "to the emotions and ritual cycles, and to bar it from participating in the activity of life, and to check its complete dominance over every human secular activity"—would reduce it to something other than the divine law. As Berman construes Qutb, "True Islam would become partial Islam: and partial Islam does not exist."[16] It would, moreover be a double affront to the divine, supplanting Allah's law and making men the gods of other men.

In Islam, it is Allah who fulfills the "tutelary deity" role of the general will (or the general will's cognates—e.g., the state, the politburo, the party, etc.—that are strewn throughout Leftist theory and history). Similarly, Qutb's "freedom of conscience" is the mirror image of Rousseau's compulsory "freedom." It is the complete submission to Allah and his law—what Rousseau described as the surrender of freedom in order to become free of physical harm, inequality, exploitation, and privation. Qutb dilated on the subject in his treatise, *Social Justice in Islam*:

> When the conscience is freed from the instinct of servitude
> to and worship of any of the servants of Allah, and when it is
> filled with the knowledge that it can of itself gain complete
> access to Allah, then it cannot be disturbed by any feeling of
> fear of life, or fear of livelihood, or fear of station. This fear is
> an ignoble instinct which lowers the individual's estimation of
> himself, which often makes him accept humiliation or abdicate
> much of his natural honor or many of his rights.[17]

As Qutb saw it, Islam corrected the flaws in Christian and Communist conceptions of freedom. Echoing Rousseau, Qutb surmised that Christians were instructed "to spurn the life of this world" in order to achieve freedom and happiness. While he agreed that the "needs of life are not paramount under all circumstances," he pointed out that earthly life required submission to the natural law—even Christians could not spurn breath, sustenance, sleep, etc. Well, Allah created *all* of earthly life: not just nature and its laws but the affairs of the world, ideally governed by sharia. There was no legitimate rationale for heeding one but not the other. To spurn the life of this world was the opposite of virtue. Certainly one should not be ruled by his desires, but neither was it appropriate to neglect them as if they, Allah's creation, were somehow unworthy.

Communism, for Qutb, was closer to the truth, for a reason that should rivet our attention. Marx, he concluded, grappled with the world, and in particular, grappled with the evil of capitalism. Qutb considered communism "the natural and logical" reaction to the fact that "the spirit of the West lacks the generous and humane aspects of true human life."[18] Islam, like Marx, *condemns capitalism*. Consider that for a moment. We are a People rooted in Judeo-Christian ethics. And in the United States, that People is the sovereign—contrary to what our elected officials sometimes appear to think, we are not ruled by a government or a "general will." Our social compact is our Constitution, and it expressly protects individual liberty and private property. As the Supreme Court has acknowledged, the Constitution forbids government from imposing onerous restrictions that prevent private entrepreneurs from seeking and securing a risk-adjusted rate of return on their investments.[19] Private property, entrepreneurial risk, the potential for profit or loss—these are the elements that make our system dynamic and that spread prosperity to more

181

people, in and out of our country, than any system in the history of man.

In stark contrast, both Marx and Qutb believed capitalism inflamed man's acquisitive instincts, resulting in gross inequality, injustice, and the degrading servitude of the have-nots when, inexorably, a few haves accumulated substantially all of the capital. This intolerable condition was exacerbated by "usury" (in this context, the charging of interest on loans), which Islam forbids—indeed, regards as worse than adultery, *a capital offense*. Like Marx, Qutb decried finance capitalism's "disgracefully swollen" agglomerations of wealth, the exploitation of workers, theft, despoliation, and other denials of social justice. A just and ethical economic system would demand adherence to sharia.[20]

So, how does Allah's law remedy this exploitation of the downtrodden by the well-to-do? Islam's answer, Qutb taught, is the redistribution of wealth. In a proper sharia state, the ruler is endowed with

> wide powers, which touch every aspect of life; and the establishment of social justice in all its aspects is a matter that is bound up with these powers. A ruler may, for example, go beyond the legal requirements in the matter of money; in addition to the *zakat*, he may introduce other taxes by which to encourage equality and justice; by these he may check malice and ill-feeling, and by these he may remove from the community the evils of luxury and penury, as well as that of artificially high prices, all of which evils are the product of the growth of excessive wealth.[21]

Wait a moment, you may be thinking. How can this be squared with Islam's protection of private property rights? Easy: this purported protection is an illusion. "Ultimately all property belongs to Allah," explains the version of the Koran published by the Saudi Ministry of Hajj and Endowments (at the King Fahd Holy Qur'an Printing Complex in Medina). It "is intended for the support of [Allah's] close relations," meaning, of course, the Muslims. "It is held in trust by a particular individual"—its Muslim owner—but his use of it, and the profits he may derive, are limited to what the Islamic authority finds "just and reasonable."[22] Qutb states the matter this way:

> The cardinal principle that Islam ratifies along with that of the right of individual possession is that the individual is in a way a steward of his property on behalf of society; his tenure of property is more of a duty than an actual right of possession. Property in the widest sense is a right that can belong only to society, which in turn receives it as a trust from Allah who is the only true owner of anything.

The individual thus exists not for himself but for the umma. He is not free and his property is not his own. Instead, it is incumbent on him, as a steward, to realize that his "property . . . is fundamentally the possession of society; this must make him accept the restrictions that the system lays upon his liberty, and the bounds that limit his rights of disposal."[23]

Communism, too, made a wrong turn in Qutb's estimation—albeit one less serious than the evil of capitalism and the otherworldliness of Christianity. It fixated on economic pressure, to the exclusion of all else, as the reason an individual in society abandons "his legal rights to justice and equality." There being more to life than materialism, the mere achievement of "economic freedom"—which, in the tortured logic of the Left, means the forfeit of one's property rights—would not guarantee justice and equality. Instead, it would result in a different kind of "tyranny": the "repression of the individual" whose "natural abilities" would be denied the outlet intended by Allah to promote his growth "in competition with others." Obsession over economic concerns would kill the human spirit, causing man to rebel or wither. "The nature of Islamic belief about human life," Qutb teaches, "makes social justice essentially an all-embracing justice which does not take account of merely material and economic factors."[24] It imposes Islam's totalitarian system so that equality is achieved in every way, down to the last detail. That, on this accounting, is social justice.

For all their differences, then, Islam and Communism are united in the imperative of achieving social justice, by compulsion, if necessary. This is not merely a slogan; it is the ballgame. It means *social* justice. Islam, like Communism, holds that the individual is subordinated to the collective. The Islamic belief is that "humanity" is what Qutb called "an essential unity" whose "scattered elements must be brought together; its diversity must give place to unity, its variety of creeds must in the end be brought into one." As in any totalitarian system, dissidents from Islam are, to borrow Rousseau's phrase, "forced to be free."

On this fundamental premise about the nature of the good life, about how we see ourselves in the world, Islam and Communism are aligned, and both are diametrically opposed to the core assumptions of American constitutional democracy: individual liberty and free-market capitalism.

Let that sink in. We in America may be convinced that capitalism, America's economic system, is both a just and peerless engine of liberty—meaning actual human freedom, not, as Islam and the Left see "freedom," the surrender of individual liberty for the purportedly greater good of being cosseted in the state's arms so we can be "free" of sundry indignities, real and imagined. We may also be convinced that wealth generation through private finance-capitalism best expands and ensures human flourishing: dramatically improving living standards in America and abroad; enabling Americans—by far and away—to be the world's most charitable donors; significantly increasing the resources available to fight disease and hunger; underwriting unparalleled military might that provides a historically unprecedented degree of global security. But our views and their supporting rationales do not matter for present purposes. This is not a debate; it's about investigating the core principles of varying ideologies in order to understand who is lining up with whom.

Islam is lined up with the Left.

chapter eleven

THE TIES THAT BIND

With the 2008 presidential election only six weeks away, it was apparently time for the legacy press to do what passed for some reporting on the background of its—er, of the Democratic Party's—candidate. So the *Boston Globe*'s Sally Jacobs filed a predictably sympathetic profile of the late Barack Obama Sr.[1]

The story related that the candidate's flawed father was a Kenyan, a member of the minority Luo tribe, political rivals of the Kikuyu, President Jomo Kenyatta's majority tribe. Jacobs, however, strictly adhered to Obama campaign protocols, which had seamlessly become media protocols: The nearly 4000-word story eschewed mention of the word "Hussein"—the middle name of both father and son. In fact, it spelled Obama Sr.'s first name as the now-familiar "Barack" (to which the candidate, once known as "Barry," had switched back years earlier) rather than "Barak," the way the father had spelled it. Though the elder Obama had been a Muslim, nowhere was the word "Muslim" or "Islam" mentioned. And despite ostensibly being an in-depth account of Obama *père's* rollercoaster career in Kenyan politics, the ideological roots of the tribal infighting went unaddressed.

Three-quarters of the way through, any readers still paying attention might have noticed a fleeting reference accompanied by another staggering omission. "In 1965," Ms. Jacobs related, "Obama published an article in the East Africa Journal in which he criticized the government's approach to economic planning." Period, no further details. The story moved swiftly back to tribal rivalries and the not so subtle undertone that the elder Obama's troubles—political ostracism, drunkenness, and early demise at age forty-six—stemmed from speaking truth to the wrong power. The *Globe* didn't find the title of Obama Sr.'s article newsworthy, much less its content.

The article was called "Problems Facing Our Socialism."[2]

The Obamedia coverage of the 2008 election was shameful. The Democratic nominee was a virtual unknown, with a record that can only generously be called "slender." He offered himself as more a screen than a projector of Hope and Change. Yet the press resisted any meaningful investigation of his background. So biased was the coverage, so determined the effort to suppress Obama's web of Leftist associations and activities, that even now, nearly halfway through his term, astonishing voids in our knowledge remain—with duped voters and commentators grumbling, "We had no idea he was this radical!"

Even taking all press neglect into account, the *Globe's* journalistic malpractice here stands out.

Senator Barack Obama was known to be ambivalent about the father he'd barely known. He made conflicting claims about the elder Obama's Islamic heritage, sometimes appearing to embrace it, other times insisting (as anxiety over the public perception of the candidate's Muslim roots gripped the campaign) that his father may have been born a Muslim but was "basically agnostic"[3]—or even "a confirmed atheist"[4]—by the time he came to America as a young college student. One thing, however, was certain: The son would burst with pride when speaking about the father's educational accomplishments and his "promise."

Obama bragged that his father had "studied econometrics" in the United States with such "unsurpassed concentration" that he'd "graduated in three years at the top of his class." Such was his mastery of the subject that "he won another scholarship—this time to pursue his Ph.D. at Harvard." Obama Sr. never actually earned the doctorate (though he did, from time to time, pass himself off as a "doctor"[5]). In the son's telling, the elder Obama had to return home, where Kenya had thrown off British rule and all of Africa was rebelling against the evils of colonialist exploitation. "A separation occurred," Obama Jr. had concluded in *Dreams from My Father*. With a young wife and newborn son staying behind in Hawaii, Obama Sr. "returned to Africa to fulfill his promise to the continent."[6]

Promise? The word is more fog from the vaporous arsenal to which Alinskyites resort when they know clarity would betray their radicalism and antagonize the public. What was this "promise" Obama incessantly invokes when speaking and writing about his father? It was communism. That was the Luo "promise" to Africa, the vision revealed in Barak Hussein Obama Sr.'s academic attainments. It was, and is, a virulently anti-capitalist, anti-Western, and anti-American brand of socialism—one that meshed comfortably with the elder Obama's Muslim roots.

Islam is a minority religion in Kenya, and most Luo are Christians, converted from Animist beliefs. But Onyango Obama,

189

President Obama's grandfather and a respected tribal elder, converted to Islam, probably while living in Zanzibar.[7] Earlier in his life, Onyango had become a Christian, even changing his name to "Johnson," according to the account given Obama by one of his grandfather's wives.[8] (The Luo traditionally practiced polygamy, long before some of them converted to Islam.) But Onyango "could not understand such ideas as mercy towards your enemies, or that this man Jesus could wash away a man's sins," the wife went on. He thought "this was foolish sentiment, something to comfort women." Compared to what he saw as Christian weakness, he found "strength" and "discipline" in Islam. So Onyango became a Muslim because Islam "conformed more closely to his beliefs."[9] He took on the name of the prophet's grandson, "Hussein," a hero in Islam's formative wars of aggression. He raised his children as Muslims, including Barak Sr., who was born to his second wife in 1936 and given the middle name Hussein.

Onyango Obama enlisted in the British army during World War II. He returned home more sympathetic to the anti-colonial movement then taking hold of Kenya, as it had taken hold of Africa generally. British rule in Kenya fell hardest on the Kikuyu. They were more pervasively dispossessed of their lands than the Luo. And as the majority tribe, they had the most to lose from the colonial policy of restricting political representation and land ownership in the highlands to white settlers. Though a Luo, Onyango involved himself with the Kikuyu Central Association, a violent independence faction that presaged the Mau Mau rebellion. As one of Onyango's wives put it, "He did not like the way British soldiers and colonialists were treating Africans, especially members of the Kikuyu Central Association, who at the time were believed to be secretly taking oaths which included promises to kill the white settlers and colonialists." Thus he exploited his position working as a cook for a British army officer in Nairobi to spy for the insurgents. Mrs. Obama claims that her husband was detained for two years at a maximum security prison in Kenya, where he endured torture that left him permanently scarred and bitterly contemptuous of the British government he had once served.[10] His young son Barak was an impressionable young teenager at the time of his father's ordeal.

Choosing Sides in Kenya

The Kikuyus' charismatic leader Jomo Kenyatta was the driving force behind the Mau Mau rebellion that began in 1952. The terror campaign lasted four years and claimed the lives of thousands of Kenyans, particularly Kikuyus. Approximately 11,000 Kikuyu insurgents were killed by British forces and 2,000 tribesmen—labeled "collaborators" because they wouldn't join the uprising—were murdered by their fellow Kikuyus.[11] Thousands of Kikuyus were jailed, with Kenyatta himself spending nearly seven years in custody. Even as the rebellion was put down, however, the momentum toward Kenyan independence was on the rise. Two major players, both Luos and yet arch-rivals, played key roles.

One was Jaramongi Oginga Odinga, the Luo leader known as "Double O," who appealed to Kenya's country peasants. He was strongly backed by the Soviet Union and openly declared "Communism is like food to me."[12] The other was Tom Mboya, a more moderate trade-unionist whose following was urban. Favored by center-Left British and American politicians, Mboya was a vigorous nationalist who eschewed both internal factionalism and the prospect of Kenya's domination by external forces.[13]

Kenya had no institutions of higher learning in the 1950s. Mboya knew independence was imminent and wanted the next generation of Kenyan leaders to be ready when it was achieved. He thought students with good potential should be educated in the West, just as he had been gotten to study at Oxford after coming to prominence in Kenyan politics. So Mboya set up the African-American Students Foundation toward that end.

Although American universities seemed eager to support the initiative with scholarships for Kenyans who could get to the U.S., funding would be needed for the students' transportation and other support. The British were unwilling to subsidize the project, pointing out that there was a perfectly good university in nearby Uganda. But the determined Mboya raised private funds in the United States, much of it from such well-known African-American celebrities as Sidney Poitier, Harry Belafonte, and Rachel Robinson (the widow of Jackie Robinson).[14]

Odinga meanwhile schemed to guide the soon to be independent Kenya into the Soviet orbit. Not to be outdone, he obtained hundreds of scholarships for young Kenyans to study in Communist countries, particularly the Soviet Union, China, and East Germany. He groomed his son, Raila, as a future leader, sending him to be educated in East Germany. In the fullness of time, Raila named one of his children after Fidel Castro.[15]

The donations secured by Mboya were enough to sponsor a first group of eighty-one Kenyan students for travel to the U.S. Included among them was the twenty-three-year-old Barak Obama, whose academic seriousness had impressed his fellow Luo, Mboya. The young man set out to attend the University of Hawaii in 1959.

It was there that Obama met Stanley Ann Dunham, a precocious seventeen-year-old who'd been infused by Marxism in the late Fifties at the unconventional Mercer Island High School in Seattle—where she was taught the *Communist Manifesto* and where the school board president acknowledged having been a member of the Communist Party.[16] Friends described Ms. Dunham as a Leftist "fellow traveler" who was aggressively atheist—the daughter of former Christians who'd become religious skeptics.[17] Obama and Dunham met in Russian language class. In short order, they conceived the child who would become our 44th president.

During the 2008 campaign, Senator Obama told the press his mother was "the dominant figure in my formative years. . . . The values she taught me continue to be my touchstone when it comes to how I go about the world of politics."[18] That is probably true. A good deal of what he said about his parents, however, was patently false. Straining to connect himself to the American civil rights movement, for example, candidate Obama told an audience in Selma, Alabama, "There was something stirring across the country because of what happened in Selma . . . so [my parents] got together and Barack Obama Jr. was born." In fact, Obama was born in 1961, four years *before* the famous civil-rights march. Straining, moreover, to connect himself to Camelot, Obama told the same audience that he owed his "very existence" to the Kennedy family, which, he claimed, had paid for his father's trip to attend the American university and thus caused his parents to meet. In fact, though the Kennedys did eventually make generous contributions to Mboya's airlift program, their donations did not start until 1960, a year after the elder Obama's trip.[19]

Further, the "separation" between Obama Sr. and his new wife and son, about which Obama Jr. would later write, was not actually due to the elder Obama's summons back to Africa to "fulfill his promise to the continent." Instead, Obama Sr. left Dunham and Obama Jr. in Hawaii because of an opportunity to continue his economics studies at Harvard—just as he had left his Kenyan wife and son to begin his studies in Hawaii. As we shall see, the abandoned Ann Dunham Obama would quickly divorce Barak and remarry; and Barak would find yet another wife while at Harvard.

In the early Sixties, while the elder Obama pursued his economics studies in America, the winds of change swept through Kenya. With both Odinga and Mboya championing his cause, the British shifted Kenyatta from prison to house arrest in 1959, and finally released him outright in 1961. By then, he had already been voted president of the main political party, the Kenyan African National Union. Kenyatta led negotiations in London that, in December 1963, won Kenyan independence within the British Commonwealth (i.e., Queen Elizabeth II was still head of state). He was named prime minister. The following year, Kenya formally severed ties with Britain: declaring a republic, adopting a new constitution, and electing Kenyatta the nation's first president. Mboya, after a brief stint at the Justice Ministry, was made Minister of Economic Planning and Development. This put him in direct confrontation with his nemesis, Odinga, who'd become vice-president.

Kenyatta had confounded expectations. Though he'd had two years of education in Moscow in the Thirties, and had been incarcerated for years by the Brits, his decades of experience convinced him that the path to prosperity led westward. Only stability and free-market policies would attract the foreign investment Kenya needed to thrive, so he implemented them. With Mboya's help, he promoted gradual change from colonialism to independence, private ownership of property, and government control of the trade unions in order to protect employers. Kenyatta also sided with the West in the Cold War. Ultimately, these policies worked: Kenya's economy dramatically outperformed its East African neighbors; its government and society were comparatively stable; and its literacy and school attendance rates were extraordinarily high, especially by African standards.[20]

At the time, though, the decision to go West brought about fierce conflict with the communists. Odinga wanted radical change:

194

free land for the landless and the Mau Mau guerrillas, nationalization of industries and foreign corporations, and muscular trade
unionism. He imported Soviet arms and, as *Time* magazine put
it in 1965, strode the countryside "heaping Red-tinged scorn on
Kenyatta's ties with the West." Kenyatta retaliated by removing
Odinga as Kenya's delegate to an important British Commonwealth conference, rebuking him publicly for serving Soviet interests, and boldly asserting that Kenya "rejected Communism" and
would not "exchange one master for a new master."[21]

These, then, were the battle-lines in mid-1965, when Kenyatta
had Mboya issue "Sessional Paper No. 10." Entitled "African
Socialism and its Applications to Planning in Kenya," the paper
was an effort to rein in the Left by ostensibly adopting the soft
socialism of Kwame Nkrumah, Ghana's champion of pan-African
independence. The substance of the Mboya plan, however, had
a decidedly capitalist flavor. It called for private property rights,
breaks for employers, and protections for foreign investors. The
proposal was stridently opposed by Odinga and the Luos.

The Dream from My Father: Marxism

It was in response to Sessional Paper No. 10 that Barak Obama
Sr. wrote his polemical essay "Problems Facing Our Socialism."

Obama had finished his master's degree in 1965, the year after
his divorce from Ann Dunham. He'd returned home to Kenya
with a third wife, Ruth Nidesand, whom he'd met while attending
Harvard. He split time between Ms. Nidesand and his first wife,
Kezia, but the two children from his first marriage, Auma and
Abango "Roy" Obama, moved in with Obama Sr. Though President Obama reports that his father was indifferent, at most, about
his Muslim religion, Auma and Roy are Muslims—Roy, in fact,
is an Islamist.

As the *Globe* reported, the time immediately after Obama Sr.'s return to Kenya was "the most prosperous period of his life." He was initially employed by an American oil company but soon landed a job working for his old mentor, Mboya, as an economist at the Ministry of Economic Planning and Development. Yet "Problems Facing Our Socialism" was not merely critical of "the government's approach to economic planning," as the *Globe* so gingerly put it. It was a scathing, comprehensive Marxist rebuke of the Mboya/Kenyatta moves toward economic liberty and the private ownership of property. Firmly in the Odinga camp, Obama Sr. belittled "African Socialism" as an incoherent doctrine that only "divert[ed] a little from the capitalistic system" compared to his clearly preferred "scientific socialism—inter alia—communism."

Though he did not discuss Islam, much of his analysis reads as if it were written by Sayyid Qutb. For example, while conceding that "in most African societies, the individual had sole right as to the use of land and proceeds from it" (just as Islam endorses such a "right"), Obama Sr. qualified that the understanding in these societies was that an "owner" held property "only as a trustee to the clan, tribe or society" (just as, in Islam, the "owner" is a trustee of the umma). The collective, Obama Sr. stressed, was the supreme unit; the function of the individual was to serve it for the greater good. Obama Sr. thus bewailed the Kenyatta government's departure from "the African tradition" of "communal ownership of major means of production and sharing of the fruits of the labours . . . to the benefit of all."

"Free enterprise," in Obama Sr.'s view, was a corrupting force that guaranteed inequitable wealth accumulations. "We need," he declared, "to eliminate power structures that have been built through excessive accumulation so that not only a few individuals shall control a vast magnitude of resources." To be avoided at all costs was the Western practice—including America's—of having political power hinge on wealth. "To rid ourselves of economic power concentration," high taxation would be necessary, he said, and there was "nothing that can stop the government from taxing 100 percent of income so long as the people get benefits from the government commensurate with their income which is taxed."

It was "important," Obama Sr. insisted, "to find means by which we can redistribute our economic gain," both to spur "future production" (evidently, the father shared the son's apathy about *current* production) and to correct economic and racial inequality. Yes, government "should tax the rich more so as to generate high tax surpluses"; but that, he explained, was not the only reason. There was also a moral imperative. Thus did the elder Obama foreshadow the illogic his son would adopt forty-three years later, namely, the claim that "social justice" mandates higher taxes on the wealthy even if the depressive effect results in less tax revenue to fund the social programs for whose support taxes are imposed in the first place. Confiscatory measures like high taxation and the even more drastic "nationalization," Obama Sr. maintained, "should not be looked at only in terms of profitability alone, but also, or even more, on the benefit to society . . . and on its importance in terms of public interest."

In a populist rationalization of his self-defeating contentions, Obama Sr. railed at the evils of British colonialism, which had "only developed the so-called white areas." He demanded that Kenya force foreign companies to "Africanize" their "key positions." He argued, in addition, for the imposition of "price controls" to punish hotels that charged "exorbitant rates" such that "only the very rich can afford to come to Kenya"—as if what the struggling infant republic then needed was an influx of yet more dependents.

Though not of much interest to the *Boston Globe* on the eve of the 2008 election, Barak Obama Sr.'s article was, and is, hugely consequential. And not just because the elder Obama had unabashedly taken firm communist positions in a public controversy— positions his son, despite rhapsodizing over Obama Sr.'s "promise to the continent" of Africa, took pains to avoid mentioning in a 442-page autobiography about the dreams he'd inherited from his father. The article placed Obama Sr. in the thick of fierce infighting between Kenyatta's pro-Western government and the Luo communists. It set him on the side of Odinga and at odds with Mboya, his longtime sponsor. The *Globe* story notes that the elder "Obama's star began to fall; he was sidelined to a job in the Ministry of Tourism." It gently suggests, though, that the demotion was due to Obama's outspokenness over the favoritism Kenyatta's government showed to Kikuyu loyalists—not to his article.

The heated dispute over Kenya's future turned explosive. Kenyatta pushed Odinga out of the vice presidency the next year and ultimately banned the opposition party he had attempted to form. Odinga was replaced as vice president by Daniel arap Moi, the Home Affairs Minister. Odinga's fall meant the rise of Mboya, who emerged as a potential successor to the aging Kenyatta. That gave Mboya enemies in two camps: Odinga, who continued to regard him as "a rabid black dog that barks furiously and bites everything in its path";[22] and the influential Kikuyus, who regarded the presidency as their tribal possession and were determined to block Mboya.

On July 5, 1969, Mboya encountered Barak Obama Sr. on a busy Nairobi street, reportedly by chance. The two stopped to chat for several minutes. Shortly afterwards, a gunman on a motorcycle shot Mboya to death on a Nairobi Street. Obama Sr. acknowledged seeing the shooter and claimed to be the only witness able to identify him. Weeks later, a Kikuyu mechanic named Issac Njenga Njoroge became the only defendant arrested and charged. He was swiftly convicted and hanged, with the help of Obama Sr.'s testimony.

The conventional wisdom, and the theory of the *Globe* story, is that the Kikuyus had Mboya killed while Obama Sr. happened to be on the scene, and that Obama Sr., realizing his mentor's death was probably the end of his career anyway, bravely threw caution to the wind and testified against the Kikuyu gunman—angering the regime and putting his life at risk. Maybe that's how it happened. But that theory lines up neatly only if one ignores Obama Sr.'s article, as the *Globe* did.

In reality, Obama Sr. had already pulled the rug out from under Mboya, aligned with the Odinga position against Kenyatta, taken very public positions against the Kikuyus, and gone out of favor. Sure, Mboya had Kikuyu enemies, but he'd made dangerous Luo enemies, too. In fact, Kenyatta rounded up Odinga and several other members of his outlawed party after Mboya's assassination and detained them for two years. Maybe Kenyatta was trying to shift suspicion from his fellow Kikuyus, or maybe he really thought the Luos were involved. We don't know: The circumstances of the murder remain murky, and the conspiracy behind it has never been solved.[23] We do know one thing, though: The ties between the Obamas and the Odingas continue to bind.

chapter twelve

MUSLIM WORLD TRAVELER

After Kenyatta died in 1978 and was replaced as president by Daniel arap Moi, Barak Obama Sr. was permitted to return to work in the Kenyan government. He was, by then, a dissipated man. He died in the last of his many car accidents in 1982. He was given an Islamic burial. That would have been unlikely if he had renounced his Muslim faith publicly, notwithstanding President Obama's occasional claim that his father had become an atheist, or at least an agnostic. The president maintains that the Islamic rites occurred at the insistence of Obama Sr.'s large Kenyan family.[1] Curious that they would be so sure that was what he wanted.

In any event, obfuscation about whether Barak Obama Sr. was a believing Muslim, an agnostic, or an atheist is central to

President Obama's carefully stitched, all-things-to-all-people narrative. It is what enabled him to tell a Florida campaign audience "My father was basically agnostic, as far as I can tell, and I didn't know him," and yet, post election, have a White House spokesman make jaws drop: "The President himself experienced Islam on three continents before he was able to—or before he's been able to visit, really, the heart of the Islamic world— you know, growing up in Indonesia, having a Muslim father— obviously Muslim Americans [are] a key part of Illinois and Chicago."[2]

The explanation behind these differently weighted statements is that Obama can put American minds at ease while signaling to Muslims that he is with them in every important way. Having "experienced Islam on three continents," the president knows that many Muslims see him as a Muslim, regardless of how he sees himself. Sharia rejects the concept of renouncing what the Koran calls "the Religion of Truth." As we've noted, Islam brands apostasy a capital crime. From the perspective of Islamic law, if Obama's father was a Muslim, then he is a Muslim. So even though he is an avowed Christian, Obama fully grasps the significance of his Islamic roots for Muslims: Not merely the son of a Muslim man, but the stepson of a second Muslim man, who actually raised him for four of his childhood years as a Muslim in Indonesia—the world's most populous Islamic country, and one of which it is very likely he became a naturalized citizen.

Shortly after divorcing Obama Sr., Ann Dunham married an Indonesian Muslim, Lolo Soetoro Mangunharjo. She had met Soetoro, just as she had met Obama Sr., when both were students at the University of Hawaii. At some point, Soetoro almost certainly adopted Dunham's son, who became known as "Barry Soetoro." Obama's lengthy, deeply introspective autobiography does not address whether he was adopted by the stepfather whose surname he shared for many years, but in all likelihood that did happen in Hawaii, before the family moved to Jakarta.

Under Indonesian law, adoption before the age of six by an Indonesian male qualified a child for citizenship. According to *Dreams from My Father*, Obama was four when he met Lolo Soetoro. His mother married Soetoro shortly thereafter. Obama was already registered for school when he and his mother relocated to Jakarta, where Soetoro was an oil-company executive and liaison to the Indonesian government. That was in 1966, when Obama was five. Obama attended Indonesian elementary schools, which, in Suharto's police state, were generally reserved for citizens (and students were required to carry identity cards that matched student registration information).[3] The records of the Catholic school Obama/Soetoro attended for three years identify him as a citizen of Indonesia.

Given the president's adamant refusal to address issues related to his birth and citizenship, it is fair to infer that Obama obtained Indonesian citizenship through his adoption by Soetoro in Hawaii. That inference is bolstered by the 1980 divorce submission of Ann Dunham and Lolo Soetoro, filed in Hawaii state court. It said "the parties" (Ann and Lolo) had a child (name not given) who was no longer a minor (Obama was 19 at the time).[4] If Soetoro had not adopted Obama, there would have been no basis for the couple to refer to Obama as *their* child—he'd have been only Ann Dunham's child.

The records of the Catholic school and the public school Obama attended during his last year in Indonesia identify him as a Muslim. As Obama relates in *Dreams from My Father*, he took Koran classes. As Obama *doesn't* relate in *Dreams from My Father*, children in Indonesia (in which several religions besides Islam are practiced) attended religious instruction in accordance with their family's chosen faith.[5]

Acquaintances recall that young Barry occasionally attended Friday prayers at the local mosque. Moreover, Maya Soetoro-Ng, Obama's half-sister (born after Lolo and Ann moved the family to Jakarta), told the *New York Times* in a 2008 interview, "My whole family was Muslim, and most of the people I knew were Muslim."[6] In fact, back in March 2007—i.e., during the early "Islamic ties are good" phase of Obama's campaign—the candidate wistfully shared with the *New York Times* columnist Nicholas Kristof his memories of the muezzin's Arabic call to prayer: "one of the prettiest sounds on earth at sunset." Kristof marveled at the "first-rate accent" with which Obama was able to repeat its opening lines.[7]

Shrouded in Mystery

Obama's formative years after Indonesia remain shrouded in mystery. His two autobiographical books, for all their breadth, tell us precious little about his years at Occidental College, Columbia College, and Harvard Law School. Some of his radical acquaintances are just skipped over—for example, Bill Ayers and Bernardine Dohrn, the former Weather Underground terrorists,[8] and Mike Klonsky, the Maoist co-founder of the radical Students for a Democratic Society, who later partnered with Ayers, his old SDS friend, on education "reform," and who ran (what else?) a "social justice" blog on Obama's campaign website until attention was called to it.[9] We don't learn that Obama studied under the Islamist theorist Edward Said at Columbia.[10] We don't learn that one of his best friends in Chicago was Rashid Khalidi, the former PLO spokesman under Arafat who now holds the Edward Said chair in Islamic studies at Columbia—and who, like the Muslim Brotherhood, has supported terrorist strikes on Israeli government targets.[11] When Obama does mention a radical associate,

like his mentor in Hawaii whose name is given only as "Frank"—
we don't learn that he is talking about the late Frank Marshall
Davis, a communist.[12]

Moreover, when Obama does occasionally give us accounts
of aspects of his past that look like they could be verifiable, they
sometimes turn out to be fictional. One typical and disturbing
example in *Dreams from My Father* is the farcical account of
Obama's first job after college:

> Eventually a consulting house to multinational corporations
> agreed to hire me as a research assistant. Like a spy behind en-
> emy lines, I arrived every day at my mid-Manhattan office and
> sat at my computer terminal, checking the Reuters machine
> that blinked bright emerald messages from across the globe.
> As far as I could tell I was the only black man in the company,
> a source of shame for me but a source of considerable pride
> for the company's secretarial pool. They treated me like a
> son, those black ladies; they told me how they expected me to
> run the company one day. . . . The company promoted me to
> the position of financial writer. I had my own office, my own
> secretary, money in the bank. Sometimes, coming out of an
> interview with Japanese financiers or German bond traders, I
> would catch my reflection in the elevator doors—see myself in
> a suit and tie, a briefcase in my hand—and for a split second
> I would imagine myself as a captain of industry, barking out
> orders, closing the deal, before I remembered who it was that
> I had told myself I wanted to be and felt pangs of guilt for my
> lack of resolve. . . .[13]

This is bunk. Obama did not work at "a consulting house to
multinational corporations." It was, a colleague who worked with

him has related, "a small company that published newsletters on international business." Obama wasn't the only black man in the company, and he didn't have an office, have a secretary, wear a suit and tie on the job, or conduct "interviews" with "Japanese financiers or German bond traders." He was a junior copyeditor.[14] And what's unnerving about the fabrication is that it is so gratuitous. It would have made no difference to anyone curious about Obama's life that he, like most of us, took a ho-hum entry-level job to start establishing himself.

But Obama misrepresents the small things just as he does the important things—depending on what he is trying to accomplish at any given time. In the above fairy tale, he sought to frame his life as a morality play: the hero giving up the cushy life of the capitalist "enemy" for the virtues of community organizing. We've now seen this dance a hundred times, though. Recall the tall tale in which he tried to tie his birth to the civil rights march in Selma. Visiting Moscow, the president obviously wanted to strike a connection with graduating students, so he made up a story about how he met his "future wife . . . in class." (In fact, Barack and Michelle Obama met at work). In trying to tap into the Leftist myth about rampant poverty in America, Obama has waxed eloquent about his single mother's surviving on "food stamps" so she could use every cent to send him "to the best schools in the country." (In fact, on returning from Indonesia, Obama was raised by his maternal grandparents, who had good jobs and were able to pull strings to get him into an elite Hawaiian prep school.) And so it goes. In America, what is supposed to save us from fraudulence of this sort is the media. Here, though, the legacy press has been deep in Obama's tank.

Consequently, we have no account about what surely must have been among the most interesting experiences of young

Barack Obama's life: his trip to Pakistan. This occurred in 1981, the year before he entered Columbia University. We know about it only because candidate Obama let it slip during a 2008 fundraiser in San Francisco. Dilating on his intimate knowledge of the Muslim world, and how it would be such a great asset for his administration's foreign policy, he declared: "When I speak about having lived in Indonesia for four years, having family that is impoverished in small villages in Africa—knowing the leaders is not important, what I know is the people. . . . *I traveled to Pakistan when I was in college*" (emphasis added).

The off-handed admission sent the Obama campaign scrambling. It was bizarre that Obama had never discussed it before. He hadn't mentioned it in *Dreams from My Father*. He hadn't referred to it earlier in the long primary and presidential campaigns, during which a major issue was Pakistan—a turbulent Taliban and al Qaeda haven where Benazir Bhutto had recently been murdered by Islamist terrorists and where the U.S. is widely despised, has tense relations with a difficult government, and was then conducting some controversial military operations.

Stressing that he had made the remark in a "private" speech (those don't count?), Obama's campaign spokesman Bill Burton explained that at Occidental, before transferring to Columbia, Obama had befriended two wealthy Pakistanis, Mohammed Hassan Chandoo and Wahid Hamid. After visiting Ann Dunham and Maya Soetoro in Indonesia, Obama traveled with Hamid to Pakistan. He remained there for "about three weeks," staying with Chandoo's family in Karachi. Burton repeated Obama's claim that the trip had somehow enhanced the candidate's "foreign policy credentials" . . . though the campaign refused to provide any further details about it.[15] Naturally, the media accepted that stance . . . after all, they needed to rest up in case there was a sudden opportunity to grill Sarah Palin's third-grade teacher in Wasilla.

Why Pakistan?

The disinterest is remarkable. Obama visited during the height of Pakistan's Islamicization under the martial law imposed by General Zia ul-Haq. In 1979, after the military's 1977 coup, Zia had executed President Zulkifar Ali Bhutto. While there was not a categorical ban, there was a State Department advisory against Americans traveling to Pakistan. For good reason: By 1981, the Islamist military regime was incarcerating political opponents, sacking judges, enforcing media censorship, and reacting to anti-government work stoppages. War was raging in neighboring Afghanistan between the Soviets and the mujahideen. In neighboring Iran, Ayatollah Khomeini's Islamist regime was now firmly in place after toppling the Shah and holding U.S. hostages for a year. Furthermore, it had been only two years since a mob had attacked the U.S. embassy in Islamabad, killing an American marine and two Pakistanis.[16]

Of all places, why would Obama travel to Pakistan at that time? And how did he enter the country? Did he use an American passport to enter a police state in which it was dangerous for Americans? If not, did he have travel documents from another country—which would raise the question also posed by his Indonesian years: Was Obama a citizen of an Islamic country? Those questions weren't pursued. Apparently the press didn't find anything newsworthy about the college friends involved in Obama's trip. Mohammed Hassan Chandoo, for example, became a New York financial consultant and a major Obama fundraiser. His brother, Mohammed Askari Chandoo, reportedly ran a crudely anti-Bush website and, besides raising money for Obama's successful 2004 Senate campaign, also organized voter registration drives in mosques.[17]

Nor was there media interest in the most intriguing (known) aspect of the trip: Obama stayed for part of it in the Jacobabad home of one of Pakistan's most prominent political families. He was hosted by the Soomros, members of the Pakistan Muslim League (a political party that is now split into several factions). Obama's host, Ahmad Mian Soomro, was a longtime Pakistani parliamentarian. His son, Muhammad Mian Soomro, who is about ten years older than Obama, not only became a very successful international banker; he was also chairman of the Pakistani Senate, became a caretaker prime minister in 2007, and served as the country's interim president when Pervez Musharraf was ousted in 2008—holding the office for a month, until the election of Benazir Bhutto's widower, Asif Ali Zadari.[18]

Nothing very interesting about that, right? Just move along . . .

The point here is not to join another crackpot conspiracy, the "Obama as Muslim Manchurian Candidate" canard. Obama's father and stepfather were Muslims. Obama, however, barely knew his father and was only ten years old when he left his stepfather in Indonesia, returning to live with his non-Muslim grandparents in Hawaii. There is no known evidence of his having made an adult choice to practice Islam. Even if that weren't the case, if you've read this far, you know that a central theme of this book is the imperative that we defend the American way of life. That means defending freedom of conscience. We needn't care what sharia says: Neither Barack Obama nor anyone else is a Muslim unless he chooses to be; that's a personal choice, not an umma choice.

Nevertheless, since he is president, Obama's private life cannot be completely separated from the life of the nation. In a time when American is targeted for destruction by a Grand Jihad, it makes a big difference whether the President of the United States was ever a Muslim, how the Islamists targeting us perceive the president, how responsive he is to such perceptions, and whether he harbors sympathy for the Islamist cause—which is, in salient particulars, consonant with his Leftist cause to transform our country.

The president knows these things. They explain why, as a candidate, he originally suggested his name and heritage would be a selling point—and not just in a policy sense. Though the legacy press has looked the other way as it typically does in things Obama, Ken Timmerman has exactingly reported that millions of dollars in illegal donations poured into the Obama campaign from Islamic countries and territories.[19] On this score, and on the pressing matter of Obama's ties to the Islamic world, the post-election commentary of the Libyan strongman Muammar Gaddafi—now among the State Department's favorite "moderate" Muslims—is especially instructive:

> There are elections in America now. Along came a black
> citizen of Kenyan African origins, a Muslim, who had studied
> in an Islamic school in Indonesia. His name is Obama. All the
> people in the Arab and Islamic world and in Africa applauded
> this man. They welcomed him and prayed for him and for his
> success, and they may have even been involved in legitimate
> contribution campaigns to enable him to win the American
> presidency.[20]

The contributions to which Gaddafi referred might have been legitimate under sharia, but donations from non-Americans overseas clearly violate American law—heretofore thought to govern American elections.[21] These staggering millions that flowed into Obama's coffers support Gaddafi's main point: Many people in the Muslim world view Obama as their own. His was the campaign of "hope," and, as the colonel elaborated, Muslims "hope that this black man will take pride in his African and Islamic identity, and in his faith, . . . and that he will change America from evil to good, and that America will establish relations that will serve it well with other peoples, especially the Arabs."

It's fashionable to roll one's eyes at Gaddafi's outbursts. His remarks here, however, accurately reflect a popular Islamic mindset that undergirds everything from the Intifada to the Muslim Brotherhood's support for the murder of American troops in Iraq to sharia's death penalty for apostates. That mindset says: If any inch of the earth's surface has ever been Islamic land, it is Islamic land forever. That is why many Muslims, not just Islamist terrorists, still call Spain "al-Andalus" even though it was reclaimed from Islamic forces over 600 years ago. Likewise, that mindset says that if a person has ever been a Muslim at any time, whether at birth or by later conversion, he or she is deemed a Muslim forever. Muslim rules governing birthright underscore this point. In Islam, there is no baptism or analogous physical act of initiation. The question of whether one is a Muslim is determined by the father's religion, and while Muslim men may marry infidel women (and keep infidel concubines), sharia does not permit Muslim women to marry non-Muslim men. In other words, if there's a Muslim parent in the mix, Islam expects to claim the offspring as its own.

But isn't there a countervailing claim of Muslim hostility to Obama? That is, doesn't Obama's proclamation of Christianity, after a Muslim upbringing, render him an apostate and thus condemnable in the eyes of Islam? This is a more complex question, but one on which the world's diverse Muslim population preponderates in the president's favor. Obama, after all, has never *renounced* Islam; his dubious claim, instead, is that he was never a

Muslim in the first place. At one end of the spectrum, there are surely Islamists (especially terrorists) who would condemn him. They are a minority, however, and they're not worth wasting much anxiety over—they can always be relied on to find a reason to condemn everyone but themselves.

At the spectrum's other end, there are hundreds of millions of Muslims (the true moderates) who take their sharia with a grain of salt. Like sensible non-Muslims, they figure being born a Muslim should be irrelevant if one never makes an adult choice to embrace the religion. To repeat, while Obama has been very sketchy about his past, there is no record of his ever having done so.

Finally, there are the Islamists—those hundreds of millions of Muslims who take their sharia quite seriously but, as we've seen, take it with varying degrees of nuance. Most of them believe that all humans, regardless of parentage, are called to Islam at birth. The question for them is whether, as an intellectual matter, a person affirms or rejects this call. Such Muslims are apt to see in Obama a man who, while never clearly affirming the call, has never really rejected it either. To the contrary, they see a man who not only has been solicitous of Muslim concerns but wants very much to be understood as being solicitous of Muslim concerns. These legions of Muslims are also apt to see Obama as a very powerful and useful man: A man in a position, if so disposed, to advance the cause of Islam in the world.

He certainly does seem so disposed.

chapter thirteen

ISLAM, THE LEFT, AND
APOCALYPSE IN KENYA

Barack Hussein Obama Jr. spent very little time in the United
States Senate after his 2004 election. In a flash, he was eyeing
the White House. All told, he spent about 140 days in attendance
at congressional sessions—at times, even seeming confused about
his committee assignments.[1]

But he did make time to spend six days in Kenya. They were
six days spent campaigning for the candidate running in opposition to Nairobi's pro-American government—in outrageous
contravention of U.S. policy and, probably, federal law. That
opposition candidate was Raila Odinga, the communist Luo who
was seeking the presidency, who agreed to impose sharia law in
Kenya in order to win the support of Islamists, and who threw
the country into murderous mayhem when his bid fell short. It

was one of the most dangerous, destabilizing, disgraceful performances in the history of the U.S. Senate—but you've probably never heard about it, because the Obamedia chose not to report it.

Odinga, as we have seen, is a Marxist. He is also a thug. He spent nearly eight years in prison for his role in the violent coup attempt against Kenyatta's pro-American successor, President Daniel arap Moi, in 1982. Though he denied involvement, and was never convicted for it (he was held without trial as a national security threat), he conceded his role while cooperating in a 2006 biography. By then, the statute of limitations had run.[2]

Odinga remained a Luo eminence, becoming the top leader after the 1994 death of his father, Oginga Odinga. For years, although Kenya's society was more stable and prosperous than most in Africa, he represented the Luo districts in the legislature and railed against what was essentially a one-party system. At the turn of the century that system gave way to free, multi-party elections, the first of which was held in 2002. Odinga joined the coalition led by Mwai Kibaki. When Kibaki won, however, he froze the tempestuous Leftist out of any influential positions in the new government. Like his father before him, Odinga reacted by starting a new opposition party (the Orange Democratic Movement) and planning to oust Kibaki in the 2007 presidential election.

One of those with whom he strategized was the newly elected American Senator from Illinois, Barack Obama.

In the *Washington Times*, Mark Hyman reported that Odinga had visited Obama in the U.S. in 2004, 2005, and 2006, and that Obama had sent an adviser, Mark Lippert, to Kenya in early 2006 to plan a trip by the senator that summer, timed to coincide with Orange Democratic Party campaign activities. Obama followed through in August. For six days, he was nearly inseparable from

Odinga as they barnstormed the countryside.[3] Obama pointedly criticized the Kibaki government for denying Kenyans' basic rights. Though he acknowledged the country's democratic tradition and strong economic growth, he decried social inequities, claimed the economy was leaving too many in poverty, and insisted that the "vast majority" of Kenyans wanted . . . "Change."

Most emphatically, he accused the Kibaki government of rampant corruption. For instance, in an interminable speech at the University of Nairobi that he provocatively entitled "An Honest Government, A Hopeful Future," Obama intoned:

> It's more than just history and outside influences that explain why Kenya lags behind. Like many nations across this continent, where Kenya is failing is in its ability to create a government that is transparent and accountable. One that serves its people and is free from corruption. . . .
>
> [T]he reason I speak of the freedom that you fought so hard to win is because today that freedom is in jeopardy. It is being threatened by corruption.
>
> [W]hile corruption is a problem we all share, here in Kenya it is a crisis—a crisis that's robbing an honest people of the opportunities they have fought for—the opportunity they deserve. I know that while recent reports have pointed to strong economic growth in this country, 56% of Kenyans still live in poverty. And I know that the vast majority of people in this country desperately want to change this.
>
> It is painfully obvious that corruption stifles development—it siphons off scarce resources that could improve infrastructure, bolster education systems, and strengthen public health. It stacks the deck so high against entrepreneurs that they cannot get their job-creating ideas off the ground. . . . And corruption also erodes the state from the inside out,

sickening the justice system until there is no justice to be found, poisoning the police forces until their presence becomes a source of insecurity rather than comfort. . . .

In the end, if the people cannot trust their government to do the job for which it exists—to protect them and to promote their common welfare—all else is lost. And this is why the struggle against corruption is one of the great struggles of our time.[4]

The Kenyan government was furious over Obama's outbursts, so transparently designed to benefit Odinga. "Sen. Obama has to look at critically about where he's receiving his advice from," said a government spokesman, Dr. Alfred Mutua. "Because somebody, somewhere wants to run for president and is using Sen. Obama as his stooge, as his puppet to be able to get to where he wants to get to."[5]

The Kibaki government had continued the Kenyan tradition of alliance with the United States. It is a relationship that it is greatly in our national interest to keep. While our government is wont to credit many suspect nations (and "Kingdoms") with being strong allies of the United States against terrorism, Kenya actually is one. It was enormously accommodating, to take just one important example, in allowing American agents and prosecutors (including me) to investigate al Qaeda's 1998 bombing of the U.S. embassy in Nairobi.

For Senator Obama—he of the Tony Rezko real estate deal—to scold such an ally as incorrigibly corrupt and to interfere in its internal politics was more than reckless. It was borderline criminal (and that's being generous). The Logan Act, which has been the law of the United States for two centuries, bars Americans who are "without authority of the United States" from conducting relations "with any foreign government . . . in relation to any disputes or controversies with the United States, or to defeat the measures of the United States."[6] Under our Constitution, the power to conduct foreign policy belongs to the president, not to individual members of Congress. Obama plainly did not have the "authority of the United States" to undermine our government's relations with an ally in a region where we badly need friends.

Hope, Change, and Islamist Socialism in Kenya

Why would he do such a thing? There are two threads to the explanation. One is the enduring tribal, and perhaps even familial, ties between the Obamas and the Odingas. According to Raila Odinga, he and President Obama are cousins: "Barack Obama's father is my maternal uncle," Odinga told the BBC in early 2008—adding that he was in phone contact with Obama during the American presidential campaign.[7] Odinga is notoriously untrustworthy, and that, combined with the media's stubborn disinterest in Obama's background, makes this claim difficult to assess. Obama aides did not confirm or deny a family tie. Reuters, however, found Said Obama, a forty-one-year-old Kenyan who claimed to be the president's uncle, and who explained that Odinga was overstating the case: "Odinga's mother came from this area, so it is normal for us to talk about cousins. But he is not a blood relative."[8] Of course, in Kenya, the pull of tribal ties can be as powerful as those of blood. Obama's autobiography, subtitled "a story of race and inheritance," attests to this: A journey through layers of racial and family relations to find identity, at last, in the "inheritance" of his Luo roots.

The second thread—and one, Hannah Arendt would caution, that is stronger even than tribal ties—is the hold of ideology. It draws its allies together, inoculated under its spell from day to day reality.[9] Obama and Odinga are Leftist ideologues, soul-mates in, and prisoners of, a flawed logic that revises the past and imposes the future, while incinerating the here and now. It is a totalitarian ideology that draws the Left irresistibly into alliance with Islamism and its cognate logic of submission.

With the Odingas and the Obamas, this is on display in matters small and large. As Obama relates in *Dreams from My Father*, his formerly hard-drinking older half-brother, Roy, decided to impose order on his troubled life by converting—submitting—to Islam. This was in the early Nineties, as the baton of Luo leadership passed from Oginga to Raila Odinga. In the conversion process, Roy "decided to reassert his African heritage," insisting that he be called by his Luo name, Abongo, planning his return to Kenya, and building a hut for himself and his mother "in accordance with Luo tradition." Suddenly ascetic in habit and arrayed in the traditional garb of African Muslims, his brother, Obama observed, had suddenly become "prone to make lengthy pronouncements on the need for the black man to liberated himself from the poisoning influences of European culture." Viewing the transformation on the day of his and Michelle's nuptials, performed by the hate-mongering Leftist Reverend Jeremiah Wright, Obama reflected that Roy/Abongo was "the person who made me proudest of all."[10]

Flashing forward to Raila Odinga's quest for the Kenyan presidency, Obama's rabble-rousing propelled Odinga from the back bench to the forefront of opposition against Kibaki. But he was still well behind. So, it later emerged, he cut a deal with the Islamist factions. Islam is decidedly a minority religion in Kenya, but many of its adherents are revolutionary and ruthless. On August 29, 2007, Odinga signed a Memorandum of Understanding with Sheikh Abdullahi Abdi, chairman of the National Muslim Leaders Forum of Kenya. The document was shocking. In exchange for Muslim support, Odinga agreed, among other things: to rewrite

218

the national constitution to install sharia as the law in all "Muslim declared regions"; to elevate Islam as "the only true religion" and give Islamic leaders an "oversight role to monitor activities of ALL other religions" (emphasis in original); to establish sharia courts in every Kenyan divisional headquarters (i.e., everywhere in Kenya, not just in Muslim areas); to ban Christian proselytism; to fire the police commissioner for "allow[ing] himself to be used by heathens and Zionists" to oppress Muslims; to adopt Islamic dress codes for women; and to ban alcohol and pork.[11]

Odinga purports to be a Christian and for months he denied that he had understandings with Muslim leaders. He retracted those denials once the Memorandum of Understanding was publicized by Sheikh Abdi.[12] The alliance, however, should have surprised no one. The cagey Odinga became a very wealthy man by setting aside his longstanding disputes with the pro-American Moi government in exchange for becoming Kenya's Energy Minister in 2001. That enabled him to establish strong ties with Colonel Muammar Gaddafi's Islamist regime in Libya, which helped establish Odinga in the oil business and materially supported his political activities.[13] More significantly, Odinga also came into the orbit of the Al Bakri oil dynasty of Saudi Arabia, headed by Sheikh Abdukeder al-Bakari. Odinga, employing good old crony capitalism, bought low and sold high.[14]

Sheikh al-Bakari's name appears on a handwritten list of twenty wealthy donors to Osama bin Laden's efforts to support the Afghan mujahideen in the late 1980s. Known within al Qaeda circles as "the Golden Chain," the list was found on a computer file, labeled "Osama's History," that was seized during a 2002 raid on the Sarajevo offices of the Benevolence International Foundation, another Islamic "charity" that has been shuttered as an al Qaeda front by both U.S. enforcement action and a United Nations resolution.[15] On its own, the list does not indicate that al-Bakari or anyone else on it funded any other bin Laden operations besides the jihad against the Soviets (which, of course, the United States also supported). But it is certainly suspicious.

Even with strong Muslim backing, Odinga was defeated in the December 2007 election, Kibaki earning 230,000 more votes out of the ten million cast. The election was marred by various irregularities on both sides. Ballistic over the result, Odinga's supporters resorted to what Peter Pham aptly called "apocalyptic violence."[16] In one atrocity, about fifty Christian worshippers—mostly women and children—were locked into the Assemblies of God Church in the village of Eldoret, northwest of Nairobi. The church was set ablaze. Those who tried desperately to flee were hacked to death by a mob, wielding machetes.[17] As Mark Hyman reported, by mid-February 2008, 1500 Kenyans had been killed and more than 500,000 displaced—with the lion's share of the violence perpetrated by Muslims.

Kibaki pleaded with leaders of all the nation's factions to come together for a summit aimed at quelling the violence. All agreed to attend, except Odinga, who was in regular communication with Obama—by then surging in the Democratic primaries and publicly calling for an end to the savagery. Odinga's strategy, the extortion strategy of Islamist intimidation, worked to a fare-thee-well. To appease his brutal supporters, he was named Prime Minister in February 2008—a position of number two in government that had to be created, a title that had not been bestowed in Kenya since the founder, Kenyatta, held it in 1963.

With Obama's helping hand, Leftists and Islamists had combined forces to overwhelm a constitutional democracy.

chapter fourteen

SOCIAL JUSTICE, OBAMA STYLE

The Warren Court "wasn't that radical" after all. Barack Obama, now a state legislator in Illinois, was giving an interview to Chicago Public Radio in 2001. Sure, the Supreme Court justices who held sway in the Sixties and Seventies had invented abortion rights under the rubric of "privacy," forged a revolution in the rights of criminals against the society on which they preyed, and put down the markers for today's imperial judiciary. In the end, though, they'd flinched. They had failed, Obama lamented, to confront "the issues of redistribution of wealth, and of more basic issues such as political and economic justice in society."[1]

It was an early iteration of the socialist philosophy Obama had learned to keep tightly under Alinskyite wraps, but for the occasional slip when he strayed from the teleprompter—as when, during the 2008 presidential campaign, he'd told Ohioan Joe Wurzelbacher, now known to America as "Joe the Plumber," that he thought social progress could come only when government "spread the wealth around." By that point, Obama was more guarded than he'd been in 2001, just as he was more coy in 2001 than he'd been in his mid-Nineties incarnation. Back then, when he first sought to represent an extremely left-wing district—debuting in the living room of the former Weather Underground terrorists Bill Ayers and Bernardine Dohrn—he had embraced his endorsement by the radical Chicago New Party, an American branch of the Socialist International and the electoral arm of his collaborators at ACORN, the Association of Community Organizers for Reform Now.[2]

By 2001, as he eyed national office, Obama put on mainstream airs. He couched his radicalism in soothing euphemisms like "economic justice." This is the finance angle of "social justice," the idée fixe of Obama and his coven of Change-agents. Such Leftists give the Warren Court high marks on non-economic "progress," but flunk the justices on redistribution: the purported right of society's ne'er-do-wells to pick the pockets of its achievers through the coercive power of government. As Obama sees it, the Warren Court failed to "break free from the essential constraints that were placed by the founding fathers in the Constitution." Instead, the justices clung to the hoary construction of the Constitution as "a charter of negative liberties": one that says only what government "can't do to you." Obama explained that real economic justice demands the *positive* case: what government *"must do on your behalf"* (emphasis added).

This philosophy is a reprise of what Jonah Goldberg elegantly calls the "apotheosis of liberal aspirations."[3] It first surfaced in FDR's 1944 proposal of a "Second Bill of Rights," a mandate that government provide "a new basis of security and prosperity." The new mandates would include, "a useful and remunerative job," "a decent home," "adequate medical care and the opportunity to achieve and enjoy good health," "adequate protection from the economic fears of old age, sickness, accident, and unemployment," and a "good education." It is the dream not only of the Left but of the Islamists, their building blocks for the umma in America . . . and beyond. It is the dream on which Obama is determined to deliver.

It is also a profound betrayal of our constitutional system. Mark Levin elaborates on FDR's vision:

> This is tyranny's disguise. These are not rights. They are the Statist's false promises of utopianism, which the Statist uses to justify all trespasses on the individual's private property. Liberty and private property go hand in hand. By dominating one, the Statist dominates both, for if the individual cannot keep or dispose of the value he creates by his own intellectual and/or physical labor, he exists to serve the state. The "Second Bill of Rights" and its legal and policy progeny require the individual to surrender control of his fate to the government.[4]

A Prescription for the House Divided

The Framers viewed government as a necessary evil. It was required for a free people's collective security but, if insufficiently checked, it was guaranteed to devour liberty. The purpose of the Constitution was not to make the positive case for *government*. The case for government is the case for *submission*. The Constitution is the positive case for *freedom*. Freedom cannot exist without order, and thus implies some measure of government. But it is a limited government, vested with only the powers expressly enumerated. As the Framers knew, a government that strays beyond those powers is necessarily treading on freedom's territory. It is certain to erode the very "Blessings of Liberty" the Constitution was designed to secure.

Relatedly, the Constitution *does* state the positive case for government in its opening lines. Government is required to safeguard the rule of law and the national security. These injunctions are vital: there is no liberty without them. Why, then, do Obama and other Leftists ignore them? Because they don't involve picking winners and losers. Because they eschew social engineering. These guarantees, instead, are for *everyone*, uniformly: Government must "provide for the *common* defense" and "promote the *general* welfare" (emphasis added). The Blessings of Liberty are to be secured "to ourselves and to our posterity"—not to yourself at the expense of my posterity.

The question isn't what government "must do on *your* behalf." It is what government must do on *our* behalf. In general, the positive power of government is for the body politic, not the individual. Of course individuals have rights. Those rights, however, comprise a sphere of personal liberty *against* government. In that sphere, each individual Joe the Plumber is free to work hard, or not; to make of his life what he will, bearing personally the consequences of his choices. Freedom, after all, includes the freedom to fail. *Pace* FDR, Obama, Qutb, and the Muslim Brotherhood, failure is a part of life. There is no right against it.

The Framers understood that there is no societal good in a government that must "do" for individuals and factions. "Doing" is a zero-sum game. Government does not inherently have anything to give. What it awards you it must seize from me. What it gives one faction it must deny to others. Islamism is more forthright than the Left on this point: It makes no bones about the fact that redistribution is compulsory because it is Allah's will, implemented through the coercive power of the Muslim state.

Its guiding force is sharia, not some gaseous palaver about "social justice." Whatever the rationale, though, the arrangement is inimical to the Constitution's purpose "to form a more perfect union." It is, in fact, a prescription for disunion, for the house divided.

Freedom accepts that we are different. The endless variety of life assures that. I had every opportunity to become just as good a basketball player as Michael Jordan, but he has natural gifts and worked harder. If we played a hundred times, he would whip me a hundred times by about 500 points. No Change, no matter how rapturously framed, could alter that result without chaining him to the bench and rendering the game no longer recognizable as basketball. That would be perversion, not justice.

Yet this is just what "economic justice" envisions: A government that hamstrings Michael Jordan and gives me enough freebies that, despite his talent and industry, he can only play me to a tie, destroying his incentive to excel while the Bulls go out of business, no longer able to afford even my mediocrity. Naturally, such an absurd system requires *change*. Redistribution smothers the freedom our Constitution is designed to foster. It is therefore antithetical to our law.

Obama professes a love for this country. So does many an Islamist. What they love, however, is a *vision* of America, not America as it *is*: *E Pluribus Unum*—the Many who are transformed into One by freedom, not ideology. For the president as for the Islamists, the object of their affection is not our *Unum*, the glorious inheritance we *pluribus* cherish through generations past, present, and (one prays) future. That *Unum* earns only their disdain.

Move through Obama's career as a community organizer, his embrace of ACORN, his radical associations: the common denominator is a purpose to break down the *Unum* at its foundations, what he calls the "grass roots." For America, he plans an atom bomb. Or, to be precise, an *atoms* bomb: countless communities in cities and towns across the land, organized along Saul Alinsky's brand of Marxism, into socialist enclaves. It fits hand in glove with Yusuf Qaradawi's voluntary apartheid, the enclave strategy of the Muslim Brotherhood. Each atom smothers the individual freedom and enterprise that have defined the American character, replacing them with welfare states that prize dysfunction and reward the rabble-rousers.

To be sure, there is an *Unum* that Obama sees. It is in his mind's eye—clearer on the horizon now than when he began his project twenty-five years ago. It will arrive when the atoms reach critical mass and finally devour the hollowing carcass of our present society. This, too, jibes perfectly with the Islamist scheme to destroy America from within, the Grand Jihad.

The Jihad against Liberty

For Obama, our society is an ineradicably racist "white world." He is more opaque than mentors like Jeremiah Wright and Bill Ayers, who mince no words in portraying America as an apartheid state. Still, as Hank De Zutter wrote in a fawning 1995 profile, Obama learned to see "integration was a one-way street, with blacks expected to assimilate into a white world that never gave ground."[5] One hears the echoes of Obama's wife, Michelle, whose Princeton thesis decried the thought of "further integration and/or assimilation into a white cultural and social structure that will only allow me to remain on the periphery of society; never becoming a full participant."[6]

What to do if one is convinced, against the weight of his Ivy League opportunities and spectacular success, that he is destined to be on the outside looking in? If you are Obama, you adopt a two-prong strategy. First, you build small, alternative realities that reject the *Unum*'s core values. Then, as those alternative realities—the communities you've organized—grow in number and sophistication, you coerce the unwilling to accept and live within the new reality, just as you believe the *Unum* has marginalized you.

For Obama and his Islamist allies, capitalist democracy is an abject failure, habituated to racism, relentless in its materialism. Coming from these accusers, it is an ironic indictment. The president and his fellow travelers are driven by nothing if not a crass materialism. They see themselves entitled to society's benefits without the burden of its toils. They are, moreover, prisoners of their own race obsessions. (Have you ever heard anyone else describe his own grandmother as "a typical white person"?) Race is their unified field theory for all of life's disparities. The power of the myth goes a long way toward explaining Islam's success in recruiting African Americans, who make up about 90 percent of the religion's American converts.[7] It is a stubborn theory, heedless of the fact that, in our free society, members of all races, ethnicities, and economic classes move up and down the ladder of opportunity by the yardstick of merit.

Obama and the Islamists purport to tolerate that yardstick, but they are poseurs. For both, merit must be harnessed by their subjective sense—masquerading as "social justice," or what Raila Odinga calls "controlled capitalism"—of how much the meritorious may be permitted to achieve. They deride the very core of what makes American society exceptional: individual liberty, freedom. "We have this strong bias toward individual action," Obama ruefully told De Zutter—and note the crafty rhetorical shift: his choice of the amorphous *action* instead of the value-laden *freedom*, lest the listener realize just what is at stake. "You know, we idolize the John Wayne hero who comes in to correct things with both guns blazing. But individual actions, individual dreams, are not sufficient. We must unite in collective action, build collective institutions and organizations."

Of course, we *already have* collective institutions and organizations. They are the branches of a limited government, designed by our Constitution precisely to promote individual liberty and national security. They are the churches, synagogues, PTAs, neighborhood clubs, and other social organizations by which each citizen may freely set the balance between his personal fulfillment and his interaction with fellow citizens. They are the arts, the sports arenas, the charities, the congeries of fulfillment for those who know the personal is not the political. That is American democracy, our *Unum*.

Enclaves of the Alienated

So if not American democracy then . . . what? De Zutter, who interviewed Obama, explained that his subject's strategy called "for organizing ordinary citizens into *bottom-up democracies* that create their own strategies, programs, and campaigns and that forge alliances with other disaffected Americans" (emphasis added).

Ah, yes, "bottom-up democracies." Like much of Obama's vaporous rhetoric, it sounds harmless enough—even admirable. Until you look closely. It turns out that these "bottom-up democracies" are phony. They are not democracies at all. They are enclaves of the alienated, where the mob strangles the achiever. They are voluntary arpartheid havens, "democratic" only in the sense that the inhabitants, enemies of our free society, have voted to withdraw. Indeed, when Ayers, Obama's long-time "education-reform" ally, conjures his ideal "participatory democracy"— fueled by what he euphemistically calls "popular empowerment" and what Obama calls "participatory politics"—the "beacon to the world" he points to is Chavez's socialist thugocracy in Venezuela.

To begin with, Obama's bottom-up democracies don't serve the *demos*. They serve the tribe at the expense of the *demos*. Obama's post-racial, post-partisanship is a pose. Back when he was an up-and-coming "community organizer" in Chicago, and more honest about his intentions, he made no bones about the fact that he was driven by a determination to "organize black folks." His preoccupation was "black America." His autobiography was "a story of race and inheritance" from his African father. He anguished over a "moral agenda" for "the African-American community," one that harnessed the "energy" and "moral fervor of black folks"— stoked in pulpits of black separatists like Wright—into a "concrete program for change."

Back then, Obama's actions spoke even louder than his words. He chose to knit himself into the fabric of Wright's church, drinking deep its Marxist Black Liberation Theology and its stated mission to sustain "an African people, and remain 'true to our native land,' the mother continent, the cradle of civilization." It was a bleak world, a defiant bottom-up community choosing to separate itself from the *Unum*. As Wright's role model, James Hal Cone, put it:

> Black theology refuses to accept a God who is not identified
> totally with the goals of the black community. If God is not
> for us and against white people, then he is a murderer, and we
> had better kill him. The task of black theology is to kill Gods
> who do not belong to the black community. . . . Black theol-
> ogy will accept only the love of God which participates in the
> destruction of the white enemy. What we need is the divine
> love as expressed in Black Power, which is the power of black
> people to destroy their oppressors here and now by any means

at their disposal. Unless God is participating in this holy activity, we must reject his love.[8]

Cone's theory was the springboard for Wright's "mission statement" for Chicago's "Trinity Church," of which Obama was a member in good standing for twenty years, and to which he contributed thousands of dollars of his own money (and steered thousands more when he and Bill Ayers ran the Leftist kitty known as the "Chicago Annenberg Challenge"[9]). From its opening lines, that mission statement proclaimed: "We are a congregation which is Unashamedly Black and Unapologetically Christian. . . . Our roots in the Black religious experience and tradition are deep, lasting and permanent. We are an African people, and remain 'true to our native land,' the mother continent, the cradle of civilization."[10]

How much of this claptrap did Obama buy? Well, he stayed at Trinity for twenty years, until political expedience tore him reluctantly away. (Talk about your "bitter clingers"!) But has he really left the fold? While he is usually careful, Delphic, with his words, he has not shrunk over the years from decrying, as De Zutter reported, "the unrealistic politics of integrationist assimilation—which helps a few upwardly mobile blacks to 'move up, get rich, and move out.'" (One hears again the echoes of Michelle, contending in her thesis that a racial "separationist" would have a better understanding of American blacks than "an integrationist who is ignorant to their plight.")

Obama was front and center at the "Million Man March" convened by Wright's intimate, the notorious Louis Farrakhan. There, Obama recalled, he basked in the "powerful demonstration of an impulse and need for African-American men to come together to recognize each other and affirm our rightful place in the society," to share their "profound sense that African-American men were ready to make a commitment to bring about change in our communities and lives." And as a state senator, Obama inveighed over the fracturing of the "Illinois Black Caucus" when black legislators sided with their diverse constituencies rather than closing ranks to force the placement of a lucrative riverboat casino in a black neighborhood. He seethed that these "lone agents" had voted their conscience, that the tribe had not effectively "enforced" unity "for the common good of the African-American community."

The politics of "bottom-up democracies," furthermore, are not the politics of the *Unum*. Our politics are premised on the rule of law—the standards of a civilized society. Obama's politics, to the contrary, are premised on a form of mob-based extortion that travels under the name of "direct action." The Obamedia never covered it during the 2008 campaign, but the young Obama used to be remarkably open, if characteristically coy, about his methods. "[G]rass-roots community organizing," he explained in 1988, "builds on indigenous leadership and direct action."

And do you know where he wrote that? In a little noticed chapter he contributed to a compendium called *After Alinsky: Community Organizing in Illinois*.[11] Alinsky, who died in 1972, was the committed Leftist revolutionary who systematized community organizing in such books as *Rules for Radicals*. Obama was not only trained in his ideology, but he also mastered it to the degree that he eventually taught "organizing." Indeed, Obama's rise to national prominence is a direct result of his stature in Alinsky's movement.

Alinsky's worldview is captured in Malcolm X's clarion call: "By any means necessary." For Alinsky, as for Obama, the point of organization is "action" which takes aim at "America's white middle class. That is where the power is." Organizers, Alinsky instructed, are "rebels" who

231

have contemptuously rejected the values and the way of life of the middle class. They have stigmatized it as materialistic, decadent, bourgeois, degenerate, imperialistic, war-monger-ing, brutalized and corrupt. They are right; but we must begin from where we are if we are to build power for change, and the power and the people are in the middle class majority.[12]

The organizer's goal is to use the system against the system: to infiltrate and alter it. What Obama calls "fundamental change." And to carry out that mission, the organizer's tool is lawlessness or "direct action."

As Obama wrote in his chapter, "Why Organize? Problems and Promise in the Inner City":

> The debate as to how black and other dispossessed people can forward their lot in America is not new. From W.E.B. DuBois to Booker T. Washington to Marcus Garvey to Malcolm X to Martin Luther King, this internal debate has raged between integration and nationalism, between accommodation and militancy, between sit-down strikes and boardroom negotia-tions. The lines between these strategies have never been simply drawn, and the most successful black leadership has recognized the need to *bridge these seemingly divergent ap-proaches*. [Emphasis added.]

Breathtaking. In essence, "direct action" is the "participatory democracy" of Raila Odinga: Take what the system will give you, then raise holy hell to extort the rest. Observe that Obama does not reject separatism, menacing, and civil disobedience. They are iterations of the hard power he "bridges" with soft power, the exploitation of the system's regular politics. And in a society that venerates dissent and free association, there is much to exploit in

232

the blurry line between critiquing our society and advocating its destruction.

The community organizer and his adherents refuse to be judged by, or to conform themselves to, bourgeois rules and values. Alinsky again: "[T]he practical revolutionary will understand . . . [that] in action, one does not always enjoy the luxury of a decision that is consistent both with one's individual conscience and the good of mankind." No, the practical revolutionary will invoke Goethe's maxim that "Conscience is the virtue of observers and not of agents of action." The organizer is an agent of action, and he has but one value: "Victory." The rest is just details.

Obama and ACORN

That explains the marriage of Obama and ACORN. Most Americans now know the organization for its serial voter-registration frauds, which seriously jeopardize the integrity of our democratic election process. But that is merely a sideline. As Sol Stern richly documented, the organization, with single-minded vigor, pursues a "1960s-bred agenda of anti-capitalism, central planning, victimology, and government handouts to the poor."[13] Its stock in trade is—wait for it—*direct action*. Obama represented ACORN as a lawyer, teamed with ACORN as an organizer, schooled ACORN radicals as a lecturer, funded ACORN while sitting on the boards of Leftist cash cows, capitalized on ACORN support as a 2004 Senate candidate, proposed ACORN-friendly legislation, and shoveled $800,000 from his campaign war chest for ACORN boots-on-the-ground—disclosure of which had to be amended because it was falsely reported the first go-round.

What does ACORN push? "Living wage" laws that kill jobs and raise taxes. The very predatory borrowing practices that ignited the credit crisis and our consequent economic meltdown.

An end to welfare reform and subsidization of the dependence-culture that breeds crime, broken families, and a swelling underclass. Government control of the economy. And the trapping of citizens and businesses in the organizers' "bottom-up democracies"—so they can't, as Obama put it, "move up, get rich, and move out" when their liberty has been strangled.

For example, ACORN, like Obama, advocates proscriptions against school vouchers that would allow parents to shield their children from the public schools. Islamists beginning with Banna and Qutb understood that a ground-up revolution requires control of the classroom. ACORN, Ayers, Obama, and their academic collaborators have helped turn America's classrooms into laboratories of political indoctrination rather than traditional education. An ACORN activist told Stern that vouchers were "a hoax to destroy the public schools," a pretext for promoting the dominant "race and class," and "capitalism at its worst," which is to say, a "life raft for a few people to get out." Welcome to the Hotel Bottom-up Democracy, where you can check out anytime you like, but you can never leave.

And rest assured that Obama-trained ACORN has plans to make sure you don't leave—plans aptly described by Stern as "undisguised authoritarian socialism." Like the imposition of an "exit visa" requirement against large companies that attempt to flee the "community" (i.e., the mini-workers' paradise the "organizer" has forged). Exit visas would extort a prohibitive payment "for losses due to relocation." How long, Stern sensibly asks, "before ACORN calls for exit visas for wealthy or middle-class individuals before they can leave a city?"

Similarly, ACORN advocates freedom-killing measures that masquerade, in Obama's best Orwellian lingo, as "sustainable development" and "regional government" regulations. The goals? To coerce the transfer of wealth from the suburbs to these bottom-up democracies, which are permanently starved for cash because their economic model cannot sustain their welfare state entitlements; to impose strictures on the suburbs' freedom to grow . . . until they are no longer viable alternatives to the organizer's statist communities.

Who would go for such a system? No one sensible, no one reared in the values of our *Unum*. So it must be achieved by "direct action." ACORN steals elections by fraud. It lies about its platform. It foments ruckuses that disrupt public hearings, shouting down its stunned, staid opposition. It organizes intimidating job actions. It storms legislative sessions, damages property and, by its sheer numbers, overwhelms police who attempt to restore order. And, as Stern and Stanley Kurtz recount, ACORN proudly brays that "direct action," legal or illegal, is used because it works.[14] The targets cave in and ACORN's recruiting swells. Naturally so: Just ask *Prime Minister* Odinga. As Osama bin Laden attests in rationalizing terror, people prefer the strong horse to the weak horse. Hamas and Hezbollah, Obama has said, have "legitimate claims"—we should try to see their murderous direct actions as tactical misjudgments, not barbarous disqualifiers. Evidently, blowing up a café or a military barracks or a skyscraper is just another way of saying "Let's renegotiate."

Destroying Liberty

Toward the end of the 2008 campaign, Obama urged a throng of supporters to "go out and talk to your friends and talk to your neighbors. I want you to talk to them whether they are independent or whether they are Republican. I want you to argue with them and *get in their face*" (emphasis added).[15] His longtime supporters will get the point: Alinsky literally wrote the book on getting in your face. Obama imbibed the lesson, and he passed it along to ACORN, which has perfected it.

And that brings us back to Joe the Plumber, our *Unum's* everyman, and the Framers. Joe asked, Aren't you going to tax me more? Aren't you going to take from the sweat of my brow, from the effort I expend to better the lives of myself and my family? Aren't you going to redistribute it as you see fit, to reward your expanding legions of something-for-nothing dependents?

"It's not that I want to punish your success," Obama replied. "I want to make sure that everybody who is behind you, that they've got a chance for success, too . . . . My attitude is that if the economy's good for folks *from the bottom up*, it's gonna be good for everybody. I think when you *spread the wealth around*, it's good for everybody" (emphasis added).

It was an answer right out of ACORN's "People's Platform": "We are the majority, forged from all the minorities. . . . We will continue our fight . . . until we have *shared the wealth*, until we have won our freedom . . . . We have nothing to show for the work of our hand, the tax of our labor" (emphasis added). These are astounding words, Stern observes, from an outfit hell-bent on destroying the individual work ethic precisely by taxing labor and rewarding sloth. They echo the intimidation and the delusional defiance of the Muslim Brotherhood's sabotage strategy.

Obama will "spread the wealth" among these "bottom up" democracies. He will encourage their alienation from the *Unum's* culture of freedom—what Obama has elsewhere condemned as "that old individualistic bootstrap myth: Get a job, get rich, and get out. Instead of investing in our neighborhoods, that's what has always happened. Our goal must be to help people get a sense of building something larger."

But we've already built something larger. *E Pluribus Unum.* Out of Many, One. It is the greatest engine of security, wealth, and dignity in human history. It does more for humankind than any nation in the world, ever. Our *Unum* doesn't need "fundamental change." It needs a determined defense against those who would destroy it from within.

chapter fifteen

THE "MOUNTAIN" GOES TO MOHAMMED

"I think what struck me is how incredibly even he is. And how frankly reassuring he is." The *New York Times'* avatar of conservatism, David Brooks, was gushing over presidential candidate Barack Obama. "It is like you're camping," he illustrated for talk-show host Charlie Rose, "and you wake up one morning, and there is a mountain. And then the next morning, there is a mountain, and there's the next morning, there's a mountain. Obama is just the mountain. He is just there. He is always the same, he doesn't hurt himself."[1]

Brooks has since had plenty of time, and cause, to reassess this unintentionally hilarious metaphor. For my money, the problems started when "the mountain" went to Mohammed.

On January 26, 2009, America's new president chose to give the first interview of his administration to al-Arabiya, an Arabic television network based in Dubai. "My job to the Muslim world," he pronounced, "is to communicate that the Americans are not your enemy."[2]

Presidents of the United States do not have a "job to the Muslim world." Their job, actually, is to preserve, protect, and defend the Constitution against all enemies, including Muslims if they happen to be Islamists seeking to destroy our society. Worse, Obama's fustian was implicitly slanderous, claiming that, until his arrival, America, despite freeing tens of millions of Muslims from tyranny in Bosnia, Afghanistan, and Iraq, had positioned itself as Islam's enemy; that, until his arrival, America, despite being subjected to serial mass-murder attacks by jihadist terrorists since the 1970s, was somehow in the wrong—needing to learn "respect" for Islam.

Of course, only Islamists contend that such nonsense is true. To say they *believe* it is true would be wrong. They *say* it is true, and for a very straightforward purpose: to destroy America's will to resist. It is Islamists who are heartened by Obama's benumbing repetition of America's "respect" for Islam; of our supposed obligation to listen with "respect" to the Iranian mullahs, the Palestinian bombers, and the rest of the Muslim world's rabid America-haters; of our purportedly renewed commitment to relations based on mutual "respect"—a commitment we supposedly lost during the Bush years, despite all the Iftaar dinners, mosque meetings, and politically correct self-flagellation.[3]

True moderate Muslims know that the United States is not Islam's enemy, that we demonstrate inordinate respect in our international relations, and that we fight to defend ourselves from the same tyranny those Muslims wish to purge from their faith. They are the Muslims whose desire is to ally with freedom. But they are not the Muslims to whom the new president chose to speak. In the Obama administration, the Islamists call the tune. It is they who are the objects of our affections, our pleadings, and our appeasements.

The al-Arabiya interview came on the heels of a flurry of Bush-bashing in the administration's initial hours. The president ordered the detention center at Guantanamo Bay to be closed within a year. He had no plan for what to do with the trained, committed, vehemently anti-American terrorists detained there—and in fact he soon found he'd have to renege. In the interim, though, he ordered a thorough review of Gitmo—by then the most thoroughly reviewed, Islam-indulgent detention center in the history of mankind. His administration later conceded it was a first-rate, Geneva Convention-compliant facility. Yet by issuing a preening order to investigate the place, Obama implied that it might still be the Bush Gulag of Leftist lore.

Similar was the effect of the president's other order, purporting to prohibit "torture." Indeed, this self-absorbed gesture is still a staple of Obama speeches, in which the president credits himself with putting a stop to this most heinous of savageries. In reality, Congress had criminalized torture fifteen years earlier. No president had ever tried to authorize it—the Bush CIA's enhanced interrogation program did not come close to the legal line of torture,[4] a fact Obama's Justice Department later implicitly conceded.[5] Nonetheless, by "banning" it, Obama fed the slander that Muslims had been subjected to systematic torture . . . until he arrived.

The president also used his first interview to flaunt his Muslim roots. It was another reversal for Obama: he'd initially played up his heritage as a post-American calling-card; then—once it was clear that America wasn't quite ready to ride off into the sunset— he bridled at the mere mention of his middle initial. But now he changed his tune again: "I have Muslim members of my family," Obama now exclaimed. "I have lived in Muslim countries."

It was a fitting warm-up act for his prostration before the Saudi king at Buckingham Palace. It also set the tone for Obama's June 2008 trip to the Middle East. The president vowed to blaze "a new beginning" in the relationship between the United States and the Muslim world. The foundation would be laid in Cairo, where he chose as his site al-Azhar University—the ancient seat of Sunni learning, whose graduates include the likes of the Blind Sheikh, Yusuf Qaradawi, and the al Qaeda founder Abdullah Azzam; whose current Grand Sheikh, Muhammad Sayyid Tantawi, construes Islamic jurisprudence to support suicide bombings; and whose faculty rallied to Qaradawi's defense when he called for terrorist operations against American troops in Iraq.[6]

The president selected not only the setting but also the audience. Invitations were issued to ten members of the Muslim Brotherhood—much to the consternation of the Egyptian government (which has officially banned the organization, though it permits members to seek office as independents) and of many American counterterrorism experts.[7] At the time, the Ikhwan had just been proved to be at the center of the most important terrorism financing case the Justice Department had ever prosecuted. A trove of documents (such as the playbook I described earlier), wiretapped meetings, and testimony had shown an ongoing sabotage strategy against the United States—a Grand Jihad that long predated the Bush administration's purported deep-sixing of our deep respect for Muslims.

Obama's speech ("A New Beginning") was excruciating: combining fictional accounts of Islamic history and doctrine, a woefully ignorant explanation of Israel's claim to its sovereign territory, and an execrable moral equivalence drawn between Southern slave owners in early America and modern Israelis besieged by Palestinian terror.[8] Perhaps worse, if worse there can be in this concatenation, America's new president signaled the gutting of a key counterterrorism tool—the "material support" statutes—that for years have enabled the United States to strangle jihadist plots in the cradle.

Airbrushing Islam

Any "partnership between America and Islam must be based on what Islam is, not what it isn't." That was the one profound truth the president did utter. Unfortunately, it was empty talk. "What Islam isn't" is a religion of peace with a legacy so overflowing in scientific, philosophical, and artistic achievement that all of civilization, Obama claimed, owes it a great "debt." In fact, the ledger runs heavily in the other direction.

Islam was spread by the sword, not by the allure of its call to submission. The president sought to whitewash this irrefragable reality even as it related to American history. "Islam," he claimed,

> has always been a part of America's story. The first nation to recognize my country was Morocco. In signing the Treaty of Tripoli in 1796, our second President John Adams wrote, "The United States has in itself no character of enmity against the laws, religion or tranquility of Muslims."

Well, not exactly. Obama skipped a teeny bit of the lead-up to the Treaty of Tripoli, namely, the predations of the Barbary pirates. Fortunately, Christopher Hitchens has filled in the missing piece explaining that, beginning in the mid-1780s,

the new United States found that it was having to deal very
directly with the tenets of the Muslim religion. The Barbary
states of North Africa . . . were using the ports of today's Algeria, Libya, and Tunisia to wage a war of piracy and enslavement against all shipping that passed through the Strait of
Gibraltar. Thousands of vessels were taken, and more than a
million Europeans and Americans sold into slavery. The fledgling United States of America was in an especially difficult
position, having forfeited the protection of the British Royal
Navy. Under this pressure, Congress gave assent to the Treaty
of Tripoli, . . . which stated roundly that "the government of
the United States of America is not, in any sense, founded on
the Christian religion, as it has in itself no character of enmity
against the laws, religion or tranquility of Musselmen." This
has often been taken as a secular affirmation, which it probably was, but the difficulty for secularists is that it also attempted to buy off the Muslim pirates by the payment of tribute.[9]

That is, it is Islamist extortion, not Islam, that has always been
part of "America's story." As far as mankind's story is concerned,
moreover, many of the cultural achievements Obama gussied
up as Muslim achievements actually occurred *despite* Islam (particularly in the areas of literature, art, and music), or are more
properly understood as the accomplishments (especially in science and architecture) of better-educated peoples whom Muslims conquered. The president rehearsed the claim that Islam
single-handedly "carried the light of learning through so many
centuries, paving the way for Europe's Renaissance and Enlightenment." This is a myth. As Robert Spencer has ably recounted,
it is not true that Muslims alone preserved the works of Aristotle,
Galen, Plato, Hippocrates, and other pillars of Western enlightenment. More significantly, arrested development in the Islamic

world owes to an anti-intellectualism that persists to this day in enclaves holding that no education beyond the study of the Koran is necessary.[10]

The president, moreover, insisted on pulling a shopworn ploy from the Muslim apologists' bag of tricks: the expurgation of Islamic scripture to render it congenial to Western sensibilities. We were thus treated to the maxim that terrorist violence simply must be anti-Islamic because "the Holy Koran" teaches that "whoever kills an innocent, it is as if he has killed all mankind; and whoever saves a person, it is as if he has saved all mankind." This conveniently decoupled Sura 5:32 from the next verse (5:33), which, though unmentioned by Obama, is well known by Muslims to read:

> The punishment of those who wage war against Allah and
> His Messenger, and strive with might and main for mischief
> through the land, is: execution, or crucifixion, or the cutting
> off of hands and feet from opposite sides, or exile from the
> land: That is their disgrace in this world, and a heavy punish-
> ment is theirs in the hereafter.

Noting a cherry-picking even this egregious does not do justice to the president's sleight of hand. Though Obama portrayed Islam as having a "proud tradition of tolerance," it has a far more consequential legacy of intolerance. Islam strives for hegemony. Islamists seek not to co-exist but to make all the world the realm of the Muslims (*dar al-Islam*). They regard parts of the world still unconquered either as the realm of war (*dar al-harb*) or the realm of sabotage (*dar al-dawa*). What Obama means by "an innocent" and what Islamists take the term to mean are starkly different.

Sura 5:33 is far from aberrant. Furthermore, "the Holy Koran," quite apart from its several other commands to violence, dehumanizes Jews in several places as the children of monkeys and pigs. It admonishes Muslims to "take not the Jews and the Christians as friends and protectors" (5:51). The hadiths of the prophet are replete with tales of non-Muslims slaughtered, forced into slavery, and reduced to humiliating dhimmitude. Mohammed's vision of the end of the world foresaw Jesus returning to abolish Christianity and impose Islam, while Jews are killed by Muslims (with the help of trees and stones, which alert the faithful, "Muslim, there is a Jew behind me—come and kill him!").

Something of basic Islamic intolerance is conveyed even by the seemingly innocuous greeting that Obama, perhaps unknowingly, offered his Egyptian audience: "*Assalaamu alaykum*" ("Peace be upon you"). In the insular, supremacist world of Islam, "Peace be upon you" is an insider salutation—akin to a solidarity gesture or the mafia's introduction of "*cosa nostra*" ("our thing"), which is only uttered in the presence of a third mafioso, known to both strangers, who can vouch that they are all members and it is thus safe to talk business. Consequently, as Spencer explains, when Muslims encounter non-Muslims, the sharia-appropriate greeting is "Peace be upon those who are rightly guided," meaning, Peace be upon *the Muslims.*[11] Between the Muslim and the non-Muslim, there doesn't have to be violence, but there is never peace.

Sweet-sounding Sell-out

Obviously, no sensible person would suggest that a U.S. president rehash these and other unpleasant facts in order to provoke Muslims gratuitously. "Respect" means never having to provoke pointlessly. But it doesn't imply a companion duty to mislead. An American president, after all, must first and foremost respect the American people. And no one forced Obama to give the Cairo speech. That was his idea. It's not as if he were put, through no fault of his own, to the awkward choice of telling a few little white lies or insulting his hosts.

These, moreover, were not little white lies. Obama's mendacity was enormously consequential. In seeming sympathy to the Zionist entity that is the bane of his audience's existence, the president asserted:

> The recognition that the aspiration for a Jewish homeland is rooted in a tragic history cannot be denied. Around the world, the Jewish people were persecuted for centuries, and anti-Semitism in Europe culminated in an unprecedented Holocaust.

This was a sweet-sounding sell-out. If you close your eyes, you can imagine those ten Muslim Brothers nodding in solemn agreement . . . trying, for decorum's sake, to mask their about-to-burst giddiness.

"The basic Arab argument against Israel," Caroline Glick observes, is that the Jewish nation was established for a single reason: "to soothe the guilty consciences of Europeans who were embarrassed about the Holocaust. By their telling, the Jews have no legal, historic or moral rights to the Land of Israel."[12] This is patently false. As Melanie Phillips put it:

> The Jews' aspiration for their homeland does not derive from the Holocaust, nor their overall tragic history. It derives from Judaism itself, which is composed of the inseparable elements of the religion, the people and the land. Their unique claim upon the land rests upon the fact that the Jews are the *only* people for whom Israel was ever their nation, which it was for hundreds of years—centuries before the Arabs and Muslims came on the scene. [Emphasis in original.] [13]

Exactly. The legal, historical, and moral claims of Jews pre-date Adolf Hitler by many centuries. As Glick elaborates, what the League of Nations mandated in 1922 was not the *creation* but the *reconstitution* of the Jewish commonwealth. Moreover, by emphasizing "anti-Semitism in Europe," Obama ignored the Nazis' alliance with the Grand Mufti of Jerusalem and the Palestinians—"and the fact," Phillips adds, "that Nazi-style Jew-hatred continues to pour out of the Arab and Muslim world to this day."

It was all well and good for the president to discourage "threatening Israel with destruction" and the repetition of "vile stereotypes about Jews." But this was just buttering-up rhet-oric, preparing the way for a wholesale adoption of Palestinian mythology. It was "undeniable," Obama claimed, that for sixty years the Palestinians had suffered in pursuit of a homeland, endured the pain of dislocation, and been confined "in refugee camps in the West Bank, Gaza, and neighboring lands," waiting, ever waiting, for "a life of peace and security that they have never been able to lead."

This is preposterous. Let's put aside that the Palestinians have controlled Gaza since 2005—any refugee camps there are cour-tesy of Hamas. The Arabs, Phillips pointed out, could easily have created a Palestinian state during the twenty years (between 1948 and 1967) that Jordan and Egypt held the West Bank and Gaza, respectively. They opted not to do so. Before that, the Palestin-ians had been offered a homeland in 1936 and 1947, and Israel renewed the offer in 1967 and 2000. They keep turning down these entreaties because their goal is to destroy Israel, not coexist in "peace and security."

How fitting it would have been, in Cairo, for an American president to look al-Azhar in the eye and observe that Egypt, too, has a border with Gaza, which they police energetically—at times, brutally—to seal off the Palestinians. But no, instead we got Islamism 101: The Israeli settlements in the Palestinian territories are illegitimate, the president declared. They "undermine efforts to achieve peace" and must stop. Unstated, naturally, were the nettlesome facts that: (a) a million Arabs live in Israel (live, in fact, with more freedom and dignity than Arabs live anywhere else in the Middle East), and (b) Palestinians demand a "right of return" to Israel (one that would destroy its character as a Jewish state) as part of any final settlement. The settlement hectoring is the world according to sharia: What's Islam's is Islam's, and what's yours is Islam's.

It was even worse than that, though. Obama treated listeners to this bit of wisdom: "*Resistance* through violence and killing is wrong and does not succeed" (emphasis added). *Resistance* is a weasel word par excellence—sort of Saul Alinsky for Islamists. It is how the Islamist can tell you, straight-faced, that he is vigorously opposed to "terrorism." In his mind, "terrorism" is American national defense and the existence of the Zionist entity. Blowing up Israelis and American troops, by contrast, is not terrorism— it's *resistance*. By using their weasel word, the president accepted a noxious premise: The Palestinians are an oppressed people, not a people trying to annihilate their unwanted neighbors. Their violence and killing is not a moral wrong but a tactical problem—"it will not succeed."

And why not? Well, because in Obama's twisted history, the Palestinians are just like "black people in America" fighting for their civil rights . . . which, of course, implicitly casts Israelis in the role of slave owners inflicting "the lash of the whip." Those civil rights, Obama maintained, were won solely "by peaceful and determined resistance."

The president occasionally fancies himself the reincarnation of Abraham Lincoln, so one wonders how he missed that little war we had from 1861 to 1865. It not only preserved the Union, it ended the lash of the whip. Barack Obama is also, without peer, a student of Barack Obama, so one wonders how he missed his own odes to "direct action." But those are side notes. In Cairo, he equated what Phillips aptly labels the Palestinians' "genocidal terrorism" with the movement led by Martin Luther King Jr. It was a despicable analogy.

Gutting Counterterrorism Law

The president, it must be acknowledged, made an eloquent case for three core American principles on which Islam frowns: freedom of expression, freedom of conscience, and equality between men and women. It was a welcome reminder of a truth often obscured by the ACLU's frequent collaborations with Islamists like CAIR: Those who cherish America's rich tradition of individual freedom—i.e., those who are *liberals* in the classical sense—should be natural allies of the struggle to turn back Islamism.

Alas, Obama giveth abstractions and taketh away where the rubber meets the road:

> Freedom of religion is central to the ability of peoples to live together. We must always examine the ways in which we protect it. For instance, in the United States, rules on charitable giving have made it harder for Muslims to fulfill their religious obligation. That's why I'm committed to working with American Muslims to ensure that they can fulfill *zakat*.

As we've seen, *zakat* is not "charitable giving." It is the obligation of Muslims to sustain the umma against outsiders. It is the underwriting of jihadist terror, of the implementation of sharia, and of Islamist ideology's march through our institutions. Even if terrorism were not an issue, it would be odd for an American president to obsess over obstacles to *Islamic* charitable giving while simultaneously proposing to burden every other category of charitable giving with new taxation—transferring to the state, from the American citizen, the determination of which social causes receive funding.

More to the point, though, the United States does not have "rules on charitable giving" that, as the president purports, make generosity especially difficult for Muslims. What we have are federal laws against financing terrorism and providing other material support to terrorists.[14] These were enacted by Congress beginning in 1996. They have been the bedrock of Justice Department's anti-terrorism enforcement ever since.

The purpose of these laws is obvious, as has been the stepped-up effort to use them since 9/11. If we are going to prevent terrorist strikes from happening, then rather than content ourselves with prosecuting any surviving terrorists after our fellow citizens have been murdered and maimed, we have to identify jihadist cells and choke off their resources *before* attacks can be planned and executed. Thus, a donor who gives to an ostensible charity that he knows to have been formally designated as a terrorist entity under U.S. law, or that he knows facilitates terrorist activity, is liable. Why should that be a problem? The law does not target *Muslim* charities or organizations. In fact, non-Islamic entities have been prosecuted.

Yet the stubborn fact is that numerous Islamic charities have proved to be fronts for terrorist activity, at least in part. As we've seen, these include the Holy Land Foundation (a Muslim Brotherhood initiative to fund Hamas, the prosecution of which exposed CAIR and ISNA as willing accomplices) and the al-Haramain Islamic Foundation, one of the world's largest Muslim charities, headquartered in Saudi Arabia (where the president stopped to pow-wow with his friend King Abdullah before moving on to Cairo).[15] So material-support statutes have become a sore subject for Muslims because the vast majority of terrorism—including virtually all anti-American terrorism—is carried out by Muslims.

In Leftist ideology, of course, there can be equal protection of the laws only if those laws produce equal (if not better) outcomes for favored grievance groups. Thus, the thinking goes, if our material-support laws are causing a peculiar problem for Muslims, that couldn't possibly be due to a peculiar nexus between Islam and terrorism. It can only be that our laws—laws that apply to everyone equally—are somehow flawed. Evidently, regardless of their vital role in keeping us safe from domestic terror attacks for the last nine years, these laws must now be kneaded into something acceptable to the Islamic activists with whom the Obama administration is so determined to "partner" in its "new beginning."

Unless that new beginning is going to supplant U.S. law with sharia, Congress has already prescribed a legal process by which charitable organizations designated as terrorist fronts can challenge that designation. In addition, the material-support statutes already carve out humanitarian exceptions for donations of medical care and religious items. No one, furthermore, can be convicted of providing material support absent proof that he knew he was giving to a terrorist organization or knew his contributions were abetting terrorist activities.

Our laws do not burden freedom of religion. They burden the forcible spread of an anti-Constitutional doctrine. That is why Islamists and Leftists object to them. The blather about "charitable giving" is a smokescreen.

The Problem, Not the Solution

This gets to the heart of the matter. In Cairo, President Obama took the risible position that "Islam is not part of the problem in combating violent extremism—it is an important part of promoting peace." To be sure, the same ground was staked out by his predecessor, President Bush. They are wrong. Islam is a huge part of the problem in combating "violent extremism." "Violent extremism"—heaven forbid we should say "Islamist terror"—is serially committed by Muslims under the influence of notable religious scholars, including more than a few educated at al-Azhar University, who invoke some of the many scriptures the president elected not to mention.

Yes, Islam must be part of the solution to the promotion of peace. But there are two reasons for this, and the president prefers not to discuss them—or, indeed, to accept them. First, while Obama is living proof that it is possible to ignore Islamic doctrine's causative connection to terrorism, it is not possible credibly to deny that connection. Therefore, the need to deal with Islam is unavoidable—not because it's an asset, but because it's a liability that can't be written off.

Second, there can be no peace unless Islam reforms. For there to be peace, Islam must purge its savage elements (we will never be able to kill or capture all the terrorists who rely on them) and it must compellingly condemn the violence committed in its name. This cannot be done, as Obama and others would like to do it, by telling Muslims everything is fine, that their religion is just peachy as is. It cannot be done by pretending the bad scriptures do not exist and that radicals are merely a tiny fringe of crazy people. That is a strategy designed by Leftists and Islamists to convince well-meaning Americans who are desperate to believe all is well—desperate to believe we don't need to get into the discomfiting business of examining other people's belief systems. This approach does nothing to discredit Islamists and Islamist terrorists in the eyes of other Muslims. In fact, it enhances their credibility because it ignores their doctrinal justifications of terror rather than offering a credible counter-construction.

Worse, as we've observed, it may well be that there is no credible counter-construction of Islam. In that case, there is a gargantuan amount of reform to be done—and that work can only be done by Muslims. They are the ones who believe there is something in Islam so worth preserving that it's better to fight than switch. We cannot rouse them to the task by telling them, as American presidents have been wont to tell them, that we think Islam, as it currently exists, is promoting peace.

To rouse them, we'd need to be honest about "what Islam is, not what it isn't," as President Obama put it. If only he'd meant it. More than "charitable giving" ought to concern an American president. Like charitable rancor. "They who bear cruelty are accomplices in it," Edmund Burke wisely cautioned. "The pretended gentleness which excludes that charitable rancor produces an indifference which is half an approbation." We cannot help the Muslims we ought to be helping without fixing ourselves unambiguously and immovably against the Islamists—not soliciting and indulging them in our deliberations. "They never will love where they ought to love," Burke concluded, "who do not hate where they ought to hate."[16]

chapter sixteen

RIGGING THE NUMBERS

In northern Virginia alone, "we boast about 250,000 to 300,000 Muslims. In the Washington metropolitan area, about 400,000." This information was gleefully broadcast by the U.S. Department of State, through its official website, "www.America. gov." It was summer 2009, and our customer-friendly foreign service was out to show the American people and the world the vibrant, moderate breed of Islam in Barack Obama's America.

State's vehicle was a short video called "Eid in America" that focused on the feast that ends "the holy month of Ramadan," as our government takes pains to call it. The feast was the occasion, State exclaimed, for "more than 400,000 ethnically-diverse Muslims" to "celebrate" right here in Washington, D.C.[1] State's source for this inflated estimate of the Washington area's Islamic population was Johari Abdul-Malik, a prominent Virginia imam—and Islamist. For Abdul-Malik, it's all about the numbers . . . and the conquest. He has insisted, even more speciously, that Islam is now "the second largest religion in America," trailing only Christianity. "Soon, before Allah closes our eyes for the last time," it will move "to being the first religion in America."[2]

It is a commonplace for Islamists to overstate wildly the number of Muslims residing in the United States. The boosterism is not just an idle habit of self-indulgence. It's a strategy.

There are, it is well-documented, nearly six million Jews living in the United States. Fully 40 percent of the world's Jewish population is comprised of American Jews. The six-million figure is symbolically meaningful. It roughly equals both the number of Jews exterminated by the Nazis and the Jewish population of Israel itself.

Consequently, six million has become the Muslim Maginot Line for Islamists. Many of them are Holocaust deniers—or, at the very least, admirers of Hitler's "final solution." (As we've observed, the Grand Mufti of Jerusalem was an ally of the Reich, and *Mein Kampf* remains a big seller in Arabic.) Islamists, moreover, are dedicated to the destruction of the Jewish state—whether by force, by such political accommodations as the so-called Palestinian "right of return," or by the sheer out-breeding of Jews on the part of Israel's growing Arab population. And received Islamist wisdom, of course, casts Jews as exercising outsize influence on American institutions and U.S. government policy. Islamist activists see a correlation between Jewish numbers and Jewish stature, and deduce that a rigged numbers game must be part of their anti-Israel strategy.

So, America's Muslim lobby, which is far more noisy than are America's Muslims, routinely claims there are as many as *ten million American Muslims*. By no means, they stubbornly maintain, can there be fewer than seven million. If there are more Muslims than Jews in the United States, the theory goes, Islam should have more influence than Judaism in the United States. Islamic culture should be as much a part of America's fabric as the Judeo-Christian rudiments of America's founding. The U.S. government should tilt in the direction of Arab terrorists and autocrats, not Israeli democrats, to resolve the Middle East impasse—an "impasse," in the Islamist worldview, being what happens when a Western-style democracy of non-Muslim character refuses to roll over and die in the face of a terrorist onslaught, and "resolve" meaning a "Palestine" that stretches from the Mediterranean Sea to the Jordan River.

America Is "One of the Largest Muslim Countries in the World"?

In point of fact, though, the Muslim American population is infinitesimal—to the point of electoral insignificance at the national level (though it clearly has important pockets—or, better yet, enclaves—of local strength). The most reliable estimates peg the figure between just under 1.4 million (the American Religious Identification Survey) and 1.8 million Muslims (the Pew Research Center studies).[3]

Now, to be sure, the Islamist premise about Jewish strength in numbers is frivolous, betraying the breadth of civilizational distance between Islam and the West. Strong Jewish and Israeli influences in the United States are explained by the American people's immanent Judeo-Christian culture, not a Judaic populace. It is a culture whose roots Paul Johnson traces back to the fifteenth century, and whose hallmarks, Mark Levin and Hadley Arkes demonstrate, course through our Declaration of Independence, our Constitution, and our jurisprudence.[4] That all men are created

257

equal, that governments derive their just powers from the consent of the governed, and that the People have an inherent right to abolish any government destructive of the ends of human liberty and reason—concepts antithetical to Islamic law—are principles basic to the Judeo-Christian tradition. If there were no Jews in America, this would not change.

Let's say, though, that you want to ignore all that is inherent in us and play the silly numbers game. In reality, the American Muslim population is about one-third the size of the American Jewish population. To be sure, it is on the rise. Still, less than 0.6 percent of the total U.S. population is American Muslim.

Obviously, restricting the count to *American* Muslims understates the presence of Islam in America. Not only do our lax immigration policies swell the non-American Islamic population through family chain-migration, student and other visas issued with virtually no background investigation (particularly to nationals of Saudi Arabia, Yemen, Egypt and other cauldrons of jihadism), and even religious-worker green-cards for clerics like the Blind Sheikh (who, at the time of issuance, was on terrorist watch-lists and known to have issued the fatwa approving the murder of Egyptian President Anwar al-Sadat).[5]

Since the Bush 41 administration, the State Department has also been running a "Diversity Visa" program, the very purpose of which is to promote immigration from countries whose citizens resist coming to the United States—i.e., to encourage our cultural disintegration. It is a hare-brained scheme, concocted by a hard-Leftist, the late Senator Ted Kennedy, because the Irish (yes, *the Irish*) were purportedly underrepresented in our gorgeous mosaic. Intended or not, Mark Krikorian, the director of the Center for Immigration Studies, describes the consequences: Fully one-third of the annual diversity-visa lottery winners now come from Islamic countries, which means that the program has become a disproportionately important immigration vehicle for Muslims.[6]

Thanks to these policies, another million or so Muslims reside in the United States (i.e., in addition to the roughly million-and-a-half American Muslims). It is impossible to say for sure what the precise number is because our crack Homeland Security Department keeps track only of immigrant entries into the U.S.—not whether these aliens leave, much less whether, once here, they adhere to their stated purpose for coming.[7] It bears repeating, however, that these aliens are not *American* Muslims. They are legal and illegal immigrants whose fealty is to some other country, or, more realistically, to the umma.[8] This is a matter of no small importance when we are well aware of the supremacist Islamist design: Immigration not to pursue the American dream but to become the American nightmare—a jihad to transform the United States.

Reliable, readily available data show the sparseness of the Muslim sector in America and its dubious ties to our society. The Islamist figures are widely known to be a gross distortion, and the Islamist purpose in inflating the numbers is easily knowable. Yet those Islamist figures create the party line dutifully channeled by the legacy media and the U.S. government. "Nearly 7 million Muslims in our country today" enjoy the "promise" of "opportunity," President Obama declared in his Cairo speech.[9] He and Secretary of State Hillary Clinton make rote references to the magic, Jew-surpassing number, our purported "7 million Muslim Americans."[10]

In a June 2009 interview with French television, Obama even contented with a straight face that "if you actually took the number of Muslim Americans, we'd be one of the largest Muslim countries in the world."[11] Maybe the president meant to say he had "created or saved" seven million Muslims. Obama obviously knew, in any event, that his numbers were off by a mile because when his fraudulent count sparked a mini-uproar, he—in a flash, and without any explanation—down-shifted the number to (the still bloated) five million American Muslims.[12] The science of counting Muslim Americans is evidently as rigorous as that for counting "the uninsured" (which plunged from sixty million to forty million with dizzying speed once questions were raised about subsidizing illegal-immigrant coverage), or for tabulating "climate change" (a term that is itself a change from "global warming" thanks to the inconvenience of global cooling).

Adopting the Brotherhood's Number

But let's pretend for a moment that the president's preferred figure of seven million is actually close to being in the ballpark. Would it be remotely reasonable to portray the United States as *one of the largest Muslim countries in the world?* What exactly does a large Muslim country look like from the standpoint of population?

Well, Obama lived as a child in Indonesia, the largest Islamic country, where there are about 200 million Muslims. That would be about 30 times as many Muslims as Obama likes to imagine are in the U.S. (or about a hundred times as many as actually are in the U.S.). Indonesian Muslims constitute over 86 percent of the total national population. That would be a little over 85 percent more than the 0.6 percent of population comprised by American Muslims.[13]

Just a quick sampling of Islamic countries (i.e., nations where Muslims are a majority) confirms the absurdity of describing the U.S. as a large Muslim country, let alone "one of the largest." There are, to cite just a few examples, 165 million Muslims in Pakistan, 132 million in Bangladesh, 75 million in Egypt, 64 million in Iran, 33 million in Morocco, 32 million in Algeria, 31 million in Afghanistan, 26 million in Iraq, and 24 million in both Yemen and Saudi Arabia. To draw a telling comparison, if we just look at sector percentage figures, Shiites make up 20 to 30 times more of Saudi Arabia's population than all Muslims do of U.S. population. More than a bow will be required when President Obama breaks it to King Abdullah that the Sunni Kingdom is actually "one of the largest Shiite countries in the world."[14]

Even if we limited our consideration to non-Muslim countries, in either the East or the West, the U.S. Muslim sector does not stack up. For example, in Kenya, the native land of Barack Obama's Muslim father and a country the president knows well, estimates of Islamic population vary widely. It can be safely said, however, that Muslims make up at least 10 percent of the country's approximately 40 million people. That is, despite a population 6.5 times smaller than America's, Kenya has about a million more Muslim citizens. In Nigeria, a large country with a bare majority of Muslims (or at least a plurality hovering around 50 percent of total population), there are about 75 million Muslims. Indian Muslims make up only 13 percent of national population (again, significantly higher than the American Muslim population), yet there are a staggering 196 million of them—an amount equal to two-thirds of the entire U.S. population. There are 25 million Muslims in Ethiopia (32 percent of population), 20 million in China (about 1.5 percent), and 15 million in Russia (about 12 percent . . . and rising in the face of the country's steep population decline).[15]

In much of Europe, immigration enforcement—particularly when it comes to immigrants from southwest Asia and northern Africa—is even more lax than in the U.S. As we've seen, moreover, unpoliced Muslim enclaves abound throughout the continent. Therefore, the rapidly expanding Islamic population is difficult to estimate.

A 2006 study commissioned by the U.S. Air Force found that the European Union's Muslim population could be 16 million, or it could be nearly 50 percent higher than that: 23 million. [16] (If Southeastern Europe, Turkey, and Russia were factored in, the figure could climb to 52 million Muslims, though, again, estimates vary.[17]) Several things explain this disparity, including the facts that (a) the Islamic population is not evenly distributed throughout the continent (while there are not yet Muslim majority countries, Muslim majority and near-majority cities are emerging); and (b) the Islamic population is younger, fecund, and thus more dynamic. But, for present purposes, just go for a stroll through Heathrow Airport. See the terminal signs inviting visits to the prayer-rooms, a visible nod to the untold thousands of travelers British authorities know will fret over the difficulty international air travel poses for diurnal *salat* obligations. Clearly, Europe's popular bent is more Islamic than America's.

In France and the U.K., each with a population slightly above 60 million, between 3 and 6 percent is comprised of Muslims. Some estimates (particularly by Islamist groups) claim Muslims have already reached the 10 percent mark in these countries. As we've already seen, it is anticipated that, in the not too distant future, Muslim immigrants will rocket England's national population ahead of Germany's—where, today, there are nearly twice as many Muslims (over 4 million) as there are in America, even though Germany's population (82 million) is only about one-third of ours. Even in Canada, our Europhile neighbor to the north, the nearly 700,000 Muslims represent more than double the percentage found in America (2 percent compared to 0.6).

That's just a smattering of the countries that would dwarf our Islamic populace even if we went with President Obama's imaginary seven million figure. If we were to be realistic, there are actually two to three times as many Muslims in tiny Burkina Faso—approximately 7.5 million—as there are in America.[18]

President Obama is not counting seven million Muslims because there are seven million Muslims. He's counting seven million Muslims because he'd like there to be seven million Muslims. He's counting seven million Muslims because that, *at the very least*, is what the Muslim Brotherhood counts. In an ideological revolution, it's critical to have allies—real or imagined. Few revolutionaries appreciate this fact as well as the president, who, as a Chicago "community organizer," ran a remarkably successful voter-registration program called "Project Vote." His partner in the venture, ACORN, has since taken it national . . . and become notorious in at least fourteen states for registering non-existent voters.

When Leftists cook the population books, it's alarming. Even in a vast, diverse country of 300 million, it matters whether there are 3 million versus 7 million Muslims. Muslims are not like any other population sector, just like Islam is not like any other religion. Islamism is a totalitarian movement, not a demographic data-point. Many Muslims—not all, but many, including some of the most influential—are looking not to settle in the West but to change the West radically. And as we've seen in place after place, when a group is on a mission to alter the playing field rather than just trying to fit in, it requires a much smaller critical mass to have real impact. Its members—its agitators—punch above their weight.

This dynamic of Muslim minorities in the West is a subset of the neocommunist Left's pathogenic intercourse with Western society. Ordinary people do not obsess over societal "progress." For the vast majority of us, the personal is not the political. Our attention and passion are reserved for our families, friends, neighborhoods, jobs, and avocations—for living life, not for prescribing how life should be lived. Ordinary people don't eat, sleep, and breathe societal engineering. They are thus at a distinct disadvantage when confronted by those who do.

The population numbers game is a small but important part of a revolution. When revolutionaries are deft enough to wage the battle inch by inch, they are apt to meet little resistance. It's not that the majority agrees with the revolutionaries. It's that the majority lacks the energy for the exhausting, day in and day out effort it takes to fight back. Often, it is without the attention span to appreciate that there is something to fight about. It's that the majority fails to see that you can't abdicate from a war when your enemies are determined to fight one, whether you engage them or not.

chapter seventeen

STARS OF STATE AND SCREEN

More distressing than its Muslim population phantasms are government's distortions about the nature of Islam in America. Even worse are the places where those distortions are willfully solicited. Thus we return to Johari Abdul-Malik.

Recall he's the Virginia imam who starred in the State Department's cinematic hagiography "Eid in America." He contributed some of the delirious population figures our government dutifully repeats. To use the clinical term, the video promoted by U.S. taxpayer funds is a big fat wet kiss on Islamist lips. And our government knows it full well. Abdul-Malik is an African-American from Brooklyn who converted to Islam. If the video is your only encounter, you'll reckon him up as the warm, avuncular "Director of Outreach" at the Dar al-Hijrah Islamic Center in Falls Church, Virginia. For the unwary viewer, the friendly Islamic Center, and its ur-tolerant companion, the Dar al-Hijrah Mosque, instantiate Muslim life in the United States.

I daresay the cutting room floor was more interesting . . . and more accurate.

State apparently thought it best not to include footage of Imam Abdul-Malik's call for "sabotage" terrorist attacks against Israel. As he put it in 2001:

> I am gonna teach you now. You can blow up bridges, but you
> cannot kill people who are innocent on their way to work. You
> can blow up power supplies . . . the water supply, you can do
> all forms of sabotage and let the world know that we are doing
> it like this because they have a respect for the lives of innocent
> people.[1]

Yes, what better way to show respect!

Of course, not alluding to this speech spared State the embarrassment of explaining that the conference at which Abdul-Malik gave it was hosted by the Islamic Association of Palestine, the epicenter of U.S. support for Hamas, itself the Palestinian terrorist branch of the Muslim Brotherhood. Perhaps Secretary of State Hillary Clinton has forgotten that the self-proclaimed "purpose" of Hamas—according to its charter—is "to create an Islamic Palestinian state throughout Israel by eliminating the State of Israel through violent *jihad*." One might have thought, however, that she'd at least vaguely recall Hamas as the thug-central her husband formally designated as a global terrorist organization, one of the first ever so recognized under U.S. law. One would assume its barbaric exertions in aid of the intifadas, which left President

Clinton's quest for Middle East peace in tatters, might have come up at the White House dinner table—perhaps during one of the Arafats' many visits.[2]

Nor, evidently, did State think it wise to include Abdul-Malik's 2004 promise of Islamic supremacy in America. He made it in a Friday "sermon," the sacerdotal cloak for many an Islamist tirade:

> *Alhamdullilah* [Praise to Allah] and we will live, will see the day when Islam, by the grace of Allah, will become the dominant way of life. . . . I'm telling you don't take it for granted because Allah is increasing this *deen* [religion] in your lifetime. *Alhamdullilah* that soon, soon . . . before Allah closes our eyes for the last time, you will see Islam move from being the second largest religion in America–that's where we are now–to being the first religion in America.[3]

As it happens, "outreach" at Dar al-Hijrah is just Abdul-Malik's day job. As a sideline, he is a director of the National Association of Muslim Chaplains. The founder and president of that outfit, Warith Deen Umar, has glorified the 9/11 hijackers, explaining that "even Muslims who say they are against terrorism secretly admire and applaud" them.[4] For his part, Abdul-Malik is a bit more circumspect. When asked by the investigative journalist Paul Sperry about other "sermons" at the mosque that lionize violent jihad and "martyrdom," he couldn't see what the problem might be. In their own way, he explained, Muslims are like United States Marines, a spiritual force in Allah's cause: "Telling people to give their all for their faith is not an unusual idea. That's the same thing as telling Marines in this country *semper fidelis.*"[5]

Notwithstanding our national infatuation with things Islamic, I somehow think our marines fighting and dying in Afghanistan would not be flattered by the comparison.

A Bridge Too Far

If the good imam sounds like he walked right out of the Muslim Brotherhood's playbook, that's not an accident. Dar al-Hijrah, which fittingly means "Land of Migration," is where the Brotherhood has settled in America. In the shadow of the White House and Capitol Hill, it is the optimal location. The $6 million complex was established in 1991, the same year the Brotherhood playbook was written. Thanks to Sperry's exacting work, we now know the realty on which the Dar al-Hijrah complex sits was purchased in the 1980s by our now familiar Ikhwan/Saudi venture, the North American Islamic Trust.[6] The Islamic Affairs Department of the Saudi embassy in Washington chipped in for the construction.[7] The trustee was the Muslim Brotherhood operative Jamal Barzinji. He, you may recall, was a formative figure in WAMY, the MSA, and the IIIT; an FBI affidavit has further tied him to Islamist terror's kissin' cousins, Palestinian Islamic Jihad and Hamas.

The original president of Dar al-Hijrah was Samir Salah, who also helped set up Bank al-Taqwa. That institution was directed by the specially designated global terrorist Youssef Nada, al Qaeda's banker in whose Swiss digs investigators found *The Project*—the Muslim Brotherhood's twelve-point plan "to establish an Islamic government on earth," written in 1982 and which we first encountered on page 60. Salah also partnered with Osama bin Laden's nephew, Abdullah from Chapter 7, in the Taiba International Aid Association, yet another of those wonderful Islamic "charities" that has been shut down by the government for bank-rolling al Qaeda.

Salah's funding lines trace back to the so-called SAAR Foun-dation, a trust fund established by the Saudi billionaire Sulaiman Abdul-Azziz Rajhi (i.e., SAAR), another fabulously flush member of bin Laden's so-called "Golden Chain" of Saudi supporters from the early days of al Qaeda. In fact, when SAAR was dis-solved in 2000 after raising $1.7 billion, much of which federal investigators believe was diverted to Islamist terror groups, Salah founded its successor organization, the "Safa Group"—located in Herndon, Virginia, conveniently close to the Dar al-Hijrah com-plex in Falls Church. The Safa offices were raided by government agents in 2002. No charges have ever been filed, though the haul was plainly a boon for the intelligence community.

Dar al-Hijrah started out as the only mosque in town, so it attracted hundreds of worshippers. Now, after two decades, it draws thousands, overrunning a once quiet Washington suburb. On Fridays, and especially during Ramadan, the faithful are known to block streets, driveways, and fire-hydrants with their parked cars, and trample across neighborhood yards while approaching the mosque on foot. If, as apologists maintain, jihad really is the internal struggle to become a better person, one wonders why manners seem to degrade as Muslim numbers increase.

But wait—if jihad is actually about struggling to implement sharia as the necessary precondition to Islamicizing a society, it all makes perfect sense. The overflow parking situation became intolerable in Falls Church, and to ease it somewhat, neighboring churches offered the use of their lots in an overture of Christian charity. Predictably, Abdul-Malik accepted the ecumenical ges-ture as a concession. "If Islam really catches on in the area," he smirked to Sperry, "maybe the neighborhood churches will come over lock, stock, and barrel, and we can all share our parking lots."[8] Islamists are happy to expand Islam's American enclaves one space at a time.

The mosque's current imam is Shaker Elsayed, a longtime Hassan al-Banna enthusiast who, for several years, ran the Muslim American Society.[9] And clearly, Dar al-Hijrah's Islamic Center conforms to the "House of Dawa" model described in the playbook and built in city after American city by MAS. It is a community "axis" of the Islamist movement. The Center encourages inter-group cooperation (its website, for example, helpfully directs viewers to the sites of the MAS, CAIR, and other Islamist groups). It serves as the "base" for the Islamist "rise," educating, preparing, and supplying "our battalions."

Founders of the Islamic Center included Ismail Elbarasse, a longtime friend and business partner of Marzook, the Hamas chieftain. The FBI alleges that Elbarasse and Marzook jointly transferred hundreds of thousands of dollars to Hamas. Marzook's underling, Mohammad Salah, confessed to Israeli authorities that money he was caught funneling for the terror organization's operations "was passed on by means of brother Musa Abu Marzuk and brother Ismail Al-Barusa [sic]."[10] In fact, Elbarasse sat on the IAP board and attended the Brotherhood's 1993 Hamas-support confab in Philadelphia—arranged, as a participant put it, to "derail" the Clinton administration's Oslo peace process. It was from his home that the Brotherhood playbook was seized.[11]

Elbarasse has seemed intrigued, to put it mildly, by Abdul-Malik's exhortations about bridge sabotage. In 2004, he was arrested for allegedly casing the Chesapeake Bridge, driving along slowly as his wife filmed the span up and down, lowering their camera out of sight when passing police vehicles drove by. It was all a misunderstanding, of course. Just recording "scenery" Mrs. Elbarasse told the FBI—as her husband urged her to pipe down.

But when the FBI reviewed the tape, they found it focused on "the cables and upper supports of the main span of the bridge, and also pan[ned] the east bound span of the bridge filming the support cables and footings of the main span of the bridge. Portions of the footage zoomed in on the bridge joints of the main support span." "It's a crime to videotape a bridge?" the agitated Mrs. Elbarasse blurted. Evidently not . . . the government decided not to pursue the case against this venerable Dar al-Hijrah elder.[12]

Integrate, But Do Not Assimilate

Uncle Sam was no doubt impressed by the way the Dar al-Hijrah community ponied up for Elbarasse's bail, several members posting their homes as collateral. Particularly charitable was Elbarasse's college roommate, Dr. Esam Omeish—an Egypt-born, Georgetown-educated surgeon and yet another Dar al-Hijrah board member who took the Ikhwan career track. While a Georgetown undergrad, Omeish headed up the Muslim Students Association. He went on to become president of the MAS. In fact, it was during a 2004 MAS conference in Kansas that he urged Muslims to adopt the Brotherhood's voluntary apartheid strategy: Integrate, but do not assimilate. Islam could "become the dominant religion," Omeish promised. Each individual Muslim just had to do his part in transforming America. All it would take was the commitment Omeish himself had taken to heart:

> making sure that I will not accept the evils of this society
> because they are putting down this society and I must do
> everything in my capacity to correct those ills. It goes towards
> perfecting the society so it can carry the light of Allah so it can
> establish a presence of what a perfect society under the guid-
> ance of Allah is.[13]

At the same conference, Omeish lavished praise on "our beloved Sheikh Ahmed Yassin," Hamas's then recently departed founder.

Dizzy enough yet? Here's more: Omeish's brother is Mohammed Omeish, the president of the U.S. branch of the International Islamic Relief Organization, another "charity" headquartered in Saudi Arabia but shut down for financing al Qaeda. Another of IIRO's favored donees was . . . brother Esam's Dar al-Hijrah Islamic Center.

Mohammed Omeish shared a Virginia address with—and his IIRO funded—Abdurahman Alamoudi, a self-professed "moderate" who became a top Clinton administration Islamic affairs adviser. It didn't matter that Alamoudi sat on the board of a Marzook Defense Committee at the very time the administration undertook to deport the Hamas kingpin, nor that he publicly defended both the Blind Sheikh and the World Trade Center bomber Mohammed Salameh, two of the most significant terrorists prosecuted by the Clinton Justice Department.[14] It later emerged that he was also a self-professed supporter of Hamas and Hezbollah. In classic Islamist style, Alamoudi bit both the American and Saudi hands that fed him. He raised a million dollars for an al Qaeda-backed Saudi opposition group, plotted with Libya to murder then-Crown Prince Abdullah, gloated to the IAP that Muslims would take over America, and bemoaned the fact that so few Americans were killed in the 1998 embassy bombings.[15] Naturally, the U.S. government lauded him as one of America's most influential Muslims and put an organization he started, the American Muslim Armed Forces and Veterans Affairs Council, in charge of vetting Islamic chaplains for service in the U.S. armed forces. He is now serving a twenty-three-year prison sentence arising out of his shenanigans with Gaddafi.

With connections like these, Esam Omeish ends up right where you'd expect: First a star turn in State's "Eid in America" extravaganza—cooing over his community's rich diversity ("diversity" in this context means everyone is a Muslim)—and then a career in Democratic Party politics. In 2009, he was defeated in his bid for a seat in Virginia's House of Delegates. He got 16 percent of the vote, an insufficient number of the Commonwealth's elusive "250,000 to 300,000 Muslims" having rallied to his platform of healthcare "reform," reduced traffic congestion, and that old Brotherhood stand-by, education. It was Omeish's second foray into the political arena. The first ended inauspiciously: He was forced to resign from a state immigration panel—to which he'd been appointed by Democratic governor Tim Kaine—when videos posted on the Internet showed him praising Palestinian resort to "the jihad way" in speeches like this one:

> We, the Muslims of the Washington metropolitan area, are
> here today in sub-freezing temperatures to tell our brothers
> and sisters in Palestine that you have learned the way, that you
> have known that the jihad way is the way to liberate your land.
> And we by standing here today . . . we are telling them that we
> are with you, we are supporting you, and we will do every-
> thing that we can, *insha Allah*, to help your cause.[16]

You'll be shocked to learn that Omeish claimed to have been "smeared" by the accurate publication of his own words.[17]

The luminaries on the Dar al-Hijrah board also include Abdelhaleem Ashqar, a former associate professor of business at Howard University. He was a key organizer of the 1993 Philadelphia meeting and, like his friend Elbarasse, became an Islamic Center hero in 1998 when he elected to go to prison rather than testify in a grand jury investigation of Hamas, a feat he repeated after the 9/11 attacks. Ashqar is now serving an eleven-year prison sentence imposed in 2007 for obstruction of justice and contempt in impeding a federal investigation of Hamas's American tentacles.[18]

With guiding forces like Elbarasse, Ashqar, and Omeish, it's no surprise that the State Department's chosen exemplar of Islam in America has featured a roster of imams that makes "Outreach Director" Johari Abdul-Malik look downright tame. Take, for instance, Mohammed al-Hanooti, the former director of the IAP who was the mosque's prayer leader in the troubled mid-nineties period after Marzook's deportation. He prepared for the Dar al-Hijrah gig with a stint running another Muslim community "axis," the Islamic Center of Jersey City, where he frequently hosted the Blind Sheikh and, according to the FBI, raised millions of dollars for Hamas. These credentials were more than enough to get him a place at the table at the 1993 Philadephia conference. They also evidently qualify him as a featured State Department speaker on the Voice of America network—flashing our very special brand of moderate Islam.[19]

And then there's Mohammed Adam El-Sheikh, a Sudanese member of the Muslim Brotherhood who served as imam from 2003 until mid-2005. El-Sheikh is a founder of the MAS. In his spare time, he was the Baltimore regional director of the Islamic American Relief Agency. Alas, in 2004 the Treasury Department named IARA a specially designated global terrorist group, concluding that it had "provided direct financial support of UBL [Osama (or "Usama") bin Laden]."[20]

With so motley a crew of founders, backers, and prayer leaders, it is no wonder that Dar al-Hijrah's worshippers are a "Who's Who" of the jihad. Besides former fixtures like Marzook and Alamoudi, congregants have included Omar Abu Ali, the valedictorian for the Class of 1999 at the Islamic Saudi Academy in northern Virginia. He is now better known for moving on to al Qaeda after graduation, plotting mass murder attacks against the United States and conspiring to murder President George W. Bush for which he was sentenced to life imprisonment.[21] Also among the faithful were Nawaf al-Hazmi and Hani Hanjour, who are now better known for crashing Flight 77 into the Pentagon, just a short distance away from the Land of Migration. They had no doubt heard about the place before they got here. The mosque's phone number was found in the Hamburg apartment shared by the 9/11 ringleaders Mohamed Atta and Ramzi bin al-Shibh.[22]

Neither the Obama administration nor its State Department is in the dark here. The 9/11 attacks, the Hamas facilitation, the bridge surveillance, the conspiracy to murder an American president, the endless waves of anti-American, anti-Semitic bile—all aspects of the Grand Jihad were well known in government circles for years before the government picked Dar al-Hijrah, of all 2300 mosques in the United States, as its showcase of American Islam. "Eid in America" continues to be featured on State Department websites in early 2010, as this book goes to press.

Back in mid-2001, as they fortified themselves at the State Department's favorite Islamic Center for the suicide-hijacking massacre that would live in infamy, Hazmi and Hanjour drew strength and other encouragement from yet another of the mosque's committed imams. Thanks to this "spiritual" guide, Anwar al-Awlaki, Dar al-Hijrah would be featured in several other videos after the summer 2009 run of "Eid in America."

As we shall see, they wouldn't be quite as flattering.

chapter eighteen

FLYING IMAMS

The Sabotage Campaign in Action

The Transportation Security Administration is the executive agency created after 9/11 to protect American travelers. *Protected* was not the feeling most Americans would have experienced, however, upon viewing the TSA's taxpayer-subsidized, official U.S. government website in January 2007. Instead, they'd have been aghast.

Right under the agency's emblem and a memorial banner depicting the late President Gerald R. Ford, Americans were treated to a press release by the Council on American-Islamic Relations, fully endorsed by—indeed, presented as if it were a statement by—the United States government itself. "CAIR Welcomes TSA Hajj Sensitivity Training" blared the big blue headline. This was unabashed proselytism, by an arm of the *Homeland*

Security Department, on behalf of the most insidious Islamist organization in the U.S.[1]

The TSA cheerily informed the nation that that it had "provided special training about Islamic traditions related to the Hajj, or pilgrimage to Mecca, to some 45,000 airport security officers." Included in this "cultural sensitivity training" were "details about the timing of Hajj travel, about items pilgrims may be carrying, and about Islamic prayers that may be observed by security personnel." And that was just the warm-up. The TSA wanted Americans to know that CAIR, or rather, *we*, as CAIR was referred to by our government,

> "welcome the fact that airport security officers nationwide will now be better informed about Islamic traditions relating to Hajj," said CAIR Communications Director Ibrahim Hooper. "This proactive effort on the part of the Transportation Security Administration demonstrates that there is no contradiction between the need to maintain airline safety and security and the duty to protect the religious and civil rights of airline passengers."

No, no contradiction at all—just ask Mohamed Atta.

In giving its megaphone over to Ibrahim Hooper, the Homeland Security Department was supporting a man who makes no secret of the fact that he would like to see the United States transformed into an Islamic country, with our Constitution supplanted by sharia law. He is, however, a man for these times: his absurd contention that there is no "contradiction" between safety and civil rights is of a piece with the gospel according to President Barack Obama and his Attorney General, Eric Holder, under which to concede the inescapable fact that liberty and security are in eternal tension—and that times of terrorist peril are thus occasions for heightened surveillance—is to be beholden to a "false choice."

In the CAIR/TSA presser, Hooper went on to brag that "CAIR chapters nationwide have met with TSA, Department of Homeland Security (DHS) and Customs and Border Protection (CBP) officials on issues related to cultural sensitivity and national security." And why not? After all, according to the TSA (cribbing *in haec verba* from the Islamists' self-description): "CAIR, America's largest Islamic civil liberties group, has 32 offices and chapters nationwide and in Canada. Its mission is to enhance the understanding of Islam, encourage dialogue, protect civil liberties, empower American Muslims, and build coalitions that promote justice and mutual understanding."

Quite apart from the impropriety of the government's Islamic evangelism (to say nothing of the unlikelihood that Americans would reach "mutual understanding" with an organization that promotes the adoption of Islamic law), this was a shockingly disingenuous portrayal of what CAIR is and what it does. Nowhere, for starters, did the TSA see fit to mention that the Justice Department had recently identified CAIR as an *unindicted coconspirator* in DOJ's most significant terrorism financing case ever, the prosecution of the Holy Land Foundation for Relief and Development (HLF). Recall that it was in the course of that prosecution, in which the HLF and several of its operatives were convicted in November 2008 on scores of felony charges arising out of a scheme to provide millions of dollars in support for Hamas, that the Muslim Brotherhood's playbook was revealed. It was also in that same prosecution that CAIR was proved beyond cavil to be the point of the Brotherhood's American spear—a key component for implementing its jihad-by-sabotage strategy to "conquer America."

279

Which is not to say that CAIR doesn't have plenty of cavil left. With the arrival of the Obama administration, CAIR is again on the rise. But as amply demonstrated by TSA's 2007 broadcast of CAIR propaganda, it didn't take an Obama administration for the United States government to engage in a suicidal dalliance with Islamism. In fact, the TSA publication of the press-release wasn't the half of it. Yes, the Homeland Security Department could not contain its glee over approbation from CAIR; nor could it pat itself on the back enough times over its recommendation of CAIR's pamphlet, "Your Rights and Responsibilities as an American Muslim," which admonishes that Muslims are "entitled to courteous, respectful and non-stigmatizing treatment by airline and security personnel," and should be alert to "treatment that . . . is discriminatory." But the agency failed to inform readers about exactly why it was suddenly thought necessary to indoctrinate tens of thousands of transportation *safety* agents in Islamic cultural practices. That, as usual, was left to Yusuf Qaradawi's admirers at the State Department. On its own website, State chimed in that the sensitivity training effort was a direct consequence of "criticism [against DHS personnel] for removing six imams from a domestic flight for what one passenger considered suspicious behavior."[2]

It would be difficult to imagine a more breathtaking misrepresentation.

"Allahu Akbar!"

The infamous "Flying Imams" incident had occurred shortly before Thanksgiving in 2006—not long after the fifth annual commemoration of the 9/11 atrocities. At Minneapolis International Airport, six ostentatiously pious imams (i.e., congregational prayer leaders), all of Middle Eastern descent, decided that boarding time at the airport gate—where passengers were gathered to enter US Airways flight 300, bound for Phoenix—was the perfect time and place to commence evening prayers.

Muslims are enjoined to pray five times a day and encouraged to do so communally. The point of prayer, however, is not to make a tawdry display. There is neither a requirement that it be done congregationally nor a restriction against private, discrete communication with the Divine. Indeed, various exigencies routinely cause Muslims to combine some of their daily prayer sessions—otherwise, things like cross-country flights, medical treatments, and business meetings (not to mention terrorism trials) would be impractical.[3]

Yet, as grippingly reported—based on eyewitness accounts—by my friend Debra Burlingame (the fearless sister of Charles F. "Chic" Burlingame, the pilot killed by the al Qaeda terrorists who crashed American Airlines flight 77 into the Pentagon on 9/11), the imams made a point of raising the decibel-level while chanting *"Allahu Akbar! Allahu Akbar! Allahu Akbar! Allahu Akbar!"*—"Allah is the greatest!"[4] That staple of Islamic prayer, as we've seen, is well known to be the anthem of Islamist terrorists . . . and the sign-off to the Muslim Brotherhood's battle-cry. As Debra recalls, and as many of the 141 passengers and crew stepping onto their flight that evening surely knew, ecstatic suicide-terrorist shouts of *"Allahu Akbar!"* were "the very last human sound on the cockpit voice recorder of United flight 93 before it screamed into the ground at 580 miles per hour," murdering everyone aboard who hadn't already been killed by the four suicide-hijackers.

In all apparent earnestness, our leaders have told us since then to report all suspicious behavior. "If you see something, say something," a ubiquitous New York City Police Department slogan admonishes. Nowhere is this presumed zeitgeist more pronounced than at the airports of America and much of the world. Heavily armed troopers and bomb-sniffing dogs patrol the by-ways, eying long passenger lines in which eighty-year-old women struggle to remove their shoes, trudge through magnetometers, and surrender their four-ounce bottles of shampoo. After all, they could be terrorists, right? Wasn't it harried octogenarians who bombed the Marine barracks in Lebanon, the World Trade Center, the Jewish centers in Buenos Aires, the Khobar Towers in Saudi Arabia, the U.S. embassies in East Africa, the nightclub in Bali, the trains and buses in London and Madrid, the luxury hotels in Mumbai? Wasn't it just average, random Americans who dragged the mutilated corpses of American servicemen through the streets of Mogadishu, who kidnapped and beheaded Daniel Pearl, and who steered jumbo jets into skyscrapers?

Well, no. Actually, those were Muslim terrorists, usually in small cells—often teams of a half-dozen or fewer men, "the battalions of Islam" as the Blind Sheikh was fond of calling them. Until the moment they strike, these sneak-attack cells appear to be exercising what CAIR and the TSA call their "religious and civil rights." To register that fact, however, we would have to acknowledge that the terrorism against us, like the less obvious sabotage against us, is fueled by Islamist ideology and carried out exclusively by Muslims. That would be "stigmatizing" and "discriminatory." After all, if a New York City cop had witnesses telling him the bank-robber was a tall man with red hair, you wouldn't expect him to search for tall men with red hair, would you? Too judgmental—better we subpoena the Manhattan telephone directory and see what turns up.

The spirit of the times—the endless lines snaking around airport terminals, around stadiums hosting major sports and entertainment events, at the entrances to public buildings, etc.—is the simulacrum of security. For when it comes to terror, government's real advice is, "If you see Muslims, say nothing."

That was certainly what the passengers on Flight 300 learned. The agitator imams had just come from attending a conference held by one of the now innumerable Muslim activist organizations, the North American Imams Federation. There, they'd had the chance to participate in discussions on "Imams and Politics" and "Imams and the Media." Now it was time to apply the lessons learned. The Minneapolis airport became what Debra describes as their "stage" and Flight 300 their "prop" in an episode of "grievance theater" in which the "*Allahu Akbar*" chants were just "the opening act." Though apparently traveling together, they dispersed to seats located throughout the plane— seats which, though assigned by the airline, might naturally have appeared to the other passengers as strategically selected by the imams to situate themselves at front, mid- and rear-cabin, just as the 9/11 hijacking teams sought to do. Several of the imams asked for "seatbelt extensions"—heavy metal buckles at the end of a long strap which are kept on airplanes for obese passengers (which the imams were not). Seatbelt extensions, like box-cutters, pose no danger if used for their legitimate purpose but also can easily be used as lethal weapons—and the men who rolled theirs up and placed them on the floor certainly didn't appear to be using them for their legitimate purpose. As Debra adds, "Lest this entire incident be written off as simple cultural ignorance, a frightened Arabic-speaking passenger pulled aside a crew member and translated the imams' suspicious conversations, which included angry denunciations of Americans, furious grumblings about U.S. foreign policy, Osama bin Laden and 'killing Saddam.'"

Contrary to our Islamophilic State Department's shameful depiction, this most certainly was not a case of a single passenger carping about "suspicious behavior." One passenger did indeed pass a note to the pilot—a note that captures the post-9/11 terror that plagues traveling Americans who, in good faith, try to do what the police claim they want us to do, *say something* ("6 suspicious Arabic men on plane, spaced out in their seats. All were together saying '. . . Allah . . . Allah' cursing U.S. involvement w/ Saddam before flight—1 in front exit row, another in first row 1st class, another in 8D, another in 22D, two in 25 E&F"). But that passenger was merely one of several who complained after scores of passengers and crew were menaced by what *was* suspicious behavior: in the end, a three-plus hour ordeal that included a front-to-back police sweep of the aircraft with a bomb-sniffing dog.

The imams were removed from the flight and detained for several hours of questioning by the FBI and other law-enforcement and air-safety agents before being released without charges being filed. Was there any other responsible way to handle the matter? Can't one can just hear the sanctimony about security incompetence and failure to "connect the dots" that would have pervaded a 9/11 Commission-type investigation had the imams actually been a terrorist cell? In short, this was a test for our government, an opportunity to demonstrate its understanding of and seriousness of purpose about the Islamist threat to the United States. It was a test government failed miserably. Concurrently, the muscle-flexing Muslim Brotherhood proved how deeply it had infiltrated our deliberations and intimidated our public officials.

The Brotherhood Swings into Action

Within hours of the ruckus, the Muslim American Society—created by the Brotherhood in 1993—sprang into action. As Debra Burlingame notes, MAS instantly issued a press release, screamed for an apology *to the imams*, and announced a "pray-in" at Reagan

National Airport in Washington: the better to command media attention and crow in the shadow of the Pentagon. MAS demonstrators bleated that African-American Muslims, already persecuted for "driving while black," must now cope with the cognate injustice of "flying while Muslim"—sheer demagoguery given not only the Flying Imams' conduct but the fact that none of them is African-American. No matter. A reliably sympathetic cable news outfit bought the contrived outrage hook, line, and sinker, making an analogy between the imams and the civil rights icon Rosa Parks. As Debra put it, "One wonders what the parents of the three 11-year-olds who died on flight 77—all African-American kids on a National Geographic field trip—would make of this stunning comparison."

The grievance machinery churned on all cylinders. Mahdi Bray, MAS's insufferable executive-director, promised to "hit [US Airways] where it hurts, the pocketbook." MAS and CAIR launched the Flying Imams on a lawfare campaign. Represented by a battery of lawyers that included the firm of Omar Mohammedi, the president of CAIR's New York chapter, the imams filed a civil rights suit in Minneapolis federal court. Not content to sue the airline, the airports commission, and one of the FBI agents who'd questioned them, the imams also roped in as defendants *the passengers who reported their conduct* to the pilot and the authorities. That last gambit was too much even for our Islamist-friendly Democratic Congress, which was finally shamed by the New York Republican Peter King into passing a law to immunize the passengers (who were dropped from the suit by the imams). Cowed, however, by shrieks of racial-profiling from the Islamist Left, lawmakers were unwilling to extend similar protection to the other defendants.

The imams hit the jackpot when their case was assigned to Judge Ann Montgomery, a Clinton appointee who refused to throw out the suit. Buying the defense claim that the imams had been arrested merely "for praying in the airport," Montgomery found the basis for their removal from the flight "dubious" and tut-tutted that they'd been subjected to "an unconstitutional custom of arresting individuals without probable cause based on their race."

Montgomery wholly discounted the imams' provocative anti-American rhetoric—the rants that so unnerved Flight 300's passengers and crew—as "protected speech under the First Amendment." If adopted nationwide, her absurd constitutional theory would suppress much of the evidence routinely admitted in terrorism cases to convict such jihadist leaders as the Blind Sheikh. The right to speak has always implied a right on the part of the listener to consider what the words spoken suggest about the speaker's intentions and actions. If, for example, a mafia don is overheard saying "Whack him" on a wiretap, his First Amendment rights are not violated if we play that tape for a jury considering a charge of murder. In Judge Montgomery's world, however, the law wears earplugs: Airline passengers subjected to menacing chants of *"Allahu Akbar!"* and vigorous denunciations of their country's policies and culture by a gaggle of angry Muslims transparently aping the behavior of 9/11 hijackers are obliged to ignore it—indeed, to feel enriched by the contribution such "political speech" makes to our diverse marketplace of ideas.

Moreover, Montgomery's constitution renders us not only deaf but blind. The judge sloughed off concerns about the seatbelt extension by pointing to the absence of any "documented instance" of their ever having been used as a weapon—a perverse application, in an era of terrorist siege, of the discredited "one free bite" rule that once protected dog-owners who neglected to control their feral canines. As Powerline's Scott Johnson astutely points out, the Montgomery standard would have tolerated the box-cutters of 9/11 and perhaps even the explosive-laden soles of would-be bomber Richard Reid's shoes; after all, before these attempts, there hadn't been any "documented instances" of terrorists using box-cutters and shoe-bombs to carry out mass-murder attacks.[5]

With the prospect of steep money damages imposed after an expensive trial before this same judge, the defendants understandably saw no alternative but to settle the case out of court. Though the pay-out was likely not large (the terms are confidential, but the airport commission announced that it was covered by its $50,000 insurance policy), there, like clock-work, was CAIR's executive-director Nihad Awad, crowing that the settlement was "a clear victory for justice and civil rights over fear and the phenomenon of 'flying while Muslim' in the post-9/11 era."

To the contrary, the evidence suggests this was a fabricated stunt that marked a telling victory for jihad by sabotage. It turns out that both CAIR and the Flying Imams' ringleader, Sheikh Omar Shahin, were well-versed in such stunts. Shahin, a forty-nine-year-old Jordanian-born sharia scholar, is the instantiation of the Muslim Brotherhood in America: mouthing occasional condemnations of terrorism and a soothing version of the Koran for gullible American media and law-enforcement admirers, while ministering to terrorists, serving as a front-man for terror-supporting Islamic "charities," and preaching a virulent, anti-Semitic strain of Wahhabism.

Immediately after 9/11, Shahin expressed doubt that Muslims had had anything to do with the attacks.[6] Yet, as detailed by the former military counterterrorism specialist P. David Gaubatz and the investigative journalist Paul Sperry in their important book *Muslim Mafia*, Shahin was an admitted "supporter of Osama bin Laden while running the Saudi-backed Islamic Center of Tucson, which functioned as one of al Qaeda's main hubs in

North America."[7] In fact, Shahin's predecessor in the Center's leadership was one of bin Laden's closest associates, Wael Hamza Julaidan, a wealthy Saudi whose assets were frozen in 2002 when the Treasury Department designated him as an international terrorist. Julaidan, one of al Qaeda's founder and, according to Treasury, the network's "logistics chief," is a central figure in the web of Brotherhood-connected non-governmental organizations that underwrite and provide other support for the terror network.[8] (As Steve Emerson explained in 2005 congressional testimony, Julaidan, now in Saudi Arabia, "continues to operate with total impunity despite (false) assurances by Saudi officials that [his] terrorist career has been shut down."[9])

That a person of Shahin's background (and we've barely scratched the surface) could not only rise to prominence in a county targeted for conquest but actually succeed in undermining its self-defense marks the triumph of a time-tested Islamist art: touting a smiley-face Islam for the consumption of credulous Westerners while the ears of the faithful are treated to a very different message.

As the public face of the Flying Imams, Shahin projected outrage at the very thought that "true Muslims" would engage in barbarous attacks. "We have been asked by God and by the prophet Muhammad to respect all human life," he told the *Washington Times*. "The Koran is very clear: To save one life he saves all human life, and whoever kills one person, he kills all humankind. And that is what Islam is all about."[10]

Thus did Shahin employ the exact same sleight-of-tongue to which President Barack Obama would resort three years later in his ballyhooed Cairo speech on Islam and the West. In point of fact, this is not what the verse in question, Sura 5:32, says. Rather, it declares that "if anyone slew a person, *unless it be for murder or for spreading mischief in the land*, it would be as if he slew the whole people" (emphasis added). As westerners and Israelis have come to learn only too well, many Muslims have rather elastic conceptions of murder and mischief when it comes to condemning non-Muslims as legitimate targets for slaying. And as we've seen, Sura 5:33 goes on to explain that those who oppose Muslims face "execution, or crucifixion, or the cutting off of hands and feet from opposite sides" and other grisly fates.

In his role as Julaidan's successor at the Islamic Center of Tucson, Shahin's following was a Wahhabist crowd who'd have been offended by such expurgations of scripture. Those believers knew Shahin for his fiery sermons. Typical was his 2002 invocation of the infamous hadith in which Mohammed calls on Muslims to exterminate all Jews in order to bring about the Day of Judgment. As Shahin put it:

> Allah will also dignify the whole Islamic Nation. Prophet Mohammed peace be upon him said: "You will keep on fighting with the Jews until the fight reaches the east of Jordan River. Then the stones and trees will say: 'Oh Muslim, oh (servant) slaves of Allah, there is a Jew behind me; come and kill him.'"[11]

In this summons to genocide, Shahin was literally cribbing from the Brotherhood game plan. The same hadith appears in Article 7 of the Hamas charter. It is also a favorite of Sheikh Yusuf Qaradawi.

We've Seen this Movie Before

Given this sort of fare, you'll not be surprised that the Islamic Center's community of worshippers looks like a mirror image of that found across the country at Dar al-Hijrah's Islamic Center.

Indeed, there is some precise duplication. Hani Hanjour was among the faithful—one of those Muslims Shahin insisted would have nothing to do with 9/11 . . . right up until he flew flight 77 into the Pentagon. Also included was Wadih El-Hage, bin Laden's personal secretary who is now serving a life sentence after convictions arising out of al Qaeda's 1998 bombings of the American embassies in Kenya and Tanzania. But two other Islamic Center denizens merit our special attention here: Hamdan al-Shalawi and Muhammed al-Qudhaieen.

Beginning in the late Nineties, this pair of young Saudis resided in Arizona on student visas. Qudhaieen's name turned up in a pre-9/11 FBI investigation of Islamic students—including some of the hijackers, such as Hanjour—who sought flight-school training in the Phoenix area. Shalawi had received terrorist training in al Qaeda's Afghanistan camps, "learning how to conduct 'Khobar Towers'-type attacks that he and a colleague planned to execute in Saudi Arabia," according to FBI reporting.[12] Eventually, they were deported back home, but not before a 1999 incident that set the stage, to borrow Debra Burlingame's fitting term, for the Flying Imams' theatrics.

In November of that year, Qudhaieen and Shalawi were removed from an America West flight from Phoenix to Washington. They had aroused suspicion by speaking loudly in Arabic (despite being fluent in English), switching their seats, roaming the length of the cabin, and, on two occasions, attempting to open the cockpit. As Gaubatz and Sperry recount, the 9/11 Commission later determined that the incident was a "dry run" for the 9/11 attacks. At the time, however, the authorities decided there was not enough evidence to file charges, so the pair was released. As night follows day, Qudhaieen and Shalawi filed civil rights suits against America West with the enthusiastic backing of CAIR. Railing at "this ugly case of racial profiling," Nihad Awad eased into his rote grousing about rampant "Islamophobia," these young Muslim men having "done absolutely nothing wrong"— their only "crime," he asserted, "was being Arab, speaking Arabic." And wouldn't you know: one of the Flying Dry-Runners' most avid supporters was none other than the future Flying Imam Omar Shahin. According to Gaubatz and Sperry, Shahin knew them, had ministered to them at his former mosque in Tucson, and quickly rushed to their defense.

You'll no doubt be shocked to learn that Shahin was also the Arizona "coordinator" for the aforementioned Brotherhood cash-cow, the Holy Land Foundation. As Shahin raised funds, the HLF branch offices proudly displayed a photo of that great moderate, Sheikh Qaradawi, posing alongside Hassan Nasrallah and Khalid al-Mishal, the chiefs, respectively, of Hezbollah and Hamas—terrorist organizations, long formally designated as such under U.S. law, which apparently never got the memo about how "whoever kills an innocent, it is as if he has killed all mankind." Qaradawi was a frequent keynoter at HLF-sponsored events, regaling all the other moderates with the reminder that "The prophet, prayer and peace be upon him, said: 'The time will not come until Muslims will fight the Jews (and kill them); until the Jews hide behind rocks and trees, which will cry: 'O Muslim! there is a Jew hiding behind me, come on and kill him!'"[13]

After a stint as a representative of "Kind Hearts," another charitable front shut down by the government for funneling money to Hamas,[14] Shahin moved on from his perch at the Islamic Center in Tucson to become president of the North American Imams Federation—the organization whose convention was the occasion for the Flying Imams' visit to Minnesota. NAIF's Board of Trustees is chockablock with Muslim activists who have associated with both notorious terrorists and organizations (e.g., the Global Relief Foundation) that have been shuddered for underwriting terrorism.[15] Besides CAIR, Shahin's organization has established "collaborative, complementary, and cooperative" ties with other "partner organizations"—as NAIF's website once gingerly put it—such as the Islamic Society of North America and the Islamic Circle of North America.[16] Like CAIR, both ISNA and ICNA are cited in the Muslim Brotherhood's 1991 memorandum as "organizations of our friends"—allies in the jihad by sabotage. (Also like CAIR, ISNA was labeled an unindicted coconspirator by the Justice Department in the Holy Land Foundation case.)

Shahin's entanglement in the Brotherhood web makes perfect sense. In his recent book, *The Muslim Family in Western Society—A Study in Islamic Law*,[17] he exhorts Muslims to turn inward, resist Western culture, and disregard any "Western laws that contradict clear-cut Islamic rulings." This is the very essence of Qaradawi's voluntary apartheid strategy to build Islamic enclaves throughout the U.S. and Europe as an intermediate stage on the journey to full Islamicization. And while Shahin, like so many other Islamists, would lull us with pleasantries about spreading Islam by peaceful persuasion, that may not exactly be the guidance his son—like his flock at the Islamic Center of Tucson—has gotten.

In March 2008, Oday Shahin (then 22) was among a group of young Muslim men who alighted from two SUVs along a dirt road near a residential area in north Phoenix, armed with assault rifles, a shotgun, a sniper rifle, and handguns. As reported by the *Arizona Republic*, "the shooters blasted away at a granite rock and empty cans in front of a hill," firing as many as a thousand rounds.[18] This tableau, scoffed at as "no big deal" by Shahin the elder, is recurrent in Brotherhood- and al Qaeda-influenced factions throughout the United States. Its driving force, typically, is a mosque or Islamic center that preaches Wahhabist ideology, with its stress on the imperative of paramilitary training. The Arizona fusillade matches up nicely with 1989 shooting sessions I detailed in *Willful Blindness*, involving teams of young Muslim men who piled into SUVs for the trip to rural Calverton, Long Island, toting firearm stockpiles they'd been storing in their Brooklyn mosque. No one thought those training exercises were a big deal either—until four years later, when several of those men bombed the World Trade Center.[19] In any event, the younger Shahin was arrested and charged with illegal firearms violations. So was Salaf Abdallah, the son of Akram Musa Abdallah, who is under indictment for allegedly lying to FBI agents about his fundraising activities on behalf of HLF. (The son of another Flying Imam, Mahmud Sulaiman, was not arrested, though he was said to be in attendance at the shooting session.) Not so coincidentally, Shahin *père* and *fils*, along with the Abdallahs, help run an Islamic school in south Phoenix—along with yet another Flying Imam, Didmar Faja. I wonder if they're teaching that whoever "saves one life, he saves all human life, and whoever kills one person, he kills all humankind." After all, as Shahin says (to Western media types), "that is what Islam is all about."

CAIR's Congressman

The most intriguing element of the Flying Imams misadventure is the use these American Islamists made of the strategy that most cleanly separates Muslim Brotherhood philosophy from al Qaeda philosophy. Mentioned explicitly in *The Project*, the 1982 plan seized from Youssef Nada and employed by Islamists from Banna forward, it is the ploy of infiltrating and co-opting government rather than levying forcible war against it. Thus was Keith Ellison a featured speaker at the 2006 NAIF conference, fresh from the national election two weeks earlier that made him the first avowed Muslim member of Congress.

At least, he is now known as Keith Ellison. The Congressman has used various aliases during his scoundrel's career: Keith Hakim, Keith Muhammad, Keith X Ellison, Keith Ellison-Muhammad, etc. Even more than President Obama, he is the embodiment of Islam and the Left, joined at the hip. Like Obama, he emerged from the Left's radical hothouse, in Ellison's case as a shock trooper for Louis Farrakhan's racist, separatist Nation of Islam. Powerline's invaluable Scott Johnson recounted in a devastating 2006 profile ("Louis Farrakhan's First Congressman"[20]) that Ellison was born a Catholic in Detroit and converted to Islam as an undergrad at Wayne State University. While at the University of Minnesota Law School, he penned two columns for the local daily, under the name "Keith Hakim," in which he defended Farrakhan's anti-Semitism and demanded reparations for slavery (though he was big enough to agree that reparations mightn't be necessary if American blacks were given a separate homeland). Ellison championed the appearance of the Black Panther icon Stokely Carmichael at the law school on the topic of "Zionism: Imperialism, White Supremacy, or Both?"—shunning pleas from Jewish law students against what they correctly anticipated would be a stridently anti-Semitic speech.

For Ellison, the practice of law (which he began in 1990) was unacquainted with the practice of lawfulness: he scoffed at the income tax laws and campaign finance laws; his driver's license was suspended numerous times for contemptuously ignoring parking and moving violations. Meantime, he became a community activist (which seems indistinguishable from a community organizer), becoming a fixture at anti-police protests and rallies in favor of thugs and cop-killers. At one rally for gangbangers who had planned and carried out the execution-style murder of Police Officer Jerry Haff as he sipped a cup of coffee in a restaurant, Ellison roused the rabble outside the courthouse with a chant of "We don't get no justice, you don't get no peace!" At a February 2000 fundraiser for the defense of the former Symbionese Liberation Army radical Kathleen Soliah, he lavished praise upon her: she had been one of those who had been "fighting for freedom in the Sixties and Seventies"—evidently, by murdering a police officer, to which she later pleaded guilty.

Attesting to the trajectory of both Minnesota and Democratic Party politics, Ellison was elected as a Democrat to the House of Representatives in 2006. He was strongly backed by CAIR, with such notables as Hamas-smooching Nihad Awad drumming up Muslim support at his campaign events. The binding tie to CAIR made the NAIF conference a busy weekend for Minnesota's newest federal lawmaker: the scheduling conflict created by the conference meant Ellison had to appear by video at CAIR's annual fundraising convention in Washington.

The congressman has more than made up for it since then, however. He has continued to appear regularly at CAIR functions—even after the Justice Department (a) identified CAIR as an unindicted coconspirator in the HLF prosecution, and (b) proved that CAIR had been formed by members of the Hamas-created Islamic Association of Palestine, who had been caught on a wiretap, only months earlier, discussing the need both to derail the Oslo Peace Accords and to create a new U.S. entity that might be able to support Hamas without being labeled as terrorist.[21] Ellison, furthermore, made time in his busy schedule to join CAIR in seeking financial support for Sami al-Arian, the founder of the murderous Palestinian Islamic Jihad who: (a) had been convicted the previous year for conspiring to support a terrorist organization, (b) had been shown by the trial evidence to be a top PIJ official and fundraiser, and (c) had praised PIJ's terrorist attacks. At the time of Ellison's appearance—during which he assured fans that he was lobbying his fellow members of Congress on al-Arian's behalf—al-Arian was fighting efforts by the Justice Department to force him to tell federal grand juries what he knows about the financing of terrorism.

In September 2009, members of Arizona's U.S. congressional delegation (Senator Jon Kyl and Congressmen Trent Franks and John Shadegg) were sufficiently alarmed by Ellison's exertions on behalf of CAIR to write him a highly unusual letter, imploring him to avoid contact with CAIR's Arizona chapter and pointing out that his support of the organization "would undermine the legitimate concerns of federal investigators about CAIR's relationship to foreign terrorist organizations." Ellison dismissed the letter as "ridiculous," risibly countering that "I would never associate myself with anyone even soft on terrorism."[22] Dr. M. Zuhdi Jasser, an authentic Muslim moderate who chides CAIR and other Islamist organizations for obfuscating the connection between Islamist ideology and terrorism, fared no better with Ellison. In a Washington debate, Ellison launched a tirade, dripping with shameful race-baiting and, as Steve Emerson's Investigative Project on Terrorism reported, as much as calling Jasser an "Islamic 'Uncle Tom'":

> I think you give people license for bigotry. I think people who want to engage in nothing less than Muslim-hating really love you a lot because you give them freedom to do that. You say, "Yeah, go get after them." . . . [African-Americans are] familiar with people who would seek to ingratiate themselves with powerful people in the white community and would there turn them on the rest of us and give license to attack us all. Arguing "African-Americans are criminally inclined, they're all in gangs, they're all on welfare." Black people who say stuff like this. But what they're really trying to do is win themselves individual benefit at the expense of everyone else. . . . I don't

know you well enough to know that's what you're doing, but I must admit that when I heard you speaking, that's what I thought of.[23]

Back in November 2006, Ellison addressed the topic of "Imams and Politics" at the NAIF convention, dovetailing nicely with Omar Shahin's workshop the previous day on "Imams and the Media." During the evening of his speech, Ellison met with Shahin. The next day, Shahin and his fellow Flying Imams carried out the shenanigans that got them booted off US Airways Flight 300. Shahin, with the media along for the ride, returned to a US Airways ticket counter the next day, making a scene and decrying anti-Muslim discrimination—while CAIR screamed for a federal investigation into Muslim "profiling." A day later, Ellison wrote to the CEO of US Airways and the director of the Minneapolis Airports Commission demanding a meeting to discuss "discrimination" and the policies involving the removal of passengers from flights. Then Shahin was off to Washington to convene his protest (along with CAIR and congressional officials) at Reagan National Airport.[24] With the legal advice he told the media CAIR was providing, he launched the lawsuit that, with the help of a Leftist federal judge, has severely compromised the capacity of airlines, other carriers, stadiums, and convention centers to detect and prevent terrorist plots—while vesting traveling Islamists with a newfangled First Amendment right to intimidate and terrorize other passengers.

Meanwhile, the State Department *bragged* that the Flying Imams incident had spurred the government to subordinate American safety concerns to Muslim cultural sensibilities. The Homeland Security Department gave CAIR—remember, an unindicted co-conspirator in a terrorism prosecution—a taxpayer-funded platform to spout its Islamist propaganda, concurrently indoctrinating tens of thousands of security agents in some fine points of Islamist ideology. And as the Flying Imams sued an FBI national-security agent for doing his job (i.e., interrogating them after they'd caused a transparently premeditated commotion to frighten airline passengers), it emerged that both the FBI and the local police had been relying on none other than Omar Shahin, that Islamist agitator and Flying Imam-ringleader, as their "Muslim community liaison" in Phoenix.[25]

Perfect: the sabotage campaign in action.

chapter nineteen

NO STRONGER RETROGRADE FORCE EXISTS IN THE WORLD

When he was in college, Keith "Hakim" took pen in hand to demand reparations for slavery. This was years before he re-reinvented himself as Congressman Keith Ellison, Democratic light of the Islamist Left. Ellison, of course, had grown up over a century after slavery had ended. Had ended *in America*, that is. Evidently, it did not dawn on young Hakim that there is still slavery aplenty in the world . . . and systematized discrimination . . . and the sexual abuse of indentured young girls. Or, more likely, he knew it but chose not to dwell it. He had, after all, just found Islam, and it is in *Dar al-Islam* where one finds these abuses.

How could that be in the twenty-first century? Well, if he were alive today, Winston Churchill—he of the bronze bust so unceremoniously expelled from the White House in the opening hours of the Obama administration—could have explained. Churchill had encountered Islam as a young man serving in the British army, both in the Afghan/Pakistan border region and in Khartoum, which is to say in places that continue, even today, to be cauldrons of Islamist terror. Ever observant, he wrote:

> How dreadful are the curses which Mohammedanism lays on its votaries! Besides the fanatical frenzy, which is as danger-ous in a man as hydrophobia in a dog, there is this fearful fatalistic apathy. Improvident habits, slovenly systems of agriculture, sluggish methods of commerce, and insecurity of property exist wherever the followers of the Prophet rule or live. A degraded sensualism deprives this life of its grace and refinement; the next of its dignity and sanctity. The fact that in Mohammedan law every woman must belong to some man as his absolute property—either as a child, a wife, or a concu-bine—must delay the final extinction of slavery until the faith of Islam has ceased to be a great power among men.[1]

Islam remains a great power among men, so slavery has not seen its final extinction. It is that simple. Though officially out-lawed, slavery is practiced still in the Kingdom of Saudi Arabia, as well as in Sudan, Mauritania, and other Muslim countries. The endorsement is in the scriptures. "Forbidden to you are . . . mar-ried women, except those whom you own as slaves," pronounces Sura 4:23–24. Robert Spencer elaborates:

> The Islamic legal manual *'Umdat al-Salik*, which carries the endorsement of Al-Azhar University, the most respected au-thority in Sunni Islam, stipulates: "When a child or a woman is taken captive, they become slaves by the fact of capture, and the woman's previous marriage is immediately annulled."

Why? So that they are free to become the concubines of their captors. . . . The Prophet Muhammad originated such legislation. After one successful battle, he told his men, "Go and take any slave girl." He took one for himself also.[2]

Next case.

Rapine, meanwhile, is the way of war in Sudan.[3] The invaluable Spencer, again, describes the sanction of the Prophet:

[W]hen Muhammad's men emerged victorious in another battle, they presented him with an ethical question: "We took women captives, and we wanted to do *'azl [coitus interruptus]* with them." Muhammad told them: "It is better that you should not do it, for Allah has written whom He is going to create till the Day of Resurrection.'" When Muhammad said "it is better that you should not do it," he was referring to *coitus interruptus*, not to raping their captives. He took that for granted.[4]

Child brides in arranged marriages are still a staple of Islamic countries and territories. When pressed about this—however rarely—by the pusillanimous press, the muftis' explanation is straightforward: Mohammed, Islam's perfect role model, took Aisha as his wife when she was six years old, then waited until she was all of nine to consummate the arrangement.[5] End of discussion. In Iran, when the parliament, in a radical move, voted to raise the minimum marriage age for girls from nine to fourteen (which would simply have put them on a par with boys—a radical concept in and of itself), the mullahs vetoed it.[6] Indeed, as Spencer points out, the Koran assumes that men will not only marry but occasionally *divorce* their prepubescent wives: Discussing the waiting period required to ensure that the woman is not pregnant at the time of divorce, Sura 65:4 instructs: "If you are in doubt concerning those of your wives who have ceased menstruating, know that their waiting period shall be three months. The same shall apply to *those who have not yet menstruated*" (emphasis added).[7]

These are truths about Islam. They are not accepted by all Muslims, or, at least, are tacitly ignored by many. Churchill appreciated the distinction between Islam and Muslims, too. "Individual Moslems," he stressed, "may show splendid qualities. Thousands become the brave and loyal soldiers of the Queen: all know how to die." The problem was not the people, it was the doctrine. "The influence of the religion paralyses the social development of those who follow it," he averred. "No stronger retrograde force exists in the world. Far from being moribund, Mohammedanism is a militant and proselytising faith."[8]

Islam is still a militant and proselytizing faith. Its influence is still paralyzing because, if strictly followed, the unadorned doctrine frowns on modernity—frowns on the engine of enlightenment, reason itself. As my friend the conservative blogger known as Tiger Hawk has observed, "The *umma* persecuted its own Thomas Aquinas." Ibn Rushd Averroes was the twelfth-century Andalusian Muslim who translated and preserved the work of Aristotle, which, Tiger Hawk notes, is "the foundation of Western scientific achievement." It is a debt the West will forever owe the Muslim world. But Averroes also proposed that Islam accommodate Aristotelian philosophy. For that, he was persecuted. The late Oriana Fallaci put it this way:

> Islam has always persecuted and silenced its intelligent men.
> I remind you of Averroes who for his distinction between
> Faith and Reason was accused of heterodoxy by the caliphs
> and forced to flee. Then, imprisoned like a criminal. Then,
> confined to his home and humiliated to such a degree that

when rehabilitated he no longer had any desire to live and died within a few months.[9]

Fallaci wrote those words in her polemical book *The Force of Reason*. A tireless advocate for human freedom, she had spent much of her life fighting fascism. That enemy was defeated because those who confronted it—the Churchills, the Fallacis— were from a different time, a time when security required a plain-spoken acknowledgment of danger. Without speaking a peril's name, without endeavoring to understand it, there could be no security.

Fallaci, like Churchill, fully understood the difference between doctrine and people, between Islam and Muslims. Her regard for the sensibility of individuals, however, did not pre-vent her from speaking plainly about the effects of ideology on the world around her—the effects of an elaborate, long-standing, painstakingly conceived Muslim Brotherhood strategy to Islami-cize the free world. Europe, she observed, was becoming "an Islamic province, an Islamic colony. . . . In each of our cities lies a second city: a Muslim city, a city run by the Quran."[10] It is not "divide and conquer." Voluntary apartheid is more a matter of "bore in and conquer."

Alas, the dangers of ignoring today's peril are the same as they were in the days of Nazi fascism, Japanese imperialism, and Soviet Communism. But the times are strikingly different. We live in an era when Yusuf Qaradawi can freely shout from the mountaintops that Islam will conquer America and conquer Europe. We live in a time when the imam of Saudi Arabia's King Fahd Defense Academy can bray with immunity: "We will con-trol the land of the Vatican; we will control Rome and introduce Islam in it. Yes, the Christians, who carve crosses on the breasts of the Muslims . . . will yet pay us the *jiziya* [poll tax], in humiliation, or they will convert to Islam."[11] Yet, speaking aloud one's witness to these proclamations, and the work being done night and day to bring them to fruition, is an indictable offense.

Again, Islam hasn't changed. From our perspective, it is exactly as it was when Jefferson matter-of-factly reported the Tripolitan ambassador's explanation: Muslim pirates would continue terrorizing infidel shippers because Islam made it the jihadists' "right and duty to make war upon them wherever they could be found, and to make slaves of all they could take as Prisoners." What has changed is the West. When he was in a position to do so, Jefferson sent the marines to confront the Barbary Pirates until the threat receded. To the contrary, Fallaci, at seventy-five and stricken with cancer, lived out her last days under indictment in her native Italy—not Iran, but Italy—for "defaming Islam."[12]

The Sacking of Stephen Coughlin

Like Winston Churchill, Stephen Coughlin first crossed paths with Islam during his military service. A lawyer and a military intelligence officer in the U.S. army reserves, he was tasked with investigating and prosecuting an intellectual property case in Pakistan. Through that experience, he first became familiar with sharia. It was the late Nineties, and the strikes against Khobar Towers, the U.S. embassies in east Africa, and then the U.S.S. *Cole* made manifest that "asymmetrical" attacks, carried out by an enemy whose motivation was Islamist ideology, were the exigencies in our threat mosaic. The 9/11 atrocities and the military response ordered by President George W. Bush ensured that a strategy fitted for such an enemy would be essential.

At least Major Coughlin assumed it would be essential. In the history of warfare, it had always been elementary that to defeat thine enemy it was first necessary to know him. Coughlin knew

Islamist ideology like no one in America's armed forces. With his inquisitive and linear mind, he had made it his business to understand sharia. Coughlin figured it was the military's business to understand it, too, since government's first duty is to secure the governed. He was dismayed, though, to find himself virtually alone in that assessment.

It wasn't just that he was the only scholar of Islamic jurisprudence—the foundation of Islamic warfare—among the intelligence advisers to the Joint Chiefs of Staff. He sometimes seemed to be the only person interested in the subject—or, with political correctness enveloping military culture, the only person who didn't want to hide under his desk when the word "Islam" came up. So in 2007—five years after Coughlin had begun briefing top Defense officials about Islamist ideology, nearly seven years after 9/11, fourteen years after the World Trade Center bombing, and over a quarter century after the Iranian Revolution and the shocking murder of 241 marines and naval personnel in their Beirut barracks—Coughlin composed a scholarly, 300-page thesis, warning of the dangers of failing to understand the history, theory, and modern-day applications of jihad.[13] He explained that America faced Islamist enemies who, in reliance on a centuries-old ideology, were committed to the global implementation of sharia, and the consequent establishment of Islamic societies, through both violent and nonviolent means. In particular, he warned that the Muslim Brotherhood had a plan to destroy America from within, and that it was using agents and front groups in the United States to carry out the strategy.

For his trouble, Steve Coughlin was fired.

Coughlin was summoned to a meeting in 2007 with Hesham Islam, a top aide to Deputy Defense Secretary Gordon England. Relying on his excellent military sources, the *Washington Times'* Bill Gertz recounted that Islam browbeat Coughlin in an effort to get him to soften his views on jihad and Islamist ideology. Coughlin refused, and the brass decided not to renew his contract. Later, Islam reportedly referred to Coughlin as a "Christian zealot with a pen."[14]

Islamist Insider

Mr. Islam is quite the piece of work. He is a native Egyptian whose personal history, as he served it up and the Pentagon swallowed it whole, appears fictitious—though it did indicate an authentic animus against Israel. He was exposed as a fraud by my friend the indefatigable Claudia Rosett.[15] Islam claimed a boyhood memory of growing up in Cairo and "huddling in terror as Israeli bombs came raining down, demolishing much of the building around him and his family." As Claudia learned, there had been no Israeli bombing of Cairo. The family later moved to Baghdad right at the time Saddam Hussein was consolidating power, but Islam evidently has no teenage memories of the place or how his father came to be invited there by the Iraqi dictator. Next, Islam portrayed himself as a young "merchant mariner adrift for three days in the Arabian Sea after an Iranian torpedo sunk his 16,000-ton cargo ship, drowning all but Islam and four of his crewmates." But Islam wouldn't name the ship, the date of the sinking, the other survivors, and so on.

Islam finally came to the U.S., quickly married an American pen-pal with whom he'd been corresponding, and eventually joined the navy. He rose to the mid-level rank of commander in an unremarkable twenty-year career as an electronics technician. Unremarkable, that is, until he was discovered by England— a former defense contractor, known by insiders as "Gullible Gordon," who suddenly found himself Secretary of the Navy in 2001, and, in the post-9/11 fashion, was hot for a Muslim pres-

306

ence to demonstrate his oceans of sensitivity.[16] When England moved into the Pentagon's number two slot in 2005 (upon Paul Wolfowitz's exit), he brought Islam along as his "special assistant for international affairs."

So what qualifies Hesham Islam as an expert in either Islamic doctrine or international affairs? Well, on the former, he's a Muslim, and that apparently carries more weight than actually having studied Islamic jurisprudence—as if, say, your cousin Ted was a better authority on American history than Paul Johnson.

As far as international affairs go, Islam brought two credentials to the table. First, a master's degree in "national-security affairs" awarded in 1992 by the Naval Postgraduate School in Monterey, California. Toward that end, Islam wrote a 139-page thesis called, "The Roots of Regional Ambition," which explained that the big problem for America in the Middle East was [drum-roll . . .] *Israel.* Claudia describes it:

> he devoted dozens of pages to lambasting Israel, and the influ-
> ence of American Jews on U.S. politics. He deplored "Israeli
> activities which have detrimentally affected U.S. objectives
> but which have continued with impunity." He argued that
> U.S. support for Israel "has negatively affected the attain-
> ment of U.S. objectives in the Middle East." He blamed the
> influence of American Jews on U.S. policy for a host of ills,
> ranging from Arab "retaliation" against Americans, to jobs
> lost overseas, to hampering sales of "defensive arms to friendly
> Arab states."

Ah yes, right. And what was Commander Islam's other qualification to be in the Pentagon's inner sanctum? To be the man England called "my personal close confidante," "my interlocutor," and "a man who represents me to the international community" and "assists me in my own outreach efforts"? To be in a position to cashier the Joint Chiefs' only scholar of Islamic jurisprudence during a war based on Islamic jurisprudence? Why, his Islamist connections, of course.

Mr. Islam, Rosett details, became England's "point man for Pentagon outreach to Muslim Groups." How shocking to learn that the groups Islam reached out and touched included none other than the Brotherhood-created Islamic Society of North America. England's energetic, highly-motivated assistant had him hosting ISNA delegations at the Pentagon and in England's office. Islam ensured that Defense Department brass was front and center at ISNA events, and even set up booths at the organization's annual convention in order to recruit Muslim chaplains and linguists.[17] (Where else but from ISNA would we want to stock up our counterterrorism resources?) The contacts and sessions continued even after the Justice Department had determined—on the basis of evidence seized from Ismail Elbarasse years before—that ISNA was a Muslim Brotherhood partner and an unindicted coconspirator in the conspiracy, orchestrated by the Brotherhood, to raise millions for Hamas.

Moreover, it later emerged, thanks to more digging by Steve Emerson, that Islam had arranged meetings for England with (a) Husam al-Dairi, a top member of the Syrian Muslim Brotherhood, and (b) Farid Aboud, a Lebanese ambassador whom the Bush administration was shunning because he was a pro-Hezbollah proxy for the Syrian government (which was then, and is still, under suspicion for the murder of the Lebanese Prime Minister Rafik Hariri).[18] The al-Dairi meeting was cancelled at the last minute when a State Department official got wind of it and went ballistic over the prospect of contacts between a senior U.S. government official and the Muslim Brotherhood—communication with which was against U.S. policy. The Aboud meeting happened, to the consternation of top administration figures.

Need more about Hesham Islam's illustrious tenure as a Pentagon insider? Paul Sperry reports that Islam met regularly with Saudi government officials lobbying for the release and repatriation of Saudi subjects who were being held at Guantanamo Bay (because for whatever peculiar reason—no doubt having to do with the weather, the moons of Saturn, or Israel—Saudis seem to account for an inordinately high percentage of the anti-American terrorist population). Relying on Islam's advice, dozens of Saudis were sprung from captivity.[19] By the way, here's a shocker: Have you heard that as many as 20 percent of the terrorists released from Gitmo have returned to the jihad? (The figure is indubitably higher: we only count those recidivists we've actually encountered on the battlefield or about whom we've gotten reliable intelligence, not the hundreds whose whereabouts and activities are unknown.) Released detainees—including graduates of the Saudi Kingdom's risible "rehabilitation program"—are now top figures in al Qaeda's satellites in Yemen and Afghanistan. Gitmo has gone from the place that keeps us safe from them to the notch on their belts that raises their stature in the Islamist pantheon.[20]

"In effect," a senior army intelligence official told Sperry, "we've got terrorist supporters calling the shots on our policies toward Muslims from the highest levels."[21] That's quite a story . . . yet the legacy media did not find anything of interest to cover in the sacking of Steve Coughlin. There was outrage in the conservative blogosphere, but the Pentagon was effective in directing Coughlin (then still under contract) to stay mum while Islam freely spoke, at least if the journalist's name wasn't Rosett or Emerson. Islam didn't provide facts, just pathos: a sob story about how he no longer had a landline telephone because, as a

Muslim, he found he "got a lot of hate messages on the phone" after 9/11. Why do I think Claudia Rosett will someday learn that those "calls" went either to the bombed-out home in Cairo or the sunken ship in the Arabian Sea?

True to form, ISNA also stepped up to the plate, swinging away on Hesham Islam's behalf. Writing for *al-Jezeera* (surprise!), ISNA's Executive Director Louay Safi lashed out at the embattled Defense official's critics, contending that the scrutiny of Mr. Islam was—you guessed it—a "neocon" conspiracy against "Muslim Americans critical of their inhumane and exploitative foreign policy agenda" (i.e., the effort, however futile, to give Muslims an alternative to Islamism), as well as against "main stream Muslim organizations" that have "expressed concerns about the dire conditions of Palestinians under occupation" (i.e., supporters of Hamas).[22]

Safi's zealous backing of his friend Islam made perfect sense, for he had forged a close relationship with the Pentagon.[23] Despite ISNA's history, and Safi's, the Defense Department brought Safi in to give our troops instruction on the finer points of Islam right before they deployed to Afghanistan and Iraq. And why not? Safi, after all, had served as the research director at the International Institute of Islamic Thought. Recall that IIIT is the Brotherhood-founded think-tank dedicated to the Islamicization of knowledge that had been a major financial backer of Sami al-Arian, the now-convicted terror-supporter.

In fact, the FBI recorded al-Arian chatting with Safi in 1995: Safi fretting that al-Arian would be negatively affected by President Clinton's then-recent executive order prohibiting financial transactions with terrorist organizations.[24] The Saudis also promoted the IIIT to the U.S. government as a go-to Islamic authority, and one eventual result was the placement of Abdurahman Alamoudi in a key position for certifying Muslim chaplains to serve in America's armed forces. Safi, furthermore, was tied to the Virginia-based Safa Group by a government search-warrant for the Safa offices.[25] As we saw in tracing the history of the Dar al-Jihrah Mosque in Virginia, the "Safa Group" is the successor to the Saudi-backed SAAR Foundation that dissolved under suspicions it was funneling millions of dollars to terrorist organizations. (Though the Justice Department continues to investigate the Safa Group, neither it nor Louay Safi has been charged with a crime.)

Obviously, why would we want Steve Coughlin directing the Islamic education of our troops when we can have Louay Safi?

Lieutenant Colonel Joseph C. Myers could tell you why. He is a flinty army adviser to the Air Command and Staff College, and he had the patriotic courage to call Coughlin's termination "an act of intellectual cowardice." LTC Myers explained:

> I have long argued and wondered why our military from senior leaders down to tactical level are so unread and unstudied on Islam, jihad in Islam, even the topic of terrorism. I have often contrasted this unconscionable wartime state of affairs, with the due diligence the US military showed since I was a cadet at West Point 30 years ago, where we lived, ate, slept and drank Soviet warfighting doctrine. . . . Today we are in the process of prosecuting a war, that from doctrinal perspective, we fundamentally do not understand. . . . We have not studied Islamic Law and few have seen or heard of even the English translation of it that has been in print for years. . . .
>
> Coughlin has briefed senior Marine Corps leaders and staff and has presented his thesis in various military educational venues . . . by all accounts the veil of ignorance is lifted for all but only a few who are afraid to face what Islamic Law, doctrinal Islam, says and means with respect to jihad and how

it plays out across the Islamic world from al Qaida, to the Saudi government, to Pakistan to the Muslim Brotherhood. . . . He argues we have in fact intellectually pre-empted our military decision-making process and intelligence preparation of the battlefield process, the critical step 3—"evaluate the threat." Strategically we have failed to do that by substituting policy for military analysis, substituting cliché for competent decision processes. . . . We began on September 12, 2001 with "Islam is a religion of peace," which soothed ideological sentiments of many but has failed us strategically, [and] short-stopped the objective, systemic evaluation of the threat doctrine.

"Islam is a religion of peace" is fine for public policy statements, but is not and cannot be the point of departure for competent military or intelligence analysis. . . . It is in fact a logical flaw under any professional research methodology. . . . You have stated the conclusion before you have done the analysis.[26]

In a 2002 BBC poll, Winston Churchill was voted the greatest Briton of all time. To be blunt, though, this is no longer Churchill's West. In Churchill's West, you did the analysis first. Now, if you intend to speak about Islam, it'd better damn well be the Koran according to ISNA, Louay Safi, and the Muslim Brotherhood, as brought to you courtesy of Hesham Islam and your Islamophilic United States government. If it's not, you will be snuffed out—by government strangulation and media isolation, if not terrorist immolation.

chapter twenty

ON LANGUAGE

C learly, it did not take an Obama administration to make talking about Islamism the equivalent of a capital crime. All the Obama Left has had to do in this regard is step up the pace.

It is one of the great ironies that George W. Bush stirred the Left to depths of dementia uncharted in American history. While President Bush had conservative instincts in significant areas— e.g, life, national defense, the need for judicial restraint—he was a starry-eyed Wilsonian on foreign policy. Remarkably, while the most deranged Leftists painted him as the unilateralist cowboy of the Christian Right (whatever that is), the beef of smart liberals like Ken Pollack was that Bush hijacked the progressive dream of remaking the Islamic World . . . and then brought the project into disrepute by purportedly implementing it incompetently and (of course) on the cheap.[1] In any event, incidents such as an afore-mentioned State Department official's having the good sense to stop Deputy Defense Secretary England from having a *tête-à-tête* with the Muslim Brotherhood were notable in the Bush era because the currents so often ran in the opposite direction.

Even in the gimlet clarity of 9/11, President Bush went to absurd lengths to absolve Islam from Islamist terror. As former Attorney General Michael Mukasey tartly observes, "Imagine FDR telling Congress on December 8, 1941 that the peaceful Shinto religion had been kidnapped by a cabal of militarists."[2] The first-term Bush, however, at least understood that it was "either with us or with them"—Islamist terrorists had to be rooted out and the rogue regimes that enabled them brought to heel. The second-term Bush, to the contrary, was an aggressive Islamophile who insisted that the "Religion of Peace" was not merely something we needed to work around but an actual asset in the war. The war, moreover, increasingly became not so much a war as a sociology experiment in a chimera called "Islamic democracy"—at least from our side; on the Islamist side, it always was and remains a war. This was all the license needed by the transnational progressives who pervade the State Department, the intelligence community, and the Washington hierarchy of such executive agencies as the FBI and the new monstrosity known as the Department of Homeland Security (DHS).

Thus it was that in mid-2008, the Bush administration declared a jihad on *jihad*—the word, that is. Based on guidance promulgated by DHS's "Office for Civil Rights and Civil Liberties" (and long championed by the executive branch's progressive legions), the government endeavored to purge from our lexicon such terms as *jihad*, *jihadism*, *Islamo-fascism*, and *mujahideen*.[3] These terms, and others like them, were, of course, the very ones security-minded Neanderthals like Steve Coughlin had had the

314

temerity to urge government officials to study, in order to know the enemy.

Not necessary, the Big Thinkers decided. What we needed, instead, was to condition ourselves, against reason and experience, to accept the premise that there is no true Islamic component in the terrorist threat confronting the United States. "The civilized world is facing a 'global' challenge, which," the guidance assured us, "*transcends* geography, culture, and *religion*" (emphasis added). To DHS, that challenge, a siege of savage strikes by Muslims—occurring the world over for what is now decades—had nothing to do with their being, you know, Muslims.

The guidance, an official explained, was a strategy for influencing an *outside* audience, Muslims living beyond our shores. No doubt, this is what DHS officials told themselves. They've probably even convinced themselves. But, based on a quarter-century in government, much of it in working on national security matters, I can attest that such a strategy comes into existence because its proponents are convinced that they need to do a better job influencing government's most important *inside* audience: the American people. For some reason, the public fails to grasp the just-must-be-truism that Islam is the solution, not the problem. And don't think the salesmen peddling this Kool-Aid have not drunk deep. Maybe they imbibe because they really believe it. Maybe they do so because that's the way the wind is blowing and they hope to ride that wind to the next career plateau. But whatever the motive, gulp it they do.

DHS cannot prove Islam is not a big part of the problem any more than it could prove that Islam is a religion of peace (or of "love and peace," as Bush's Secretary of State Condoleezza Rice liked to say). Instead, as LTC Myers lamented, government enshrines as policy its most fervent hopes, as if hopes were facts. Naysayers are dared to naysay . . . at the risk of ostracism from

315

polite, media-driven society—with the occasional renegade like Coughlin served up as a public warning not to dare leave the ideological plantation.

Thus, for example, the guidance asserts: "The fact is that Islam and secular democracy are fully compatible—in fact, they can make each other stronger. Senior officials should emphasize this positive fact." Well, while saying so may explain my being dropped from the Christmas—er, Holiday card list, this "positive fact" is not a fact at all. It's a theory, and a wayward one. Islamic culture does not have a secular democratic tradition. As we've seen, the very concept of *secular* is foreign to Islam, which aspires to be not just a religious creed but a full-blown cultural, legal, and political system, sprung from precepts dictated to Mohammed by Allah Himself.

Free democratic systems, moreover, are based on notions of liberty, private property, and equality. In stark contrast, many Islamic traditions reject freedom of conscience, freedom to make law that countermands *sharia*, economic freedom, equality for Muslims and non-Muslims, and equality for men and women, to name just a few key divergences. But even if none of this were so, mightn't Occam's razor have reared its head by now? After fourteen centuries, there is no secular democratic tradition in Islamic society. Given that secular democracy is the best guarantor of liberty and prosperity, is it not self-evident that some precinct of the umma would have adopted it by now, without any help from us, if Islamic society were innately receptive?

After paying lip-service to the notion that "the terms we use must be accurate and descriptive," the DHS guidance urged that we drop *jihad* from our lexicon, despite its being a perfectly accurate descriptor. According to DHS and the "influential Muslim Americans" with whom it consulted, the true meaning of *jihad* is the subject of honest-to-goodness dispute. Indeed, DHS, in its best moral equivalence, framed the disputants in this supposed controversy as "polemic[ists]"—rather than, as is actually the case, one group accurately invoking *jihad* as a divinely sanctioned war to implement sharia versus another trying, whether out of good intentions or duplicity, to reinvent *jihad* as the virtuous striving to become a better person.

And who are these "influential Muslim Americans" the government consults? Somehow, it never seems to be Muslims like M. Zuhdi Jasser who advocate for a separation of mosque and state, who want to be seen in this society as Americans who happen to be Muslims. Instead the Pentagon finds its Hesham Islams and Louay Safis, the Transportation Safety Administration turns to CAIR, and DHS leans on the Muslim Public Affairs Council—the Islamists we found campaigning for Obamacare in Chapter 9. MPAC was quick to issue a press release lauding the new DHS guidance and patting itself on the back for both its "regular . . . engagement with government agencies including [DHS]," and its long advocacy of a "nuanced approach" that stresses "the importance of decoupling Islam with [*sic*] terrorism." Unmentioned, of course, was MPAC's history of lobbying the government for the removal of Hezbollah, Hamas, and Palestinian Islamic Jihad from the government's lists of designated terrorist organizations.

The incentive of government's Islamist advisers is patent—to anyone willing to open his eyes. With the Islam bleached out of Islamic terror, it becomes a simple matter to portray the inevitable Muslim violence as driven by "regional" concerns, as a predictable reaction to bad American policies, or as legitimate "resistance" against purported oppressors. It becomes far easier to camouflage creeping sharia as just another form of "progress," "reform," or "diversity." With Islam off the table, we no longer worry about—or defend ourselves against—a global movement, driven by a common religious ideology which, far from a perversion of Muslim doctrine, is both well-rooted in scripture and a lot more mainstream than DHS's consultants let on.

With such splendid advisers, should we be surprised that government preposterously sees as much validity in the revisionist smiley-face jihad as in the holy war of rich historical pedigree? And all the while, officials miss the nonviolent advances in this civilizational struggle that are being choreographed by these self-same advisers.

Then there's the heart of the DHS's rationale for the proposed language purge: "Many so-called [*so-called?*] 'Islamic' terrorist groups *twist* and exploit *the tenets of Islam to justify violence*" (emphasis added.) *Really?* The Koran (which, again, Muslims take to be the verbatim word of Allah) commands, in Sura 9:123 (to take just one of many examples), "O ye who believe, fight those of the disbelievers who are near you, and let them find harshness in you, and know that Allah is with those who keep their duty unto him." What part of that does DHS suppose needs to be "twisted" by terrorists in order to gull fellow Muslims into believing Islam commands Muslims to "fight those of the disbelievers who are near you, and let them find harshness in you"?

The "Overseas Contingency Operation" against "Violent Extremists"

The Obama administration has been roundly ridiculed, and deservedly so, for its aversion to the language of war—indeed, for the word *war* itself. From the Bush language purge, though, it was but a short hop to this sorry destination. Short and inevitable.

Saul Alinsky, Obama's community-organizing inspiration, waxed at length about language in *Rules for Radicals*, about the power of words to inspire . . . or to enervate. "In communication as in thought, we must ever strive toward simplicity" when it is our purpose to inspire. Such a purpose calls for "a determination not to detour around reality." (E.g., you say things like: *You're either with us, or you're against us.*) Symmetrically, an opposite purpose calls for an opposite approach. Avoid the "force, vigor, and simplicity" of the right word, Alinsky wrote, and "we soon become averse to thinking in vigorous, simple, honest terms." For those who wish to deaden rather than invigorate the spirit, the task is "to invent sterilized synonyms." Alinksy taught that such "new words mean something different, so that they tranquilize us, begin to shepherd our mental processes off the main, conflict-ridden, grimy, and realistic power-paved highway of life."[4]

The president learned his lessons well: bloodless prolixity deftly imposed from who knows where within Leviathan's sprawl. It was not DHS, the FBI, or even the National Intelligence Directorate but *the Office of Management and Budget* that advised the Pentagon that the word *war* is now out. "This administration prefers to avoid using the term 'Long War' or 'Global War on Terror,'" said the new, March 2009 guidance. Our warriors were curtly told, "Please use 'Overseas Contingency Operation.'"[5]

That this "overseas contingency" on which we are "operating" has left a rather large (and still unfilled) hole in the ground in lower Manhattan apparently was beside the point. Or, better, was exactly the point. *War* is a powerful word, redolent of power, force, zeal, and national purpose. That is why the Left routinely invokes *war* in its beloved campaigns against poverty, obesity, and other abstractions. Real wars, the forcible defense of our nation and the pursuit of our interests, are to be avoided. So are real enemies. Thus came the complementary announcement (an affirmation filed in federal court by Attorney General Eric Holder) that "enemy combatants" aren't *enemy combatants* anymore. They are simply "individuals currently detained at Guantanamo Bay."

Unfortunately, that formulation ran the risk that we might confuse jihadists with Cuban refugees. During the Clinton administration, in which Holder served as Deputy Attorney General, those apprehended while seeking to escape Communist tyranny also became known as "individuals currently detained at Guantanamo Bay"—a policy aggressively defended by the Justice Department at the time, without much harrumphing from the Left. Perhaps that's why Holder interchangeably used "individuals captured or apprehended in connection with armed conflicts and counterterrorism operations"—more precise, though not quite as catchy.

As in the final Bush years "Islam" is not to be uttered in conjunction with "terror." Our "contingency" is only with "violent extremists," and we wouldn't presume to suggest that they are motivated by anything other than, say, George Bush, Abu Ghraib, or the existence of Guantanamo Bay. In Obamalogic, people who live in foreign sharia societies where women are stoned for adultery somehow appreciate the American jurisprudential distinction between detention under the laws of war and detention under civilian due process. And what do you know? Just like the American Left, they turn out to be profoundly offended by the military detention. That, we're told, is the root cause of terro— er, violent extremism . . . notwithstanding that there was no Gitmo on 9/11 or during the raft of atrocities that predated it. The word *terror* is passé. We wouldn't want to use a term that comes straight out of the Koran. Rather than *terrorism*, Obama's hapless Homeland Security Secretary Janet Napolitano explained, she prefers the term "man-caused disaster."

Bloodless is one thing, but mindless?

Your Universal Human Rights Under Sharia

None of this happens in a vacuum, of course. In 1990, the fifty-seven-nation bloc known as the Organization of the Islamic Conference promulgated the "Cairo Declaration," its answer to the Universal Declaration of Human Rights adopted by the nascent UN General Assembly in the aftermath of World War II. Indeed, the Cairo Declaration is also known as the "Universal Declaration of Human Rights In Islam." It "reaffirm[s] the civilizing and historic role of the Islamic Ummah which Allah made the best nation." President Obama may have a problem with American Exceptionalism, but the umma is not so diffident. The Cairo Declaration also demands that there be "no crime or punishment except as provided for in the Sharia," and it transparently rejects freedom of conscience.[6]

Sharia makes blasphemy a capital offense. It considers blasphemy to be any form of expression that casts Islam and its prophet in a poor light. Islamists refer to this concept as "defamation," and their apologists follow the script. But the equivalence is absurd. Defamation is *slander*: harming the reputation by the publication of things that are untrue. It is not defamation to call attention to the true parts of a doctrine that believers are embarrassed by or on which they would, for strategic reasons, prefer that you didn't focus. Islamists don't see, or at least won't acknowledge, this distinction because they see Islam as the one true religion, and therefore anything said against it must, by definition, be false . . . and punishable by death. In fact, in a recent case in Afghanistan, now under a new, U.S.-supported constitution that installed sharia as part of the fundamental law, merely expressing criticism of the crime of "insulting Islam" was itself deemed an offense against Islam by the court.[7] The other five billion of us, however, are under no duty to abide these Kafkaesque constructions.

Or are we? In March 2008, the UN's Orwellian "Human Rights Council," a subsidiary of the General Assembly, adopted a resolution proposed by Pakistan and sponsored by the OIC, entitled "Combating the Defamation of Religions." As Ibn Warraq and Michael Weiss recount, it defines *any* intellectual or moral criticism of "religion"—by which, transparently, is meant *Islam*—as "a human rights violation." By the OIC's lights, now endorsed by the UN, the legacy of 9/11 is not barbaric Islamist violence but an "intensification of the overall campaign of defamation of religions and incitement to religious hatred in general." Thus the resolution exhorts states to "deny impunity" to those guilty of words or deeds that the HRC deems critical of what it calls "religion"—again, meaning Islamism's totalitarian program.[8]

When Islamists say, "*Jump*," the West says, "How high?" It's no longer necessary for an Ayatollah Khomeini to issue a fatwa calling for the death of Salman Rushdie, or for Sheikh Qaradawi to stir the umma into a frenzy over unflattering cartoon depictions that portrayed the warrior prophet as, well, a warrior prophet. The culture will carry out all necessary stifling, and where social pressure doesn't suffice, the legal system will oblige.

Preemptive Capitulation

The Danish cartoons usefully trace the path from extortion by riot to what Roger Kimball calls society's "preemptive capitulation." In 2009, Yale University Press agreed to publish the author Jytte Klausen's scholarly book on the cartoon controversy . . . provided she agreed to strip out photos of the cartoons, as well as of such classic representations of Mohammed as Gustave Doré's illustration for Canto 28 (the "sowers of religious discord") of Dante's *Inferno*.[9]

Yale claimed its "reluctant" decision resulted from consultation with a panel of experts—including former government officials—who were concerned that Muslims could be stoked to violence if the images were not censored. The panel included such luminaries as *Newsweek*'s Fareed Zakaria, who supported censorship despite having only recently lectured readers that it was time to "learn to live with radical Islam," "to stop treating all Islamists as potential terrorists," and to mount "a spirited defense of our views and values."[10] Professor Klausen went along with the arrangement even though the purge undermined the core theory of the book—i.e., that the cause of rioting was not anything peculiar about Islam but rather merely the grubby political opportunism to which all humans are prone.[11]

In Canada, publishing the Danish cartoons got Ezra Levant hauled before one of the execrable Human Rights Commissions (HRCs) that have largely killed free speech (formerly known as a fundamental freedom in the Canadian Charter of Rights). At the same time, the irrepressible Mark Steyn was cited, along with *MacLean's*, when a handful of Muslim law students complained to a Canadian HRC about an excerpt of his bestselling book, *America Alone*, that the magazine had published under the title "The Future Belongs to Islam." Steyn and Levant fought back and won—as Mark points out in a foreword to *Shakedown*, Ezra's superb book on the debacle, "Canada's 'human rights' racket could not withstand the glare of publicity."[12]

Nevertheless, as they are the first to point out, Steyn and Levant had not only the invincibility of spirit but the platform and the means to fight the beast toe-to-toe. Most people do not. We are talking about a system in which the government brings the case in the name of the purportedly aggrieved Islamist and the target—i.e., the Canadian who has dared express himself— must bear both the indignity of the allegation and the expense of defending himself.

Terrorism researcher Rachel Ehrenfeld experienced a similar arrow in the Islamist quiver: "libel tourism." In 2003, she wrote a book entitled *Funding Evil*. Largely echoing assertions that had been made by the U.S. Treasury Department and former government officials, Ehrenfeld recounted that the Saudi banker Khalid bin Mahfouz, an intimate of the royal family, was alleged to have funneled money to terrorists.[13] Bin Mahfouz, who died in 2009, had conceded funding bin Laden at least once during the Afghan jihad against the Soviets. He was almost certainly the "bin Mahfouz" referred to on the aforementioned "Golden Chain" list of bin Laden donors. He ran an Islamic "charity," the Muwafaq Foundation, that the Treasury Department alleged was involved in terrorism financing. In addition, the man he retained to run it, one Yasin al-Qadi, was later formally designated as a global terrorist under U.S. law.[14]

Ehrenfeld recounted these facts and faithfully reported that Mahfouz had denied being involved in financing terrorism. Yet she was sued anyway . . . *in England*, where she had not attempted to market her book—but where as few as two dozen copies may have been purchased over the Internet, enough, a British judge said, to warrant exercising his jurisdiction.

It turned out that Mahfouz had discovered quite the racket. Unlike U.S. libel law, Britain imposes the burden of proof on the journalist to establish the truth of her allegations—an impossible standard for a reporter who lacks the power to subpoena her sources and free access to government files. On the one hand, since Mahfouz was one of the world's richest men (reportedly worth $3 billion), many journalists—and, more importantly, their potential publishers—could not afford the prospect of litigating against him before a hostile court in a foreign and exorbitantly expensive jurisdiction. On the other hand, ignoring the case meant a default judgment would be entered. Potentially, Mah-fouz could execute against any property held by the journalist or publisher overseas, and it would raise the specter of their arrest during any foreign travel.

So the Saudi sheikh became a serial "libel tourist" in the friendly British court. Voting with their wallets, journalists and publishers decided it wasn't worth the hassle and the expense to fight. Most of the three dozen libel tourism defendants caved in when Mahfouz merely threatened to sue them. The Cambridge University Press shamefully issued a public apology for publishing an academic book called *Alms for Jihad*—agreeing to pay damages, retrieve the books, and then pulp any unsold copies.

Ehrenfeld attempted to fight back by suing Mahfouz in the U.S., but the court found it did not have jurisdiction over him. She has since sought legislative fixes. So far, she's only gotten New York to agree that she should be able to prevent Mahfouz from enforcing the judgment against her in that state. But this is close to useless. He had no intention of trying to enforce the judgment in the U.S. For him, a $200,000 judgment against Ehrenfeld was chump change. What he wanted was to *have* the judgment as a weapon of intimidation against publishers. The message is plain: If you try to tell the story of Saudi complicity in jihadist terror, be prepared to pay dearly.

Publishers are hearing the message loud and clear. Before my *Willful Blindness* was published in 2008, a British book distributor contacted my friend and publisher Roger Kimball to inquire whether "there are any references to Saudis and terrorist[s] in the book. We are just concerned that this book could potentially create libel lawsuits as it could offend Saudis living in England."[15]

Cassandra Is Shown the Door

"I am not Geert Wilders." That was Professor Jytte Klausen's curt justification for acceding to Yale University Press's bowdlerizing of the cartoon-rioting study over which she'd labored so long. Wilders is a Dutch Parliamentarian in whose vocabulary the word *accede* does not appear.

In the great tradition of the Enlightenment, and to the horror of post-sovereign Europe, he faithfully reports what his senses perceive. Studying the Koran, he found exhortations to violence. Reading Allah's command in Sura 9:5 that "when the sacred months have passed," Muslims must "slay the idolaters wherever ye find them," he entertained the notions that it meant exactly what it said and that many Muslims would understand it as such. He noticed, moreover, that this passage reflected a recurrent theme in the Koran, and that the sentiment is even more pronounced in the Hadiths and other Islamic scriptures. He further noticed that Muslim militants seem to slay the idolaters and other unbelievers with some regularity. So he made a short film about the phenomenon called *Fitna*—an Arabic word for the cause of a deep, chaotic rift.

Fitna runs about fifteen minutes. It juxtaposes the faithful rendition of verses from the Koran, often recited by influential Islamic clerics, with acts of terrorism committed by Muslim militants who profess that they are simply putting those scriptures into action. For this *reporting* of hatred, he has been charged criminally in the Netherlands for *inciting* hatred—a case the prosecutors declined to bring only to be overruled by Amsterdam's craven court of appeals, which is paralyzed by dread of upsetting Muslims. The Netherlands, of course, was the home of Theo van Gogh, the producer whose film about the abuse of women in Islamic societies, *Submission*, inspired his brutal 2004 murder by a jihadist named Mohammed Bouyeri, and the flight to America of the screenplay's brilliant author, Ayaan Hirsi Ali. The Dutch takeaway from the van Gogh slaying is analogous to Sheikh Qaradawi's on the rape of women arrayed in Western fashion: He had it coming.

The censorious jurists fulminated over more than Wilder's irrefutable demonstration of the tight nexus between doctrine and savagery. The lightning rod had also drawn a disquieting parallel between the Koran and Adolf Hitler's polemic, *Mein Kampf*.

Let's set aside the fact that the German *kampf* and the Arabic *jihad* convey the same meaning: *struggle*. The judicial harrumphing against Wilders got me to wondering. A prosecutor always wants to begin his case with a bang: a piece of evidence that rivets the jury, making a powerful, lasting impression. In the Blind Sheikh prosecution, the most important case I ever tried, and one in which the challenge was to seize on something that would frame for the jury the many months of proof that were to follow, we finally settled on a blood-curdling videotape. It was the Blind Sheikh, speaking forcefully at a Hamas rally in the early Nineties: the cleric would make bold pronouncements, interrupted every few moment's by the mobs' refrain, *Allahu akbar! Allahu akbar!*

None of this was in English. We played it for our non-Arabic speaking jury all the same. Even without understanding the words, one could not help but be struck by the spell of ideology on the assembled mass and the power of the speaker to stir them. Anyone who had ever seen film of the Führer's orations to

National Socialists—and the throng's antiphonic chants of *Heil Hitler!*—could not fail to be chilled by the parallel. And you didn't need to speak the Mother Tongue to get the point.

The Sheikh, given his infirmities, never built a bomb or fired a gun in the jihad. His power to command barbarities was his recognized mastery of Islamic doctrine. From the Hamas tape, our case against him generally proceeded as follows: We proved his exhortations to violence, liberally invoking Muslim scripture; then we proved his followers' murderous mayhem. For this, the jury convicted him and the judge sentenced him to life imprisonment. For merely presenting this cause and effect, I received professional acclaim, was presented high honors by the Justice Department, and was invited to the White House to meet President Clinton and be on hand as he signed major anti-terrorism legislation.

Geert Wilders got indicted. Has that much changed in fifteen years?

In England it certainly has. Wilders was banned from the realm, despite the fact that the vision of Europe as a "union" is supposed to mean that Europeans may travel freely within it. Quite apart from the fact that he is a government official of the Netherlands, he was not visiting the U.K. on a lark. He was the invited guest of Malcolm Pearson, a member of the House of Lords. Lord Pearson and Baroness Caroline Cox (a human-rights activist who has worked tirelessly on behalf of enslaved and oppressed Christians and Muslims in Sudan) asked Wilders to screen *Fitna* for Parliament.

Westminster was once the domain of Churchill. As we've seen, the man whom the British people just voted the "greatest Briton of all time" was a keen observer of the Muslim world. As noted by two scholars of Islam, Daniel Pipes and Andrew Bostom, Churchill's inestimable history of the Second World

War describes *Mein Kampf* as "the new Koran of faith and war: turgid, verbose, shapeless, but pregnant with its message."[16] One needn't accept the analogy (Pipes, for example, does not) to concede it is not a frivolous one.

Today's Westminster, however, is the domain of Nazir Ahmed, a Labour lord and grievance-industry agitator of the first order. Lord Ahmed threatened to mobilize 10,000 rabble-rousers to prevent Wilders from entering Parliament.[17] Cowed, the Home Secretary Jacqui Smith issued a curt letter telling Wilders that he would not be admitted into the country. According to the Right Honourable Ms. Smith, Wilders's "statements about Muslims and their beliefs, as expressed in your film *Fitna* and elsewhere, would threaten community harmony and therefore public security in the U.K." Later, the Home Office laughably maintained that by barring Wilders it was perforce barring "extremism, hatred, and violent messages."

But extremism, hatred, and violent messages have found a comfortable home in the birthplace of Western civil rights. There, "community harmony" now means that Islamists talk and you listen. In 2005, Lord Ahmed hosted a book launch for Joran Jermas, a notorious Swedish anti-Semite who predictably ranted about the "Jewish supremacy drive," the Jews as the "one reason for wars, terror and trouble" in the Middle East, and Zionist "control" of Western mass media.[18] The following year, Ahmed's guest at Westminster, a building that happens to be one of al Qaeda's most coveted targets, was Mahmoud Suliman Ahmed Abu Rideh. Before his release in 2005, Abu Rideh, a Palestinian, had been detained under Britain's anti-terrorism laws due to al Qaeda connections and threats to carry out a bombing plot.[19]

So suspected al Qaeda members are welcome in Parliament, but not a member of the Dutch parliament. Britain has a revolving door for Islamists but a closed door for their democratic critics.

In 2004, British authorities insisted that the Bush administration return to the U.K. all Britons who, having been captured fighting with the enemy in Afghanistan and elsewhere, were held at Guantanamo Bay. Not content with President Bush's accommodation on that score, the Brits proceeded to demand that non-British detainees be shipped to England from Gitmo if they had any basis, no matter how tenuous, to claim legal U.K. residence. The Bush administration again relented, and British authorities promptly set the jihadists free.[20] When this move aroused grave public concern, Lord Peter Henry Goldsmith, a former attorney general, gave voice to the Labour government's dismissive party line: It did not matter whether the men were dangerous, because at stake was a "principle . . . which is more important." "The principle," Lord Goldsmith piously proclaimed, "is fundamental civil liberties."[21]

Indeed. Fundamental civil liberties for those committed to destroying the ever-diminishing British way of life. Cassandra, meantime, was shown the door: When Wilders attempted to enter London despite the ban, he was arrested, detained at the airport, and put on the next plane back to Holland.

A civilization fights to preserve itself or it dies. Has ours become so hollow, such a pale imitation of its former self? Do we lack the capacity even to speak of the evils arrayed against us? Have we become so cowardly that our censure is reserved for our saviors, not our pillagers?

The Grand Jihad is banking on it.

chapter twenty-one

THE ENCLAVE OF MINNESOTA

The questions came rat-tat-tat at this townhall meeting for Amy Klobuchar. A member of Minnesota's hard Left Democratic Farm Labor Party, she was campaigning as the Democrats' nominee for the United States Senate. Her answers sounded like babble, or perhaps clipped laughter: *Haa, haa, haa*. But she wasn't laughing. Klobuchar was speaking Somali.

And she was saying "yes": Yes to "comprehensive immigration reform"; yes to foreign language programs; yes to helping Somali money-service businesses that her constituents used to send the American dollars they earned back "home"; yes to meeting regularly with the Somali community so they could monitor that she was producing on the commitments that, absolutely *haa*, she was making.[1]

The two hundred Somalis in the audience seemed pleased. They were no doubt happier still when Klobuchar won in a landslide. She rode the same wave that carried Keith Ellison into Congress. Another Farm Labor Party member, Ellison became the first Muslim to sit in the House of Representatives. He credited his victory to the enthusiastic support of Somalis.[2] He took the oath of office, swearing on the Koran, to represent Minnesota's fifth congressional district. In that district lies the entire City of Minneapolis. It is the Muslim enclave.

The local Somali population that has been estimated at 100,000, representing somewhere between half and two-thirds the total number of Somalis now living in the United States. The actual population size is unknowable because of rampant illegal immigration, widespread identity and documentation fraud, and what the FBI gingerly describes as "a cultural reluctance to share personal information with census takers [that] has prevented an accurate count of the ethnic Somali population inside the United States."[3]

Somalis began pouring into America in the mid-Nineties thanks to the State Department's refugee resettlement efforts, such as the "Africa Priority Three Program" that gives special attention to Somalis, Ethiopians. and Liberians. These initiatives were robust and incompetently supervised. They targeted dire African countries without any evident concern about cultural differences that made assimilation unlikely. In 2008, State was forced to concede that there had been immigration fraud on a massive scale: nearly 40,000 aliens admitted into our country after falsely claiming family ties to immigrants already here.[4] If Klobuchar delivers on her promises to push for an immigration "reform" package that would not just legalize aliens who are here unlawfully but streamline the process for importing their chains of family members, the numbers could increase geometrically.[5]

The Somalis are the dominant Islamic group in Minnesota, but hardly the only one. As we've seen, CAIR was a prominent player in Ellison's campaign, which appealed to Muslims across the board, including American- and Arab-born Muslims, as well as to the Islamists' reliable allies on the Left. But the Somalis are an especially potent, aggressive force. That is the case here as it is in their war-torn homeland, where life-expectancy for men is less than forty-eight years (for women, it hovers just above fifty-one), where the dead-end of Islamism is thriving, and where the scourge of piracy is again on the rise.[6]

Besides Minneapolis, insular Somali communities have sprung up in Seattle, San Diego, Columbus, Atlanta, and—it almost goes without saying—Washington.[7] There are other pockets throughout the country. The Tennessee town of Shelbyville is one. Hundreds of Somalis found work there in the local Tyson's Chicken plant, and two were soon elected to the union's eight-member board. When it came time for a new collective bargaining agreement to be struck in 2008, the union pressured the company to abandon Labor Day. In its place, the Somali workers demanded a Muslim holiday: the Eid (*Eid ul-Fitr*), which marks the end of Ramadan. The company capitulated, to much gnashing of teeth by the majority, non-Muslim employees.[8]

It is in Minneapolis, though, where the greatest political and legal strides are being made by Somalis, and thus by Islamism. The Fifth District has become such a safe seat for Ellison that, on the campaign trail, he is more needed than in need. In 2008, he stumped vigorously for Al Franken's Senate bid. During his Minneapolis appearances, by his side was Abdullahi Ugas Farah, described in one press account as a "highly regarded prominent Somali traditional leader"—which, my friend Diana West acidly observed, translates to "a Somali leader from Somalia, not Minnesota." Farah urged the faithful that "in order for Keith to be helpful to the situation in Somalia, you must also elect Al Franken to the Senate."[9] That's the job of the U.S. Congress, right? To fix the situation in Somalia.

What exactly is the situation in Somalia? Well, the failed state has been engulfed in a civil war for well over a decade, going back to the shattering "Black Hawk Down" days of the early Nineties. Islamists seek to take over the country and impose strict sharia law under the auspices of leadership known as the "Islamic Courts Union," together with the local al Qaeda affiliate, al-Shabaab ("the lads"). As Diana West found, Abdullahi Ugas Farah was one of two speakers who presided in 2003 over the opening ceremony for a new sharia court in Mogadishu's Shirkole area.[10] It was apparently a short distance from there to Democratic Party politics in Minneapolis.

Import Somali Aliens, Export Islamist Militants

In Somalia, the Islamist factions are linked to the al Qaeda cells that bombed the American embassies in Nairobi and Dar es Salaam in 1998. They also maintain ties with al Qaeda leaders in Northwest Pakistan. Somalia has thus become crucially important to bin Laden's network as both a rich recruiting vein and a staging ground for regional and global terrorist operations—including strikes against the United States.[11] Reciprocally, al Qaeda training has proved critical to the Somali Islamists. Recruits, who have often been led to Somalia from mosques or diverted there while on pilgrimage to Saudi Arabia, are steeped in Salafist ideology while being trained in military assault tactics and the use of machine guns, rocket-propelled grenades, and other explosives. Terror tactics apt to intimidate civilian populations are stressed. In late 2008, for example, al-Shabaab "produced a videotape depicting the slow decapitation of an accused spy," according to the FBI.[12]

Incorporating familiar al Qaeda tactics like simultaneous bombings (frequently using suicide attackers), the campaign has been frightfully successful. The Islamists took over much of Somalia in 2006 before being beaten back by U.S.-backed Ethiopian forces. By 2009, the Islamists had surged back as Ethiopia retreated under the usual pressure from "human rights" groups— ever notice how they always seem preternaturally interested in the humans doing the killing versus the humans being killed? Shabaab terrorists and the Islamic Courts Union seized much of the country's south again, including the strategically important port city of Kismayo.[13] Ayman al-Zawahiri, bin Laden's deputy, was moved to proclaim that Shabaab gains were "a step on the path of victory of Islam."[14]

The recent offensives had significant, U.S.-based help. Our Somali immigration pipeline, you see, does not run in just one direction. We not only import Somali aliens, including their "traditional leaders." We also send back aspiring Islamist militants, including suicide bombers. Since 2006, the FBI has detected that many Somalis are returning to fight on behalf of al-Shabaab, and more are launched from Minneapolis than from any other U.S. haven.

Despite the extensive history of Muslims flocking to any "field of jihad" where Islamists are in combat, the Bureau was instinctively quick to rationalize that "the primary motivation" for their travel to Somalia was "to defend their place of birth [i.e., the place they couldn't get out of fast enough] from the Ethiopian invasion." But the criminal charges filed by the Justice Department tell a different story: one of a call to jihad that sounded in mosques from Minneapolis to Mecca. Thus, even the FBI has had to concede, however grudgingly, that "an appeal was also made based on their shared Islamic identity."[15] You don't say? In fact, Somali Islamists have been bold in stressing their attachment to the global Islamist project. They've issued public statements of solidarity with their allies in al Qaeda's rambunctious Yemeni satellite (al Qaeda in the Arabian Peninsula). Moreover, on New Year's Day 2010, a Somali Islamist in Denmark attempted to murder Kurt Westergaard, the cartoonist who drew one of the riot-inspiring depictions of Mohammed in 2005.[16]

Shabaab recruitment drives have become intense in the United States and Canada. Some relatives of the young men who've gone missing from Minneapolis point to the Abubakar as-Saddique mosque as the catalyst that radicalized them. And then there is the familiar Brotherhood route. Omar Hammami grew up as a Baptist in Alabama before converting to Islam while studying at the University of South Alabama. He became president of the Muslim Students Association, duly opposed "terrorism," and was quick to express his "shock" at the time of the 9/11 attacks that "a Muslim could have done this." In short order, though, the young American gravitated to Somali areas of Toronto before joining al-Shabaab, taking on the *nom de guerre* Abu Mansour al-Amriki.* He is now a top Shabaab commander who regularly appears in recruiting videos, denouncing democracy and Western notions of human rights as being implacably set against sharia principles.[17]

The recruitment drive is taking its toll. Shirwa Ahmed, a twenty-seven-year old Somali who had lived with his family in Minneapolis, blew himself up at a UN checkpoint in 2008, killing twenty-nine people. In September 2009, another Somali immi-

---

Al-Amriki means "the American." Most Islamists have an *Abu*-[fill in the name] in their string of aliases; it indicates that one is the "father of" someone.

grant left his Seattle community to return home and carry out a truck bombing in Mogadishu, killing twenty-one people.[18] The case of Ahmed is especially grating. Thanks to the State Department's refugee resettlement mania, he'd become a naturalized American citizen. So, after his mass-murder attack against U.S.-supported allies in northern Somalia, the FBI, at the expense of the American taxpayer, had his remains (which had become evidence in the Bureau's terrorism-support investigation) transported back to America so he could be given a proper Islamic burial at "home."[19]

To be fair, the Bureau, however ham-handedly, is trying to ingratiate itself within the community for intelligence purposes. The palpable fear of American and Canadian investigators is that the young men who leave North America with a jihadist fervor will return as trained, lethally capable terrorists, committed to carrying out terrorist strikes against the West. As David Harris, the former chief of strategic planning for the Canadian Security Intelligence Service starkly puts it, "it is just a matter of time before someone who went abroad comes back to North America in an effort to carry out an attack."[20]

Implementing Sharia

Beyond what they hear from al Qaeda in Kismayo, Somali immigrants certainly get plenty of stoking once they get here. Besides agitators like Congressman Ellison and the "traditional leader" Abdullahi Ugas Farah, there are such priceless academics as Abdi Sheikhosman, a professor of Islamic law at the University of Minnesota. "We have a saying in Somalia," he said to the *Star Tribune* in 2008. "He who approaches the lion does not know what a lion is." That's how it is for Somali immigrants, the good professor groused. They "arrive here not knowing the history of racial divide in this country. They don't know the lion they are up against." And what abuse had the lion heaped on them that might make them long once again to be in the placid bosom of Mogadishu? It seems the tortilla factory in New Brighton adopted a company uniform, which Muslim workers decided was a violation of their religious beliefs. "For me," said Fatuma Hassan, a twenty-two-year-old Somali immigrant, "wearing pants is the same as being naked." The company was also resistant to accommodating prayer breaks throughout the work day. But Minnesotans would have to adjust to such novelties, opined another academic, Bruce Corrie, of Concordia University. "The Somali community is highly assertive and politically engaged. . . . It's part of who they are as a people."[21]

American travelers found that out soon enough. At the Minneapolis-St. Paul International Airport—the same place where the Flying Imams decided it was opportune to play out their hijinks—Somali taxi drivers, who make up three-quarters of the busy terminal's 900 cabbies, began refusing service to passengers who were carrying alcohol (shopping bags from the duty free shop are a tell-tale sign).[22] The ball, it turned out, got rolling in 2006 when the local chapter of the Muslim American Society issued a fatwa admonishing Muslim taxi drivers that transporting passengers with alcohol in their baggage was a violation of sharia.[23] As one learns to expect, the resistance soon expanded to other sharia culprits: passengers accompanied by dogs, and even some who appeared overtly homosexual.[24] The reluctance to ferry dogs— which are often needed by passengers with disabilties—was predictable. In 1997, Daniel Pipes has reported, a New Orleans taxi driver, Mahmoud Awad, was so incensed when a passenger tried to bring a dog into his cab that he yanked her out of the vehicle by her broken arm screaming, "No dog, no dog, get out, get out!" CAIR rushed to his defense, helpfully pointing out that "the saliva of dogs invalidates the ritual purity needed for prayer."[25] Good to know that.

The transportation authorities, who would not for a moment countenance a driver's refusal to serve Muslim passengers, reacted to this affront by . . . consulting the MAS. With their sensitivity thus enriched, the authorities opted to respond not by withdrawing licenses but by engaging the cabbies on the finer points of sharia. To wit, Muslim law, they counseled, proscribed the *consumption* of alcohol, not its *transportation*. Of course, this fecklessness served only to imply that, in clearer cases of sharia violation, American equal-protection principles would yield as necessary to give sharia its newfangled due. Adroitly, the MAS had first provoked a controversy, taken the measure of the spineless opposition, and come away with a precedent that American law could be trumped by sharia—which, it cannot be stressed enough, is a corpus of political and social directives, not just religious commandments.

Sharia, the Muslim aversion to canines, and the traditional Islamist focus on dominating the education system proved to be too toxic a brew for Tyler Hurd. Because the twenty-three-year-old St. Cloud State University student was prone to seizures, he attended school in the company of his service dog. The black lab, called "Emmitt," was specially trained to protect Hurd, toting a pouch that contained items that would help passersby aid him in the event of an episode. Hurd was enrolled in a teacher-training program that required field work at local high schools. At Technical High, this brought Hurd into communion with scores of Somali students. Their Muslim faith, the *St. Cloud Times* deferentially reported, "forbids the touching of dogs." As a result, there was much taunting and, finally, threats to kill the canine.

Fearing for himself and his animal, Hurd complained to officials at his college. St. Cloud State bravely resolved . . . to waive

Hurd's remaining training hours: giving him credit for completing the course without doing the required work in order to avoid a confrontation with menacing Muslims. A university official, the paper recounts, opined that it was "important to respect different cultures and the rights of disabled students." He added, "I think this is part of the growth process when we become more diverse."[26]

The growth process also includes suspending students out of fear for their safety. That's what happened to an Owatonna High School senior who, in an assignment to write a class paper, chose the topic "Somalian Privileges," complaining that the Muslim students were not required to adhere to various school rules. He and his mother were promptly summoned to the school and advised that he would be suspended, officially for "language and inappropriate comments," but unofficially because school officials feared he would be attacked. After a few days that officials hoped would be a "cooling off period," the boy returned to school . . . and was mauled by a gang that grew to somewhere between twenty and forty Somali students. He had to be hospitalized for head injuries.[27]

Jihad in the Classroom

In the classroom, Islamicization is seeping into the learning process as well—and not only in Minnesota. The American Textbook Council (ATC) has released a jaw-dropping study called "Islam in the Classroom."[28] History and "social studies" texts routinely indoctrinate children of middle and high school age that the prophet of Islam was a trader who "taught equality" and was animated by the desire to "help the poor." The texts "feature manifold contributions of Islam to the arts and science"— including "textiles, calligraphy, design, books, city building, architecture, mathematics, medicine, polo, and chess." Students are informed that music, and particularly singing, was "an essential part of Muslim Spain's musical culture"—which is said to have "undoubtedly influenced later musical forms in Europe and North Africa" . . . though the text in question later admits that this music is "lost," so just how much "undoubted influence" it actually had can only be imagined.

The concept of jihad is whitewashed in a way that would surely bring an envious smile to government experts. Gone is the once straightforward recitation that Islam spread by the sword. Now, as the pages turn, Islam "moves peacefully with traders." It is "brought" to seemingly willing populations and spontaneously "spreads" throughout the Middle East to people who simply "become" Muslims. A McDougal Littell volume explains, "There was much blending of cultures under Muslim rule. Over time, many peoples in Muslim-ruled territories converted to Islam. They were attracted by Islam's message of equality and hope for salvation." Islamic tolerance is a leitmotif. Students are informed, for example, that "[a]nother factor in helping the Arabs [in the "spread of Islam"] was their tolerance for other religions." As the study summarizes, "Once non-Arabs have been conquered, students learn, those societies and civilizations with non-Islamic systems of belief live in a wonderland of interreligious cooperation." A teacher's edition of the McDougal Littell text poses the "Essential Question":

Q: How did the caliphs who expanded the Muslim empire treat those the conquered?

A: They treated them with tolerance.

Review:

Q: Why were the caliphs tolerant of the people they conquered?

A: Because the Qur'an did not allow Muslims to force people to convert to Islam.

Islam's legacy of dhimmitude and enslavement is assiduously suppressed, as is its official sanction of booty-taking. Indeed, what the Koran did and did not allow is left a mystery. On sharia, children are vapidly taught that Islamic law "makes no distinctions between religious beliefs and daily life," and that "Shari'ah sets rewards for good behavior and punishments for crimes"—but they are informed neither of how profound a departure the melding of mosque and state is from Western traditions of religious freedom, nor of the particular rewards (such as an orgiastic paradise for martyrdom in the cause of jihad) and punishments (such as stoning, decapitation, dismemberment, for such offenses as apostasy, a woman's refusal to enter an arranged marriage, and petty theft).

Since the mid-1990s, the message that it is a "common misrepresentation" to frame jihad as "holy war" has been drummed into students. A widely used Prentice-Hall high school text says: "Some Muslims look on *jihad*, or effort in God's service, as another duty. Jihad has often been mistakenly translated simply as 'holy war.' In fact, it may include acts of charity or an inner struggle to achieve spiritual peace, as well as any battle in defense of Islam." Seventh graders in California and Arizona are schooled that jihad

> represents the human struggle to overcome difficulties and
> do things that are pleasing to God. Muslims strive to respond
> positively to personal difficulties as well as worldly challenges.
> For instance, they might work to become better people, re-
> form society, or correct injustice.

As the ATC incisively observes, since jihad is so often described as a "struggle against oppression," how can students who hear of repeated calls to jihad against Christians and Jews not consider that the United States and Israel are likely the culprits?

As combustible as the clash of cultures is, it may be the least of the education problem. There is also the elevation and subsidization of the single Muslim culture. To accommodate Muslims, the state of Minnesota is using its charter school law to operate an Islamic public school, a benefit accorded no other religious group. Taxpayers foot the bill for the 'Tarek ibn Ziyad Academy in suburban St. Paul, to the tune of nearly $4 million per annum. That is the allegation of the American Civil Liberties Union of Minnesota, which has filed a suit, claiming a breach of the First Amendment's proscription against establishing a state religion.[29]

Besides information derived from the lawsuit, much is known about the school because of diligent investigative reporting by the *Star Tribune*'s Katherine Kersten.[30] "TIZA," as it is known for short, is named after the Muslim general who conquered medieval Spain in the Eighth Century. It was founded by a pair of imams who doubled as top leaders of MAS-Minnesota: MAS-MN Vice President Asad Zaman served as principal, while MAS-MN President Hesham Hussein chaired TIZA's board until being killed in car accident in Saudi Arabia. The school is physically located in the MAS-MN headquarters, as is a mosque. Besides the MAS-MN, the most important backer of TIZA is its sponsor, the Islamic American Relief Agency. While the Islamic American Relief Agency is likened to the Red Cross in several TIZA documents, the Israeli government observes that its parent organization, Islamic Relief Worldwide, "provides support and assistance" to Hamas.

Minnesotan law requires its public schools to be nonsectarian. Visitors to TIZA, however, found themselves greeted by a Muslim prayer posted in the entryway. The school sports a centrally carpeted prayer room, and the ACLU alleges both that MAS-MN has conducted prayer sessions there during school hours, and that—after teachers encouraged students to partake in Islam's pre-prayer ablution ritual—the school breaks for a half-hour of prayer service on Fridays (time that is not made up). Moreover, the MAS-MN runs a Muslim studies program for an hour immediately after school has officially concluded for the day. In effect, this makes Muslim studies part of the regular curriculum: Although school officially ends at 3:30pm, buses don't depart from TIZA until 4:30. Further, the school requires girls (but not boys) to cover their bare arms, and the uniform for older girls (as well as the dress code for female teachers) calls for them to be covered from the neck to the wrist and ankle, with virtually all wearing headscarves. Students refer to their teachers as "Brother" or "Sister." The cafeteria serves halal food only, and students fast from dawn until dusk during Ramadan.

Publicly, TIZA claims to conform to the standard secular curriculum. A different picture, though, is painted for Muslim audiences. Katherine Kersten explains:

> At MAS-MN's 2007 convention, for example, the program featured an advertisement for the "Muslim American Society of Minnesota," superimposed on a picture of a mosque. Under the motto 'Establishing Islam in Minnesota," it asked: "Did you know that MAS-MN . . . houses a full-time elementary school"? On the adjacent page was an application for TIZA. . . . Meanwhile, MAS-MN offers on its web site "beneficial and enlightening information" about Islam, which includes statements like "Regularly make the intention to go on jihad with the ambition to die as a martyr." At its 2007 convention, MAS-MN featured the notorious [Sheikh]

Khalid Yasin, who is well-known in Britain and Australia for teaching that husbands can beat disobedient wives, that gays should be executed and that the United States spreads the AIDS virus in Africa through vaccines for tropical diseases. Yasin's topic? "Building a Successful Muslim Community in Minnesota."

Jihad in the Financial System

Meanwhile, taxpayers in the state—and, derivatively, throughout the United States—are underwriting the spread of Islam in another significant way: special Muslim mortgages, which the state housing agency refers to as *Murbaha* financing. It is another stealth importation of sharia into our law. As we've seen, Islamic law does not tolerate interest, the root of all capitalist evil. So the game is to structure transactions that would not occur absent interest payments without *calling* those payments "interest." In Minnesota, the state purchases a home from a realtor and sells it to a predetermined Muslim buyer at an increased up front price that factors in what the payments (plus interest) would have been on, say, a thirty-year mortgage. The payments are stretched out over the usual period but—*presto!*—you have something you can pretend is all payments and no interest.

Is it the most dicey financial gimmick anyone's ever heard of? Of course not. It never is . . . at the start. Apologists predictably argue that it is an arm's length transaction for a good cause, so no one is getting hurt. But *we're* getting hurt. It is not a proper governmental function to buy and sell homes. Government's job is to protect the housing market from fraud . . . by enforcing *American* law. What makes a state government think it has to, or should, use American public funds to structure financial transactions that accord with a religious code?

The initiative, moreover, is just one aspect of a comprehensive financial sector project known as "sharia compliant finance." In increasing numbers, troubled American banks, anxious to tap into Islamic oil wealth, set up sharia advisory boards for the purpose of avoiding Islamic injunctions against not only interest, but certain forms of risk and investments in industries (pork, alcohol, investment funds, etc.) whose operations transgress Muslim law. Financial arrangements that run afoul of these standards can be "purified" by, for example, diversion of interest payments to Islamic charities under the auspices of *zakat*—the troublesome principle we encountered in Chapter 6.

Again, it sounds innocuous enough. Yet, there are a slew of problematic consequences. Many of the sharia advisors turn out (surprise!) to be vehemently anti-Western clerics. As we've seen, Muslim charities are notoriously co-opted for terror financing purposes. Sharia "compliance" bears the earmarks of fraud since it is meant to disguise the reality of interest income. The availability of such Islam-certified devices puts pressure on authentic moderates to refrain from assimilating Western financial practices—implicitly facilitating the Brotherhood's apartheid strategy. The upshot of the entire scheme, finally, is to legitimize and regularize sharia as part of the American legal system—without disclosing to would-be investors (as U.S. securities laws would seem to require) that Islamic law purports to be indivisible. That is, recognition of its financial aspects invites acceptance, or at least conscious avoidance of, its suppression of freedom of conscience, its legal iniquities against women and non-Muslims, its promotion of polygamy and child marriage, its persecution of homosexuals and apostates, and its resort to violence as necessary to advance the Muslim cause.

The lobster never notices the water is starting to boil until it's too late.

chapter twenty-two

BACK IN THE FOLD

Finally, it was over. The Age of Obama had arrived in America, and no one was more ecstatic than the Islamist Left. "After eight years of enduring religious racism, the Muslims are now leading a movement to help others and serve the community," exclaimed a jubilant Dalia Mogahed.[1]

Her statement was prominently displayed on the Muslim Brotherhood's website, ikhwanweb.com. It was two days before the eighth anniversary of the attacks on the World Trade Center and the Pentagon. Mogahed, the executive director of the Gallup Center for Muslim Studies, was reveling in the new president's determination to change the way America thought about 9/11. It wasn't a day to dwell on barbaric attacks by terrorists who just happened to be Muslims. Henceforth, the community-organizer-in-chief had decided to make every September 11th a national day of community service.

"It was Islam's core teachings of affirming faith with good deeds that formed the heart of [the president's] call to action," Mogahed explained. She would know: Obama had recently appointed her as one of his top advisers on all things Islam, giving her a plum seat on the President's Advisory Council on Faith-Based and Neighborhood Partnerships. Already, Mogahed had the party line down cold: We are against "violent extremists" but they've got nothing to do with Islam; when it comes to Islam, we are willing to work with any Muslims. After all, if you're a Muslim, you are by definition not a violent extremist: Islam has to be perverted for a Muslim to resort to terro—um . . . we don't even want to say the T-word. And if you're not a "violent extremist," you are by definition a moderate, no matter what you are trying to accomplish.

Even if what you are out to accomplish is the imposition of sharia on the West. See, sharia is really terrific, especially for women, Mogahed explained. It's just that "the media" raises all these unwarranted concerns about "oppression, injustice [and] second-class citizenship." The president's adviser held forth on "Muslimah Dilemma," a television program on Britain's popular Islam Channel. Muslim women "have a very different understanding of sharia," she countered, not this "oversimplified" caricature. Women actually "associate . . . gender justice or justice for women with sharia *compliance*" (emphasis added). It is "only a small fraction," she insisted, that associate sharia with "oppression of women."

Mogahed added that what women really want, especially in Muslim-majority countries, is to find ways to integrate Islamic law into public law.[2] In effect, we need more sharia. But the columnist Supna Zaidi begged to differ. As she observed in assessing Mogahed's dreadful performance, "Muslims who do not want to live under Islamic law are not oversimplifying. Rather, they are accepting that Mogahed's vapid description bears no resemblance to Islamic law in practice."[3]

A crucial part of Mogahed's Islamic "outreach" on the president's behalf is to "dialogue" with influential Muslims. The administration wants not only to do it but to be seen doing it. So in this European television setting, Mogahed agreed to appear with Nasreen Nawaz. Dr. Nawaz is one of those moderates from Hizb ut-Tahrir, the international movement to establish a global caliphate. It advocates overthrowing the U.S. political system.

Though it is supportive of al Qaeda and the Taliban, Hizb ut-Tahrir claims to be strictly nonviolent in its own activities. For years, it has operated in the U.S. only in the shadows, but the organization decided the Age of Obama was the perfect time to go overt in an effort to reach new American recruits. When Mogahed and Nawaz appeared together, it had been only a few weeks since Hizb had held its first ever American "Khalifa Convention"— in the suburbs of the president's hometown, Chicago. It called the confab "The Fall of Capitalism and the Rise of Islam." The challenge, a Hizb spokesman explained, was to end the scourge of "economic terrorism" known as "capitalism." There would be no cure for the world's social and economic ills until the Constitution was abandoned, sharia was adopted, government was in control of all major industries, *zakat* and other compulsory levies were in place to address "economic inequality," and lenders were barred from charging interest on loans.[4]

As anyone could have predicted, Nawaz relished the opportunity to spew Hizb's platform publicly for forty-five minutes while Obama's representative sat by in seeming agreement. Mogahed let it all pass without objection. The impression created was one of unanimity on the virtues of sharia, including Nawaz's depiction of sharia as a "pioneer" for women's rights.[5]

We're Engaged!

That is the way it is in the Obama administration. American officials are to project consensus and cooperation with Islamists. The tone is set from the very top, by a president whose very first judicial nominee to the all-important federal appellate courts was the Leftist jurist David F. Hamilton. As a district judge in Indiana, Hamilton infamously ruled that the First Amendment's Establishment Clause barred state legislators from uttering the name of Jesus Christ in any invocations . . . but that referring to the name of Allah was fine.[6] Even more alarmingly, Obama's first months featured a hand that, when not outstretched in friendship, was penning saccharine overtures of "respect" to the likes of the Iranian supreme Ayatollah Ali Khamenei and the Organization of the Islamic Conference.[7] It matters not how many times the mullahs and their henchmen spurn him. This president is hellbent on "engaging"—even to the point of averting his gaze from the regime's slaughter of its desperate citizens.

Iran's popular rebellion was being brutally repressed. General Ray Odierno, the commander of U.S. forces in Iraq, acknowledged that Tehran was "still supporting, funding, and training surrogates who operate inside of Iraq" and target American troops. The mullahs went defiantly about the business of building their nukes. How did Obama respond to these provocations from "the Islamic Republic"? By freeing the five top Iranian commanders our military had captured coordinating anti-American insurgent operations in Iraq. And then freeing the two top leaders of the Iran-backed jihadist network, the Qazali organization, responsible for the execution-style murders in 2007 of five American soldiers abducted in Karbala.[8]

Meantime, a mere presidential "we can work it out" letter was not good enough for the OIC. The world's sharia alliance is now on a jihad to snuff out free speech through its "defamation of religion" resolution. The president's reaction? He extended a standing invitation for OIC's secretary general, Professor Ekmeleddin Ihsanoglu, to visit the White House and strategize on how the United States and the Islamist bloc can work together.[9]

Invitations to Islamists to visit White House and to participate in other executive branch events now roll off the printing press faster than deflated U.S. treasury notes. The entreaties reflect not only the new face of government but the insinuation of America's enemies into America's policy-making apparatus. For example, long before President Obama invited the Muslim Brotherhood to attend his Cairo speech, his administration began cultivating the Islamic Society of North America. As we've seen, ISNA is the Brotherhood's U.S. umbrella organization. It exists "to advance the cause of Islam and service Muslims in North America so as to enable them to adopt Islam as a complete way of life." At the recently concluded HLF trial, the Justice Department had shown ISNA to be complicit in ongoing Brotherhood conspiracies to sabotage the West and to fund the terrorist organization Hamas.

No matter. Obama asked ISNA President Ingrid Mattson to lead prayers at the Democratic National Convention and at his inauguration. Mattson is a Muslim convert who compares Wahhabism to the protestant reformation in Europe; rationalizes al Qaeda's "extremism" as something its operatives see as "the only rational choice, because extreme actions are the only actions that seem to have an effect"; and denies there have been Muslim terror cells operating inside the United States.[10] Mattson was front and center with official Washington when the Obama White House hosted its first Iftar dinner. And, with Iftar dinners having replaced cherry blossoms as official Washington's signature observance, Mattson also joined the leadership of the Muslim Public Affairs Council at the Treasury Department's separate Iftar celebration. There, she pressed Secretary Timothy Geithner on Obama's commitment to remove impediments to Islamic "charity."[11]

With CAIR on the ropes, the FBI continues to cultivate a robust relationship with ISNA—even though it was the Bureau that cracked the HLF case. Our domestic national security agency gives awards to ISNA officials and places ads in ISNA publications, soliciting ISNA members to consider applying for FBI jobs. The "outreach" efforts directed from headquarters in Washington are maddening to agents in the field. "FBI leadership is relying on the Muslim leaders, who are known Muslim Brotherhood, to give them direction on how to go after the enemy in the community," one former agent groused to Rowan Scarborough of *Human Events*. "These are the very people who have advocated overthrowing the American government."[12] Such warnings don't faze the Obama White House. Valerie Jarrett, the president's top adviser and close Chicago friend, appeared as the headliner at ISNA's annual convention in 2009. Another featured speaker was Warith Deen Umar, the Islamist who was forced out as the head of the New York State prison chaplain program because of his praise for the 9/11 hijackers and his Koran-based calls for Muslims to "strike terror into the heart of the disbeliever."[13]

ISNA's resurgence is not singular. It was recently joined by MPAC and MAS, among other groups, for a private pow-wow with DHS Secretary Janet Napolitano. She listened with the Obama administration's patented empathy as the Islamist leaders called for a rescission of enhanced scrutiny for travelers from *Dar al-Islam*'s notorious terror havens and demanded severe limits on power of customs agents to search and interrogate Muslim immigrants at border crossings.[14]

CAIR is also rising from the ashes in Obama's presidency. Politically, this is a more delicate process because of the FBI's public break with the group, after years of "partnering," when evidence of CAIR's Hamas pedigree became too embarrassing. But the Obama administration is steadily returning CAIR to the fold, mostly at the branch-office level.

CAIR's very active Michigan affiliate, for example, has access to Department of Homeland Security officials and the leadership of DHS's Immigration and Customs Enforcement agency, which it lobbies for immigration reform and an easing of enforcement policies. Similarly, CAIR's Philadelphia office is consulting with the U.S. Citizenship and Immigration Services. The organization's Florida satellite joined with Justice Department officials at a September "Hate Crimes Awareness Summit." Its Washington branch in Seattle met with DHS officials and the leadership of DHS's Customs and Border Protection agency to complain that Muslims were being "profiled" when attempting to enter the U.S. at the Canadian border.[15]

With the ground thus prepared, CAIR's old, Hamas-tainted leaders are reemerging. After the HLF trial and the eye-popping publication of *Muslim Mafia* (by P. David Gaubatz and Paul Sperry), the public may see them as a farce. The administration, however, does not. "Tonight is a true representation of what America stands for," observed a gushing Nihad Awad according to one press account of the Pentagon's Iftar dinner.[16]

In fact, it is not just ISNA and CAIR. There is also the International Institute of Islamic Thought. Recall that it is a Saudi/Ikhwan venture dedicated to the Islamicization of knowledge, and that it considered the convicted terror-monger Sami al-Arian's Florida organization to be an extension of itself. The IIIT has also been recruited into Obama's go-to team. Three weeks after the administration's accession to power, Hillary Clinton's State Department had the IIIT join a contingent of "Interfaith Community" members that met with a delegation of Turkish imams brought to the U.S. under State's International Visitor Program.[17]

Speaking of the State Department, you'll be thrilled to hear that, hard on the raging success that was "Eid in America," our foreign service is getting back into the movie business. Members of a Middle East media venture who also came to the U.S. under the International Visitor Program in 2009 announced that they were producing a documentary, "Muslim Life in America." So naturally, for guidance, State steered them directly to the Brotherhood's primary U.S. arm, the Muslim American Society.[18]

Leftward Toward Sharia

To meet with the media moguls, the MAS took time out from its ongoing campaign to make healthcare a human right. Consistent with "the tenets of the Islamic faith," MAS explains, Muslims are compelled "to work for social justice and compassion, which means, in the context of this political issue, universal health care in the United States."[19]

Islamists have taken that campaign to Capitol Hill, where they won lavish praise for pushing universal health care from three hard Left allies: Democratic Representatives Dennis Kucinich, Pete Stark, and Andre Carson. Indeed, in 2008, thanks to enthusiastic Islamist support, Carson became the second Muslim member of Congress (from Indiana).[20]

Like the first, Keith Ellison, Carson is a convert to Islam with embarrassing ties to the Jew-bashing black separatist Louis Farrakhan of the Nation of Islam. The congressional seat Carson won was long held by his late grandmother, Julia Carson, who was a Farrakhan disciple. Indeed, at Rep. Carson's 2007 funeral, the family had Farrakhan give the eulogy . . . which occasion he used to endorse Carson.[21] The new congressman is a regular congregant at the Nur-Allah Islamic Center in Indianapolis, one of those centers that the Brotherhood predicted would be the "axis" of the Islamist movement in each city. Nur is led by Imam Warith Deen Mohammed, a frequent ISNA collaborator who brought the Nation of Islam (founded by his father, Elijah Mohammed) more into line with the Sunni Islamic principles favored by the Muslim Brotherhood.[22]

The September 2009 "citizens' hearing" on healthcare at the Rayburn House office building featured such Islamist notables as the MAS's Mahdi Bray, CAIR's Nihad Awad, the IIIT's Jamal Barzinji, and the former MAS President Esam Omeish—always willing to make himself available for efforts to bend America toward sharia.[23] The presence of Omeish along with Congressman Carson at a universal healthcare summit convened by Islamists and the radical Left was a timely reminder of the Dar al-Hijrah mosque and its profound influence. Omeish, of course, served on *Dar*'s board of directors. *Dar*'s "Outreach Director" Johari Abdul-Malik was among Carson's biggest fundraisers.

There would soon be other reminders.

chapter twenty-three

ISOLATED EXTREMISTS

On November 5, 2009, a Dar al-Hijrah worshipper named Nidal Malik Hasan walked into the readiness center on the Fort Hood U.S. army base in Texas. The center is a final launch point for young American men and women who are about to deploy overseas to put their lives on the line for their country. That afternoon, it was bustling as soldiers about to ship off to Afghanistan engaged in meetings and had last-minute medical check-ups.

Allahu Akbar! Allahu Akbar! Hasan was shouting . . . and shooting. Armed with a pair of handguns, he'd begun blasting away. When the smoke cleared, he had been critically wounded by military guards who'd returned fire, but not before Hasan had murdered thirteen Americans, including twelve U.S. troops, and wounded another thirty-eight.

Hasan had been seen on the base in the hours before the shooting. It seemed highly unusual because he was garbed in traditional Arabic Muslim clothing, a flowing white gown and skull cap. But by the time of the shooting, he had shed his Islamic duds for the outfit he more regularly wore on the base: his uniform. Hasan was a major in the United States army: an American-born, American-educated psychiatrist, assigned by the military to Fort Hood to treat our soldiers.[1]

He was also an Islamist terrorist. It seemed impossible, though, to get anyone to acknowledge that—to concede an obvious fact: the atrocity that had just occurred, claiming twice as many lives as the 1993 World Trade Center bombing, was an act of terrorism. Was, in fact, one of the worst ever committed on American soil. Before a shred of investigation could be done, the FBI quickly told the media that terrorism had not been involved.[2]

This, again, was the gospel according to the government: Islam has nothing to do with terrorism, and therefore the common denominator that links all the savagery is an irrelevancy to be ignored. Sure there are terrorists who, by some coincidence, happen to be Muslims; but they are from al Qaeda, and they are perverters of the true Islam, not real Muslims. To be a called a terrorist, you must be from al Qaeda. (Hamas and Hezbollah are now armed political resistance movements, not global terrorists. And, remember, nobody is a jihadist, because *jihad* is a noble Islamic concept that has been hijacked by the bad terrorists—we don't even mention it anymore). So, you see, if you are not a member of al Qaeda and you are a Muslim, you are by definition not a terrorist. Case closed.

President Obama was quick to reinforce this pious syllo-
gism—which is so palpable that it needs to be repeated constantly
lest you forget that it simply must be so. "It may be hard to com-
prehend the twisted logic that led to this tragedy. But this much,"
the president pronounced, "we do know: No faith justifies these
murderous and craven acts; no just and loving God looks upon
them with favor."[3]

That's not what Nidal Malik Hassan learned at Dar al-Hijrah.
He had attended the mosque earlier in the decade, when he was
assigned to the Walter Reed Army Medical Center. Back then,
the mosque had undergone a transition of sorts. Mohammed al-
Hanooti stepped down. He was *Dar* founder and former IAP
president who, in 1999, had described Dar al-Hijrah as "the
greatest example in sacrifice, execution, and in carrying out the
jihad that Allah calls for"—jihad, he said, that would "give us
the victory over our tyrannical enemies . . . the infidel Americans and British," as well as "the infidel Jews."[4] To fill Hanooti's
enormous shoes, the *Dar* board turned to Anwar al-Awlaki, a
Yemeni-trained scholar of Islam who claims to have been born
in New Mexico.

After lying on an application to obtain a $20,000 U.S. Agency
for International Development grant, Awlaki drifted from Islamist mosque to Islamist mosque. Finally, he landed in San Diego,
where, as the local imam, he ministered to the 9/11 hijackers
Nawaf al-Hazmi and Khaled al-Midhar.[5] In 2001, when Awlaki
got the gig at Dar al-Hijrah, Hazmi caught up with him there as
did fellow hijacker Hani Hanjour. Under Awlaki's direction, the
mosque helped the eventual hijackers obtain housing and identification in Virginia.[6]

Our friendly outreach director Johari Abdul-Malik now
insists that, as the imam at *Dar*, Awlaki "was articulating the same

message that I articulate today." Given what we've learned about Imam "You can blow up bridges" Abdul-Malik, maybe that's an accurate description. Awlaki, in any event, claimed that Muslims were 9/11 "victims rather than hijackers"; that "no Muslim . . . advocates killing American civilians" (as Awlaki knew, bin Laden, to name just one Muslim, had done so publicly and repeatedly); and that Palestinian terrorists were actually "freedom fighters fighting an illegal occupation." [7] Furthermore, when the FBI grilled him a week after the plane had plowed into the Pentagon, Awlaki claimed to be shocked that some of the hijackers seemed to have followed him from San Diego to Virginia. He also denied having contact with Hazmi and Hanjour at Dar al-Hijrah. And, though he admitted seeing Hazmi in San Diego, Awlaki claimed neither to know Hazmi's name nor remember anything they might have talked about.[8]

It was during Awlaki's suicide-hijacker ministry that he first met Nidal Hasan. Hasan's mother died in early 2001, and Awlaki presided over the funeral. The officer and the imam struck up a relationship that continued for years. Not surprisingly, Awlaki figured he'd better skip town after the FBI's post-9/11 questioning, leaving some investigators furious because they were convinced he'd been complicit.[9] But Awlaki was permitted to flee to Yemen, where he openly became an al Qaeda recruiter, exhorting young Muslims to go fight the Americans in Iraq and Afghanistan. In that role, he was echoing a long-held Brotherhood/Qaradawi principle calling for combat against infidel armies, including U.S. forces, that operate in Islamic countries.

Hasan kept the relationship up by email. By 2008, they were regular interlocutors, exchanging numerous messages. Because it continued to investigate Awlaki, the FBI was well aware that a Muslim psychiatrist responsible for treating our soldiers was in fairly constant contact with the suspected terrorist imam. Incredibly, however, counterterrorism agents dismissed these communications as somehow consistent with Hasan's academic research into the psychological effects combat in Muslim countries had on American troops.[10]

Diversity über Alles

Hasan, meanwhile, was a five-alarm jihadist in our midst. It is not even possible to say he was hiding in plain sight because he made no secret of his sympathies. The army major opposed the war in Afghanistan and Iraq. He urged Islamist ideology on his patients, some of whom he wanted prosecuted for war crimes based on what he learned from them in sessions.[11] At what was supposed to be a scholarly presentation on a psychiatric topic during his residency at Walter Reed, he chose, instead, to lecture on the Koranic justifications of violent jihad. He'd been moved to anger, he explained, because it was "getting harder and harder for Muslims in the service to morally justify being in a military that seems constantly engaged against fellow Muslims." So he defended suicide terrorism, argued that non-believers should be savagely killed (including by pouring boiling oil down their throats), and presented a power-point slide that invoked the prophet Mohammed's words:

> I have been commanded to fight people until they testify that there is no God but Allah and that Muhammad is the Messenger of Allah, and perform the prayer, and pay *zakat*. If they say it, they have saved their blood and possessions from me, except for the rights of Islam over them. And the final reckoning is with Allah.

In the now-infamous bin Laden locution, the slide concluded, "We love death more then [*sic*] you love life."[12]

It was patent that Hasan should be removed from our armed forces. In his mind, he was not a member of the U.S. Army. He was "a soldier of Allah" as the business cards he designed attested—cards that were seized from his apartment after the massacre. Fellow soldiers who knew him fulminated when he appeared pleased by an Islamist terrorist's June 2008 murder of a U.S. soldier outside a Little Rock recruiting station. Some complained to superiors that he was anti-American. Many feared he could commit a fragging incident of the type carried out by another Muslim soldier, Sergeant Hasan Akbar, who killed two fellow troops and injured several others by rolling a grenade into their tent in 2003.[13]

Nevertheless, when the FBI decided not to proceed with an investigation of Hasan, neither the Bureau nor the Defense Department investigator on the FBI's Joint Terrorism Task Force thought the fact that Hasan was in communication with Awlaki was important enough to share with the army brass.[14] Who knows if that would have mattered? Nothing else did. Hasan was a Muslim, and the military was deathly afraid to enforce military discipline against a Muslim. It didn't seem worth enduring the Flying Imams treatment. It didn't seem worth the torrents of grief that would be sure to follow from CAIR and ISNA and the MAS and the rest of the Islamic grievance industry that now has Washington's ear.

So they didn't remove him. They promoted him to major in May 2009.[15] Five months later, he slaughtered thirteen of our best and bravest.

Naturally, in the recriminations that followed, there were congressional finger-waggings and internal investigations. In January 2010, the Defense Department completed its review, which it called "Protecting the Force—Lessons from Fort Hood."[16] Nowhere does it refer to Hasan's atrocity as a terrorist attack or address the Islamist ideology that drove him to it. In fact, in the fifty-three-page whitewash, none of the words *Islam*, *jihad*, *Yemen* or *Awlaki* is mentioned a single time.

At Fort Hood, nothing changed. ISNA's Louay Safi continued the work there, doing what our Defense Department retained him to do: giving Islam classes to our soldiers as they were about to deploy to the Muslim world. On December 2, less than a month after the massacre, commanders on the base permitted him to conduct a brief ceremony: The presentation of a check on behalf of ISNA to the victims' family, a demonstration of Islamic charity and thoughtfulness. One military official anonymously boiled, "This is nothing short of blood money. This is criminal and the Fort Hood base commander should be fired right now."[17]

There wasn't much chance of that. The army's chief-of-staff, General George W. Casey Jr., spoke of the massacre not as a terrorist act of war but as a "tragedy." The real concern, he nattered, was the risk to "our diversity." As he put it in an NBC News interview, "Our diversity, not only in our Army, but in our country, is a strength. And as horrific as this tragedy was, if our diversity becomes a casualty, I think that's worse."[18]

Of course, the greatness of America, and of America's Army, is the opposite of diversity. It is *E Pluribus Unum*, the fact that the many become one. The beauty of the military as an institution is that Americans from all walks of life volunteer because they want to be part of the single culture it forges . . . just as people from all parts of the world once came to America to be part of the unique American identity. To the contrary, what General Casey venerates is the Tower of Babel—to the mind-blowing point that the prospect of its toppling is, in his mind, worse than the killing of American soldiers.

Surrender to Sabotage

That is not how the Islamists see it. They believe they are, as the Organization of the Islamic Conference put it, "the Islamic Umma that Allah made the best Nation." They intend to fight to the end because they believe they will win, and that they fully deserve to win. Islamists have no qualms about mentioning the names of their enemies. Islamists have no reservations about fighting for conquest until their enemies unconditionally surrender or are utterly destroyed. In the wake of the Fort Hood massacre, Anwar al-Awlaki publicly praised Nidal Malik Hasan—took credit, in fact, for issuing the Islamic fatwa that justified the attack.[19]

Then the former Dar al-Hijrah imam and his Islamist terrorist confederates in Yemen had another surprise for their enemies.

On Christmas Day, one of the highest Christian holidays in the West and the one almost universally observed by Americans, they dispatched Umar Farouk Abdulmutallab on a plane to the United States. As it descended to land in Detroit, Abdulmutallab attempted to detonate a chemical bomb concealed in his pants. Alert passengers and crew tackled him, put out the fire, and prevented what could otherwise have been the killing of 288 people.

The commander-in-chief, on vacation in Hawaii, waited three days to make a public statement about this act of war. In the interim, his administration implemented its strategy of treating Islamist terrorist attacks as mere crimes—an effort to improve America's image in the Muslim world by demonstrating that we are not "at war with Islam." As a result, investigators got only fifty minutes of polite interrogation with Abdulmutallab before he was given *Miranda* warnings, invoked his right to counsel, and ceased taking questions.[20] Despite this blunder, U.S. agents had still learned that Abdulmutallab was an al Qaeda operative who had spent the preceding four months being trained by terrorists in Yemen. Al Qaeda, moreover, had publicly claimed responsibility for the attempted airliner bombing.[21]

Finally, there was the public reporting, available not just to intelligence agents but to anyone who could read a newspaper or flip on a television set. This terrorist's path to Yemen had begun, it turned out, in the United Kingdom. While attending University College in London, he had joined the Muslim Brotherhood–inspired Student Islamic Society (the British equivalent of the Muslim Students Association), becoming president of that organization in 2006. In class, he had defended the Taliban and its program to Islamicize Afghanistan. Out of class, he had regularly attended a London mosque run by the Muslim World League, the seminal Saudi/Muslim Brotherhood collaboration.[22] Abdulmutallab had run the full Islamist course: from theory, to commitment, to deadly practice.

This was all known when President Obama took to the microphone. Yet, he reported to the American people that Abdulmutallab was an "isolated extremist."[23]

No Yemen, no Britain, no Islam, no ideology. Most of all, no Grand Jihad. A lone "isolated extremist." Just like Nidal Malik Hasan, Abdulmutallab had spontaneously combusted: without rhyme or reason, impossible to predict, impossible to prevent. From this kind of threat, America could not, would not, defend itself.

A half a world away, King Abdullah smiled. He knew a bow when he heard one.

EPILOGUE

To produce tirades of victimhood was why the Muslim Brotherhood and their Saudi backers created the Muslim Students Association. The speaker at the 2004 MSA conference in Chicago did not disappoint.

He insisted that the terrorism indictment against Sami al-Arian was "politically motivated." As al-Arian's daughter Laila, an oft-featured star at such events, looked on, the speaker groused that the prosecution was "truly a sad commentary on our legal system" and "a travesty of justice." Most disgraceful, he added, was "the process that has been used" which was "atrocious," such that the case against al-Arian fit a "common pattern . . . of politically-motivated prosecutions," exaggerating the "threat to American security."[1]

In actuality, the sad commentary was how common, and how willfully false, was the repetition of this Islamist party line. As described in the government's indictment, al-Arian had been a top American operative of the Palestinian Islamic Jihad terrorist organization. The trial evidence indicated that al-Arian (who eventually admitted to having been a member of the Muslim Brotherhood) may have been the author of PIJ's "manifesto." That Islamist clarion call rejects "any peaceful solution to the Palestinian cause" and "affirm[s] . . . the Jihad solution and the martyrdom style as the only choice for liberation."[2]

PIJ killed massively in Israel and the Palestinian territories, and its murder victims included American citizens. That never troubled al-Arian. The invaluable David Horowitz recounts:

> An FBI surveillance video of al-Arian's fund-raising tour of American mosques shows al-Arian being introduced as "the president of the Islamic Committee for Palestine . . . the active arm of the Islamic *Jihad* Movement." While others in the video praise the killing of Jews and Christians, al-Arian states, "Let us damn America . . . . Let us damn [her] allies until death." In another speech al-Arian said, "We assemble today to pay respects to the march of the martyrs and to the river of blood that gushes forth and does not extinguish, from butchery to butchery, and from martyrdom to martyrdom, from *jihad* to *jihad*."[3]

Al-Arian raised hundreds of thousands of dollars to keep the river of blood in full-time gush, jihad-to-jihad being a full-time business. He monitored both the coordination of attacks between PIJ and Hamas and also the "Pact of Brotherhood and Cooperation" the two Islamist terrorist organizations entered with each other. He bragged in fund-raising pleas that terror attacks demonstrated PIJ's efficiency.[4] When he finally pled guilty to conspiring to support terrorism, the judge who had presided over his case called him a "master manipulator" who had serially lied to cover up his exertions on PIJ's behalf. After he was sentenced, he refused to testify in the grand jury regarding his knowledge of other terrorists and their activities, resulting in yet another indictment for criminal contempt.

The process that resulted in al-Arian's case *was* atrocious—but for reasons quite the opposite of those posited by the MSA conference speaker. The real "travesty" lay in the fact that, prior to the 9/11 attacks, self-imposed Justice Department restrictions prevented the FBI's counterterrorism agents from communicating effectively with criminal investigators and Justice Department prosecutors. This was the Clinton Justice Department's infamous "wall." Consequently, al-Arian was able to carry on his deadly business for years. Not until the wall was razed did agents connect the intelligence dots that yielded a prosecutable case. The inexcusable delay armed al-Arian's lawyers with a formidable argument. Regardless of the mountains of evidence against him, they looked jurors in the eye and quite sensibly asserted that no government in its right mind would let someone it truly believed was a terrorist parade about for years, like al-Arian had done, teaching impressionable young people and hobnobbing with high public officials—including presidents. Far from being fundamentally unfair to al-Arian, this legal process and the political connections it helped him make along the way worked to his tremendous advantage. Before he finally pled guilty, a jury acquitted him on several counts and hung on others. The process very nearly derailed what should have been a slam-dunk case.

In the meantime, al-Arian, the committed Islamist, became a darling of the American Left. In Brotherhood fashion, his bloviations about "civil rights" and "social justice" camouflaged his attacks on the laws that would eventually undo him: the material support to terrorism law (the law President Obama targeted in his Cairo speech when he pandered to Muslims about easing restrictions on Islamic "charity") and the Patriot Act (the vehicle that finally knocked down Clinton's wall). Al-Arian's partners in these campaigns included such Leftist bastions as the Center for Constitutional Rights, the National Lawyers Guild, the ACLU, and, of course, CAIR and the American Muslim Council. It was Islam and the Left, sabotaging America.[5]

Naturally, the speaker at the MSA conference mentioned none of this. In fact, when he wasn't championing al-Arian's cause, the speaker was lambasting the Patriot Act. That legislation, he claimed, was "horrible" and "dangerous" because of its dismantling of the wall—the curative measure that even most Patriot opponents have conceded is essential if we are to thwart jihadist attacks and prosecute the likes of al-Arian. The speaker went on to regurgitate the standard Brotherhood/CAIR laundry list of purported "persecutions" against Muslims, including the case of José Padilla (who plotted a post-9/11 second-wave of attacks and was ultimately convicted on separate terrorism charges); the case of Yasser Hamdi (whose capture and detention as an enemy combatant in the War on Terror was upheld by the Supreme Court); and the prosecution of an imam and a pizzeria owner in Albany for plotting to launch missiles at a Pakistani diplomat (the men were later convicted and sentenced to fifteen years' imprisonment despite claiming they'd been entrapped. Question: Would a provocateur, no matter how persuasive, be able to entrap *you* into launching missiles at someone?).[6]

By now, such speechifying at MSA conferences is old hat. This instance would not be worth mentioning were it not for the identity of the speaker. He was Yale law student Rashad Hussain. Only four years after his tirade, Hussain was selected by President Barack Obama to be, as the president puts it, "a trusted member of my staff."

And what exactly are the thirty-two-year-old Hussain's qualifications to serve as Deputy Associate Counsel to the President of the United States? Obama bragged that Hussain is a "*hafiz* of the Koran"—meaning, a Muslim who has memorized Islamic scriptures in the original Arabic—and a "respected member of the Muslim community."[7] He also co-wrote a study urging the Islamist Left's standard, counterfactual conceit: Terrorism is somehow antithetical to the teachings of Islam, therefore we must look elsewhere (like at economic and social injustice) to find what actually causes it, and we must work closely with "mainstream" Islamic organizations—even if they oppose Western democracy and culture—as long as they reject "violent extremism."[8]

Ironically, this position is often taken by people who turn out to have advocated on behalf of the likes of al-Arian, a "violent extremist" who believed he was doing what his religion commanded him to do. The contradiction never seems to register: Hussain's effusions of sympathy for al-Arian, Padilla, Hamdi, and other violent jihadists were obviously of no concern to a president who began his public career in the living room of Bill Ayers and Bernardine Dohrn—the Weather Underground terrorists who saw blowing up buildings and targeting U.S. military personnel as just another way to achieve social justice. And being a headliner at what predictably became an al-Arian support confab arranged by the MSA—the Ikhwan-created precursor of the Islamic Society of North America—was clearly more a credential than a drawback. Hussain spent part of his year as a trusted Obama staffer attending training sessions run by CAIR (ISNA's fellow unindicted co-conspirator in the Hamas terrorism financing case).[9]

The White House was quick to credit Hussain as one of the most important contributors to—you guessed it—Obama's fatuous Cairo speech on Islam and the West.[10]

Then came the *pièce de resistance*: the president named Hussain to be his special envoy to the Organization of the Islamic Conference, the fifty-seven-member Islamist bloc dedicated to spreading sharia across the globe.[11] The move is yet another example of Obama geometrically worsening an Islamophilic misstep by his predecessor. Despite its staunchly anti-American, anti-liberty outlook, George W. Bush became the first president to name an envoy to the OIC and to trumpet the purported importance of working cooperatively with an entity whose most devout wish is an American decline and fall. Yet President Bush's ambassador, Sada Cumber, at least understood his job as attempting to move the OIC toward a condemnation of suicide bombing and the sorts of terrorism tactics that Sami al-Arian promoted.[12] With Hussain, by contrast, one is left to wonder whether America's representative believes America and its Constitution, as opposed to the OIC and its Cairo Declaration, present the superior vision of human freedom and dignity.

Human dignity was not much on display in Hussain's OIC appointment. The White House vigorously denied that he had championed al-Arian's cause. Hussain was more restrained, claiming a case of amnesia, but appearing tacitly to concur with the administration's claims that the disputed remarks had been made by al-Arian's daughter. Alas, Hussain was eventually confronted with a recording of his diatribe—whereupon he somehow instantly remembered that he had made the statements, that he had merely been a law student concerned about civil rights, and that he now thought Sami al-Arian was guilty after all.

Meantime, it emerged that, before the controversy became public, Hussain had pressured a journal to purge from its report of the event the remarks he supposedly hadn't been able to remember. (Naturally, the Obama-friendly journal complied, even though its reporter had insisted, correctly as it turned out, that her report was accurate.)[13] These developments stirred worthy controversy over both Hussain's fitness to represent the United States and the whole concept of extending the hand of friendship to the OIC, an organization that, like Obama, believes America requires radical change. But the president is standing by his man . . . and his plan.

He is also standing by his national security team, which is more like an Islamist outreach team, as if the two tasks were the same rather than at odds. Thus did John Brennan, Obama's top advisor on homeland security and counterterrorism, troop up to New York University to address what the media referred to as "Islamic law students," creating some confusion about whether Brennan had met with students of U.S. law who happened to be Muslim (as was the case) or students of sharia—these days, you have to ask.

The president's adviser ended up (unwittingly, it seemed) in an exchange with none other than Flying Imam extraordinaire Omar Shahin, who bleated about how "We feel that since September 11, we aren't enjoying these [American] values anymore. . . . Also, we feel that there's a big lack of trust between Muslims' community and our government. . . . My question: Is there anything being done by our government to rebuild this trust?" Shahin, of course, is beholden to sharia values, with which he urges Muslims to supplant American principles. No matter: Brennan played right into the narrative that it was the United States, rather than the likes of Shahin, whose basic trustworthiness was in question. Rather than challenging Shahin, he accepted the Islamist's premise and promised that Obama was "determined to put America on a strong course"—meaning a course that would correct the Bush administration approach to counterterrorism that had been so "over the top" and "excessive."[14]

Because the irrepressible Michelle Malkin was on the case, we know that things soon went from bad to worse:

> Brennan then went on to decry the "ignorant feelings" of Americans outraged at the jihadi attacks on American soil. And then he told Shahin and the audience of Muslim students that he "was very concerned after the attack in Fort Hood as well as the December 25 attack that all of sudden there were people who went back into this fearful position that lashed out, not thinking through what was reasonable and appropriate."[15]

So, with fourteen innocent lives lost to what the Obama administration can't bring itself to call Islamist terrorism fomented by Islamist ideology, the president's counterterrorism guru is channeling army chief-of-staff General George Casey, who thinks the real threat is not to our lives but to our "diversity." Jihadists kill, and Brennan frets over those notorious violent reactionaries, the American people.

Most hair-raising of all, was Brennan's answer when he was pressed by an obvious intruder on the matter of Guantanamo Bay detainees who, upon release, are returning to the jihad at alarming rates—rates that stun Americans who've bought the party line that terror has nothing to do with Islamist ideology. Recent reports have raised the recidivism rate to 20 percent—which, for reasons already explained, is absurdly low. Yet for Brennan, it was somehow a sign of progress: "You know," he countered, in "the American penal system, the recidivism rate is up to something about 50 percent or so, as far as return to crime. Twenty percent isn't that bad."[16]

One in five mass-murdering, anti-American jihadists goes back to mass-murder, and the Obama administration figures we're doing pretty well considering all those pick-pockets who are back picking pockets. Why not go back to seeing "violent extremism" as just another criminal justice issue?

Meanwhile, with the Justice Department once again the epicenter of counterterrorism as it was throughout the nineties, government policy is now being made by lawyers recruited by the Obama administration after spending much of the last eight years volunteering their services to America's enemies. That includes Attorney General Eric Holder himself. He has recently acknowledged that, as a private lawyer, he filed Supreme Court briefs arguing that al Qaeda "Dirty Bomber" Jose Padilla should be treated as an ordinary criminal defendant, not a war prisoner—a fact he withheld from the Senate during his confirmation hearings. His hires at Justice include Jennifer Daskal, formerly of the leftist Human Rights Watch, who has no prior prosecutorial experience. Her qualifications appear to be that she spent the last several years tirelessly advocating for the enemy combatants held at Guantanamo Bay, helping compromise a covert CIA program involving the detention of captured terrorists in European prisons, and urging the United Nations to investigate the United States for torture, war crimes, and international law violations (purportedly committed in what she called "the so-called 'war on terror'").

For eight years, the Left has portrayed such "progressive" lawyers as the embodiment of American "values," fearlessly putting America's government on trial in America's courts over the manner in which Bush administration officials have prosecuted a war Americans overwhelmingly support. Now, the Obama Justice Department is rewarding the worst war criminals with the gold-plated due process of civilian trials, replacing enhanced interrogations with *Miranda* warnings, and releasing some terrorists while failing to appeal when judges order others released. Still, we are told to accept as an article of faith that their prior, voluntary representation of terrorists does not mean these lawyers would countenance a policy of coddling terrorists. No, of course not.

In the interim, more details are emerging about the Homeland Security Department's high-level pow-wows with tentacles of the Muslim Brotherhood. DHS Secretary Janet Napolitano, along with her top aides, personally held two days of intensive briefings in late January 2010 for, among others, ISNA, MPAC (the Muslim Public Affairs Council), and the Muslim American Society. The concept, imported from the United Kingdom, is to treat these anti-Western sharia organizations as allies and devise, in collaboration with them, a "two-way information-sharing" framework. As one exasperated former U.S. intelligence officer explained to Pajamas Media:

> The "counter-radicalization" program is something that the other side created for us. . . . It initially started in Britain. The Muslim Brotherhood groups suggested it. We went over there and got it. We thought it was a great idea and now we're using it. It's the enemy giving us a way to destroy ourselves.[17]

Just so. If you didn't know better, you'd think Islamists had developed "a kind of grand jihad in eliminating and destroying the Western civilization from within and 'sabotaging' its miserable house."

Why, it's almost as if they now had a government that was helping them do it.

NOTES

Chapter One

1. Andrew C. McCarthy, "Sistani and the Democracy Project—A useful measure of the divide between 'To Hell with Them' and 'Anything Goes'" (*National Review Online*, March 20, 2006) (http://www.nationalreview.com/mccarthy/mccarthy200603200816.asp); Andrew G. Bostom, "Is Shi'ism the Iranian Regime's Achilles Heel?" (*The American Thinker*, Dec. 26, 2009) (ttp://www.americanthinker.com/2009/12/is_shiism_the_iranian_regimes.html).

2. Susan Katz Keating, "The Wahhabi Fifth Column" (*Frontpage Magazine*, Dec. 30, 2002) (http://97.74.65.51/readArticle.aspx?ARTID=20523).

3. Sujit Das, "A Tribute to a Muslim Genius" (*Islam Watch*, Nov. 12, 2006) (http://www.islam-watch.org/SujitDas/MuslimGenius.htm), citing Carl Sagan, *The Demon-haunted World: Science as a Candle in the Dark* (Ballantine Books, 2007), p. 2. In 1993, the supreme religious au-

thority of Saudi Arabia, Sheik Abdel-Aziz bin Baaz, issued an edict, or fatwah, declaring that the world is flat. Anyone of the round persuasion does not believe in God and should be punished." See also Ibid., citing Judith Miller, *God Has Ninety-nine Names* (Touchstone, 1996), p. 114 (recalling Sheikh bin Baaz's condemnation of the "Copernican 'heresy'" of a heliocentric cosmos).

4. Center for Religious Freedom, "Saudi Publications on Hate Ideology Invade American Mosques" (Freedom House, 2005), p. 4 (http://www.freedomhouse.org/uploads/special_report/45.pdf).

5. Mohammad Jamjoom and Saad Abdedine, "Saudis order 40 lashes for elderly woman for mingling" (CNN, March 9, 2009) (http://www.cnn.com/2009/WORLD/meast/03/09/saudi.arabia.lashes/index.html).

6. Bret Stephens, "A President, Not a Symbol" (*Wall Street Journal*, March 11, 2008) (http://online.wsj.com/article/SB120519540222325779.html#).

7. See Suras 33:21 and 61:5–6.

8. See generally Saul Alinsky, *Rules for Radicals*; see also Barack Obama, "Why Organize? Problems and Promise in the Inner City," a chapter Obama contributed to an Alinsky retrospective called *After Alinsky: Community Organizing in Illinois* (*Illinois Issues*, University of Illinois at Springfield, reissued in 1990) (originally issued in 1988 by Sangamon State University, which is now the University of Illinois at Springfield) (http://www.edwoj.com/Alinsky/AlinskyObamaChapter1990.htm); David Horowitz, *Barack Obama's Rules for Revolution: The Alinsky Model* (David Horowitz Freedom Center, 2009).

9. David Horowitz, *Unholy Alliance: Radical Islam and the American Left* (Regnery, 2004), p. 69.

Chapter Two

1. U.K. Office of National Statistics Release on Most Popular Names (Sept. 8, 2009); *CIA World Fact Book* (entries for United Kingdom and Germany) (accessed Sept. 11, 2009); Rebecca Lefort and Ben Leapman, "Mohammed is most popular name for baby boys in London" (*Telegraph*, Sept. 15, 2009) (http://www.telegraph.co.uk/news/newstopics/religion/6194354/Mohammed-is-most-popular-name-for-baby-boys-in-London.html); Nick Allen, "Jack pips Mohammed to be most

popular boys' name" (*Telegraph* Sept. 9, 2009) (http://www.telegraph. co.uk/news/uknews/6156803/Jack-pips-Mohammed-to-be-most-popular-boys-name.html); Max Hastings, "Mohammed is now the third most popular boy's name in Englad. So why this shabby effort to conceal it?" (*Daily Mail*, Sept. 11, 2009) (http://www.dailymail.co.uk/debate/ columnists/article-1212368/Mohammed-popular-boys-England-So-shabby-effort-conceal-it.html#).

2. Pew Research Center, "Muslim Americans: Middle Class and Mostly Mainstream" (May 22, 2007) (http://pewresearch.org/assets/ pdf/muslim-americans.pdf); see also Steven Emerson, "MPAC: Who's Changing the Subject?" (*Counterterrorism Blog*, June 8, 2007) (republished by the Investigative Project on Terrorism at http://www.investigativeproject.org/292/mpac-whos-changing-the-subject).

3. Allahpundit, "Poll ~ 15 % of British Muslims have a rod for jihad" (Hot Air, July 3, 2006) (http://hotair.com/archives/2006/07/03/ poll-15-of-british-muslims-have-a-rod-for-jihad/) (collecting polling data from the *Times* of London and the Pew Research Center).

4. Smadar Haran Kaiser, "The World Should Know What He Did to My Family" (*Washington Post*, 2003) (http://www.washingtonpost. com/ac2/wp-dyn?pagename=article&contentId=A2740-2003May17); Baruch Gordon, "PA Grants Murderer of 4-Year-Old Girl Honorary Citizenship" (IsraelNationalNews.com, March 15, 2006) (http://www. israelnationalnews.com/News/News.aspx/100254); Andrew C. McCarthy, "Swapped for Live Terrorists, two Israeli Soldiers Confirmed Dead" (*National Review Online, The Corner*, July 17, 2008) (http://corner. nationalreview.com/post/?q=MGE3NzYyYmNkYjI5ZmM4Y2U1Zm Q1MGU3MDUzN2NhODk=).

5. Andrew C. McCarthy, "Our Terrorists Are Better Than Your Terrorists—Supporting Fatah, the Bush administration makes a deal with the devil" (*National Review Online*, June 21, 2007) (http://article.nationalreview.com/?q=MDg2NTNkOTMoZjI5ZTEzNzBjNzc4ODNj ZjRhMmRlZjQ=); see also Itamar Marcus and Barbara Cook, "Denial of Youth" (*Frontpage Magazine*, March 2, 2007) (http://www.frontpagemag. com/readArticle.aspx?ARTID=25787) (collecting polling data).

6. Abdurrahman Wahid, "Right Islam vs. Wrong Islam—Muslims and non-Muslims must unite to defeat the Wahhabi ideology" (*Wall Street Journal*, Dec. 31, 2005) (http://www.opinionjournal.com/

extra/?id=110007743), reprinted in *Current Trends in Islamist Ideology*, Vol. 3 (2006).

7. Andrew G. Bostom, "The Muslim Mainstream and the New Caliphate" (*American Thinker*, April 27, 2007) http://www.american-thinker.com/2007/04/the_muslim_mainstream_and_the.html), citing "Muslims Believe US Seeks to Undermine Islam" (WorldPublicO-pinion.org, April 24, 2007) (http://www.worldpublicopinion.org/incl/printable_version.php?pnt=346).

8. Sadanand Dhume, "Adultery in Aceh—The latest sign of creeping Shariah" (*Wall Street Journal*, Opinion Asia, Sept. 15, 2009) (http://online.wsj.com/article/SB10001424052970203917304574414111062066186.html).

9. Diana West, "Britain's Silence Ammo for a Sharia-Run Future" (*Townhall*, Aug. 1, 2008) (http://townhall.com/columnists/DianaWest/2008/08/01/britains_silence_ammo_for_a_sharia-run_future).

10. "Poll: Bin Laden tops Musharraf in Pakistan" (CNN, Sept. 11, 2007) (http://edition.cnn.com/2007/POLITICS/09/11/poll.pakistanis/index.html).

11. Andrew G. Bostom, "The Muslim Mainstream and the New Caliphate."

12. Niniek Karmini, "Indonesians torch Muslim sect's mosque" (Associated Press, April 27, 2008) (URL no longer available); Robert Spencer, "Indonesia: Muslim mob chanting "Kill, kill" torches mosque of heretical Islamic sect" (Jihad Watch, April 28, 2008) (http://www.jihadwatch.org/archives/020822.php) (citing and excerpting Karmini's report).

13. Robert Spencer, *The Truth about Muhammad—Founder of the World's Most Intolerant Religion* (Regnery 2006).

14. Robert Spencer, "A few reflections on Wahid's 'Right Islam vs. Wrong Islam'" (*Jihad Watch*, Dec. 31, 2005) (http://www.jihadwatch.org/archives/009623.php).

15. George Pell, "Islam and Western Democracies" (Legatus Summit, Naples, Florida, 2005) (reprinted by David Virtue, "Virtue On Line," May 4, 2006 (http://virtueonline.org/portal/modules/news/article.php?storyid=3980).

16. Campus Watch Report, "Esposito: Apologist for Militant Islam" (*Frontpage Magazine*, Sept. 3, 2002) (http://www.frontpagemag.com/readArticle.aspx?ARTID=22984), citing "'Jihad' not Necessarily a Call to Religious War" (*All Things Considered*, National Public Radio, host Robert Siegel, May 18, 1994 [4:30 pm ET], Transcript # 1486–9); see also Andrea Levin, CAMERA Media Report, October 2, 1995. http://world.std.com/~camera/docs/oncamera/ocmm.html.

17. Zeyno Baran, "The Muslim Brotherhood's U.S. Network" (*Current Trends in Islamist Ideology*, Vol. 6, p. 96) (Hudson Institute Center on Islam, Democracy and the Future of the Modern World) (http://www.currenttrends.org/research/detail/the-muslim-brotherhoods-us-network).

18. Andrew G. Bostom, "Islamism or Islam? Islamist or Islamic?" (*The American Thinker*, Nov. 14, 2009) (http://www.americanthinker.com/2009/11/islamism_or_islam_islamist_or.html).

Chapter Three

1. Richard P. Mitchell, *The Society of Muslim Brothers* (Oxford University Press, 1969), pp. 193–4.

2. Eric Brown, "After the Ramadan Affair: New Trends in Islamism in the West" (*Current Trends in Islamist Ideology*, Vol. 2, 2005), p. 9.

3. Michael Pollock, *A Path Out of the Desert* (Random House, 2008).

4. McCarthy, *Willful Blindness*.

5. Bernard Lewis, *Islam and the West* (Oxford University Press, 1993), p. 155.

6. Daniel Benjamin and Steven Simon, *The Age of Sacred Terror—Radical Islam's War Against America* (Random House Trade Paperback, 2003), pp. 54–55 & n.

7. Mark R. Levin, *Liberty & Tyranny* (Threshold Editions, 2009).

8. Ian Johnson, "The Brotherhood's Western Expansion" (*Current Trends in Islamist Ideology*, Vol. 6) (2008), p. 80. (http://www.futureofmuslimworld.com/research/pubID.80/pub_detail.asp#).

9. Robert B. Bork, *The Tempting of America* (Free Press, 1990).

10. Wahid, "Right Islam vs. Wrong Islam."

11. Raymond Ibrahim, "When Will Westerners Stop Westernizing Islamic Concepts?" (*Middle East Forum* Aug. 25, 2009) (http://www.me-forum.org/2441/westernizing-islamic-concepts).

12. Robert Spencer, "A few reflections on Wahid's 'Right Islam vs. Wrong Islam.'" The Koran is not arranged in chronological order but according to the length of its suras (or chapters).

13. Qutb, *Milestones*, p. 63; see also Bostom, *The Legacy of Jihad*, p. 237; see also Benjamin & Simon, *The Age of Sacred Terror*, pp. 64–66.

14. Richard P. Mitchell, *Society of Muslim Brothers* (Oxford University Press, Middle Eastern Monographs series, 1969) (Oxford University Press paperback ed., 1993), p. 207. The study was originally presented as Mitchell's doctoral thesis at Princeton in 1960. See also Stephen A. Emerson, "Report on the Roots of Violent Islamist Extremism and Efforts to Counter It: The Muslim Brotherhood" (hereafter, "The Muslim Brotherhood") (July 10, 2008 Testimony before the Senate Committee on Homeland Security and Governmental Affairs) (http://www.investigativeproject.org/documents/testimony/353.pdf).

15. Hassan al-Banna, "Jihad," http://www.youngmuslims.ca/online_library/books/jihad/ (see Emerson, "The Muslim Brotherhood").

16. Ibid.

Chapter Four

1. Investigative Project on Terrorism, Document Archive at http://www.investigativeproject.org/documents/misc/20.pdf.

2. Ian Johnson, "The Brotherhood's Westward Expansion," pp. 77–78 & n. 23.

3. Jean-Charles Brisard, "Swiss Supreme Court Keeps Youssef Nada on the Terrorist List" (Brisard blog, Nov. 30, 2007) (http://jcb.blogs.com/jcb_blog/2007/11/swiss-supreme-c.html).

4. Patrick Poole, "The Muslim Brotherhood 'Project'" (*Frontpage Magazine*, May 11, 2006) (http://www.frontpagemag.com/Articles/Read.aspx?GUID=67736123-6864-4205-B51E-BCBDEF45FCDE). As Poole details, the fruits of the raid remain the private preserve of American and foreign intelligence agencies, but much is known about "*the Project*" thanks to the investigative reporting of the French journalist Sylvain Besson, particularly his book, *La conquête de l'Occident: Le projet secret des Islamistes* (*The Conquest of the West: The Islamists' Secret*

Project) (Seuil, 2005). In a footnote to his important 2008 essay "The Brotherhood's Westward Expansion" (supra, p. 82, n. 19), Ian Johnson throws cold water on what he calls Besson's "master plan" theory, arguing that the document "is anonymous" and that "no concrete evidence exists that the plan was ever implemented." Rather, Johnson says, "such documents are probably illustrative of the general desire to push the Brotherhood's ideology, but not an actionable plan to do so." But the fact that *the Project's* author is not identified is not nearly as significant as the fact that the document was found in the home of Nada, who was formally designated as a terrorist under both American and U.N. legal processes and who, Poole notes, has conceded that the authors were Brotherhood associates. Moreover, Johnson himself contends that there is a "network of political Islam in the West" that was "created through determination and persistence," based on "a vision that was vigorously pursued over decades." Ibid. at 76. Clearly, the existence of such a vision is entirely consistent with the occasional generation by movement leaders of strategic plans—such as *the Project* and the 1991 memo—to achieve the vision. And the fact that the Brotherhood has proceeded in the manner spelled out by these strategic plans underscores their significance.

5. Joseph Myers, "Homeland Security Implications of the Holy Land Foundation Trial" (*The American Thinker* Sept. 18, 2007) (http://www.americanthinker.com/2007/09/homeland_security_implications_1.html).

6. Mitchell, *Society of Muslim Brothers*, p. 14; see also Emerson, "The Muslim Brotherhood."

7. Caroline Fourest, *Brother Tariq—The Doublespeak of Tariq Ramadan* (Encounter, 2008), p. 8.

8. Bernard Lewis, *The Middle East—A Brief History of the Last 2,000 Years* (Scribner, 1995); Paul Berman, *Terror and Liberalism* (W.W. Norton & Co., 2003) (Norton paperback ed., 2004), p. 59.

9. Wahid, "Right Islam vs. Wrong Islam," p. 6; see also Emerson, "The Muslim Brotherhood," n. 15 (the "pious predecessors").

10. Andrew G. Bostom, "Von Grunebaum: Islam as Inherently Political" (Andrew Bostom.org, April 19, 2009) (http://www.andrew-bostom.org/blog/2008/04/19/von-grunebaum-islam-as-inherently-political/) (quoting Gustave E. von Grunebaum, "Problems of Muslim

Nationalism," published in *Islam and the West*, edited by Richard Frye, The Hague, 1957).

11. Fourest, *Brother Tariq*, pp. 10–11. Fourest refutes the claims of Banna's grandson, the Swiss Islamist Tariq Ramadan, that Banna was heir to the rationalist reform tradition of Mohammed Abdu, pointing out that Rida, while a prominent student of Abdu's, "was determined to rigidify this aspect of his thought and to rid it of all rationalism." (Quoting Ali Merad, a specialist in Muslim reform movements.) Banna was more plainly influenced by Rida, and notwithstanding Ramadan's efforts to harmonize Abdu and Rida into one reformist current, they were significantly different thinkers.

12. Ibid.; see also, Berman, *Terror and Liberalism*; Trevor Stanley, "Understanding the Origins of Wahhabism and Salafism" (The Jamestown Foundation, *Global Terrorism Analysis* Vol. 3, Issue 14, July 15, 2005).

13. See, e.g., Wahid, "Right Islam vs. Wrong Islam."

14. See, e.g., Brown, "After the Ramadan Affair: New Trends in Islamism in the West."

15. See, e.g., Gilles Kepel, *Muslim Extremism in Egypt* (University of California Press, 2003 ed.), p. 58.

16. Mitchell, *Society of Muslim Brothers*, p. 195.

17. Fourest, *Brother Tariq*, p. 17.

18. Banna, "Jihad" (http://www.youngmuslims.ca/online_library/ books/jihad/) (see Emerson, "The Muslim Brotherhood").

19. Fourest, *Brother Tariq*, p. 8.

20. Mitchell, *Society of Muslim Brothers*, pp. 185–91.

21. Ibid., pp. 206–07.

22. Ibid., p. 14; see also Emerson, "The Muslim Brotherhood."

23. Lt. Col. (res.) Jonathan Dahoah Halevi, "The Muslim Brotherhood: A Moderate Islamic Alternative to al-Qaeda or a Partner in Global *Jihad?*" *Jerusalem Viewpoints*, Jerusalem Center for Public Affairs, November 1, 2007; Emerson, "Report on the Roots of Violent Islamist Extremism and Efforts to Counter It: The Muslim Brotherhood."

24. See, e.g., Raymond Ibrahim, "What Piracy? This Is the Same Old Jihad" (*Pajamas Media*, April 17, 2009) (citing canonical hadith, collected by al-Tirmidhi) (http://pajamasmedia.com/blog/what-piracy-

this-is-the-same-old-jihad/) (see canonical hadith at http://hadith.al-islam.com/Display/Display.asp?Doc=2&Rec=2695).

25. Interview with Mohammad Akef, *Elaph*, May 23, 2008, http://65.17.227.80/ElaphWeb/AkhbarKhasa/2008/5/332823.htm; Emerson, "Report on the Roots of Violent Islamist Extremism and Efforts to Counter It: The Muslim Brotherhood."

26. Emerson, "The Muslim Brotherhood"; "The Muslim Brotherhood Movement in Support of Fighting Americans Forces in Iraq" (MEMRI Special Dispatch Series, Sept. 3, 2004), and "Cleric Says It's Right to Fight U.S. Civilians in Iraq" (Reuters, Sept. 2, 2004).

27. Ibid.

28. Ibid.

29. MEMRI Report No. 794, "Reactions to Sheikh Al-Qaradhawi's Fatwa Calling for the Abduction and Killing of American Civilians in Iraq" (Oct. 6, 2004) (http://www.memri.org/bin/articles.cgi?Page=subjects&Area=jihad&ID=SP79404#_edn4).

30. Ibid.

31. Raymond Ibrahim (editor and translator), *The Al Qaeda Reader* (Doubleday, 2007), pp. 282–82.

32. Robert Spencer, "Al-Qaradhawi at Solidarity Conference: 'I Hope to Die a Virtuous Death Like a Jihad Warrior, with the Head Severed from the Body'" (*Jihad Watch*, Feb. 25, 2005) (http://www.jihadwatch.org/archives/005160.php), citing MEMRI Report No. 869 (Feb. 25, 2005) (http://memri.org/bin/latestnews.cgi?ID=SD86905).

33. Israel Elad Altman, *Strategies of the Muslim Brotherhood Movement—1928–2007* (Hudson Institute, Center on Islam, Democracy, and the Future of the Muslim World, January 2009), p. 1.

34. Fourest, *Brother Tariq*, p. 13.

35. Ibid.; see also Altman, *Strategies of the Muslim Brotherhood Movement—1928–2007*, p.1.

36. Yusuf al-Qaradawi, "The importance of Islam Online" (Islam Online.net, accessed Sept. 1, 2009) (http://www.islamonline.net/english/qaradawi/index.shtml).

37. Ibid; see also Gilles Kepel, *Muslim Extremism in Egypt—The Prophet and Pharaoh* (University of California, 2003 ed.), p. 55.

38. Fourest, *Brother Tariq*, p. 15.

Notes

39. See, e.g., Fawaz A. Gerges, *The Far Enemy—Why Jihad Went Global* (Cambridge University Press, 2005), p. 109.

40. McCarthy, *Willful Blindness*.

41. Wright, *The Looming Tower*, p. 25. Consistent with the arc of his thought, Qutb, too, saw liberal democracy as a form of repression because it effectively imposes on people "the servitude to other men." Qutb, *Milestones*, p. 61; see also Bostom, *The Legacy of Jihad*, p. 234.

42. Mitchell, *Society of Muslim Brothers*, p. 14.

43. Ibid., pp. 14–15.

44. Emerson, "The Muslim Brotherhood," citing Mona El-Ghobashy, "The Metamorphosis of the Egyptian Muslim Brothers," *International Journal of Middle East Studies* (Cambridge University Press, 2005) p. 385; see also, e.g., Owen Bowcott and Faisal al Yafai, "Scholar with a streetwise touch defies expectations and stereotypes" (*The Guardian*, July 9, 2004) (http://www.guardian.co.uk/politics/2004/jul/09/religion.immigrationpolicy).

45. Andrew C. McCarthy, "Your Honey or Your Lyin' Eyes—The myth of a vibrant moderate Islam" (*National Review Online*, Feb. 15, 2006) (http://article.nationalreview.com/?q=MWRkNGMzZTdmZjRh MTNiOGMzYjFmM2RkM2E5YTYzMTU=).

46. Andrew C. McCarthy, "American 'Stupidity' and 'Arrogance' in Iraq—The State Department's Alberto Fernandez strikes again" (*National Review Online*, Oct. 23, 2006) (http://article.nationalreview.com /?q=OGFhYmIoZTAzYmM5MDYyZWYwZDI5NGIwZWY3YmZ kNTA=); Associated Press, "Envoy concedes U.S. arrogance in Iraq" (*Washington Times*, Oct. 21, 2006) (http://www.washingtontimes.com/ news/2006/oct/21/20061021-113644-1545r/).

47. Youssef Qaradawi interview, al-Jezeera Television (Qatar) (June 19, 2001), "The Prophet Muhammad as a Jihad Model," Middle East Media Research Institute (MEMRI) Report No. 246 (July 26, 2001) (http://memri.org/bin/articles.cgi?Page=archives&Area=sd&ID=SP24 601.

48. Daniel Pipes, "The Qaradawi Fatwas" (*Middle East Quarterly*, Summer 2004) (http://www.meforum.org/article/646).

49. Qaradawi interview, MEMRI Report No. 246.

Chapter Five

1. Baran, "The Muslim Brotherhood's U.S. Network."
2. Ibid.
3. Brown, "After the Ramadan Affair: New Trends in Islamism in the West."
4. Qaradawi interview, MEMRI Report No. 246.
5. Ana B. Soage, "Shaykh Yusuf al-Qaradawi: Portrait of a Leading Islamist Cleric" (*Global Politician*, March 25, 2008) (http://www.globalpolitician.com/24328-islam).
6. Ibid.
7. MEMRI Report No. 2277, "Scandinavian Islamic Groups Distance Themselves from Sheikh Yousef Al-Qaradhawi, Following MEMRI Translation of His Statements on Al-Jazeera TV Calling Holocaust 'Divine Punishment' for Jews, Warning 'Allah Willing, The Next Time Will Be at the Hand of the Believers'" (March 11, 2009) (http://www.memri.org/bin/latestnews.cgi?ID=SD227709).
8. Brown, "After the Ramadan Affair: New Trends in Islamism in the West."
9. Barbara F. Stowasser, "Reading Shaykh Yusuf al-Qaradawi on Women's Political Rights in Islam" (*Center for Contemporary Arabic Studies Newsletter*, March 2007) (http://ccas.georgetown.edu/files/Newsletter%203.07.pdf).
10. Asaf Romirowski, "Balancing the Bias" (*Jerusalem Post*, Feb. 2, 2009) (reprinted by the Middle East Forum) (http://www.meforum.org/2058/balancing-the-bias); Lee Kaplan, "The Saudi Fifth Column on Our Nation's Campuses" (*Frontpage Magazine*, April 5, 2004) (http://www.frontpagemag.com/readArticle.aspx?ARTID=13551).
11. Soage, "Shaykh Yusuf al-Qaradawi: Portrait of a Leading Islamist Cleric"; see also, e.g., Rajeev Syal and Julia Henry, "For her to be absolved from guilt, a raped woman must have shown good conduct" (*The Telegraph*, July 11, 2004) (http://www.hvk.org/articles/0704/107.html); Sharon Lapkin, "Western Muslims' Racist Rape Spree" (*Frontpage Magazine*, Dec. 27, 2005) (http://97.74.65.51/readArticle.aspx?ARTID=6161).
12. Soage, "Shaykh Yusuf al-Qaradawi: Portrait of a Leading Islamist Cleric."

13. Stowasser, "Reading Shaykh Yusuf al-Qaradawi on Women's Political Rights in Islam."

14. Joseph Schacht, *An Introduction to Islamic Law* (Oxford/Clarendon Press, 1982), pp. 69–71; Robert Spencer, *The Politically Incorrect Guide to Islam (and the Crusades)* (Regnery, 2006) p. 38.

15. Soage, "Shaykh Yusuf al-Qaradawi: Portrait of a Leading Islamist Cleric."

16. Brown, "After the Ramadan Affair: New Trends in Islamism in the West," p. 24.

17. Andrew G. Bostom, "Shari'a for All—Khaled 'Odd Job' El-Fadl Does Harvard" (AndrewBostom.org, March 7, 2008) (http://www.andrewbostom.org/blog/2008/03/07/shari%e2%80%99a-for-all%e2%80%94khaled-%e2%80%9codd-job%e2%80%9d-el-fadl-does-harvard/print/).

18. Douglas Jehl, Obituary for "Mohammed al-Ghazali, 78, An Egyptian Cleric and Scholar" (*New York Times*, March 14, 1996) (http://www.nytimes.com/1996/03/14/world/mohammed-al-ghazali-78-an-egyptian-cleric-and-scholar.html).

19. MEMRI Report No. 208, "Accusing Muslim Intellectuals of Apostasy" (Feb. 18, 2005) (http://memri.org/bin/latestnews.cgi?ID=IA20805).

20. See, e.g., Fawaz A. Gerges, *The Far Enemy—Why Jihad Went Global* (Cambridge University Press, 2005), pp. 108–09.

21. Brown, "After the Ramadan Affair: New Trends in Islamism in the West," pp. 8, 12–13

22. Baran, "The Muslim Brotherhood's U.S. Network," p. 116.

23. Brown, "After the Ramadan Affair: New Trends in Islamism in the West," pp. 9–10.

24. Sami A. Muhammad, "Integration Tops European Fatwa Council Meeting" (*IslamOnLine News*, Feb. 24, 2005) (http://www.islamonline.net/English/News/2005-02/24/article04.shtml).

25. Christopher Caldwell, "Islamic Europe?—When Bernard Lewis speaks . . ." (*Weekly Standard*, Oct. 4, 2004).

26. Theodore Dalrymple, "Our prisons are fertile grounds for cultivating suicide bombers—Why convicts are susceptible to the lure of radical Islam" (*London Times*, July 30, 2005) (http://www.timesonline.co.uk/tol/comment/columnists/guest_contributors/article549567.ece).

THE GRAND JIHAD

27. Leo McKinstry, "How the Government Has Declared War on White English People" (*Daily Express*, Aug. 9, 2007) (http://www.express.co.uk/posts/view/15991/How-the-Government-has-declared-war-on-white-English-people).

28. John O'Sullivan, "Sharia-UK: Brits Head Toward Islamic Law (*New York Post*, Sept. 18, 2008) (http://www.nypost.com/seven/09182008/postopinion/opedcolumnists/sharia_uk_129620.htm?page=0).

29. Diana West, "We Are Losing Europe to Islam" (*Townhall.com*, Sept. 18, 2008) (http://townhall.com/columnists/DianaWest/2008/09/18/we_are_losing_europe_to_islam); O'Sullivan, "Sharia-UK."

30. Simon Hughes, "£9k 'terror aid'" (*The Sun*, Feb. 25, 2009) (http://www.thesun.co.uk/sol/homepage/news/article2270404.ece).

31. A. Millar, "The State of Englishness" (*The Brussels Journal*, May 26, 2008) (http://www.brusselsjournal.com/node/3288); Fjordman, "The Execution of Britain" (*The Brussels Journal*, June 5, 2008) (http://www.brusselsjournal.com/node/3322).

32. Fjordman, "The Execution of Britain"; see also Steve Doughty and Andy Dolan, "You can't preach the Bible here, this is a Muslim area" (*The Daily Mail*, June 2, 2008) (http://www.dailymail.co.uk/news/article-1023483/You-preach-Bible-Muslim-area-What-police-told-Christian-preachers.html#).

33. Lapkin, "Western Muslims' Racist Rape Spree."

34. See, e.g., Lapkin, "Western Muslims' Racist Rape Spree"; Fjordman, "Immigrant Rape Wave in Sweden" (Fjordman Blog, Dec. 12, 2005) (http://fjordman.blogspot.com/2005/12/immigrant-rape-wave-in-sweden.html); Fjordman, "Rape: Nothing to do with Islam?" (Fjordman Blog, Aug. 1, 2005) (http://fjordman.blogspot.com/2005/08/rape-nothing-to-do-with-islam.html); Fjordman, "The Norwegian Government—Covering Up Immigrant Rapes (*Fjordman Blog*, July 24, 2005) (http://fjordman.blogspot.com/2005/07/norwegian-government-covering-up.html).

35. Theodore Dalrymple, "Our prisons are fertile grounds for cultivating suicide bombers."

36. Lapkin, "Western Muslims' Racist Rape Spree."

37. Richard Kerbaj, "Race riot flared after Muslims were urged to confront right-wing protests" (*London Times*, Sept. 7, 2009) (http://www.timesonline.co.uk/tol/news/uk/article6823767.ece); Andrew C. McCa-

rthy, "Liberal (Spin On) Fascism Alert" (*National Review Online, The Corner*), Sept. 7, 2009) (http://corner.nationalreview.com/post/?q=M2 NkYTQ3OTViOTZiNzI1ZGNjMzJhNzViYjk5NDhkOTg=).

38. "EU 'should expand beyond Europe'—Miliband on the EU" (BBC, Nov. 15, 2007) (http://news.bbc.co.uk/go/pr/fr/-/2/hi/uk_news/politics/7095657.stm); see also Fjordman, "The Execution of Britain."

39. Robert Spencer, "France, Germany to create Eurabia: Mediterranean Union" (*Jihad Watch*, March 5, 2008) (http://www.jihadwatch.org/2008/03/france-germany-to-create-eurabia-mediterranean-union.html) (quoting "Merkel and Sarkozy Find 'Club Med' Compromise," *Spiegel Online*, April 3, 2008) (http://www.spiegel.de/international/europe/0,1518,539247,00.html); see also Fjordman, "The Execution of Britain."

40. "Sharia law move quashed in Canada" (BBC, Sept. 12, 2005) (http://news.bbc.co.uk/2/hi/americas/4236762.stm).

41. Baran, "The Muslim Brotherhood's U.S. Network," pp. 116–17.

Chapter Six

1. Gilles Kepel, "The Brotherhood in the Salafist Universe" (*Current Trends in Islamist Ideology*, Vol. 6) (Hudson Institute, 2008), p. 23.

2. Berman, *Terror and Liberalism*, p. 69–70.

3. Trevor Stanley, "Understanding the Origins of Wahhabism and Salafism" (Jamestown.org, "Terrorism Monitor," Vol. 3, Issue 14, July 15, 2005) (http://www.jamestown.org/terrorism/news/article.php?articleid=2369746).

4. Ibid; see also Kepel, "The Brotherhood in the Salafist Universe," pp. 23–24.

5. Kepel, "The Brotherhood in the Salafist Universe," p. 23.

6. Susan Katz Keating, "The Wahhabi Fifth Column" (*Frontpage Magazine*, Dec. 30, 2002) (http://97.74.65.51/readArticle.aspx?ARTID=20523).

7. Kepel, "The Brotherhood in the Salafist Universe," p. 24; see also Erick Stakelbeck, "The Saudi Hate Machine" (*The National Interest*, Dec. 17, 2003) (republished by the Investigative Project on Terrorism at http://www.investigativeproject.org/171/the-saudi-hate-machine); Daniel Pipes and Sharon Chada, "CAIR: Islamists Fooling the Estab-

lishment" (*Middle East Quarterly*, Spring 2006) (http://www.meforum.org/916/cair-islamists-fooling-the-establishment).

8. In 2004, the U.S. Treasury Department conservatively estimated the figure at about $75 billion. Baran, "The Muslim Brotherhood's U.S. Network," pp. 98–99 & n. 11. In 2005, former CIA Director Jim Woolsey estimated that, just since the 1970s, the figure was then $90 billion. R. James Woolsey, "Saudi Government Propaganda in the United States: Avowed Ally or Secret Enemy?" (Presentation at the American Enterprise Institute, February 16, 2005); see also Evgenii Novikov, "The Muslim World League: Agent of Wahhabi Propagation in Europe" (The Jamestown Foundation, *Terrorism Monitor*, Vol. 3, Issue 9) (May 6, 2005) (http://www.jamestown.org/single/?no_cache=1&tx_ttnews%5Btt_news%5D=472).

9. Claudia Rosett, "Givers and Misers" (*Forbes*, Jan. 22, 2010) (http://www.forbes.com/2010/01/21/haiti-earthquake-aid-united-nations-opinions-columnists-claudia-rosett.html?boxes=opinionschannellighttop).

10. Qutb, *Social Justice in Islam*, p. 67.

11. Faraz Rabbani, "Zakat Cannot Be Given To Non-Muslims" (*Sunni Path*, July 3, 2005) (http://qa.sunnipath.com/issue_view.asp?HD=1&ID=1527&CATE=5).

12. Raymond Ibrahim, "Why Muslim Charities Fund Jihad" (*Pajamas Media*, Aug. 15, 2009) (http://pajamasmedia.com/blog/why-muslim-charities-fund-the-jihad/).

13. Matthew Levitt, *Hamas: Politics, Charity, and Terrorism in the Service of Jihad* (Yale University Press and The Washington Institute for Near East Policy, 2006), pp. 63–64.

14. Ibrahim, "Why Muslim Charities Fund Jihad."

15. Raymond Ibrahim, "What Piracy? This Is the Same Old Jihad" (citing canonical hadith, collected by al-Tirmidhi) (see canonical hadith at http://hadith.al-islam.com/Display/Display.asp?Doc=2&Rec=2695).

16. Ibrahim, "What Piracy? This Is the Same Old Jihad" (citing Suras 9:20, 9:60, 49:15, and 61:10–11).

17. Ibrahim, "What Piracy? This Is the Same Old Jihad" (citing Khadduri, *War and Peace in the Law of Islam*, pp. 119, 131).

18. Levitt, *Hamas*, pp. 63–64.

19. Ibid.

20. Ibid., citing Center for Religious Freedom, "Saudi Publications on Hate Ideology Invade American Mosques," supra.

21. Alfred B. Prados and Christopher M. Blanchard, "Saudi Arabia: Terrorism Financing Issues" (Congressional Research Service Report for Congress, No. RL32499, Dec. 8, 2004), p. 2 & n. 2 (http://www.fas.org/irp/crs/RL32499.pdf), p. 1; see also Andrew C. McCarthy, "To Be Charitable, They're Terrorists—The Justice Department Indicts Hamas's American Funding Arm" (*National Review Online*, July 29, 2004 (http://article.nationalreview.com/?q=YzFiZDYwODRjZmUoZTIxZj g4MTY1Zjg1YWMoZjRkN2M=).

22. Prados and Blanchard, "Saudi Arabia: Terrorism Financing Issues" p. 2 & n. 2.

23. Christopher Hitchens, "Jefferson's Quran—What the founder really thought about Islam" (*Slate*, Jan. 9, 2007) (http://www.slate.com/id/2157314/).

24. Ibrahim, "What Piracy? This Is the Same Old Jihad" (citing Majid Khadduri, *War and Peace in the Laws of Islam* (The Johns Hopkins University Press, 1955), p. 113.

Chapter Seven

1. Zeyno Baran, "The Muslim Brotherhood's U.S. Network" (*Current Trends in Islamist Ideology*, Vol. 6, p. 96) (Hudson Institute Center on Islam, Democracy and the Future of the Modern World) (http://www.currenttrends.org/research/detail/the-muslim-brotherhoods-us-network); see also Joseph Kaufman, "MSA, the Missing Co-Conspirator" (*Frontpage Magazine* July 11, 2007) (http://97.74.65.51/readArticle.aspx?ARTID=27342); see, e.g., Noreen S. Ahmed-Ullah, Sam Roe, and Laurie Cohen, "A Rare Look at Secretive Brotherhood in America" (*Chicago Tribune*, Sept. 19, 2004) (www.chicagotribune.com/news/watchdog/chi-0409190261sep19,0,3008717.story).

2. Steven A. Emerson, Testimony before the Third Public Hearing of the 9/11 Commission (July 9, 2003) (http://govinfo.library.unt.edu/911/hearings/hearing3/witness_emerson.htm); see also Baran, "The Muslim Brotherhood's U.S. Network."

3. Emerson, 9/11 Commission Testimony; see also Jonathan Levin, "The Roots of Terror" (*National Review Online*, Dec. 5, 2002)

(reproduced by the Investigative Project on Terrorism at http://www.
investigativeproject.org/165/the-roots-of-terror).

4. Emerson, 9/11 Commission Testimony.

5. History Commons Profile, "World Assembly of Muslim Youth
(WAMY)" (http://www.historycommons.org/entity.jsp?entity=world_
assembly_of_muslim_youth); Emerson, 9/11 Commission Testimony;
Discover the Networks Profile: Benevolence International Foundation
(http://www.discoverthenetworks.org/groupProfile.asp?grpid=6416);
Combatant Status Review Board, Unclassified Summary of Eveidence
for Combatant Status Review Tribunal—HAMED, Adel Hassan (Nov.
19, 2004) (published by the *New York Times* on-line ["The Gitmo Dock-
et"] at http://projects.nytimes.com/guantanamo/detainees/940-adel-
hassan).

6. Eric Lichtblau, "White House Approved Departure of Saudis
After Sept. 11, Ex-Aide Says" (*New York Times*, Sept. 4, 2003) (http://
www.nytimes.com/2003/09/04/politics/04SAUD.html?ex=1063252800
&en=808be44aeob6c3aa&ei=5062&partner=GOOGLE).

7. Susan B. Trento and Joseph J. Trento, *Unsafe at Any Altitude:
Failed Terrorism Investigations, Scapegoating 9/11, and the Shocking Truth
about Aviation Security Today* (Steerforth 2006); see also History Commons Profile, "World Assembly of Muslim Youth (WAMY)."

8. See, e.g., Daniel Pipes and Sharon Chadha, "CAIR: Islamists Fooling the Establishment" (*Middle East Quarterly*, Spring
2006 ed.) (http://www.meforum.org/916/cair-islamists-fooling-the-
establishment).

9. Susan Schmidt, "Spreading Saudi Fundamentalism in U.S.—
Network of Wahhabi Mosques, Schools, Web Sites Probed By FBI"
(*Washington Post*, Oct. 2, 2003) (http://www.washingtonpost.com/ac2/
wp-dyn/A31402-2003Oct1?language=printer); see also Rita Katz and
Josh Devon, "Terror Tools—Saudi-funded front in Michigan" (*National
Review Online*, March 11, 2003) (http://article.nationalreview.com/print
/?q=YmU1NWRjZDkwYzNmMWZjYjFmYWViY2I1Y2YyOTc4MT
g=); Discover the Networks Profile: Islamic Assembly of North America
(http://www.discoverthenetworks.org/groupProfile.asp?grpid=6457);
Discover the Networks Profile: Dr. Fafil Dhafir (http://www.discover-
thenetworks.org/individualProfile.asp?indid=1030).

10. Baran, "The Muslim Brotherhood's U.S. Network," pp. 99–100; Kaufman, "MSA, the Missing Co-Conspirator."

11. Baran, "The Muslim Brotherhood's U.S. Network," p. 100 & n. 20 (citing testimony of J. Michael Waller before the Senate Judiciary Committee, Subcommittee on Terrorism, Technology and Homeland Security, Oct. 14, 2003).

12. Baran, "The Muslim Brotherhood's U.S. Network," p. 100; Kaufman, "MSA, the Missing Co-Conspirator."

13. Kaufman, "MSA, the Missing Co-Conspirator"; "White House Senior Official Addresses ISNA Convention" (ISNA press release, July 6, 2009) (http://www.isna.net/articles/News/White-House-Senior-Official-Addresses-ISNA-Convention.aspx).

14. Kaufman, "MSA, the Missing Co-Conspirator."

15. Baran, "The Muslim Brotherhood's U.S. Network," pp. 99–101; Investigative Project on Terrorism, "Islamic Society of North America—An IPT Investigative Report" (http://www.investigativeproject.org/documents/misc/275.pdf).

16. *United States* v. *Sami Amin Al-Arian*, No. 08 Cr. 131, Affidavit of Dr. Sami Amin Al-Arian, p. 5, para. 6 (July 14, 2008) (admitting "involvement" with the Muslim Brotherhood from 1978 through 1982) (http://www.investigativeproject.org/documents/misc/152.pdf).

17. Levitt, *Hamas*, pp. 40–47; Baran, "The Muslim Brotherhood's U.S. Network," pp. 102–04; Discover the Networks, Profile of Sami al-Arian (http://www.discoverthenetworks.org/individualProfile.asp?indid=671).

18. Noreen S. Ahmed-Ullah, Kim Barker, Laurie Cohen, Stephen Franklin and Sam Roe, "Hard-liners won battle for Bridgeview mosque" (*Chicago Tribune*, Feb. 8, 2004) (www.chicagotribune.com/news/local/chi-0402080265feb08,0,3486861.story).

19. Ahmed-Ullah, Barker, Cohen, Franklin and Roe, "Hard-liners won battle for Bridgeview mosque." Salah spent five years in Israeli custody. He was eventually indicted in the United States for racketeering in connection with his admitted Hamas activities. He ultimately retracted his confession, but his main defense at trial was that he'd withdrawn from the Hamas enterprise, not that he'd never been part of it. He was acquitted of the racketeering charges but convicted of obstructing justice for lying under oath about his Hamas fundraising activities. He was sen-

tenced to 21 months' imprisonment and fined $25,000. The Bridgeview Mosque encouraged worshippers to help his defense and organized a campaign as the result of which hundreds of letters were submitted to the court on his behalf, pleading for leniency in the imposition of sentence. Marzook was also indicted in the case, but remains a fugitive. See Steven Emerson, "Tribune's Former Public Editor: Hamas Operative Is an Asset to Chicago Community" (*Counterterrorism Blog*, July 24, 2007) (republished by the Investigative Project on Terrorism at http://www. investigativeproject.org/286/tribunes-former-public-editor-hamas-operative-is-an-asset); see also Levitt, *Hamas*, pp. 42–43, 74–75); "21 Months for Man Once Accused of Funding Hamas" (*CBS 2 Chicago*, July 11, 2007) (republished by the *Militant Islam Monitor* at http://www. militantislammonitor.org/article/id/3045.

20. Investigative Project on Terrorism, "Al-Arian Indicted for Contempt" (June 26, 2008) (http://www.investigativeproject.org/700/al-arian-indicted-for-contempt) (citing Letter of Dr. Taha Jaber al-Awani, IIIT President, to Sami al-Arian, Nov. 6, 1992) (http://www.investigativeproject.org/redirect/Exhibit325.pdf)).

Chapter Eight

1. Andrew C. McCarthy, "The Father of Modern Terrorism—The true legacy of Yasser Arafat" (*National Review Online*, Nov. 12, 2004) (http://article.nationalreview.com/?q=MjhiMjI3NDIyMzgzY2JmMTY 2YTk1NmJhYjJhMWZlZjQ=).

2. Olivier Roy, *The Politics of Chaos in the Middle East* (Columbia University Press, 2008).

3. Baran, "The Muslim Brotherhood's U.S. Network," p. 103; see also Levitt, *Hamas*, p. 9.

4. Levitt, *Hamas*, pp. 40–47, 240–41; McCarthy, "To Be Charitable, They're Terrorists"; see also Shane Bauer, "Hamas: We will win war in Gaza" (*Al-Jezeera* [English], Jan. 13, 2009) (interview with Mousa Abu Marzook from Hamas's headquarters in Damascus) (http://english. aljazeera.net/news/middleeast/2009/01/20091815533331118900.html).

5. See Koran Suras 2:63–66, 5:59–60, and 7:166; see also Robert Spencer, *The Complete Infidel's Guide to the Koran* (Regnery, 2009), p. 126.

6. Andrew C. McCarthy, "The Father of Modern Terrorism."

7. Itamar Marcus and Barbara Cook, Denial of Youth (Palestinian Media Watch, March 2, 2007) (republished in *Frontpage Magazine* at http://97.74.65.51/readArticle.aspx?ARTID=25787); see also Andrew C. McCarthy, "Our Terrorists Are Better Than Your Terrorists—Supporting Fatah, the Bush administration makes a deal with the devil" (*National Review Online*, June 21, 2007) (http://article.nationalreview.com/?q=MDg2NTNkOTMoZjI5ZTEzNzBjNzc4ODNjZjRhMmRlZjQ=).

8. Levitt, *Hamas.*

9. Emerson, 9/11 Commission Testimony.

10. McCarthy, "To Be Charitable, They're Terrorists"; Baran, "The Muslim Brotherhood's U.S. Network," pp. 102–03, Stephen Schwartz, "The Holy War Foundation" (*Frontpage Magazine*, July 30, 2004) (http://97.74.65.51/Printable.aspx?ArtId=12009); Discover the Networks Profile of the Holy Land Foundation for Relief and Development (HLF) (http://www.discoverthenetworks.org/groupProfile.asp?grpid=6181); Investigative Project on Terrorism, "Holy Land Foundation for Relief and Development" (Biographies of Major Players) (http://www.investigativeproject.org/redirect/HLF-Bios.pdf).

11. *United States* v. *Holy Land Foundation for Relief and Development*, No. 04 Cr. 240-P, Government's Memorandum in Opposition to Petitioners Islamic Society of North America and North American Islamic Trust's Motion for Equitable Relief (July 10, 2008), p. 14 (http://www.investigativeproject.org/documents/case_docs/623.pdf).

12. Daniel Pipes, "That List of Islamist Organizations under U.S. Senate Scrutiny" (Daniel Pipes.org, Jan. 14, 2004) (citing Letter of Senators Charles Grassley and Max Baucus to the IRS) (http://www.danielpipes.org/blog/2004/01/that-list-of-islamist-organizations-under-us).

13. Schwartz, "The Holy War Foundation."

14. Levitt, *Hamas*, pp. 43–43.

15. Investigative Project on Terrorism, "CAIR's Origins," (http://www.investigativeproject.org/documents/misc/109.pdf); see also Baran, "The Muslim Brotherhood's U.S. Network," p. 103.

16. Ahmed-Ullah, Roe & Cohen, "A Rare Look at Secretive Brotherhood in America"; see also Investigative Project on Terrorism, Dos-

sier on the Muslim American Society (http://www.investigativeproject.
org/documents/misc/85.pdf); Baran, "The Muslim Brotherhood's U.S.
Network"; Muslim American Society, "About MAS" (http://masnet.
org/aboutmas.asp).

17. Ibid.

18. Ahmed-Ullah, Roe & Cohen, "A Rare Look at Secretive Brotherhood in America."

19. Daveed Gartenstein-Ross, *My Year Inside Radical Islam: A Mem-
oir* (Tarcher, 2007).

20. Daveed Gartenstein-Ross, "MAS's Muslim Brotherhood Problem" (*The Weekly Standard*, May 30, 2005) (republished by *Frontpage
Magazine* at http://97.74.65.51/readArticle.aspx?ARTID=8471).

21. See, e.g., Peace Watch, "PLO Charter Was Not Changed"
(April 25, 1996) (published by Information Regarding Israel's Security
(IRIS) at http://www.iris.org.il/pncvote.htm); Palestine Facts, "Didn't
the PLO finally revise its charter on Israel, opening the way to peace?"
(*Palestine Facts.org*, History: Israel 1991 To Present) (http://www.pal-
estinefacts.org/pf_1991to_now_plo_charter_revise.php).

22. Investigative Project on Terrorism, "CAIR's Origins."

23. Investigative Project on Terrorism, "CAIR's Origins."

24. P. David Gaubatz and Paul Sperry, *Muslim Mafia: Inside the
Secret Underworld That's Conspiring to Islamize America* (WND Books,
2009), pp. 42–45; see also Pipe and Chada, "CAIR: Islamists Fooling
the Establishment" (Elashi at Philadelphia meeting, along with Omar
Ahmad and others).

25. Mary Jacoby, "FBI Cuts Off CAIR over Hamas Questions"
(IPT News, Jan. 29, 2009) (http://www.investigativeproject.org/985/
fbi-cuts-off-cair-over-hamas-questions).

26. Ibid.

27. Investigative Project on Terrorism, "CAIR's Origins"; see also
McCarthy, "Singing CAIR's Tune on Your Dime."

28. IPT News, "HLF Founders Sentenced to Long Prison Terms"
(May 27, 2009) (http://www.investigativeproject.org/1046/hlf-founders-
sentenced-to-long-prison-terms).

29. Meeting Agenda for the Palestine Committee 7/30/1994, *United States* v. *Holy Land Foundation*, No. 3:04-CR-240-G, Gov't Ex. 3–78

(published by the Investigative Project on Terrorism at http://www.investigativeproject.org/documents/case_docs/717.pdf).

30. Ibid.; see also Gaubatz and Sperry, *Muslim Mafia*, pp. 43–45.

31. McCarthy, "Singing CAIR's Tune On Your Dime," citing *Council on American-Islamic Relations* v. *Andrew Whitehead*, Defendant's Answer, Grounds of Defense, and Counterclaims (April 30, 2004) (http://www.anti-cair-net.org/Response.html).

32. Investigative Project on Terrorism, Dossier: "CAIR's Origins," p. 1 & n. 2 (http://www.investigativeproject.org/documents/misc/109.pdf).

33. U.S. Department of the Treasury, "Shutting Down the Terrorist Financial Network" (Dec. 4, 2001) (http://www.ustreas.gov/press/releases/po841.htm).

34. Andrew C. McCarthy, "Singing CAIR's Tune on Your Dime," citing Testimony of Steven Emerson before the United States Senate Committee on Banking, Housing, and Urban Affairs, "Money Laundering and Terror Financing Issues in the Middle East" (July 13, 2005) p. 9 & n. 53 (http://www.investigativeproject.org/documents/testimony/19.pdf); Testimony of Matthew Epstein before the Senate Judiciary Committee—Subcommittee on Terrorism, Technology, and Homeland Security (Sept.10, 2003) p. 11 & n. 20 (citing IRS Form 1023, Holy Land Foundation for Relief and Development) (http://kyl.senate.gov/legis_center/subdocs/091003_epstein.pdf); and Nihad Awad Letter to The Honorable Senator John [sic] Kyl (Sept. 9, 2003).

35. Pipes and Chada, "CAIR: Islamists Fooling the Establishment," citing Joe Kaufman, "The CAIR-Terror Connection" (*Frontpage Magazine*, April 29, 2004) (http://97.74.65.51/readArticle.aspx?ARTID=13221).

36. McCarthy, "Singing CAIR's Tune on Your Dime"; Pipes and Chadha, "CAIR: Islamists Fooling the Establishment."

37. Pipes and Chadha, "CAIR: Islamists Fooling the Establishment" (citing *Estate of John P. O'Neill Sr.* v. *Al-Baraka Investment and Development Corporation*, No. 04 Civ. 1923 [SDNY 2004]).

38. Pipes and Chadha, "CAIR: Islamists Fooling the Establishment."

39. McCarthy, "Singing CAIR's Tune on Your Dime" (citing Pipes and Chadha, "CAIR: Islamists Fooling the Establishment").

Chapter Nine

1. See, e.g., Andrew C. McCarthy, "Nazis for Me, but Not for Thee—Why shouldn't socialized medicine prompt comparisons to National Socialism?" (*National Review Online*, Aug. 14, 2009) (http://article. nationalreview.com/?q=YjIoN2E5ZjMoMGUoZWVkZTdmYTBjNDQ4YTM4YTgzODA=).

2. "Stop Changing the Subject, Mr. Emerson" (Muslim Public Affairs Council) (http://www.mpac.org/article.php?id=510).

3. Investigative Project on Terrorism press release: "Congressman Sherman Turns the Tables on MPAC—Group Tried to Block Emerson Testimony" (July 30, 2008) (http://www.investigativeproject.org/ article/734), citing Hassan Hathout, Maher Hathout, and Fathi Osman, *In Fraternity: A Message to Muslims in America*, The Minaret Publishing House, 1989; *The Minaret*, July-August 1997, p. 20; and Maher Hathout, Debate on Terrorism, L.A. radio station, November 13, 1998, posted on the *Voice of Islam* website.

4. Ibid., citing Larry Stammer, "After the Attack: Jewish-Muslim Dialogue Newly Tested," *The Los Angeles Times*, September 22, 2001.

5. Steven Emerson, "Ms. Lekovic . . . A Dozen Printing Mistakes?" (*Counterterrorism Blog*, May 30, 2007) (http://counterterrorismblog. org/2007/05/ms_lekovica_dozen_printing_mis.php); see also Steven Emerson, "MPAC: Who's Changing the Subject?" (*Counterterrorism Blog*, June 8, 2007) (republished by the Investigative Project on Terrorism at http://www.investigativeproject.org/292/mpac-whos-changing-the-subject).

6. Investigative Project on Terrorism press release: "Congressman Sherman Turns the Tables on MPAC—Group Tried to Block Emerson Testimony."

7. M. Zahdi Jasser, "Islamists Insert Themselves into Healthcare Debate—Wake-Up Call," (*Hudson Institute*, Sept. 9, 2009) (http://www. mzuhdijasser.com/6190/islamists_healthcare_debate). Andrew C. McCarthy, "DHS Wants to Know What You're Thinking—The Obama

administration defines extremism down" (*National Review Online*, April 17, 2009) (http://article.nationalreview.com/?q=OTI1MTYwMjhmMj ZkMmNiYjg1NGJhNmIyYzQ2NTk4Yjg=).

9. McCarthy, *Willful Blindness*.

10. Berman, *Terror and Liberalism*, p. 62.

11. Gilles Kepel, "The Brotherhood in the Salafist Universe" (*Current Trends in Islamist Ideology*, Vol. 6, p. 23) (Hudson Institute Center on Islam, Democracy and the Future of the Modern World).

12. Kepel, supra.

13. McCarthy, *Willful Blindness*.

14. Frantz Fanon, *Les Damnés de la Terre* (*The Wretched of the Earth*) (Présence Africaine, 1963); Yussur Simmonds, "Legends: Frantz Fanon" (*Los Angeles Sentinel*, May 8, 2008) (http://www.lasentinel.net/Frantz-Fanon.html); Robert Fulford, "Frantz Fanon: a poisonous thinker who refuses to die" (*National Post*, Feb. 2, 2002) (http://www.robertfulford.com/FrantzFanon.html).

15. Stanley Kurtz, "Context,' You Say? A guide to the radical theology of the Rev. Jeremiah Wright" (*National Review*, May 19, 2008); Joseph Cardinal Ratzinger, "Liberation Theology" (*The Ratzinger Report*, Dec. 9, 2004) (reprinted at *Christendom Awake*) (http://www.christendom-awake.org/pages/ratzinger/liberationtheol.htm).

16. Paul Berman, *Terror and Liberalism* (Norton 2003) (2004 ed.), p. 105.

17. Andrew C. McCarthy, "Our Terrorists Are Better Than Your Terrorists—Supporting Fatah, the Bush administration makes a deal with the devil" (*National Review Online* June 21, 2007) (http://article.nationalreview.com/?q=MDg2NTNkOTMoZjI5ZTEzNzBjNzc4OD NjZjRhMmRlZjQ=); Andrew C. McCarthy, "The Father of Modern Terrorism—The True Legacy of Yasser Arafat" (*National Review Online* Nov. 12, 2004) (http://article.nationalreview.com/?q=MjhiMjI3NDIyM zgzY2JmMTY2YTk1NmJhYjJhMWZlZjQ=).

18. Steve Coll, *Ghost Wars: The Secret History of the CIA, Afghanistan, and bin Laden, from the Soviet invasion to September 10, 2001* (Penguin, 2004), pp. 297–329; Rosie DeManno, "Bhutto helped create Taliban monster" (*The Star* (Canada), Jan. 2, 2008) (http://www.thestar.com/News/World/article/290372); Andrew G. Bostom, "End the Moral Idiocy on Kashmir" (AndrewBostom.org, July 10, 2008) (http://

www.andrewbostom.org/blog/2008/07/10/end-the-moral-idiocy-on-kashmir/).

Chapter Ten

1. Berman, *Terror and Liberalism*, p. 86.

2. Robert C. Tucker, editor, *The Marx-Engels Reader* (Norton 1978) (2d ed.), pp. 20, 35; David Horowitz, *Unholy Alliance: Radical Islam and the American Left* (Regnery, 2004), pp. 129–30 (quoting Karl Marx, *Introduction to a Contribution to the Critique of Hegel's Philosophy of Right*).

3. Conor Cruise O'Brien, *The Great Melody: A Thematic Biography of Edmund Burke* (University of Chicago Press, 1992) (1993 paperback ed.), p. 598.

4. Paul Johnson, *Intellectuals—From Marx and Tolstoy to Sartre and Chomsky* (Harper & Row, 1988) (Harper Perennial ed., 2007), pp. 24–26.

5. Amir Taheri, "End of Discussion—In Iran, there is a growing consensus that it is time to move beyond Khomeinism" (*National Review Online* July 27, 2009) http://article.nationalreview.com/?q=Mjc3YTU1NWExYmJhNmNhOWQxZjM2YmEyZDI2ZTBiMmE=).

6. Berman, *Terror and Liberalism*, pp. 58, 62.

7. McCarthy, *Willful Blindness*.

8. Paul Johnson, *Intellectuals*, p. 24.

9. Qutb, *Social Justice in Islam*, p. 97.

10. Conor Cruise O'Brien, *The Long Affair: Thomas Jefferson and the French Revolution, 1785–1800* (University of Chicago Press, 1996), p. 302 (citing James H. Smylie, "The President as Prophet, Priest, King" (*Civil Religion in America: Manifest Destiny and Historical Judgment: A Symposium*).

11. Sayyid Qutb, *Social Justice in Islam* (American Council of Learned Societies, 1953) (Islamic Publications International ed. 2000), p. 69.

12. Ibid, p. 58.

13. Ibid, p. 41.

14. Ibid, p. 90.

15. Ibid, pp. 120–22.

16. Berman, *Terror and Liberalism*, pp. 91–92.

17. Qutb, *Social Justice in Islam*, pp. 57–58.

18. Qutb, *Social Justice in Islam*, p. 77.

19. See, e.g., Richard Epstein, "Impermissible Ratemaking in Health-Insurance Reform: Why the Reid Bill is Unconstitutional" (PointofLaw.com, Dec. 18, 2009) (http://www.pointoflaw.com/columns/archives/2009/12/impermissible-ratemaking-in-he.php) (citing *Duquesne Light Co.* v. *Barasch*, 488 U.S. 299 [1989]).

20. Qutb, *Social Justice in Islam*, pp. 146–50; Berman, *Terror and Liberalism*, p. 80.

21. Qutb, *Social Justice in Islam*, p. 125.

22. *The Holy Qur'an—English translation of the meanings and Commentary*, p. 207, Sura 4:5, n. 511 (Kingdom of Saudi Arabia, King Fahd Holy Qur'an Printing Complex [undated]).

23. Qutb, *Social Justice in Islam*, pp. 132–134.

24. Qutb, *Social Justice in Islam*, pp. 51, 54.

Chapter Eleven

1. Sally Jacobs, "A father's charm, absence—Friends recall Barack Obama Sr. as a self-confident, complex dreamer whose promising life ended in tragedy" (*Boston Globe*, Sept. 21, 2008) (http://www.boston.com/news/politics/2008/articles/2008/09/21/a_fathers_charm_absence/).

2. Barak H. Obama, "Problems Facing Our Socialism" (*East Africa Journal*, July 1965) pp. 26 & ff. (republished by Politco.com at http://www.politico.com/static/PPM41_eastafrica.html).

3. Jim Kuhnhann, "Obama walks fine line in fighting false links to Islam" (Associated Press, Feb. 28, 2008).

4. Barack Obama, "My Spiritual Journey" (*Time Magazine*, Oct. 6, 2006) (http://www.time.com/time/printout/0,8816,1546579,00.html); see also Bill Sammon, "Can a past of Islam change the path to president for Obama?" (*The Examiner*, Jan 19, 2007) (http://www.examiner.com/a-534540~Can_a_past_of_Islam_change_the_path_to_president_.html).

5. Jacobs, "A father's charm, absence" (noting that Obama Sr. earned a master's degree from Harvard, did not complete a Ph.D., but would occasionally introduce himself as "Dr. Obama").

6. Barack Obama, *Dreams from My Father: A Story of Race and Inheritance* (Crown, 1995) (2004 ed), pp. 9–10.

7. It is known that Onyango Obama traveled widely—for example, to Burma, India, Tanzania, Europe, and elsewhere—but the exact

time and place of his conversion to Islam is not reported. See, e.g., Joe Ambuor, "Obama's father and the origin of Muslim name" (*Star Media* [Kenya], April 11, 2008) (conversion at some point during service in British army, perhaps in Zanzibar) (http://www.standardmedia.co.ke/sports/InsidePage.php?id=1143998542&cid=4&); Kimberly Powell, "Ancestry of Barack Obama" (family members reportedly said conversion was in Zanzibar, where he lived after military service in Europe and India) (*About.com*; http://genealogy.about.com/od/aframertrees/p/barack_obama.htm); Ben Macintyre and Paul Orengoh, "Beatings and abuse made Barack Obama's grandfather loathe the British" (*London Times*, Dec. 3, 2008) (Onyango served with the British army in Burma during World War II) (http://www.timesonline.co.uk/tol/news/world/africa/article5276010.ece). It is noteworthy that Barak Obama Sr., was born in 1936, before World War II started. He was given the name Hussein, the name his father took upon converting to Islam. It is not clear, however, whether this was done at birth or sometime later.

8. Barack Obama, *Dreams from My Father*, p. 407.

9. Sammon, "Can a past of Islam change the path to president for Obama?"; see also Barack Obama, *Dreams from My Father*, p. 407.

10. Macintyre and Orengoh, "Beatings and abuse made Barack Obama's grandfather loathe the British"; but see Obama, *Dreams from My Father*, pp. 417–18 (stating that the imprisonment lasted approximately six months, not two years).

11. "History of Kenya" (HistoryWorld.net) (http://www.historyworld.net/wrldhis/PlainTextHistories.asp?historyid=ad21); see also Macintyre and Orengoh, "Beatings and abuse made Barack Obama's grandfather loathe the British."

12. "Kenya: Why We Reject Communism" (*Time Magazine*, June 11, 1965) (http://www.time.com/time/magazine/article/0,9171,833698,00.htm).

13. E.S. Atieno-Odhiambo and John Kiriamiti, *Jaramogi Oginga Odinga* (East African Educational Publishers Ltd.,1997); *Time*, "Kenya: Why We Reject Communism."

14. Michael Dobbs, "Obama Overstates Kennedys' Role in Helping His Father" (*Washington Post*, March 30, 2008) (http://www.washingtonpost.com/wp-dyn/content/article/2008/03/29/AR2008032902031.html); "Tom Mboya: Kenyan trade unionist and statesman, assassinated

six years into independence" (*African History.com*) (http://africanhistory. about.com/od/countrieseast/p/bio_mboya.htm).

15. Jack Wheeler, "Obama in Kenya" (*To the Point News*, 2007), excerpted in Pamela Geller, "Kenya, Islam and Obama Hussein" (*Atlas Shrugs*, Jan. 4, 2008) (http://atlasshrugs2000.typepad.com/atlas_ shrugs/2008/01/obama-islam-and.html); see also E.S. Atieno-Odhiambo and John Kiriamiti, *Jaramogi Oginga Odinga* (East African Educational Publishers Ltd.,1997), p. 15; Pamela Geller, "Kenya, Islam and *Obama Hussein*" (*Atlas Shrugs*, Jan. 4, 2008) (http://atlasshrugs2000.typepad. com/atlas_shrugs/2008/01/obama-islam-and.html).

16. Tim Jones, "Barack Obama: Mother Not Just a Girl from Kansas" (*Chicago Tribune*, March 27, 2007) (www.chicagotribune.com/news/ politics/obama/chi-0703270151mar27-archive,0,2623808.story).

17. Alexander LaBrecque, "Obama's Religious Ruse: 'I've Always Been a Christian'" (*The American Thinker*, Oct. 14, 2008) (http://www. americanthinker.com/2008/10/obamas_religious_ruse_ive_alwa.html), citing Tim Jones, "Barack Obama: Mother Not Just a Girl from Kansas."

18. Tim Jones, "Barack Obama: Mother Not Just a Girl from Kansas."

19. Michael Dobbs, "Obama Overstates Kennedys' Role in Helping His Father."

20. Side Goodo, "Kenya's Political Crisis: Lessons for Africa" (*The American Chronicle*, March 15, 2008) (http://www.americanchronicle. com/articles/view/55435).

21. *Time*, "Kenya: Why We Reject Communism."

22. Murithi Mutiga, "The one leader who could have stopped Kenya's descent into a polarised nation" (Kenya.com, July 6, 2009) (http:// majimbokenya.com/home/2009/07/06/the-late-tom-mboyathe-one- leader-who-could-have-stopped-kenya%E2%80%99s-descent-into-a- polarised-nation/).

23. Obituary, "Jaramogi Ajuma Oginga Odinga (1911–1994)" (*Liberal International* Jan. 1994) (http://www.liberal-international.org/ editorial.asp?ia_id=1039); "Tom Mboya: Kenyan trade unionist and statesman, assassinated six years into independence" (*African History.*

com) (http://africanhistory.about.com/od/countrieseast/p/bio_mboya. htm).

Chapter Twelve

1. Obama, *Dreams from My Father*; see also Sammon, "Can a past of Islam change the path to president for Obama?"

2. Jake Tapper & Sunlen Miller, "The Emergence of President Obama's Muslim Roots" (ABC News June 2, 2009) (http://blogs.abcnews. com/politicalpunch/2009/06/abc-news-jake-tapper-and-sunlen-miller-report-the-other-day-we-heard-a-comment-from-a-white-house-aide-that-neverwould-have.html).

3. Aaron Klein, "Was young Obama Indonesian citizen? Document, travel suggest 'Barry Soetoro' member of world's largest Muslim country" (*World Net Daily*, Aug. 17, 2008) (http://www.wnd.com/index. php?pageId=72656).

4. *Stanley Ann Soetoro* v. *Lolo Soetoro*, Complaint for Divorce and Summons, No. 117619 (Family Court for the First Circuit, State of Hawaii) (Aug. 20, 1980) (published at http://decalogosintl.org/documents/ Soetoro_Divorce.pdf).

5. Daniel Pipes, "Barack Obama's Muslm Childhood" (*Frontpage Magazine*, April 29, 2008) (republished at Daniel Pipes.org, http://www. danielpipes.org/5544/barack-obamas-muslim-childhood).

6. Jodi Kantor, "A Candidate, His Minister, and the Search for Faith" (*New York Times*, April 30, 2007) (http://www.nytimes. com/2007/04/30/us/politics/30obama.html?_r=3&oref=slogin&pagew anted=print).

7. Nicholas D. Kristof, "Obama: Man of the World" (*New York Times*, March 6, 2007) (http://select.nytimes.com/2007/03/06/ opinion/06kristof.html?_r=4&oref=slogin&pagewanted=print).

8. See, e.g., Andrew C. McCarthy, "The Company He Keeps—Meet Obama's circle: The same old America-hating Left" (*National Review Online*, April 11, 2008) (http://article.nationalreview.com/354119/ the-company-he-keeps/andrew-c-mccarthy); Andrew C. McCarthy, "The Real Ayers Issue—It's about revolution, not terrorism" (*National Review*, Nov. 3, 2008); Andrew C. McCarthy, "What kind of education

reform did Ayers & Obama have in mind?" (*National Review Online, The Corner*, Oct. 11, 2008) (Ayers' speech at Hugo Chavez's education summit in Venezuela) (http://corner.nationalreview.com/post/?q=NjRkOW UzMTVjMTU5YjIxYmQyMjY3YjUoNWJkY2QxZjY=).

9. Andrew C. McCarthy, "Another Communist in Obama's Orb—Meet Michael Klonsky, Obama's 'social justice' education expert" (*National Review Online*, Oct. 22, 2008) (http://article.nationalreview. com/376079/another-communist-in-obamas-orb/andrew-c-mccarthy).

10. Peter Wallsten, "Allies of Palestinians see a friend in Obama" (*Los Angeles Times*, April 10, 2008) (http://articles.latimes.com/2008/ apr/10/nation/na-obamamideast10); see also Andrew C. McCarthy, "Why Won't Obama Talk About Columbia? The years he won't discuss may explain the Ayers tie he keeps lying about" (*National Review Online*, Oct. 7, 2008) (http://article.nationalreview.com/374119/why-wont-obama-talk-about-columbia/andrew-c-mccarthy).

11. McCarthy, "Why Won't Obama Talk About Columbia?"; see also, Andrew C. McCarthy, "The *L.A. Times* Suppresses Obama's Khalidi Bash Tape" (Oct. 27, 2008) (http://article.nationalreview. com/376504/the-ila-timesi-suppresses-obamas-khalidi-bash-tape/ andrew-c-mccarthy).

12. Candace de Russy, "Radical Mind—Understanding Obama" (*National Review Online*, Sept. 12, 2008) (http://article.nationalreview. com/370783/radical-mind/candace-de-russy); "Obama mentor identified as communist—Frank Marshall Davis 'discussed American imperialism, colonialism, exploitation'" (*World Net Daily*, Feb. 19, 2008) (http:// www.worldnetdaily.com/index.php?fa=PAGE.view&pageId=56859); Cliff Kincaid, "AP Lies About Obama's Red Mentor" (Accuracy in Media, Aug. 4, 2008) (http://www.aim.org/aim-column/ap-lies-about-obamas-red-mentor/); Gerald Horne, "Rethinking the History and Future of the Communist Party (*Political Affairs Magazine*, March 28, 2007) (speech at the reception of the Communist Party USA) (http://www. politicalaffairs.net/article/articleview/5047/1/32/).

13. Obama, *Dreams from My Father*, p. 135.

14. Dan Armstrong, "Barack Obama Embellishes His Resume" (*Analyze This*, July 9, 2005) (http://www.analyzethis.net/2005/07/09/ barack-obama-embellishes-his-resume/); see also "Co-Workers: Obama

Inflated His Resume" (*Sweetness & Light*, Sept. 14, 2008) (http://sweet-ness-light.com/archive/did-obama-turn-down-a-wall-street-career).

15. Patrick Goodenough, "Few Details Known About Obama's Three Weeks in Pakistan" (CNS News, Nov. 3, 2008); Jake Tapper, "Obama's College Trip to Pakistan" (ABC News, Aprl 8, 2008) (http://blogs.abcnews.com/politicalpunch/2008/04/obamas-college.html).

16. Goodenough, "Few Details Known About Obama's Three Weeks in Pakistan."

17. "In 1981, Barack Obama visited Pakistan stayed with Mohammed Hasan Chandoo, who are the Chandoo Brothers?" (MikeFrancesa.com, Sept. 18, 2008) (http://www.mikefrancesa.com/wordpress/?p=1190), citing, among other things, Larry Rohter, "Obama Says Real-Life Experience Trumps Rivals' Foreign Policy Credentials" (*New York Times*, April 10, 2008) (http://www.nytimes.com/2008/04/10/us/politics/10obama.html?_r=1&bl&ex=1208059200&en=b73a8a7a2664d856&ei=5087); and entries from www.chandoo.com (e.g.: "The Organization for Incestuous Living (OIL) threw its firm support behind President George W. Bush in his bid for a second term. OIL said that the President was just like them: 'We're both from the south; we love beer; we love our families (only we love them literally); and we have the same IQ.'")

18. Goodenough, "Few Details Known About Obama's Three Weeks in Pakistan"; "Soomro was among Obama's hosts in Pakistan" (*The News.com* [Pakistan], April 24, 2008) (http://www.thenews.com.pk/daily_detail.asp?id=108690).

19. Ken Timmerman, ""Obama's Secret Campaign Cash: Has $63 Million Flowed from Foreign Sources?" (Newsmax Oct. 19, 2008) (http://www.newsmax.com/headlines/obama_illegal_dona-tions/2008/10/19/141979.html).

20. "Libyan Leader Mu'ammar Al-Qadhafi: Obama Suffers Inferiority Complex That Might Make Him Behave 'Whiter Than the White.'" (Middle East Media Research Institute, June 11, 2008) (republished at *Sweetness & Light*, http://sweetness-light.com/archive/qaddaffi-says-barack-obama-is-a-muslim).

21. Kenneth R. Timmerman, "Secret Foreign Money Floods Into Obama Campaign" (*Newsmax*, Sept. 29, 2008) (http://www.newsmax.com/timmerman/Obama_fundraising_illegal/2008/09/29/135718.

html); see also Timmerman, "Obama's Secret Campaign Cash: Has $63 Million Flowed from Foreign Sources?"

Chapter Thirteen

1. See, e.g., Katie Fretland, "Obama claims he's on banking committee" (*The Swamp*, July 23, 2008) (http://www.swamppolitics.com/news/politics/blog/2008/07/barack_obama_gaffe.html).

2. Mark Hyman, "Obama's Kenya Ghosts" (*Washington Times*, Oct. 12, 2008) (http://www.washingtontimes.com/news/2008/oct/12/obamas-kenya-ghosts/).

3. Ibid.

4. Barack Obama, "An Honest Government, A Hopeful Future" (Speech as delivered at University of Nairobi, Aug. 28, 2006) (http://obamaspeeches.com/o88-An-Honest-Government-A-Hopeful-Future-Obama-Speech.htm).

5. Mike Flannery, "Obama's Criticism Irks Kenyan Government—Government Says Obama Is A Stooge For Political Opposition" (CBS-2 News Chicago, Aug. 28, 2006) (http://cbs2chicago.com/topstories/Barack.Obama.Kenya.2.331658.html).

6. Title 18, United States Code, Section 953.

7. Hyman, "Obama's Kenya Ghosts."

8. Thomas Mukoya and Leon Mahherbe, "Some Kenyans forget crisis to root for Obama" (*Reuters*, Jan. 8, 2008) (http://www.reuters.com/article/idUSL0872724120080108).

9. Hannah Arendt, *The Origins of Totalitarianism* (Schocken Books ed., 2004) (originally published in 1948), pp. 603–610 (on "ideologies—isms").

10. Obama, *Dreams from My Father*, pp. 440–41.

11. Hyman, "Obama's Kenya Ghosts"; Geller, "Kenya, Islam and *Obama Hussein*."

12. Hyman, "Obama's Kenya Ghosts."

13. "How rich is Raila, the ODM-Kenya Presidential aspirant" (*African Press*, April 26, 2007) (http://africanpress.wordpress.com/2007/04/26/how-rich-is-raila-the-odm-kenya-presidential-aspirant/).

14. Ibid.; see also, "Odinga, Obama and the lack of courage" (A Jacksonian blog, Jan. 5, 2008) (republishing profile of Odinga published by *The Standard* of Kenya, July 31, 2007).

15. See *Final Report of the National Commission on Terrorist Attacks Upon the United States* ("*9/11 Commission Report*") (Norton, 2004), p. 15; see also *United States* v. *Arnaout*, No. 02 Cr. 892, Government's Proffer Supporting the Admissibility of Coconspirator Statements (Jan. 6, 2003), pp. 20–21, 31–32; "The Golden Chain" (*Sharia Finance Watch*, Oct. 19, 2008) (http://shariafinance.blogspot.com/2008/10/golden-chain.html).

16. J. Peter Pham, "The Kenyan Tragedy and the Future of Democracy in Africa" (*World Defense Review.com*, Jan. 17, 2008) (http://shariafinance.blogspot.com/2008/10/golden-chain.html).

17. Hyman, "Obama's Kenya Ghosts"; see also Pham, "The Kenyan Tragedy and the Future of Democracy in Africa."

Chapter Fourteen

1. Michelle Malkin, "Obama in 2001: How to bring about 're-distributive change'") (Michelle Malkin.com, Oct. 26, 2008) (http://michellemalkin.com/2008/10/26/obama-in-2001-how-to-bring-about-redistributive-change/).

2. Stanley Kurtz, "Something New Here—Radical? Check. Tied to ACORN? Check. Redistributionist? Check" (*National Review Online*, Oct. 20, 2008) (http://article.nationalreview.com/375696/something-new-here/stanley-kurtz); see also Stanley Kurtz, "Inside Obama's ACORN—By their fruits ye shall know them" (*National Review Online*, May 29, 2008) (http://article.nationalreview.com/358910/inside-obamas-acorn/stanley-kurtz); Stanley Kurtz, "Life of the New Party—A redistributionist success story" (*National Review Online*, Oct. 30, 2008) (http://article.nationalreview.com/376951/life-of-the-new-party/stanley-kurtz).

3. Jonah Goldberg, *Liberal Fascism: The Secret History of the American Left from Mussolini to the Politics of Meaning* (Doubleday, 2008), p. 223; see also Amity Shlaes, *The Forgotten Man: A New History of the Great Depression* (Harper Collins, 2007) (paperback ed., 2008).

4. Mark Levin, Liberty & Tyranny (Simon and Shuster, Threshold Editions, 2009).

5. Hank de Zutter, "What Makes Obama Run?" (Chicago Reader 1995) (http://www1.chicagoreader.com/obama/951208/).

6. Jeffrey Ressner, "Michelle Obama thesis was on the racial divide" (Politico, Feb. 22, 2008) (providing links to thesis, in four parts" (http://www.politico.com/news/stories/0208/8642.html).

7. Dinah Wisenberg Brin, "More Black Americans Finding Peace, Freedom through Living Lhe life of Islam (Associated Press, Nov. 2, 1996) (citing The Oxford Encyclopedia of the Modern Islamic World) (article republished at http://www.themodernreligion.com/convert/ convert_black.htm); see also Wendy Murray Zoba, "Islam, U.S.A." (Christianity Today, 3 April 2000,) p. 42 (cited in James Dretke, "Islam Grows Into a Strong Presence in America" (Christian Research Journal, Vol. 23, No. 4 (2001)) (republished by Arabic Bible.com at http://www. arabicbible.com/christian/islam_in_america.htm).

8. James Hal Cone, Black Theology and Black Power (1969) (re-published by Orbis Books, 1997), see also "James Hal Cone Speaks— Father of Black Theology" (Hiphop Republican.com, March 27, 2008) (http://hiphoprepublican.com/2008/03/james-hal-cone-speaks-father-of-black.html).

9. Stanley Kurtz, "Wright 101" (*National Review Online*, Oct. 14, 2008) (http://article.nationalreview.com/374927/wright-101/stanley-kurtz).

10. The mission statement has been removed from Internet access. It was excerpted in McCarthy, "The Company He Keeps."

11. Barack Obama, "Why Organize? Problems and Promise in the Inner City," (*After Alinsky: Community Organizing in Illinois, Illinois Issues* (University of Illinois at Springfield, 1990 ed.), Chapter 4, pp. 35–40) (republished at http://www.edwoj.com/Alinsky/AlinskyObamaChapter1990.htm).

12. Saul d. alinsky, *Rules for Radicals: A Pragmatic Primer for Realistic Radicals* (1971) (Vintage Books, 1989), p. 185.

13. Sol Stern, "ACORN's Nutty Regime for Cities" (*City Journal*, Spring 2003 ed.) (http://www.city-journal.org/html/13_2_acorns_nutty_regime.html).

14. Ibid, see also Kurtz, "Inside Obama's ACORN."

15. Kathleen Hennessey, "Obama mocks McCain in Nevada stops" (Associated Presss, Sept. 17, 2008) (http://www.sfgate.com/cgi-bin/article.cgi?f=/n/a/2008/09/17/politics/p185733D40.DTL&type=politics); see also Jim Geraghty, "Did ACORN Take Obama's 'Get In Their Face' Rallying Cry Literally?" (*National Review Online, Campaign Spot Blog*,

Oct. 9, 2008) (http://campaignspot.nationalreview.com/post/?q=MjNl
NTc4ZjdmNWMwMWJlYTY1MDE2ZjFjMTQwMzIwYTU=).

Chapter Fifteen

    1.   Tim Graham, "David Brooks on Obama: Redwood Forest or
Sturdy Mountain?" (*Newsbusters*, Media Reearch Center, Oct. 16, 2008)
(http://newsbusters.org/blogs/tim-graham/2008/10/16/david-brooks-
obama-redwood-forest-or-sturdy-mountain).

    2.   "President gives first interview since taking office to Arab TV—
Obama tells Al Arabiya peace talks should resume" (*Al Arabiya.net*,
Jan. 27, 2009) (http://www.alarabiya.net/articles/2009/01/27/65087.
html#004); Ben Smith, "Obama: U.S. not your enemy" (*Politico*, Jan. 26,
2009) (http://news.yahoo.com/s/politico/20090127/pl_politico/18016).

    3.   Daniel Pipes, "Obama, 'Respect' and Muslims" (Jan. 26, 2009)
(with updates) (http://www.danielpipes.org/blog/2009/01/obama-
respect-and-muslims).

    4.   Andrew C. McCarthy, "Waterboarding and Torture—Jonathan
Turley's irresponsible attack on Judge Mukasey" (*National Review Online*,
Oct. 26, 2007) (http://article.nationalreview.com/331968/waterboard-
ing-and-torture/andrew-c-mccarthy); Andrew C. McCarthy, "The
'Moral Authority' Canard—Senator McCain is heroic, awe-inspiring, and
wrong." (*National Review Online*, Nov. 28, 2005) (http://article.national-
review.com/277299/the-moral-authority-canard/andrew-c-mccarthy).

    5.   Andrew C. McCarthy, "The Justice Department's Torture
Hypocrisy—Investigate Bush lawyers' torture analysis one day, cite it
favorably the next" (*National Review Online*, May 6, 2009) (http://article.
nationalreview.com/393415/the-justice-departments-torture-hypocri-
sy/andrew-c-mccarthy); Andrew C. McCarthy, "On Torture, Holder
Undoes Holder—The attorney general reveals his legal ignorance—or
his willful inconsistency" (*National Review Online*, May 19, 2009) (http://
article.nationalreview.com/394480/on-torture-holder-undoes-holder/
andrew-c-mccarthy).

    6.   Robert Spencer, "Platitudes and naivete: Obama's Cairo speech
(*JihadWatch*, June 4, 2009) (http://www.jihadwatch.org/archives/026426.
php); on Azzam, see McCarthy, *Willful Blindness*.

7. "Muslim Brotherhood Members to Attend Obama's Cairo Speech" (Fox News, June 3, 2009) (http://www.foxnews.com/politics/2009/06/03/muslim-brotherhood-members-attend-obamas-cairo-speech/).

8. President Barack Obama, "A New Beginning" (Cairo speech as delivered, June 4, 2009) (republished by *National Review Online* at http://corner.nationalreview.com/post/?q=YjNkOTI5MDIyMTRiZW NkMjFlN2JkOWU1OGU4NDVjYWU=).

9. Hitchens, "Jefferson's Quran."

10. Spencer, "Platitudes and naivete: Obama's Cairo speech." ("The idea that Islamic culture was once a beacon of learning and enlightenment is a commonly held myth. In fact, much of this has been exaggerated, often for quite transparent apologetic motives. The astrolabe was developed, if not perfected, long before Muhammad was born. The zero, which is often attributed to Muslims, and what we know today as "Arabic numerals" did not originate in Arabia, but in pre-Islamic India. Aristotle's work was preserved in Arabic not initially by Muslims at all, but by Christians such as the fifth century priest Probus of Antioch, who introduced Aristotle to the Arabic-speaking world. Another Christian, Huneyn ibn-Ishaq (809–873), translated many works by Aristotle, Galen, Plato and Hippocrates into Syriac. His son then translated them into Arabic. The Syrian Christian Yahya ibn 'Adi (893–974) also translated works of philosophy into Arabic, and wrote one of his own, The Reformation of Morals. His student, another Christian named Abu 'Ali 'Isa ibn Zur'a (943–1008), also translated Aristotle and others from Syriac into Arabic. The first Arabic-language medical treatise was written by a Christian priest and translated into Arabic by a Jewish doctor in 683. The first hospital was founded in Baghdad during the Abbasid caliphate—not by a Muslim, but a Nestorian Christian. A pioneering medical school was founded at Gundeshapur in Persia—by Assyrian Christians"); see also Robert Spencer, *The Politically Incorrect Guide to Islam (and the Crusades)* (Regnery Publishing, 2005); Ibn Warraq, *Why I Am Not a Muslim*, (Prometheus Books 2003) (originally published in 1995).

11. Spencer, "Platitudes and naivete: Obama's Cairo speech."

12. Caroline Glick, "Obama's Arabian Dreams" (*Jerusalem Post*, June 5, 2009) (http://www.jpost.com /servlet/Satellite?cid=124403500 8682&pagename=JPArticle%2FShowFull).

13. Melanie Phillips, "Obama in Cairo" (*The Spectator*, June 4, 2009) (http://www.spectator.co.uk/melaniephillips/3670626/obama-in-cairo.thtml).

14. Title 18, United States Code, Sections 2339A, 2339B, and 2339C.

15. On al-Haramain, see Andrew C. McCarthy, "Getting FISA Wrong . . . Again" (*National Review Online*, July 5, 2007) (http://article.nationalreview.com/362612/getting-fisa-wrong——again/andrew-c-mccarthy).

16. O'Brien, "The Great Melody," p. 551.

Chapter Sixteen

1. Video, "Eid in America" (http://www.america.gov/multimedia/video.html?videoId=1883577479) (June 22, 2009).

2. "Dar al-Hijrah Official's Deception on Awlaki" (Investigative Project on Terrorism, IPT News, Nov. 18, 2009) (http://www.investigativeproject.org/1521/dar-al-hijrah-officials-deception-on-awlaki).

3. Daniel Pipes, "How Many Muslims in the United States" (Nov. 22, 2009) (http://www.danielpipes.org/blog/2003/04/how-many-muslims-in-the-united-states), citing Barry A. Kosmin and Ariela, "American Religious Identification Survey" (Trinity College, March 2009) (http://b27.cc.trincoll.edu/weblogs/AmericanReligionSurvey-ARIS/reports/ARIS_Report_2008.pdf), and Pew Research Center (The Pew Forum on Religion & Public Life), "U.S. Religious Landscape Survey" (http://religions.pewforum.org/affiliations).

4. Paul Johnson, *A History of the American People* (Harper Collins, 1997), p. 23 & ff.; Levin, *Liberty & Tyranny*, pp. 24–35; Hadley Arkes, *Beyond the Constitution* (Princeton University Press, 1990), pp. 35–39.

5. McCarthy, *Willful Blindness*.

6. Mark Krikorian, U.S. House of Representatives, Judiciary Committee testimony before the Subcommittee on Immigration, Border Security, and Claims (June 15, 2005) (http://www.cis.org/arti-

cles/2005/msktestimony061505.html); Matt Cover, "State Department
Using 'Diversity Visas' to Encourage Immigration to U.S. from Terror-
Ridden Yemen" (CNS News.com, Jan. 5, 2010) (http://www.cnsnews.
com/news/article/59270); Mark Krikorian and Andrew C. McCarthy
exchange of posts, "The System Still Works" (*National Review Online*,
The Corner, Jan. 6, 2010) (http://corner.nationalreview.com/post/?q=M
Tk3NGY0M2ExNDhmYTUzNWUzODQwNTU3YTIwYzk2ND
g=).

7. Andrew C. McCarthy and Bill West, "'Enforcement First'
Doesn't Stop at the Border—US VISIT needs fixing—and opportunity for McCain" (*National Review Online*, July 29, 2008) (http://
article.nationalreview.com/364704/enforcement-first-doesnt-stop-at-
the-border/bill-west-andrew-c-mccarthy?page=1).

8. Ibid. As Daniel Pipes recounts, a 2007 Pew survey estimated the
total population of Muslims in America to be 2.35 million, of which 1.5
million were counted as adult Muslim Americans.

9. President Obama, "A New Beginning."

10. Ibid.

11. Jeff Zelney, "Obama Says U.S. Could Be Seen as a Muslim
Country, Too" (*New York Times*, "The Caucus" blog, June 2, 2009) (http://
thecaucus.blogs.nytimes.com/2009/06/02/obama-signals-themes-of-
mideast-speech/?hp).

12. Pipes, "How Many Muslims in the United States" (citing Anwar
Iqbal, "Beat Extremists you can, says Obama" (*Dawn.com* of Pakistan,
June 21, 2009) (http://www.dawn.com/wps/wcm/connect/dawn-con-
tent-library/dawn/the-newspaper/front-page/beat-extremists-you-
can,-says-obama-169)).

13. For national population breakdowns, see *CIA World Fact Book*
(https://www.cia.gov/library/publications/the-world-factbook/index.
html); for Muslim population breakdowns, Pew Research Center, Pew
Forum, "Mapping the Global Muslim Population" (Oct. 2009) (http://
pewforum.org/docs/?DocID=450) (see also Wikipedia List of Countries
by Muslim Population relying on Pew numbers) (http://en.wikipedia.
org/wiki/Islam_by_country).

14. Estimates of the Shiite population in Saudi Arabia vary widely,
from a high of around 15 percent—see, e.g., Scott Wilson, "Shiites See
an Opening in Saudi Arabia" (*Washington Post*, Feb. 28, 2005) (http://

www.washingtonpost.com/wp-dyn/articles/A58262-2005Feb27.html—to slightly under 10 percent—see, e.g., International Crisis Group, "The Shiite Question in Saudi Arabia" (ICG Middle East Report No. 45, Sept. 19, 2005) (http://merln.ndu.edu/archive/icg/shiitequestion.pdf).

15. On Russia's population decline, see Mark Steyn, *America Alone* (Regnery, 2006), pp. 8, 21–31.

16. Leon Perkowski (Major, U.S. Air Force), "Muslim Demographics in the European Union: Widening the Gap with US Foreign Policy" (Air University Research Bulletin, 2006); Adrian Michaels, "Muslim Europe: the demographic time bomb transforming our continent" (*The Telegraph*, Aug. 8, 2009) (http://www.telegraph.co.uk/news/worldnews/europe/5994047/Muslim-Europe-the-demographic-time-bomb-transforming-our-continent.html).

17. Novikov, "The Muslim World League: Agent of Wahhabi Propagation in Europe," citing Craig S. Smith, "Islam in Jail: Europe's Neglect Breeds Angry Radicals" (*New York Times*, Dec. 8, 2004).

18. Andrew C. McCarthy, "Welcome to America, 'One of the Largest Muslim Countries in the World'!" (*National Review Online, The Corner*, June 3, 2009) (http://corner.nationalreview.com/post/?q=NTk1Z DVjODNmMjBlY2YoMTQ5Nzc2OWU1NjA3MmIxNTA=) (citing Wikipedia List of Countries by Muslim Population and Pew Research Center, Pew Forum, Mapping the Global Muslim Population).

Chapter Seventeen

1. "State Department Site Features Radical Mosque" (IPT News, June 22, 2009) (http://www.investigativeproject.org/blog/2009/06/state-department-site-features-radical-mosque).

2. Andrew C. McCarthy, "To Be Charitable, They're Terrorists—The Justice Department indicts Hamas's American funding arm" (*National Review Online*, July 29, 2004) (http://article.nationalreview.com/?q=YzFiZDYwODRjZmUoZTIxZjg4MTY1Zjg1YWMoZjRkN2M=).

3. IPT News, "State Department Site Features Radical Mosque."

4. Paul Sperry, *Infiltration* (Nelson Current, 2005), pp. 113–14, 196–97.

5. Sperry, pp. 113–14.

6. Sperry, *Infiltration*, pp. 110–18; see also Gaubatz and Sperry, *Muslim Mafia*, p. 202.

7. Caryle Murphy, "Facing New Realities as Muslim Americans" (*Washington Post*, Sept. 12, 2004) (http://www.washingtonpost.com/wp-dyn/articles/A14497-2004Sep11.html).

8. Sperry, *Infiltration*, p. 114.

9. Baran, "The Muslim Brotherhood's U.S. Network"; IPT Dossier: "Muslim American Society," p. 2 (http://www.investigativeproject.org/documents/misc/85.pdf); Noreen S. Ahmed-Ullah, Sam Roe and Laurie Cohen, "A Rare Look at Secretive Brotherhood in America") (*Chicago Tribune*, Sept. 19, 2004) (http://www.chicagotribune.com/news/watchdog/chi-0409190261sep19,0,3008717.story).

10. FBI affidavit in support of the search of Elbarasse's residence in Annandale, Virginia (United States District Court, Eastern District of Virginia, Alexandria Div., Aug. 20, 2004), pp. 5–6 (http://www.investigativeproject.org/documents/case_docs/885.pdf); Levitt, *Hamas*, p. 43.

11. *United States* v. *Holy Land Foundation for Relief and Development*, No. 04 Cr. 240-P, Government's Exhibit "Elbrasse Search 3" (http://www.txnd.uscourts.gov/judges/hlf2/09-25-08/Elbarasse%20Search%203).

12. Ibid., pp. 7–8.

13. Investigative Project on Terrorism, "MAS' Esam Omeish Seeks Virginia Office—Campaign Mum on MAS Ties, Radical Omeish Speeches" (IPT News, May 1, 2009) (http://www.investigativeproject.org/1025/mas-esam-omeish-seeks-virginia-office).

14. Discover the Networks Profile: Abdurahman Alamoudi (Alamoudi on Marzook: "I am honored to be a member of the committee that is defending Musa Abu Marzook in America. . . . I really consider him to be from among the best people in the Islamic movement, Hamas . . . and I work together with him.") (Alamoudi on Salameh: "All their [law enforcement] facts . . . are flimsy. . . . We don't think that any of those facts that they have against him, or the fact that they searched his home and they found a few wires here or there—are not enough.") (http://www.discoverthenetworks.org/individualProfile.asp?indid=1311).

15. "Treasury Designates MIRA for Support to Al Qaida" (United States Treasury Department Press Release, July 14, 2005) ("In 2003, MIRA [the Movement for Islamic Reform, a U.K.-based Saudi opposition organization] and [Saad al-Faqih, a formally designated terrorist

tied to Osama bin Laden] received approximately $1 million in funding through Abdulrahman [sic] Alamoudi. According to information available to the U.S. Government, the September 2003 arrest of Alamoudi was a severe blow to al Qaida, as Alamoudi had a close relationship with al Qaida and had raised money for al Qaida in the United States. In a 2004 plea agreement, Alamoudi admitted to his role in an assassination plot targeting the Crown Prince of Saudi Arabia and is currently serving a 23 year sentence.") (http://www.treasury.gov/press/releases/js2632.htm); "The al-Amoudi terror charges" (*Washington Times*, Oct. 5, 2003) (http://www.washingtontimes.com/news/2003/oct/05/20031005-111130-4622r/); "Alamoudi: 'You can be violent anwhere else . . . '" (Investigative Project on Terrorism, Dec. 28, 1996).

16. Marc Fisher, "From Fairfax to Richmond, 'The Jihad Way?'" (*Washington Post*, April 29, 2009) (http://voices.washingtonpost.com/rawfisher/2009/04/from_fairfax_to_richmond_the_j.html); Robert Spencer, "Virginia: The jihad candidate" (*Jihad Watch*, April 29, 2009) (http://www.jihadwatch.org/2009/04/virginia-the-jihad-candidate.html).

17. Ibid.

18. Robert Spencer, "Former prof gets 11 years for refusing to testify in Hamas funding case" (*Jihad Watch*, Nov. 22, 2007) (explaining that Ashqar and co-defendant Mohammad Salah were acquitted of racketeering conspiracy but shown to be in contact with Hamas leaders, and that sentencing judge found Ashqar's motive in obstructing the investigation was to "promote terrorism," dictating a severe sentence under the U.S. sentencing guidelines) (http://www.jihadwatch.org/2007/11/former-prof-gets-11-years-for-refusing-to-testify-in-hamas-funding-case.html);"Ashqar Gets 11 Years for Contempt" (IPT News, Nov. 21, 2007) (http://www.investigativeproject.org/554/ashqar-gets-11-years-for-contempt); IPT News, "Dar al-Hijrahh Official's Deception on Awlaki."

19. Sperry, *Infiltration*, p. 113; see also IPT News, "Dar Al-Hijrahh Official's Deception on Awlaki."

20. IPT News, "Dar Al-Hijrahh Official's Deception on Awlaki"; "Treasury Designates Global Network, Senior Officials of IARA for Supporting bin Laden, Others" (United States Treasury Department Press Release, Oct. 13, 2004) (http://www.investigativeproject.org/

documents/misc/32.pdf); Murphy, "Facing New Realities as Muslim Americans."

21. IPT News, "Life Sentence for Virginia Man Who Plotted to Kill President Bush" (Investigative Project on Terrorism, July 27, 2009) (http://www.investigativeproject.org/1333/life-sentence-for-virginia-man-who-plotted-to-kill); IPT News, "State Department Site Features Radical Mosque."

22. Sperry, *Infiltration*, pp. 117–18.

Chapter Eighteen

1. Andrew C. McCarthy, "Singing CAIR's Tune on Your Dime—As the Bush administration squanders a trust, Democrats prepare a new 'Sister Souljah Moment,' (*National Review Online*, Jan. 2, 2007) (http://article.nationalreview.com/?q=NjY4M2VjNmE2NmIxNzM3YjYyNTJjMjI4Y2JkOTE1YWI=).

2. Andrew C. McCarthy, "Relativism: paving the road to radicalism" (*The New Criterion*, Jan. 2009) (http://www.newcriterion.com/articles.cfm/Relativism—paving-the-road-to-radicalism-3984).

3. See, e.g., M. Zhudi Jasser, "From a Muslim outlook, imams have missed the point on flight behavior" (*Arizona Republic*, Dec. 11, 2006) (http://www.azcentral.com/arizonarepublic/viewpoints/articles/1211jasser1210.html).

4. Debra Burlingame, "On a Wing and a Prayer—Grievance theater at Minneapolis International Airport" (*Wall Street Journal*, Dec. 6, 2006) (http://www.opinionjournal.com/editorial/feature.html?id=110009348).

5. Scott Johnson, "Ascent of the Flying Imams: The Settlement" (*Powerline*, Oct. 21, 20009) (http://www.powerlineblog.com/archives/2009/10/024758.php).

6. Dennis Wagner and Tom Zoellner, "Arizona Was Home to bin Laden 'Sleeper Cell'" (*Arizona Republic*, Sept. 28, 2001) (http://www.hvk.org/articles/1106/126.html).

7. Gaubatz and Sperry, *Muslim Mafia*, pp. 221–24.

8. *In re: Terrorist Attacks on September 11, 2001* (Sept. 21, 2005 Opinion & Order of Hon. Richard Conway Casey, U.S. District Judge) (03 MDL 1570 (RCC), op. at p. 17 (available at the website of the In-

vestigative Project on Terrorism, http://www.investigativeproject.org/documents/case_docs/232.pdf).

9. Steven A. Emerson, Testimony before the U.S. Senate Committee on Banking, Housing, and Urban Affairs hearing on "Money Laundering and Terror Financing Issues in the Middle East" (July 13, 2005), p. 24 (http://www.investigativeproject.org/documents/testimony/19.pdf).

10. Audrey Hudson, "Imam disputes tie to Hamas" (*Washington Times*, Dec. 1, 2006) (http://www.washingtontimes.com/news/2006/dec/01/20061201-121239-7193r/).

11. Joe Kaufman and Gary Gross, "Fifth Column Imam Flyers" (*Frontpage Magazine*, April 19, 2007) (http://97.74.65.51/readArticle.aspx?ARTID=26185); *Americans Against Hate*, collected lectures of Imam Omar Shahin at the Islamic Center of Tucson (http://www.americansagainsthate.org/Omar_Shahin's_ICT_Lectures.htm) (accessed Nov. 2, 2009); see also Hadith: Sahih Muslim Coolection, Book 41, Nos. 6981 through 6985 (http://www.muslimaccess.com/sunnah/hadeeth/muslim/041.html); Robert Spencer, "USC MSA removes, does not repudiate, genocidal hadith (*Jihad Watch*, Aug. 22, 2008) (collecting variants of the same hadith, e.g. Bukhari Collection, Vol. 4, Book 52, No. 177 "Allah's Apostle said, "The Hour will not be established until you fight with the Jews, and the stone behind which a Jew will be hiding will say. 'O Muslim! There is a Jew hiding behind me, so kill him.'") (http://www.jihadwatch.org/2008/08/usc-msa-removes-does-not-repudiate-genocidal-hadith.html).

12. 9/11 Commission Final Report (2004), p. 521 n.60.

13. Investigative Project on Terrorism, "Hamas Leaders Dominate HLF Speakers List" (Oct. 7, 2008) (http://www.investigativeproject.org/787/hamas-leaders-dominate-hlf-speakers-list).

14. Gaubatz and Sperry, *Muslim Mafia*, p. 224; see also *Discover the Networks*, profile of the North American Imams Federation (http://www.discoverthenetworks.org/groupProfile.asp?grpid=7357) (accessed Nov. 2, 2009).

15. Kaufman and Gross, "Fifth Column Imam Flyers."

16. *Discover the Networks*, profile of the North American Imams Federation.

17. Cloverdale Books, 2007.

18. Sean Holstege and Dennis Wagner, "Ariz. Muslim leaders face increased FBI scrutiny—Monitoring grew after charity probe, 2 incidents" (*Arizona Republic*, Nov. 16, 2008) (http://www.azcentral.com/arizonarepublic/news/articles/2008/11/16/20081116scrutiny1116.html).

19. McCarthy, *Willful Blindness*.

20. Scott W. Johnson, "Louis Farrakhan's First Congressman—Why was the press so incurious about the past of Keith Ellison?" (*The Weekly Standard*, Oct. 9, 2006 ed.) (http://www.weeklystandard.com/content/public/articles/000/000/012/764obcsx.asp).

21. Investigative Project on Terrorism, "Congress Cozying Up to CAIR" (Oct. 17, 2008) (citing *USA v. Holy Land Foundation for Relief and Development*, Government Exhibit 16–53, p. 14) (http://www.investigativeproject.org/791/congress-cozying-up-to-cair).

22. Investigative Project on Terrorism, "Arizona Politicians Concerned By Minnesota Rep.'s Relationship with CAIR" (Sept. 22, 2009) (http://www.investigativeproject.org/blog/2009/09/arizona-politicians-concerned-by-minnesota-reps); Jim Walsh, "U.S. Rep. meets group accused of terror ties" (*Arizona Republic*, Sept. 19, 2009) (http://www.azcentral.com/news/articles/2009/09/19/20090919ellison0919.html).

23. Investigative Project on Terrorism, "Jasser Challenges Congressman on Reform's Value" (October 2, 2009) (http://www.investigativeproject.org/1448/jasser-challenges-congressman-on-reforms-value).

24. Gaubatz and Sperry, *Muslim Mafia*, p. 223; Burlingame, "On a Wing and a Prayer."

25. Holstege and Wagner, "Ariz. Muslim leaders face increased FBI scrutiny"; Robert Spencer, "Phoenix Imam Tells Muslims To Disregard U.S. Laws" (*Human Events*, Nov. 19, 2008) (http://www.humanevents.com/article.php?print=yes&id=29545).

Chapter Nineteen

1. Adrian Morgan, "Winston Churchill on Islamism" (*Family Security Matters*, April 10, 2007) (quoting Churchill, *The River War: An Account of the Reconquest of Sudan*, Vol. II, pp. 248–50 [Longmans, 1899]) (http://www.fsmarchives.org/article.php?id=877480).

2. Robert Spencer, "Muslim Target" (*Frontpage Magazine*, June 14, 2005) (http://97.74.65.51/readArticle.aspx?ARTID=8334) (citing

Nuh Ha Mim Keller, editor and translator, *Reliance of the Traveller* ['*Umdat al-Salik*], Amana Publications, 1994, 09.13).

3. See, e.g., Robert Spencer, "The Rape Jihad" (*Frontpage Magazine*, Sept. 24, 2004) (http://97.74.65.51/readArticle.aspx?ARTID=11278).

4. Spencer, "Muslim Target," citing *Sahih Bukhari*, vol. 5, book 59, no. 459.

5. See Bukari Hadith, Vol. 5, Book 58, Nos. 234–36 (e.g., no. 236: "Khadija died three years before the Prophet departed to Medina. He stayed there for two years or so and then he married 'Aisha when she was a girl of six years of age, and he consumed [sic] that marriage when she was nine years old.") (published at http://www.usc.edu/schools/college/crcc/engagement/resources/texts/muslim/hadith/bukhari/058.sbt.html).

6. Robert Spencer, "Child Marriage in the Islamic World" (*Frontpage Magazine*, Sept. 18, 2009) (http://97.74.65.51/readArticle.aspx?ARTID=36336).

7. Ibid.

8. Morgan, "Winston Churchill on Islamism."

9. Tiger Hawk, "The Muslims of Invention" (*Tiger Hawk*, March 12, 2006) (http://tigerhawk.blogspot.com/2006/03/muslims-of-invention.html), quoting Oriana Fallaci, *The Force of Reason* (Rizzoli International Publications, 2004), pp. ____.

10. See "FrontPage Magazine's Woman of the Year: Oriana Fallaci" (*Frontpage Magazine*, Editorial, Dec. 30, 2005) (http://97.74.65.51/readArticle.aspx?ARTID=6073).

11. Spencer, "Muslim Target," citing Steven Stalinsky, "The Next Pope and Islamic Prophecy" *Frontpage Magazine*, April 14, 2005 (http://97.74.65.51/readArticle.aspx?ARTID=8931).

12. The complaint was approved by a judge. The ministry of grace and justice did not support the suit but Italian law permits a judge to level criminal charges on the basis of complaints by private persons. If convicted, she could have been sentenced to two years' imprisonment. See Tunku Varadarajan, "Prophet of Decline—An interview with Oriana Fallaci" (*Wall Street Journal*, June 23, 2005) (http://www.opinionjournal.com/columnists/tvaradarajan/?id=110006858); Having taken up residence in the U.S., Fallaci did not answer the charges and died before the trial. Robert Spencer examined the 18 specifications of purported

defamation. See Spencer, "Muslim Target." They were certainly unflattering, but did not come close to legal defamation. In the main, they were fact-rooted expressions of Fallaci's opinion.

13. Stephen Collins Coughlin, "To Our Great Detriment: Ignoring What Extremists Say About *Jihad.*" Submitted to the National Defense Intelligence College in pursuit of Coughlin's master of science degree in the field of strategic intelligence, July 2007 (http://www.strategycenter. net/docLib/20080107_Coughlin_ExtremistJihad.pdf).

14. Bill Gertz, "Coughlin Sacked" (*Washington Times*, "Inside the Ring," Jan. 4, 2008) (http://www.washingtontimes.com/news/2008/ jan/04/inside-the-ring-83234302/).

15. Claudia Rosett, "Questions for the Pentagon" (*National Review Online*, Jan. 25, 2008) (http://article.nationalreview.com/345339/ questions-for-the-pentagon/claudia-rosett).

16. Paul Sperry, "Penetration Even At The Pentagon: Muslim Spies Setting Muslim Policy" (*Investor's Business Daily*, Dec. 17, 2009) (http:// www.investors.com/NewsAndAnalysis/Article.aspx?id=515712).

17. Ibid.

18. Steven Emerson, "Pentagon Aide's Invitations Contradicted U.S. Policy" (IPT News, Feb. 4, 2008) (http://www.investigativeproject. org/596/pentagon-aides-invitations-contradicted-us-policy).

19. Sperry, "Penetration Even At The Pentagon."

20. See Thomas Joscelyn, "Obama Wrong On Al Qaeda in the Arabian Peninsula's 'Rationale'" (*The Weekly Standard*, Jan. 6, 2010) (http://www.weeklystandard.com/weblogs/TWSFP/2010/01/obama_ wrong_on_al_qaeda_in_the.asp); Adam Entous and Phil Stewart, "U.S. believes 1 in 5 ex-detainees joining militants" (*Reuters*, Jan. 6, 2010) (http://news.yahoo.com/s/nm/20100106/ts_nm/us_yemen_guantana-mo_usa); Stephen F. Hayes and Thomas Joscelyn, "Rehab for Jihadists— The Gitmo problem is also a Yemen problem" (*The Weekly Standard*, Feb. 23, 2009) (http://www.weeklystandard.com/content/public/ articles/000/000/016/153krrgy.asp); Thomas Joscelyn, "The Taliban's surge commander was Gitmo detainee" (*The Long War Journal*, March 11, 2009) (http://www.longwarjournal.org/archives/2009/03/the_tali-bans_surge_c.php).

21. Sperry, "Penetration Even At The Pentagon."

22. IPT News, "Hesham Islam's Friend in Low Places" (Feb. 14, 2008) (http://www.investigativeproject.org/blog/2008/02/hesham-islams-friend-in-low-places).

23. Andrew C. McCarthy, "Somebody at Fort Hood Should Be Walking the Plank" (*National Review Online, The Corner*, Dec. 3, 2009) (http://corner.nationalreview.com/post/?q=Y2QxNWFlZDM5MDQo NzM4MDg3ZjA3MDE5ZjNmYzBjYzU).

24. IPT News, "Denials Carry a Familiar Ring" (Investigative Project on Terrorism, Oct. 10, 2007) (http://www.investigativeproject. org/510/denials-carry-a-familiar-ring).

25. Evan McCormick, "Pentagon Madrassas" (*Frontpage Magazine*, Dec. 2, 2003) (http://97.74.65.51/readArticle.aspx?ARTID=15222).

26. Robert Spencer, "The termination of Stephen Coughlin on the Joint Staff is an act of intellectual cowardice" (*Jihad Watch*, Jan. 5, 2008) (http://www.jihadwatch.org/2008/01/the-termination-of-stephen-coughlin-on-the-joint-staff-is-an-act-of-intellectual-cowardice. html).

Chapter Twenty

1. Andrew C. McCarthy, "Riddle of the Sands" (*Claremont Review of Books*, Vol. IX, No. 2, Spring 2009) (http://www.claremont.org/publications/crb/id.1613/article_detail.asp#), reviewing Pollack, *A Path Out of the Desert: A Grand Strategy for America in the Middle East*.

2. Michael B. Mukasey, *How Obama has Mishandled the War on Terror* (Encounter, "Encounter Broadsides," 2010).

3. Department of Homeland Security, Office for Civil Rights and Civil Liberties, "Terminology to Define the Terrorists: Recommendations from American Muslims" (Jan. 2008) (http://www.investigative-project.org/documents/misc/126.pdf); see Andrew C. McCarthy, "The Government's Jihad on Jihad—Still lookin' for love in all the wrong places" (*National Review Online*, May 13, 2008) (http://article.nationalreview. com/357443/the-governments-jihad-on-ijihadi/andrew-c-mccarthy).

4. Alinsky, *Rules for Radicals*, p. 50.

5. Scott Wilson and Al Kamen, "'Global War On Terror' Is Given New Name—Bush's Phrase Is Out, Pentagon Says" (*Washington Post*, March 25, 2009) (http://www.washingtonpost.com/wp-dyn/con-

tent/article/2009/03/24/AR2009032402818.html?wprss=rss_politics/ administration).

6. Andrew G. Bostom, "Islamism or Islam? Islamist or Islamic?" (*The American Thinker*, Nov. 14, 2009) (http://www.americanthinker. com/2009/11/islamism_or_islam_islamist_or.html).

7. Nina Shea, "'Insulting Islam': One Way Street in the Wrong Direction" (*Hudson Institute*, Jan. 26, 2009) (http://www.hudsonny. org/2009/01/insulting-islam-one-way-street-in-the-wrong-direction. php).

8. Michael Weiss and Ibn Warraq, "Inhuman Rights—The UN's Human Rights Council, friend to Islamistst and tyrants everywhere" (*City Journal*, Spring 2009) (http://www.city-journal.org/2009/19_2_ UN-human-rights-council.html).

9. Roger Kimball, "Villain or Fall Guy? Yale and the Case of the Missing Cartoons" (*Pajamas Media*, "Roger's Rules," Aug. 14, 2009) (htt://pajamasmedia/com/rogerkimball/2009/08/14/villain-or-fall-guy-yale-and-the-case-of-the-missing-cartoons/).

10. Mark Steyn, "Learning to Live with Islam" (*National Review Online, The Corner*, Aug. 24, 2009) (http:corner.nationalreview.com/p ost/?q=Njg5NjFhZDczYWM1M214YWFIYmUxZDA1MWE4MzA2 ODc=); Michael Rubin, "Fareed Zakaraia, Yale Press, and Censorship" (*National Review Online, The Corner*, Aug. 24, 2009) (http://corner.na-tionareview.com/post?q=M2YyMjhiZWFmOWNmZGUxMTRmMT UzNTBmZjU2)DM2YTM=); Fareed Zakaraia, "Learning to Live with Radical Islam—We don't have to accept the stoning of criminals. But it's time to stop treating all Islamists as potential terrorists" (*Newsweek*, Feb. 28, 2009) (http://www.newsweek.com/id/197093).

11. Diana West, "No Lux, More Dhimmitude" (Diana West.com, Aug. 14, 2009) (http://www.dianawest.net/Home/tabid/36/EntryId/983/ No-Lux-More-Dhimmitude.aspx); Andrew C. McCarthy, "More on Preemptive Capitulation at Yale (Part 2 of 2)" (National Review Online, "The Corner," Aug. 15, 2009) http://corner.nationalreview.com/post/? q=ZDBjN2NkOTM2YWJlNTlkMjIzZGY2MWY0ZTg3MjljN2Y).

12. Ezra Levant, *Shakedown: How Our Government Is Undermining Democracy in the Name of Human Rights* (McClellan & Stewart, 2009);

see also Mark Steyn, *Lights Out: Islam, Free Speech and the Twilight of the West* (Stockade Books, 2009).

13. Rachel Ehrenfeld, *Funding Evil, Updated: How Terrorism Is Financed and How to Stop It* (Bonus Books 2005).

14. Andrew C. McCarthy, "Can Libel Tourism Be Stopped" (*Commentary*, Sept. 2008).

15. Roger Kimball, "Terrorizing Publishing" (*New York Sun*, April 10, 2008) (http://www.nysun.com/editorials/terrorizing-publishing); Clifford D. May, "The Big Chill" (Scripps Howard News Service, Aug. 28, 2008) (http://www.cliffordmay.org/2213/the-big-chill).

16. Winston S. Churchill, *The Second World War: The Gathering Storm* (Houghton Mifflin Company, 1948) (relevant excerpt published by Amazon at http://books.google.com/books?id=JjvnPJnk57cC&pg=PA5 0&lpg=PA50&dq=%22here+was+the+new+koran+of+faith+and+war% 22&source=web&ots=k9fcgXFV4P&sig=WElr7pLH8Y_JUyQ5JLUy T6QAAOs#v=onepage&q=%22here%20was%20the%20new%20ko- ran%20of%20faith%20and%20war%22&f=false); Daniel Pipes, "Winston Churchill Compares 'Mein Kampf to the Koran'" (Daniel Pipes. org Feb. 21, 2008) (http://www.danielpipes.org/blog/2008/02/winston-churchill-compares-mein-kampf-to-the); Andrew G. Bostom, "The Koran and Mein Kampf: From Winston Churchill to Geert Wilders" (Andrew Bostom.org, March 4, 2008) (http://www.andrewbostom.org/ blog/2008/03/04/the-koran-and-mein-kampf-from-winston-churchill-to-geert-wilders/).

17. Thomas Landen, "Dutch MP Wilders Denied Entry to UK (*Hudson Institute*, Feb. 10, 2009) (http://www.hudsonny.org/2009/02/ dutch-mp-geert-wilders-denied-entry-to-uk.php); John O'Sullivan, "England's Muslim Spleen—Brits Ban a Foe of Islamism" (*New York Post*, Feb. 16, 2009) (http://www.nypost.com/seven/02162009/postopinion/ opedcolumnists/englands_muslim_spleen_155468.htm?page=0).

18. Stephen Pollard, "Lord Ahmed's unwelcome guest—The Labour peer must admit his error in inviting an extreme anti-Semite to air his views" (*London Times*, April 7, 2005) (http://www.timesonline. co.uk/tol/comment/columnists/guest_contributors/article378140.ece); Andrew Stuttaford, "Wilders" (*National Review Online, The Corner*, Feb.

12, 2009) (http://corner.nationalreview.com/post/?q=YzA1NzNhMTV jZDM2NWIwMTAxYmZlZWE2MGJkNzVjYTY=).

19. Michael Lea, "'Al Qaeda' in Commons" (*The Sun* (UK), March 18, 2006) (http://www.thesun.co.uk/sol/homepage/news/article41733. ece).

20. "Freed 'terror 3' held in the UK" (*The Sun* (UK), Dec. 20, 2007) (http://www.thesun.co.uk/sol/homepage/news/article604588.ece).

21. Natalie Paris, "Tories: Are Guantanamo detainees dangerous?" (*The Telegraph* (UK), Dec. 8, 2007) (http://www.telegraph.co.uk/news/ worldnews/1571925/Tories-Are-Guantanamo-detainees-dangerous. html).

Chapter Twenty-One

1. Diana West, "Somaliology" (Diana West.net, Nov. 20, 2008) (http://www.dianawest.net/Home/tabid/36/EntryId/599/Somaliology. aspx).

2. Diana West, "Pay Attention to the Somalis" (http://townhall. com/columnists/DianaWest/2008/11/20/pay_attention_to_the_ somalis).

3. Philip Mudd, Associate Executive Assistant Director, National Security Division, Federal Bureau of Investigation (March 11, 2009 Testimony before the Senate Committee on Homeland Security and Governmental Affairs) (http://www.fbi.gov/congress/congress09/ mudd031109.htm).

4. "State Department close to reopening previously fraud-ridden program" (*Refugee Resettlement Watch*, Nov. 20, 2009) (linked AP story has been removed from the AP site) (http://refugeeresettlementwatch. wordpress.com/2009/11/20/state-department-close-to-reopening-pre-viously-fraud-ridden-program/); West, "Pay Attention to the Somalis."

5. West, "Somaliology."

6. See Bret Stephens, "Why Don't We Hang Pirates Anymore?" (*Wall Street Journal*, Nov. 25, 2008) (http://online.wsj.com/article/ SB122757123487054681.html).

7. Mudd Testimony.

8. "Tyson Plant Drops Labor Day for Muslim Holiday" (Fox News, Aug. 5, 2008) (http://www.foxnews.com/story/0,2933,397645,00.html); Steven Greenhouse, "Muslim Holiday at Tyson Plant Creates Furor

(*New York Times*, Aug. 6, 2008) (http://www.nytimes.com/2008/08/06/us/06muslim.html).

9. West, "Pay Attention to the Somalis."

10. West, "Pay Attention to the Somalis."

11. Mudd Testimony; see also, IPT News, "It's Official: Al-Shabaab Ties the Knot with Al Qaeda " (Investigative Project on Terrorism, Sept. 22, 2009) (http://www.investigativeproject.org/1425/its-official-al-shabaab-ties-the-knot-with-al).

12. Michael N. Cannizaro, Special Agent, Federal Bureau of Investigation, affidavit in support of criminal complaint, *United States* v. *Cabdulaahi Ahmed Faarax and Abdiweli Yassin Isse* (United States District Court, District of Minnesota, Oct. 8, 2009), pp. 3–4. (http://graphics8.nytimes.com/packages/pdf/us/20091124_TERROR_DOCS/faarax.pdf); see also IPT News, "How al-Shabaab Targets Western Youth" (Investigative Project on Terrorism, Jan. 29, 2010) (http://www.investigativeproject.org/1764/how-al-shabaab-targets-western-youth).

13. Mary Harper, "Profile: Somalia's Islamist 'lads'" (BBC, March 21, 2008) (http://news.bbc.co.uk/2/hi/7307521.stm); "Militants Patrol Captured Somali City (Associated Press, Aug. 24, 2008) (http://www.nytimes.com/2008/08/24/world/africa/24somalia.html?ref=world).

14. Mudd Testimony.

15. Cannizaro affidavit, pp. 8–9; Mudd Testimony.

16. IPT News, "How al-Shabaab Targets Western Youth."

17. Ibid; see also John Goddard, "Fanatic convert to terrorism spent year in Toronto (*The Star* [Canada], Jan. 4, 2010) (http://www.thestar.com/news/gta/article/745524—fanatic-convert-to-terrorism-spent-year-in-toronto).

18. IPT News, "A Busy Day for Terror" (Investigative Project on Terrorism, Sept. 25, 2009) (http://www.investigativeproject.org/blog/2009/09/a-busy-day-for-terror-1); Cannizaro affidavit, pp. 3–5; IPT News, "How al-Shabaab Targets Western Youth."

19. Andrew C. McCarthy, "Your Tax Dollars at Work: Burying Somali Suicide Bombers . . . in Minnesota" (*National Review Online, The Corner*, Dec. 5, 2008) (http://corner.nationalreview.com/post/?q=MDE1ZGQ1MzdiY2NhMTdhYWJlZmM2MTUoOWJhNjgoNWU=);Pamela Geller, "Muslim Suicide Bomber Given Decent Burial in Minnesota" (*Atlas Shrugs*, Dec. 4, 2008) (http://atlasshrugs2000.typepad.com/

atlas_shrugs/2008/12/muslim-suicide.html); "Somali terrorist group wants to throw the West 'into hell'" (*Refugee Resettlement Watch*, Nov. 25, 2008) (http://refugeeresettlementwatch.wordpress.com/2008/11/25/somali-terrorist-group-wants-to-throw-the-west-into-hell/).

20. IPT News, "How al-Shabaab Targets Western Youth."

21. Chris Serres, "On the job, their way" (*Star Tribune*, June 15, 2008) (http://www.startribune.com/business/19934184.html?location_refer=Most%20Viewed:Homepage).

22. Daniel Pipes, "More on Those Alcohol-shy Minnesota Taxi Drivers" (Daniel Pipes.org, Sept. 10, 2008) (http://www.danielpipes.org/blog/2006/10/more-on-those-alcohol-shy-minnesota-taxi); Daniel Pipes, "Don't Bring the Booze into my Taxi" (Daniel Pipes.org, Sept. 10, 2008) (http://www.danielpipes.org/4046/dont-bring-that-booze-in-to-my-taxi); Barbara Pinto, "Muslim Cab Drivers Refuse to Transport Alcohol, and Dogs" (ABC News, Jan 26, 2007) (http://abcnews.go.com/International/story?id=2827800&page=1).

23. Katherine Kersten, "Are Taxpayers Footing the Bill for an Islamic Public School in Minnesota?" (*Star Tribune*, March 9, 2009) (http://kerstenblog.startribune.com/kerstenblog/?p=392).

24. Pipes, "More on Those Alcohol-shy Minnesota Taxi Drivers"; Pinto, "Muslim Cab Drivers Refuse to Transport Alcohol, and Dogs."

25. Daniel Pipes, "Muslim Taxi Drivers v. Seeing-Eye Dogs" (Daniel Pipes.org, Nov. 14, 2005) (http://www.danielpipes.org/blog/2005/11/muslim-taxi-drivers-vs-seeing-eye-dogs).

26. Andrew C. McCarthy, "Internal Struggle for Personal Betterment Alert" (*National Review Online*, May 13, 2008) (cited article from *St. Cloud Times* removed from Internet) (http://corner.nationalreview.com/post/?q=YjY4M2NlMzU3MWQyMzg1ODEzNmM1MjhkMTBjODBmZmI=).

27. Jeffrey Jackson, "Tensions Mount at OHS" (*Owatonna News*, Nov. 18, 2009) (http://www.owatonna.com/news.php?viewStoryPrinter=111955); Pamela Geller, "Imposing Shariah in America: Somali Muslims 'Out for Blood' at Minnesota High School" (*Atlas Shrugs*, Dec. 28, 2009) (http://atlasshrugs2000.typepad.com/atlas_shrugs/2009/12/imposing-sharia-in-america-.html).

28. Gilbert T. Sewall, "Islam in the Classroom—What the Textbooks Tell Us" (American Textbook Council, 2008) (http://www.news-wwk.com/is/187093).

29. Civil Complaint, *American Civil Liberties Union of Minnesota* v. *Tarek ibn Ziyad Academy* Civ. No. 09–138 (United States District Court, District of Minnesota, Jan. 2009) (http://www.aclu-mn.org/downloads/TIZAComplaint.pdf).

30. Kersten, "Are Taxpayers Footing the Bill for an Islamic Public School in Minnesota?"; see also Scott Johnson, "TIZA Swings and Misses" (*Powerline*, Dec. 10, 2009) (http://www.powerlineblog.com/archives/2009/12/025125.php).

Chapter Twenty-Two

1. "Muslim Americans unite in response to Obama's call for change" (*Ikhwanweb.com*, Sept. 9, 2009) (http://www.ikhwanweb.com/article.php?id=20981).

2. IPT News, "Dalia Mogahed, Hizb ut-Tahrir Representative Tout Sharia for Women" (Investigative Project on Terrorism, Oct. 8, 2009) (http://www.investigativeproject.org/blog/2009/10/dalia-mogahed-hizb-ut-tahrir-representative-tout).

3. Supna Zaidi, "Exporting American anti-Americanism to Muslim world" (*Washington Examiner*, Oct. 28, 2009) (http://www.washington-examiner.com/opinion/columns/OpEd-Contributor/Exporting-American-anti-Americanism-to-Muslim-world-8445809.html).

4. IPT News, "Hizb Ut-Tahrir: Shariah Takes Precedence over U.S. Constitution—Imam Promises to Fight 'Until Islam Becomes Victorious or We Die in the Attempt" (Investigative Project on Terrorism, July 20, 2009) (http://www.investigativeproject.org/1100/hizb-ut-tahrir-shariah-takes-precedence-over-us).

5. IPT News, "Dalia Mogahed, Hizb ut-Tahrir Representative Tout Sharia for Women"

6. *Hinrichs* v. *Bosma*, No. 05 Civ 813 (S.D. In., Indianapolis Div., Nov. 30, 2005) (http://www.insd/uscourts.gov/news/1-05-cv-0813%20opinion.pdf); J. Edward Whelan, "Seventh Circuit Nominee David Hamilton: 'Allah' Yes, 'Jesus' No" (*National Review Online*, Bench

Memos, March 26, 2009) (http://bench.nationalreview.com/post/
?q=ZmRiZGVkYzZmZGFhMDM4MTE2ZmE1ZTMxOTAxM
2RkNmM=); "Thank Allah it's Friday" (*Washington Times*, Editorial, Jan. 22, 2010) (http://www.washingtontimes.com/news/2010/
jan/22/thank-allah-its-friday/?source=newsletter_must-read-stories-
today_more_news_carousel).

7.   Robert Tait and Ewen MacAskill, "Revealed: the letter Obama
team hope will heal Iran rift—Symbolic gesture gives assurances that US
does not want to topple Islamic regime" (*The Guardian*, Jan. 29, 2009)
(http://www.guardian.co.uk/world/2009/jan/28/barack-obama-letter-
to-iran); "Obama say US can work with Muslims: OIC" (*Agence France
Presse*, Feb. 1, 2009) (http://www.khaleejtimes.com/DisplayArticle08.
asp?xfile=data/middleeast/2009/February/middleeast_February30.
xml&section=middleeast); see also Barbara Slavin and Iason Athana-
siadis, "Obama sent second letter to Khamenei" (*Washington Times*, Sept.
3, 2009) (http://www.washingtontimes.com/news/2009/sep/03/obama-
sent-second-letter-to-irans-khamenei/); Barbara Slavin, "U.S. contacted
Iran's ayatollah before election—Administration overture to Khamenei
ridiculed in sermon" (*Washington Times*, June 24, 2009) (http://washing-
tontimes.com/news/2009/jun/24/us-contacted-irans-ayatollah-before-
election/?feat=home_cube_position1); Christiane Amanpour, "Obama
sent letter to Iran leader before election, sources say" (CNN, June 24,
2009)   (http://www.cnn.com/2009/POLITICS/06/24/iran.obama.let-
ter/index.html).

8.   Andrew C. McCarthy, "Obama Frees Iranian Terror Masters—
The release of the Irbil Five is a continuation of a shameful policy"
(*National Review Online*, June 24, 2009) (http://article.nationalreview.co
m/?q=ZjYoMjkwOWVkYTNlYzE2ZjM1N2E5M2MoMTdiYTI3Mz
M=); Andrew C. McCarthy, "Negotiating with Terrorists—The Obama
administration ignores a longstanding—and life-saving—policy" (*National Review Online*, June 24, 2009) (http://article.nationalreview.com
/?q=ODFkYTU2MjBmMTE5MDUzZTEzZWMyMTE5ZWZjNWI
4Mjg=); Andrew C. McCarthy, "It's Not Yet Friday, But It Is New Year's
Eve—What Better Time to Release an Iran-Backed Terror Master Who
Murdered American Troops" (*National Review Online*, The Corner, Dec.
31, 2009) (http://corner.nationalreview.com/post/?q=NmZjZmMyNm
FmODUoZGE5NjRlYTA4MzMzYmUwMzk2OGE).

9. Robert Spencer, "Obama Invites Organization of the Islamic Conference chief to White House" (*Jihad Watch*, April 7, 2009) (http://www.jihadwatch.org/2009/04/obama-invites-organization-of-the-islamic-conference-chief-to-white-house.html).

10. IPT Profile, "Ingrid Mattson and the Islamic Society of North America" (http://www.investigativeproject.org/profile/174#_ftnref13), quoting Ingrid Mattson, speech at the Kenndy School at Harvard University (March 12, 2007).

11. White House, Office of the Press Secretary, Official Guest List for White House Dinner Celebrating Ramadan (Sept. 1, 2009) (http://www.whitehouse.gov/the_press_office/Expected-attendees-at-tonights-White-House-dinner-celebrating-Ramadan/); "ISNA Leadership Attend Treasury Iftar (*ISNA.net*, Sept. 23, 2009) (http://www.whitehouse.gov/the_press_office/Expected-attendees-at-tonights-White-House-dinner-celebrating-Ramadan/).

12. Rowan Scarborough, "FBI Partners with Jihad Groups." (*Human Events*, Sept. 10, 2009) (http://www.humanevents.com/article.php?id=33472).

13. IPT News, "'Mainsteam' Islamist Convention Features Hate Speech and Hezbollah Defense" (Investigative Project on Terrorism, July 8, 2009) (http://www.investigativeproject.org/1085/mainstream-islamist-convention-features-hate).

14. Arab American Institute Press Release, "Arab, Muslim, Sikh & South Asian American Community Leaders Meet with DHS Secretary Napolitano" (Jan. 29, 2010) (available at www.aaiusa.org).

15. CAIR-Michigan Press Release, "CAIR-MI Meets with DHS Assistant Secretary Regarding Immigration Reform" (Sept. 1, 2009) (http://www.cairmichigan.org/news/press_releases/cair_mi_meets_with_dhs_assistant_secretary_regar); see also CAIR-Michigan Newsletter (Oct. 29, 2009), p. 1; CAIR-Pennsylvania, Philadelphia Newsletter (Spring 2009 ed., Issue No. 3); "CAIR-WA Meets with DHS, CBP on Border Profiling" ("Local Muslims testify to mistreatment when returning to U.S.," http://www.facebook.com/note.php?note_id=118640019441 [Facebook] Notes, Aug. 20, 2009).

16. Barbara Ferguson, "Iftar at Pentagon sends a message" (*Arab News*, Sept. 5, 2009) (http://www.arabnews.com/?page=4&section=0&article=126110&d=5&m=9&y=2009).

17. "Turkish Imams Meet with Interfaith Leaders in Washington" (IIIT.org, Feb. 6, 2009) (http://www.iiit.org/NewsEvents/News/tabid/62/articleType/ArticleView/articleId/122/Default.aspx).

18. Muslim American Society Freedom Foundation, "MAS Freedom Visited by Muslim Foreign News and Journalist Team as Part of U.S. State Department Visitation Program" (MASnet.org, July 17, 2009) (http://www.masnet.org/takeaction.asp?id=5392).

19. Muslim American Society Freedom Foundation, "Muslim Health Professionals Hold Capitol Hill Citizens' Hearing on Universal Healthcare" (MASnet.org, Sept. 16, 2009) (http://www.masnet.org/takeaction.asp?id=5419).

20. "Second Muslim elected to Congress" (Reuters, March 11, 2008) (http://www.reuters.com/article/idUSN1164415020080312).

21. "Carson Blames Grandmother for Farrakhan Ties" (*Advance Indiana*, Feb. 25, 2009) (http://advanceindiana.blogspot.com/2008/02/carson-blames-grandmother-for-farrakhan.html).

22. Beila Rabinowitz and William Mayer, "Andre Carson Joins Ellison's Stealth Jihad in Congress" (*PipeLineNews.org*, March 14, 2008)(http://www.pipelinenews.org/index.cfm?page=carson3.14.08%2Ehtm).

23. MAS, "Muslim Health Professionals Hold Capitol Hill Citizens' Hearing on Universal Healthcare."

Chapter Twenty-Three

1. IPT News, "Introspection, Not Rationalization, Needed in Wake of Fort Hood Slaughter" (Investigative Project on Terrorism, Nov. 6, 2009) (http://www.investigativeproject.org/1500/introspection-not-rationalization-needed-in-wake).

2. Andrew C. McCarthy, "Dare to Call It Terrorism—The FBI will not admit that what happened in Texas is part of the jihad" (*National Review Online*, Nov. 10, 2009) (http://article.nationalreview.com/413891/dare-to-call-it-terrorism/andrew-c-mccarthy).

3. Andrew C. McCarthy, "Still Willfully Blind" (*National Review Online*, Nov. 10, 2009) (http://corner.nationalreview.com/post/?q=OWE4YTM3MmZlODFjYjUxYzg3MzNlZWIzMjEoMmIwMWU=).

4. Steven Emerson, "Buried Videos Surface in HLF Trial" (*Counterterrorism Blog*, July 26, 2007) (republished by the Investigative Project

on Terrorism at http://www.investigativeproject.org/278/buried-videos-surface-in-hlf-trial).

5. Paul Sperry, "Fiend's easy escape" (*New York Post*, Jan. 10, 2010) (http://www.nypost.com/p/news/international/fiend_easy_escape_no4I3fUgiSmzc7WxrV2LLN).

6. Ibid; see also Sperry, *Infiltration*, pp. 121–23.

7. IPT News, "Dar Al-Hijrah Officia's Deception on Awlaki."

8. 9/11 Commission Report, pp. 221, 230; Sperry, *Infiltration*, pp. 121–23.

9. Sperry, "Fiend's easy escape."

10. Thomas Joscelyn, "See No Evil—The Pentagon's Fort Hood investigation is a pathetic whitewash" (*The Weekly Standard*, Feb. 1, 2010) (http://www.weeklystandard.com/print/articles/see-no-evil).

11. Brooks Egerton, "Fort Hood: Hasan wanted patients to face war crimes charges" (*Dallas Morning News*, Nov. 17, 2009) (http://www.dallasnews.com/sharedcontent/dws/dn/latestnews/stories/111709dntexshooter.3f2db30.html).

12. Dana Priest, "Fort Hood suspect warned of threats within the ranks—Cited stress facing Muslims[;] Hasan spoke at Walter Reed in 2007" (*Washington Post*, Nov. 10, 2009) (http://www.washingtonpost.com/wp-dyn/content/article/2009/11/09/AR2009110903618.html); Joscelyn, "See No Evil—The Pentagon's Fort Hood investigation is a pathetic whitewash"; Jonah Goldberg, "Connecting the Dots—Many people saw signs that the Fort Hood shooter could become violent" (*National Review Online*, Nov. 10, 2009) (http://article.nationalreview.com/413968/connecting-the-dots/jonah-goldberg).

13. IPT News, "Introspection, Not Rationalization, Needed in Wake of Fort Hood Slaughter."

14. Julian E. Barnes and Josh Meyer, "Military not told about Ft. Hood suspect's emails" (*Los Angeles Times*, Nov. 11, 2009) (http://articles.latimes.com/2009/nov/11/nation/na-fort-hood-army11).

15. Joscelyn, "See No Evil—The Pentagon's Fort Hood investigation is a pathetic whitewash."

16. Department of Defense Independent Review, "Protecting the Force—Lessons from Fort Hood" (Jan. 2010) (http://www.defense.gov/pubs/pdfs/DOD-ProtectingTheForce-Web_Security_HR_13Jan10.pdf).

17. Andrew C. McCarthy, "Somebody at Fort Hood Should Be Walking the Plank" (*National Review Online, The Corner*, Dec. 3, 2009) (http://corner.nationalreview.com/post/?q=Y2QxNWFlZDM5MDQ0 NzM4MDg3ZjA3MDE5ZjNmYzBjYzU).

18. *Meet the Press*, Transcript of Interview with Gen. George Casey (NBC News, Nov. 8, 2009) (http://www.msnbc.msn.com/id/33752275/ ns/meet_the_press/).

19. Joscelyn, "See No Evil—The Pentagon's Fort Hood investigation is a pathetic whitewash."

20. Andrew C. McCarthy, "Holder's Haste Makes Waste of Intel" (*National Review Online*, Jan. 7, 2010) (http://article.nationalreview. com/420098/holders-haste-makes-waste-of-intel/andrew-c-mccarthy); Andrew C. McCarthy, "Still Time to Get It Right—But only if Obama reverses course on Abdulmutallab" (*National Review Online*, Jan. 22, 2010) (http://article.nationalreview.com/422496/still-time-to-get-it-right/andrew-c-mccarthy).

21. "U.S. cleric: Accused plane bomber was my student" (Associated Press, Feb 4. 2010) (http://www.suntimes.com/news/ world/2029613,yemen-plane-bomber-student-020410.article); see also Jason Keyser, "Bin Laden Endorses Bomb Attempt on US Plane" (Associated Press, Jan. 24, 2010) (http://abcnews.go.com/International/ wireStory?id=9647388).

22. "Profile: Umar Farouk Abdulmutallab" (BBC, Jan. 7, 2010) (http://news.bbc.co.uk/go/pr/fr/-/2/hi/americas/8431530.stm); "Attempted Airline Bomber Headed Campus Society With Muslim Brotherhood Ties" (*Global Muslim Brotherhood Report*, Jan. 6, 2010) (http:// globalmbreport.com/?p=1761); "Attempted Plane Bomber Attended Muslim World League Mosque" (*Global Muslim Brotherhood Report*, Jan. 6, 2010) (http://globalmbreport.com/?p=1769); John Thorne and Hanna Stuart, "Islam on Campus" (Centre for Social Cohesion Monograph, 2008) (http://www.socialcohesion.co.uk/files/1231525079_1. pdf); "U.K. Student Societies Tied to Muslim Brotherhood Most Likely To Hold Intolerant Views" (*Global Muslim Brotherhood Report*, July 31, 2008) (http://globalmbreport.com/?p=1014).

23. Susan Jones, "Obama Describes Nigerian As 'Isolated Extremist,' Despite Ties to Yemen" (CNS News, Dec. 29, 2009) (http://www. cnsnews.com/news/article/59115).

Epilogue

1. Josh Gerstein, "Islam envoy retreats on terror talk" (*Politico*, Feb. 19, 2010) (http://dyn.politico.com/printstory.cfm?uuid=E9590C34-18FE-70B2-A88C9208B93FC804).

2. Indictment, *United States* v. *Sami Amin al-Arian, et al.*, No. 03 Cr. 77 (United States District Court, Middle District of Florida, 2003) (http://www.fas.org/irp/ops/ci/al-arian_indict_022003.pdf); Investigative Project on Terrorism, Sami al-Arian Profile (http://www.investigativeproject.org/profile/100#_ftn5).

3. Horowitz, *Unholy Alliance*, p. 188.

4. Indictment, *United States* v. *Sami Amin al-Arian*; see also Scott Johnson, "The Case of Rashad Hussain, Part 3" (*Powerline*, Feb. 24, 2010) (http://www.powerlineblog.com/archives/2010/02/025671.php).

5. Horowitz, *Unholy Alliance*, p. 189; Scott Johnson, "The Case of Rashad Hussain."

6. Gerstein, "Islam envoy retreats on terror talk."

7. Scott Johnson, "The Case of Rashad Hussain, Part 3."

8. Rashad Hussain, Al-Husein N. Madhany, "Reformulating the Battle of Ideas: Understanding the Role of Islam in Counterterrorism Policy" (Brookings Institution, Aug. 2008) (http://www.brookings.edu/papers/2008/08_counterterrorism_hussain.aspx).

9. Jennifer Rubin, "Re: Obama Envoy Vouched for a Convicted Terrorist" (*Commentary, Contentions*, Feb. 17, 2010) (http://www.commentarymagazine.com/blogs/index.php/rubin/238836).

10. Gerstein, "Islam envoy retreats on terror talk."

11. See, e.g., Claudia Rosett, "Pandering to the Islamic Conference" (*Forbes*, Feb. 18, 2010) (http://www.forbes.com/2010/02/17/rashad-hussain-islam-obama-opinions-columnists-claudia-rosett_2.html).

12. Jennifer Rubin, "Re: Obama Envoy Vouched for a Convicted Terrorist" (*Commentary, Contentions*, Feb. 17, 2010) (http://www.commentarymagazine.com/blogs/index.php/rubin/238836).

13. Gerstein, "Islam envoy retreats on terror talk"; Scott Johnson, "The Case of Rashad Hussain, Part 3"; Robert Spencer, "Rashad Hussain's Samigate" (*Jihad Watch*, Feb. 17, 2010) (http://frontpagemag.com/2010/02/17/rashad-hussain%e2%80%99s-samigate/).

14. Michelle Malkin, "The *other* stupid things John Brennan said" (Creators Syndicate, Feb. 17, 2010) (republished at Michelle Mal-

kin.com, http://michellemalkin.com/2010/02/17/national-security-nightmare-john-brennan-and-the-notorious-flying-imam/).

15. Ibid.

16. Thomas Joscelyn, "John Brennan on Gitmo Recidivism—Terrorism is not an ordinary crime" (*Weekly Standard, The Blog*, Feb. 14, 2010) (http://www.weeklystandard.com/blogs/john-brennan-gitmo-recidivism).

17. Richard Pollack, "Napolitano Meets with Muslim Brotherhood Leaders—As part of a new 'counter-radicalization' program, the Homeland Security secretary quietly met with individuals tied to the outlawed terror group" (*Pajamas Media*, Feb. 17, 2010) (http://pajamasmedia.com/blog/napolitano-meets-with-muslim-brotherhood-leaders-pjm-exclusive/).

INDEX

Abbas, Mohammed, 137
Abdallah, Akram Musa, 293
Abdallah, Salaf, 293
Abdel Rahman, Omar, 75–76 ,
    94–95, 178, 242, 258, 272, 274,
    282, 286, 327–328
Abdi, Sheikh Abdullahi, 218–219
Abdrahaman, Sidi Haji, 118–119
Abdul-Malik, Johari, 256,
    265–267, 269–270, 274, 355,
    359–360
Abdullah, King of Saudi Arabia,
    1–8, 16–17, 44, 91, 242, 252,
    261, 365; Libyan assassination
    plot against, 272

Abdulmutallab, Umar Farouk,
    365–366
Aboud, Farid, 308–309
Abu Abbas, 23
Abu Ali, Omar, 274
Abu Baker, Shukri, 139, 148, 150
Abu Ghraib, 320
Abu Khabi, 128
Abu Rideh, Mahmoud Suliman
    Ahmed, 329
Abubakar as-Saddique Mosque
    (Minneapolis), 336
ACLU, 155, 250, 343–344, 370
ACORN, 222, 225, 233–235, 263
Adams, John, 118, 243

Afghani, Jamal al-Din al-, 90
Afghanistan, al Qaeda in, 290,
    309; Muslim population in, 35,
    261; sharia in, 77, 321; Soviet
    invasion of, 167, 208, 324;
    Taliban in, 365; U.S. forces in,
    240, 268, 360–361
Aflaq, Michal, 173
Ahmad, Omar, 149–151
Ahmadi, the (Indonesia), 30, 35,
    49
Ahmadinejad, Mahmud, 162
Ahmed, Nazir, 329
Ahmed, Shirwa, 336–337
AIDS, 38, 345
Air Command and Staff College,
    311
Ajaj, Ahmed, 123
Akbar, Sergeant Hasan, 362
Akef, Mohammed Mahdi, 68–69,
    142–143
Akram, Mohamed, 58, 140–142
Al-Aqsa Martyrs Brigades, 168
Al-Arabiya, 240–241
Al-Azhar University, 71, 76, 90,
    107–109, 135, 164, 242, 248–
    249, 253, 300
Al Bakri oil dynasty, 219
Al-Haramain Islamic Foundation,
    252
Al-Jezeera, 77, 81, 86, 310
Al Qaeda, in Afghanistan, 309;
    beliefs of, 6, 8, 34, 71, 110,
    135–137; founders of, 242;
    funding of, 59, 124–125,
    268–269, 272; "Golden Chain"
    donor list, 219, 269, 324; in

Kenya, 216; and 9/11, 281; in
    Pakistan, 207; supporters in
    U.S. of, 159, 162, 274–275,
    287, 292, 349; targets of, 329;
    as terrorist network, 43, 51, 73,
    78, 113–114, 312, 358; violent
    acts of, 15, 24, 68–69, 290; in
    Yemen, 309
Al-Taqwa Bank, 59, 268
Alamoudi, Abdurahman, 272,
    274, 310
Algeria, 261
Alhazmi, Nawaf, 124
Alinsky, Saul, 9–11, 189, 221,
    226, 231–233, 236, 249; *Rules
    for Radicals*, 231, 319
Alms for Jihad, 325
Altman, Israel Elad, 73–74
American Muslim Armed Forces
    and Veterans Affairs Council,
    272
American Muslim Council, 370
American Religious Identification
    Survey, 257
American Textbook Council
    (ATC), 340–343
Aquinas, Thomas, 302
Arafat, Yasser, 38, 80, 134, 137–
    138, 145–147, 149–150, 167,
    204, 267
Arap Moi, Daniel, 198, 201, 214,
    219
Arendt, Hannah, 217
Arian, Laila al-, 367, 372
Arian, Sami al-, 128–129, 132,
    139–140, 295–296, 310, 353,
    367–372

Aristotle, 244, 302

Arizona Republic, 292

Arkes, Hadley, 257

Ashqar, Abdelhaleem, 273–274

Assad regime, 136

Associated Press, purged stories from archives, 30

Ataturk, Kemal, 61–62, 164

Atta, Mohamed, 275, 278

Auda, Salman al-, 110, 125

Australia, Lebanese gangs in, 100; Muslim "no-go" zones in, 96; Muslim views of women's attire in, 99

Averroes, Ibn Rushd, 302–303

Awad, Mahmoud, 338

Awad, Nihad, 150–152, 287, 290, 295, 353, 355

Awali, Safer al-, 110, 125

Awlaki, Anwar al-, 275, 359–360, 362–364

Ayers, Bill, 11, 204, 222, 226, 228–230, 371

Azzam, Abdullah, 242

Baath Party, 173

Bakari, Sheikh Abdukeder al-, 219–220

Bangladesh, 260

Banna, Hassan al-, on controlling education, 234; in Egypt, 74–77; and Hamas, 136; for Islamic hegemony, 80–81, 83, 85, 293; *Jihad*, 55–56; killing of, 163; *The Message of the Teachings*, 144–145; Muslim Brotherhood, 38–40, 61–68, 72, 106–108,

121, 132, 159, 171, 270; Salafism, 90, 93, 177

Baran, Zeyno, 103–104, 122, 129, 132

Barbary pirates, 118–119, 243–244, 304

Barusa, Ismail Al-, 270

Barzinji, Jamal, 132, 268, 355

Bayyoumi, Abd Al-Mu'ti, 71

BBC, 217, 312

Begin, Menachem, 166

Belafonte, Harry, 192

Benedict, Pope, speech at Regensburg, 33

Benevolence International Foundation, 124, 219

Benjamin, Daniel, *The Age of Sacred Terror*, 46

Berman, Paul, *Terror and Liberalism*, 173, 180

Bhutto, Benazir, 168, 207, 209

Bhutto, Zulkifar Ali, 168, 208

Bin Baz, Abd al-Aziz bin Abdullah, 7

Bin Laden, Abdullah (brother of Osama), 123, 268

Bin Laden, Abdullah Awad (nephew of Osama), 123–124

Bin Laden, Omar, 124

Bin Laden, Osama, in Afghanistan, 219–220; family of, 123–124; and the Flying Imams, 283, 290; and jihad, 93, 110, 154, 159, 178, 235, 360, 362; in Kenya, 8, 71; and the Muslim Brotherhood, 68, 75; Muslim views of, 26; outside

funds for, 269, 274, 287–288, 324; in Somalia, 334
Black Liberation Theology, 166, 229
Black Panthers, 166, 294
Blair, Tony, 3, 84
Blind Sheikh, the, *see* Abdel Rahman, Omar
Bork, Judge Robert, 52
Bosnia, 116, 240
Bostom, Andrew, 26, 39, 328
Boston Globe, 187–188, 198–199
Bouyeri, Mohammed, 327
Bray, Mahdi, 285, 355
Brennan, John, 373–374
Bridgeview Mosque (Chicago), 129–131
Brookings Institution, 45
Brooks, David, 239
Brown, Eric, 84, 87, 90
Brown, Gordon, 3
Brussels Journal, 98
Buenos Aires, Jewish centers bombed, 282
Burke, Edmund, 254
Burkina Faso, 263
Burlingame, Charles F. "Chic," 281
Burlingame, Debra, 281, 283–284, 290
Burton, Bill, 207
Bush, George H.W., 146, 258
Bush, George W., administration, 155, 241–242, 330, 372, 374; anti-, 208; euphemisms on Islamic matters of, 117, 253, 313–318, 320; and King

Abdullah, 7–8; murder plot against, 275; in Muslim polls, 26; Obama's opinion of, 9; at war, 163, 304

Cambridge University Press, 325
Canada, CAIR in, 279; charity from, 112; Danish cartoons in, 323; Human Rights Commissions (HRCs) in, 323–324; Muslims in, 262; Security Intelligence Service, 337; Shabaab recruitment in, 336–337; sharia proposals in, 102–103
Carmichael, Stokely, 294
Carson, Andre, 354–355
Carson, Julia, 355
Carter, Jimmy, 167
Casey, General George W., Jr., 363, 374
Castro, Fidel, 192
Center for Constitutional Rights, 162, 370
Center for Immigration Studies, 258
Chandoo, Mohammed Askari, 208
Chandoo, Mohammed Hassan, 207–208
Chavez, Hugo, 162, 229
Chicago Annenberg Challenge, 230
Chicago New Party, 222
Chicago Public Radio, 221
Chicago Tribune, 130–131, 143–144

China, Muslims in, 261
Christmas bombing attempt,
  364–365,
Churchill, Winston, 3, 299–300,
  302–304, 312, 328
Clinton, Bill, 145–147, 266–268,
  270, 328, 370; appointees, 285;
  staffing/administration, 38, 45,
  46, 272, 272, 320, 369, 374
Clinton, Hillary, 259, 266, 354
College of Europe (Bruges), 101
Columbia State University
  (Louisiana), 128
Columbia University, 151, 207;
  College, 204
Concordia University, 338
Cone, James Hal, 166, 229–230
Congressional Research Service,
  117–118
Corrie, Bruce, 338
Coughlin, Steve, 304–306, 309,
  311, 314, 316
Council on American Islamic
  Relations (CAIR), and the
  ACLU, 250; euphemisms of,
  282; and the Flying Imams,
  285, 287, 290–292; history of,
  150–155; influence of, 160,
  270, 277–280, 295–298, 317,
  333, 338, 352–353, 355, 362,
  370–371
Cox, Baroness Caroline, 328
Cumber, Sada, 372

Dairi, Husam al-, 308
Dalrymple, Theodore, 99
Dante, 323

Dar al-Hijrah Islamic Center and
  Mosque, 266–275, 289, 355,
  357, 359–360
Darfur, 98
Daskal, Jennifer, 357
Davis, Frank Marshall, 205
Dawa, 43, 83–104, 110–111, 116,
  122, 132, 137, 141, 270
De Zutter, Hank, 226–228, 230
Declaration of Independence,
  119, 257
Democratic National
  Convention, 351
Denmark, cartoons from, 91, 101,
  322–323, 336; Muslims in, 99
Dhume, Sadanand, 26
Dictionary of Islam, 46, 52
Dogs, dislike of in Islam, 338–340
Dohrn, Bernardine, 11, 204, 222,
  371
Doré, Gustave, 322–323
Dosari, Abdelrahman, 125
Dubai, 230
DuBois, W. E. B., 232
Dunham, Stanley Ann, 192–193,
  195, 207

East Africa Journal, 188
Egypt, during WWII, 134; Fouda
  murder trial, 90; immigration
  and visas to US from, 258;
  Muslim Brotherhood in, 45,
  61, 74–75, 105–109, 143, 163–
  167, 242; Muslim population
  in, 260; and Palestinians, 248–
  149; socialists in, 15; terrorists
  from, 136

Ehrenfeld, Rachel, *Funding Evil*, 324–325

"Eid in America" (short film), 255–256, 265–266, 272–273, 275, 354

Elashi, Ghassan, 139, 148, 152–153

Elbarasse, Ismail, 273, 308; and wife, 270–271

Elizabeth II, 2–3, 194

Elkadi, Ahmed, 142

Ellison, Keith, 293–297, 299, 332–333, 337, 354

Elsayed, Shaker, 144, 270

Emerson, Steven, 66, 70–71, 122–123, 152, 160, 288, 296, 308–309

England, Gordon, 305–307, 314

Erdogan, Recep Tayyip, 39

Esposito, John, 38

Ethiopia, 261; immigrants to the US from, 332; US-backed forces in, 335

European Council for Fatwa and Research (Dublin), 77, 96

European Court of Human Rights, 98

European Union, 101–102, 262

Fahd, King of Saudi Arabia, 7, 44

Faisal, King of Saudi Arabia, 142

Faja, Didmar, 293

Fallaci, Oriana, 302–304; *The Force of Reason*, 303

Fanon, Frantz, 166

Farah, Abdullahi Ugas, 333–334, 337

Farm Labor Party, 331–332

Farouk, King of Egypt, 163

Farrakhan, Louis, 230, 294, 354–355

Fatah, 24, 134, 137, 168–169

Fawwaz, Khalid al-, 123

FBI, and al-Arian, 310, 368; and CAIR, 155; counterterrorism, 154, 369; Dar al-Hijrah mosque, 268, 270–271, 274; Flying Imams, 284–285, 290, 298; and Fort Hood, 362; and Hamas, 147, 274; Holy Land Foundation case, 58, 293, 352–353; Joint Terrorism Task Force, 362; Khobar Towers, 16, 290; after 9/11, 314, 360; Palestine Committee, 150; Somali enclaves and Shabaab, 332, 335, 337; WAMY, 124–126; World Trade Towers bombing, 358

Fernandez, Alberto, 77–78

Fjordman, 98–99

Florida Board of Medicine, 142

Flying Imams, 277–298, 338, 362, 373

Ford, Gerald, 277

Fort Hood massacre, 357–365, 374

Fouda, Farag, murder of, 90–91

Foundation for Defense of Democracies, 144

Fourest, Caroline, 61–62, 73

France, Algerian immigrants to, 167; Muslim "no-go" zones in, 96; Muslim objections to national flag in, 98; Muslim population in, 262; Muslim prison population in, 96–97

Franken, Al, 332–333

Franks, Trent, 296

Freedom House, 117

Frontpage Magazine, 100

G-20 Summit (London), 2

Gaddafi, Muammar, 210–211, 219, 272

Galen, 244

Gallup Center for Muslim Studies, 347

Gartenstein-Ross, Daveed, 144–145

Garvey, Marcus, 232

Gaubatz, P. David, *Muslim Mafia*, 287–288, 290–291, 353

Geithner, Timothy, 352

Geneva Convention, 241

Georgetown University, 38, 271; Center for Contemporary Arabic Studies, 87

Gerges, Fawaz, 75

Germany, population of, 20, 262

Gertz, Bill, 305

Ghana, 195

Ghazali, Mohammed al-, 90–92

Gibbs, Robert, 4

Glick, Caroline, 247–248

Global Relief Foundation, 153, 291

Goethe, Johann Wolfgang von, 233

Goldberg, Jonah, 222

Goldsmith, Lord Peter Henry, 330

Great Britain, *see* United Kingdom

Guantanamo Bay, 31, 124, 241, 309, 320, 330, 374–375

Gulf War (1991), 24, 85, 138, 146

Haddad, Rabih, 153

Haff, Police Officer Jerry, murder of, 294

Hage, Wadih El-, 290

Haiti, earthquake relief for, 111–113

Halevi, Jonathan Dahoah, 68

Hamas, fundamental beliefs of, 24; funding for, 59, 131, 251, 266, 268, 270, 279, 291, 295, 310; history of, 134–155, 167–169; Izz el-Din al-Qassam Brigades, 137, 140; raising money for, 308, 343; rally, 327–328; terrorism financing of, 371; as terrorist organization, 73, 114–115, 129, 160, 235, 248, 272–274, 317, 351, 358, 368

Hamdi, Yasser, 370–371

Hamid, Wahid, 207

Hamilton, David F., 350

Hammami, Omar (aka Abu Mansour al-Amriki), 336

Haniyeh, Ismail, 136

Hanjour, Hani, 124, 275, 290, 359–360

Hanooti, Mohammed al-, 274, 359

Hariri, Rafik, murder of, 308
Harris, David, 337
Harvard University, 189, 193, 195; Law School, 204
Hasan, Nidal Malik, 357–365
Hassan, Fatuma, 338
Hathout, Hassan, 159
Hathout, Maher, 159
Hazmi, Nawaf al-, 275, 359–360
Hezbollah, 43, 73, 114, 116, 137, 167, 235, 272, 291, 317, 358
Hippocrates, 244
Hirsi Ali, Ayaan, 29, 101, 327
Hitchens, Christopher, 118–119, 243–244
Hitler, Adolf, 134, 162, 248, 256; *Mein Kampf*, 256, 327, 329
Hizb ut-Tahrir, 349–350; "Khalifa Convention," 349
Holder, Eric, 278, 320, 375
Holocaust, the, 86, 247; deniers, 256
Holy Land Foundation (HLF), 139, 147–148, 150, 154, 251, 279, 291; case, 137, 160, 292–293, 295, 352; trial, 58, 351
Hooper, Douglas aka Ibrahim, 152, 154, 278–279
Horowitz, David, 13–14, 368
Howard University, 273
Hudson Institute, 73, 84; Center on Islam, Democracy, and the Future of the Modern World, 51
Hughes, Thomas Patrick, 46
Human Events, 352
Huntington, Samuel, 35–36

Hurd, Tyler, 339–340
Hurgronje, C. Snouck, 26–27
Hussain, Rashad, 370–373
Hussayen, Saleh, 124–126
Hussayen, Sami Omar, 125–126
Hussein, Hesham, 343
Husseini, Haj Amin el-, 134
Hyman, Mark, 214, 220

Ibn Ishaq, 31
Ibn Warraq, 29, 322
Ibrahim, Raymond, 114–115, 119
Ihsanoglu, Ekmeleddin, 351
Ikhwan, the, *see* Muslim Brotherhood
Ila Filastin (IAP magazine), 148
India, 168; Mumbai hotel bombings, 282
Indonesia, Bali nightclub bombing, 282; Islamic fundamentalists in, 30–31, 35; Muslim population in, 260; Obama in, 202–204, 206–208, 260
International Association of Muslim Scholars, 90
International Institute of Islamic Thought (IIIT), 131–132, 142, 268, 310, 353–355
International Islamic Relief Organization (IIRO), 272
Investigative Project on Terrorism, 296
Iran, under Ahmadinejad, 162, 350; bombing of Khobar Towers, 16; charity from, 113; communism in, 15; Islam in,

35, 73; Muslim population,
260; 1979 revolution in, 15, 47,
127, 208, 305
Iraq, Iraqi forces in, 85; Muslim
population in, 261; U.S. forces
in, 6, 69, 71, 77, 211, 240, 350,
360–361
Islam, Hesham, 305–312, 317
Islamic American Relief Agency
(IARA), 274, 343
Islamic Assembly of North
America (IANA), 125–126, 153
Islamic Association of Palestine
(IAP), 129, 138, 142, 147–152,
266, 272, 274, 295, 359
Islamic Center of Gaza, 139
Islamic Center of Tucson, 287–
293
Islamic Center of Washington,
117
Islamic Circle of North America
(ICNA), 292
Islamic Committee for Palestine,
368
Islamic Relief Worldwide, 343
Islamic Saudi Academy (Virginia),
274
Islamic Society of North America
(ISNA), 127–128, 139, 142,
251, 292, 308, 310–312, 351–
355, 362–363, 371, 376
Islamic Views, 122
Islamism, 16–17, 19–41 153, 155
Israel, Arab arguments against,
247–248; Arabs in, 256; bin
Laden on, 72; and Egypt, 146;
elimination of, 266; imputed

racism in, 5; jihad against, 38;
and Palestine, 6, 86, 146–148,
256; as scapegoat, 31, 84;
terrorism in, 22–24

Jaber, Rafeeq, 151
Jacobs, Sally, 188
Japan, 112
Jarrett, Valerie, 128, 352
Jasser, Dr. M. Zuhdi, 161, 296,
317
Jay, John, 118
Jefferson, Thomas, 118–119, 304
Jermas, Joran, 329
Jerusalem Center for Public
Affairs, 68
Jesus, 10
Johnson, Ian, 51, 59
Johnson, Paul, 174, 307
Johnson, Scott, 286–287, 294
Jones, Van, 13
Jordan, 128, 248
Jordan, Michael, 225
Julaidan, Wael Hamza, 288–289
Justice Department, under
Clinton, 272, 328, 369; and
Holy Land Foundation
case,137, 152–153, 242, 251,
279, 292, 295–296, 351; and
international terrorist groups,
335; and ISNA, 128; and the
Muslim Brotherhood, 242;
under Obama 241, 375; and the
Safa Group, 311

Kaine, Tim, 273
Kaiser family, murders of, 23, 65

Kennedy, Ted, 258
Kennedy family, 193
Kenya, 187–199, 213–220;
    Muslim population in, 261
Kenyatta, Jomo, 187, 191, 194–
    199, 201, 213, 220
Kepel, Gilles, 106–107
Kersten, Katherine, 343–345
Khafagi, Bassem, 153
Khalidi, Rashid, 204
Khalife, Mohammed Jamal, 124
Khamenei, Ayatollah Ali, 350–
Khomeini, Ayatollah Ruhollah,
    15, 127, 173, 208, 322
Kibaki, Mwai, 214–216, 218, 220
Kimball, Roger, 322, 325
Kind Hearts (charity), 291
King, Jr., Martin Luther, 232,
    250
King, Peter, 285
King Abdulaziz University
    (Jeddah), 110
King Fahd Defense Academy
    (Saudi Arabia), 303
Klausen, Jytte, 322–323, 326
Klobuchar, Amy, 331–332
Klonsky, Mike, 204
Koran, the, on apostasy, 202–
    203; used as constitution, 7;
    history of, 31–34, 76, 92; on
    infidels, 6–8, 318; on Jews,
    137, 289; memorizing, 76, 371;
    pacific selections from, 287,
    on personal property, 183;
    swearing on the, 332; "Verse
    of the Sword," 34, 53, 70;
    violence advocated in, 46, 115,

245–246, 320, 326–327, 352;
    on women, 97, 300–302
Krikorian, Mark, 258
Kristof, Nicholas, 204
Kucinich, Dennis, 354
Kuntar, Samir, 23
Kurtz, Stanley, 235
Kuwait, American military in,
    24; Muslim Brotherhood in,
    128–129; Palestinian refugees
    in, 128
Kyl, Jon, 296

Lapkin, Sharon, 100
League of Nations, 248
Lebanon, Hamas in, 140; Marine
    barracks bombing, 282; murder
    of prime minister of, 308
Lekovic, Edina, 159
Levant, Ezra, *Shakedown*, 323
Levin, Mark, 223, 257–258
Levitt, Matthew, 114, 135, 140;
    Hamas, 116–117
Lewis, Bernard, 46, 96
Libel tourism, 324–325
Liberation Theology, 166
Liberia, immigrants to the US
    from, 332
Libya, 153, 210, 219, 272
Lincoln, Abraham, 249
Lippert, Mark, 214
Little Rock recruiting station
    murder, 362
Logan Act, 216

Mafia, 46
Mahfouz, Khalid bin, 324

Malcolm X, 231–232
Malkin, Michelle, 374
Mao, 123; Maoism, 204
Marayati, Salam al-, 159–160
Marx, Karl, 171–172, 181–182;
    Communist Manifesto, 192
Marxism, 13, 166, 171–185, 196,
    214, 229
Marzook, Mousa abu, 128–129,
    131, 136, 139–140, 147–148,
    152–154, 270, 274; Defense
    Committee, 272
Mattson, Ingrid, 351–352
Mau Mau rebellion, 190–191, 195
Mauritania, slavery in, 300
Mboya, Tom, 191–196
McCarthy, Andrew, *Willful
    Blindness*, 40, 47, 75, 293, 325
McDougal Littell, 341–342
McKinstry, Leo, 97
Mitchell, Robert P., *The Society of
    Muslim Brothers*, 55, 66–67
Mehdi, Shahid, 99
Midhar, Khaled al-, 124, 359
Miliband, David, 101–102
Million Man March, 230
Mishal, Khalid al-, 128–129,
    135–141, 291
Mogahed, Dalia, 347–349
Mohammed, and Aisha, 301;
    cartoons about, 322–323, 336;
    history of, 27, 33–34, 37, 46,
    53, 62, 81, 85, 122, 178, 288;
    on jihad, 115; on killing Jews,
    289–290; as prophet, 10, 30–
    31, 49, 76, 246, 361; on raping
    wartime captives, 301

Mohammed, Elijah, 355
Mohammed, Khalid Sheikh, 178
Mohammed, Sheik Faiz, 99
Mohammed, Warith Deen, 355
Mohammedi, Omar, 285
Montgomery, Judge Ann, 285–
    287
Morocco, 260
Moses, 10
Moussa, Bashir, 129
Mubarak regime, 45, 91
Mukasey, Michael, 314
Munich Olympics, 167
Murbaha financing, 345–346
Musharraf, Pervez, 26, 209
Muslim American Society (MAS),
    270–271, 274, 284–285, 338–
    339, 343–344, 352, 354–355,
    362, 376
Muslim Arbitration Council, 97
Muslim Brotherhood, anti-
    Semitism in, 204; beliefs
    and strategies of, 91, 93–95,
    161, 171, 211, 224, 226, 236,
    270–275, 287–288, 346, 355,
    360; in England, 365; founding
    in Egypt, 15, 38, 43–46, 54–
    81,159; and Hamas, 134–136,
    138–155, 251, 266; and the
    Holy Land Foundation, 291–
    293; influence with Homeland
    Security, 376; at Obama's Cairo
    speech, 242, 247, 351–352;
    plans for worldwide dominance
    of, 83–84, 87, 119, 303–305,
    310, 312, 314; playbook, 57–58,
    140–141, 268, 279; population

projections from, 263; *The Project*, 60, 268, 293; and Saudi Arabia, 105–110, 113, 116, 121–132, 367–370; in Syria, 308; training, 336; website, 347
Muslim Public Affairs Council (MPAC), 159–161, 317, 352, 376
Muslim Students Association (MSA), 121–122, 126–128, 132, 142–145, 268, 271, 336, 365, 367, 369–371; *al-Talib*, 159
Muslim World League, 108, 111, 124, 365
Mutaween (Commission for Promotion of Virtue and Prevention of Vice), 7
Mutua, Dr. Alfred, 216
Muwafaq Foundation, 324
Myers, LTC Joseph C., 60, 311–312, 315

Nada, Youssef, suspected money-laundering of, 59–60; as terrorist, 268, 293
Naguib, General Muhammad, 163
Nahdlatul Ulama, 31, 35
Napolitano, Janet, 320, 352, 376
Nasrallah, Sheikh Hassan, 116, 291
Nasser, Gamal Abdel, 15, 75, 105–109, 134–135, 163–165, 167
Nation of Islam, 294, 354–355

National Association of Muslim Chaplains, 267
National Geographic Association, 285
National Lawyers Guild, 370
Naval Postgraduate School, 307
Nawaz, Nasreen, 349–350
NBC News, 363
Netherlands, the, Geert Wilders case, 326–330; Muslim objections to national flag in, 98; treatment of Hirsi Ali in, 101, 327
New York City Police Department, 281–282
New York Times, 90, 204, 231
New York University, 373
Newsweek, 323
Nidesand, Ruth, 195
Nigeria, 261
9/11, aftermath, 117, 124, 251, 305, 322, 370; anniversary, 347–348; attacks, 3, 51, 59, 69, 71, 125, 154, 273, 287, 290, 304, 369; Commission, 122–123, 284, 290; Flying Imams parallels, 280–281, 283–284, 286, 373; hijackers, 16, 110, 267, 275, 359–360; as inside job, 13; Israel suspected in, 159; Pentagon flight, 275, 281, 285, 290; reactions to, 336, 352
Njoroge, Issac Njenga, 199
Nkrumah, Kwame, 195
Nobel Peace Prize, 146

North American Imams
Federation (NAIF), 283, 291–
293, 295, 297
North American Islamic Trust
(NAIT), 126–129, 139, 142,
153, 268
North Carolina State University,
128
Nur-Allah Islamic Center
(Indianapolis), 355

O'Brien, Conor Cruise, 172
O'Neill, John P., 154
O'Sullivan, John, 97
Obama, Abango "Roy," 195, 218
Obama, Auma, 195
Obama, Barack Hussein,
and ACORN, 233–236;
administration, 241, 275, 350,
352, 371, 373, 375; Advisory
Council on Faith-Based and
Neighborhood Partnerships,
348–350; *After Alinsky*,
231–232; al-Arabiya interview,
240; *The Audacity of Hope*, 13;
bowing of, 1–5, 8, 17, 44, 91,
242; Cairo speech, 242–250,
253–254, 259, 288, 351, 370,
372; campaign contributions
to, 210; on Christmas
bombing attempt, 365–365;
as community organizer, 263,
319; on the Constitution,
224; *Dreams from My Father*,
189, 203, 205, 207, 218; early
history, 201–237; euphemisms
on Islamic matters of, 34, 313,

318–320; Fort Hood massacre,
359; French tv interview, 259;
friends of, 11; grandmother,
227; healthcare, 157–162,
355; in Illinois legislature, 12,
221, 231; and Islamists, 19,
241–243; Kenyan relations
of, 2, 187–199; Kenyan trip,
213–217; Marxism and, 2, 13;
middle name of, 1–2, 9–10,
187; Million Man March,
230–231; and MPAC, 157–159,
161; Nairobi speech, 215–216;
and national security, 278; in
Pakistan, 208–210; religion
and, 11–13, 201–204, 211–212;
Selma march, 193, 206;
spending of, 14; UK views,
1–3; views on as presidential
candidate, 239; White House
staffing of, 13, 128
Obama, Barak, Sr., 187–199,
201–202
Obama, Kezia, 195
Obama, Michelle, 2, 206, 218,
226
Obama, Onyango, 189–191
Occidental College, 204, 207
Occupied Land Fund/
Committee, 139, 147; *see also*
Holy Land Foundation
Odeh, Abdul Azziz, 129
Odierno, General Ray, 350
Odinga, Jaramongi Oginga, 191–
192, 194–200, 214, 218
Odinga, Raila, 192, 213–220, 227,
232, 235

Olmert, Ehud, 23

Omeish, Esam, 271–274, 355

Omeish, Mohammed, 272

Organization of the Islamic
Conference (OIC), 350–351,
364, 372; "Cairo Declaration,"
321

Oslo Accord, 146, 270, 295

Ottoman Empire, 4, 26, 61

Owatonna High School (MN),
Somali students in, 340

'Owhali, Mohammed Daoud al-,
8

Oxford Centre for Islamic
Studies, 77

Padilla, José, 370–371

Pajamas Media, 376

Pakistan, al Qaeda in, 334;
banned WAMY, 124; 167–169;
Muslim League, 209; Muslim
population in, 35, 260; Obama's
visit to, 207–209; sharia in, 26,
304

Palestine, homeland "right of
return" claims, 79, 248, 368;
Intifada, 80, 133–134, 145,
211; and Israel, 6, 23–24,
129, 133–138, 243; jihad in,
273; liberation of, 122; under
occupation, 310; suicide
bombers from, 113, 240

Palestine Committee, 139, 147–
148, 150–151

Palestine Liberation Front, 23

Palestine Liberation Organization
(PLO), 80, 134, 146, 167–168,
204

Palestinian Islamic Jihad (PIJ),
129, 146, 167, 268, 295, 317,
368–369

Palin, Sarah, 208

Parks, Rosa, 285

Patriot Act, 154, 370

PBS, 9–10

Pearl, Daniel, 282

Pearson, Malcolm, 328

Pell, George, Cardinal, 35

Pelosi, Nancy, 158

Pew Research Center, 22, 257

Pham, Peter, 220

Phillips, Melanie, 247–248, 250

Pipes, Daniel, 153–154, 328–329,
338

Plato, 243

Poitier, Sidney, 192

Pollack, Kenneth, 45, 313

Poole, Patrick, 59–60

Powerline (website), 286

Prentice-Hall, 342–343

Priest, Tim, 100

Qadi, Yasin al-, 324

Qaradawi, Sheikh Yusuf al-,
background of, 76–81, 242;
banned from US, 78; and the
Muslim Brotherhood, 58–59,
69–72, 83–96, 291, 360; "Sharia
and Life," 77; and the State
Department, 280; teachings

of, 74, 108–109, 116, 145, 180, 226, 303, 322, 327

Qassam Brigades, *see* Hamas

Qatar, 77; University, 81

Qazali organization, 350–351

Qudhaieen, Muhammed al-, 290

Qutb, Mohammed, 110, 121

Qutb, Sayyid, 54, 75, 77, 80, 90, 105–110, 113, 123, 163–165, 171–185, 196, 224, 234; *Social Justice in Islam*, 180

Rabbani, Shaykh Faraz, 113–114

Rajhi, Sulaiman Abdul-Azziz, 269

Ramadan, Said, 93

Ramadan, Tariq, 93–94

Rantisi, Abdel Azziz al-, 135

Reagan National Airport, 284–285

Red Crescent, 115

Red Cross, 343; International Committee (ICRC), 112–113

Reid, Richard, 287

Rice, Condoleezza Rice, 23–24, 30, 315

Rida, Rashid, 62, 90

Robespierre, Maximilien, 178

Robinson, Jackie, 192

Robinson, Rachel, 192

Roman Catholicism, 33, 49

Roosevelt, Franklin Delano, 222–224, 314

Rose, Charlie, 239

Rosett, Claudia, 112–113, 306–310

Rousseau, Jean-Jacques, 172–184; *The Social Contract*, 173

Roy, Olivier, 135

Royer, Randall, 153

Rushdie, Salman, 322

SAAR Foundation, 269, 311

Sadat, Anwar al-, 146, 165–168, 258

Saddam Hussein, 109, 146, 166, 283, 306

Safa Group, 311

Safi, Louay, 310–312, 317, 363

Said, Edward, 151, 204

Said, Jamal, 131

St. Cloud State University, 339–340

St. Cloud Times, 339

Salafism, 32–33, 61, 64, 90, 93, 105–107, 167, 177, 334

Salah, Mohammad, 131, 270

Salah, Samir, 268–269

Salameh, Mohammed, 272

Sarkozy, Nicolas, 4, 102

Saud, Muhammad ibn, 6

Saudi Arabia, American military in, 24; Armed Forces Printing Press, 122; and bin Laden, 136; British and, 4; as burial place of Ghazali, 91; charity from 113, 252, 272; funding from, 58–59, 87, 107, 121–132, 134, 153, 272, 288, 324, 325–326; history of, 4–6; immigration and visas to US from, 258;

Khobar Towers bombing, 16, 282, 290, 304; Korans printed by, 183; Ministry of Islamic Affairs, Endowment and Dawa, 122; Muslim Brotherhood and, 109–111, 116–118, 121–123, 167, 268, 365, 367; Muslim population in, 261; oil in, 4; royal family, 89; slavery in, 300; subjects in Guantanamo Bay, 309; US and, 2, 4; Wahhabism in, 6–8, 32–36, 63, 106–107; Wassatiyyah in, 44

Scarborough, Rowan, 352

Schwartz, Stephen, 139

Shabaab, al- (Somalian terrorist group), 334–337

Shadegg, John, 296

Shahin, Oday, 292–293

Shahin, Sheikh Omar, 287–289, 291–293, 297–298, 373–374; *The Muslim Family in Western Society*, 292

Shalawi, Hamdan al-, 290

Sharia, creep, 95–104; defined and applied, 7, 87, 93, 179, 202, 209, 211, 246, 249, 316, 321, 348; enclaves, 40, 103–104, 292, 331–346; in Kenya, 213, 219; organizations, 376; planned spread of, 25–26, 44, 46–47, 53–56, 64, 372; scholars of, 32, 287; in the US, 19, 355, 373

Sheikh, Mohammed Adam El-, 274

Sheikhosman, Abdi, 337–338

Shibh, Ramzi bin al-, 275

Shikaki, Fathi, 129

Siddiqi, Faisal Aqtab, 97

Simon, Steven, *The Age of Sacred Terror*, 46

Sistani, Grand Ayatollah Ali al-, 6

Siyash, 43, 45, 75

Smith, Jacqui, 30, 53, 329

Smylie, James H., 174

Socialist International, 222

Soetoro Mangunharjo, Lolo, 202–204

Soetoro-Ng, Maya, 204, 207

Soliah, Kathleen, 295

Somalia, al Qaeda in, 334–336; "Black Hawk Down" murder and mutilation, 145, 282, 334; immigrants to the US from, 331–340; sharia in, 334; taxi drivers from, 338–339

Soomro, Ahmad Mian, 209

Soomro, Muhammad Mian, 209

Soros, George, funding by, 159

South America, 112

Southern Illinois University, 128

Spain, as al-Andalus, 211, 341; Madrid bombing in, 282

Spencer, Robert, 34, 53, 99–100, 244, 246, 300–301

Sperry, Paul, 267–269, 309; *Muslim Mafia*, 287–288, 290–291, 353

Stalin, Joseph, 166

Star Tribune (Minneapolis-St. Paul), 337, 343

Stark, Pete, 354

Stern, Sol, 233–236

Steyn, Mark, *America Alone*, 323
Stowasser, Barbara, 87–88
Student Islamic Society, 365
Students for a Democratic
  Society (SDS), 204
Submission (film), 101, 327
Sudan, 274; National Islamic
  Front, 159; rape in, 98, 100,
  300; slavery in, 300, 328
Sulaiman, Mahmud, 293
"Sunni Path," 113
Sweden, loss of police control
  in Muslim parts of, 100–101;
  Muslim objections to national
  flag in, 98
Syeed, Sayyid, 132
Symbionese Liberation Army,
  295
Syria, 136, 153; Muslim
  Brotherhood in, 308

Taiba International Aid
  Association, 268–269
Taliban, 168, 207, 349, 365
Tantawi, Muhammad Sayyid, 242
Tarek ibn Ziyad Academy
  (TIZA), 343–345
Tarin, Haris, 161
Thomas, Cal, 23
Tiger Hawk, 302
Time (magazine), 195
Times (London), 22
Timmerman, Ken, 210
Treaty of Tripoli, 243–244
Turabi, Hassan al-, 159
Turkey, 35, 39, 61–62, 101, 164,
  166, 262

Twin Towers, 15, 53
Tyson's Chicken, 333

Ubeid, Mansur Al-Rifa'i, 71
Umar, Warith Deen, 267, 352
United Association for Studies
  and Research (UASR), 139,
  142, 147, 150, 153
United Kingdom, Birmingham
  mosque, 101; and Geert
  Wilders, 328–330; Heathrow,
  262; Home Office, 329; Islam
  Channel, 348; libel laws, 324–
  325; "Muslimah Dilemma,"
  348–349; Muslims in, 20–22,
  97–98; Muslim objections to
  national flag in, 98; popularity
  of "Mohammed" as name in,
  20, 37; Obama's visit to, 1–4,
  44, 242; Office of National
  Statistics, 20; population of,
  20, 262; prison population in,
  99; 7/7 bombings in, 22, 282;
  sharia in, 26; terrorists from
  and indoctrinated in, 365–366,
  376
United Nations, General
  Assembly, 146; Human
  Rights Council (HRC), 322;
  resolution, 219; terrorist
  designations by, 59; Universal
  Declaration of Human Rights,
  321; U.S. contributions to
  relief efforts of, 112
United States, Air Force, 16,
  262; "Africa Priority Three
  Program," 332; charity from,

112–113; Christmas in, 5; CIA, 241; Constitution, 5, 48, 158, 181, 223–225, 258, 349, 372 ; Customs and Border Protection (CBP), 279, 353; Defense, 362–363; "Diversity Visa" program, 258; FBI, *see main entry*; First Amendment, 286, 297; IRS, 139, 152; Homeland Security (DHS), 163, 259, 277–280, 297, 314–319, 352–353, 373, 376; International Visitor Program, 354; Jews in, 256, 307; Kenyan alliance, 216; Marine Corps., 119, 267–268; Muslims in, 21–22, [more], 331–346, Muslim population estimates in, 255–264; Nairobi embassy bombing, 8, 71, 123, 154, 159, 216, 272, 282, 290, 304, 334; National Intelligence Directorate, 319; Justice Department, *see main entry*; National Security Agency, 155; Office of Management and Budget, 319; religion in, 48–49; Senate Banking Committee, 139; Saudi religious financing in, 111–118; Shabaab recruitment in, 336–337; State Department, 210, 255, 258, 274–275, 283, 314, 332, 337, 354; Supreme Court, 181, 221–222; Tanzania embassy bombing, 71, 123, 154, 159, 272, 282, 290, 304,

334; textbooks in, 340–343; Transportation Security Administration (TSA), 277–282, 317; Treasury, 274, 288, 324, 352
University College (London), 365
University of Hawaii, 192–193, 202–203
University of Illinois Urbana-Champaign, 121
University of Maryland, poll, 25–26
University of Medina, 110
University of Minnesota, 337; Law School, 294
University of Nairobi, 215
University of South Alabama, 336
University of South Florida, 128
U.S.S. *Cole*, 304

Van Gogh, Theo, murder of, 101, 327
Venezuela, 162, 229
Voice of America, 274

Wahhab, Muhammad ibn Abd al-, 6, 63
Wahhabism, 6–7, 32–36, 63, 93, 287, 289
Wahid, Abdurrahman, 25, 31–36, 53
Wall Street Journal, 31, 35, 51
Walter Reed Hospital, 359, 361
Washington, Booker T., 232
Washington Post, 126
Washington Times, 214, 288, 305

Wassatiyya, 44, 84, 86–87, 89–90, 93
Wayne State University, 294
Weather Underground, 204, 222, 371
Weiss, Michael, 322
West, Diana, 333–334
Westergaard, Kurt, 336
Wilders, Geert, 326–330; *Fitna*, 326, 328–329
Wolfowitz, Paul, 307
World Assembly of Muslim Youth (WAMY), 122–126, 132, 268; "Military Lessons in the Jihad Against the Tyrants," 123
World Bank, 112
World Health Organization, 157
World Islamic Study Enterprise (WISE), 132
World Public Opinion poll, 25–26
World Trade Center, 1993 bombing of, 47, 75, 123, 145, 154, 178, 272, 282, 293, 305, 358; security chief of, 154
World War I, 26, 61
Wright, Jeremiah, 11–12, 166, 218, 226, 229–230

Wright, Lawrence, 75–76
Wurzelbacher, Joe "the Plumber," 222, 224, 236

Yaktun, Fathi, *To Be a Muslim*, 145
Yale University, Law, 370; Press, 322–323, 326
Yasin, Khalid, 345
Yassin, Sheikh Ahmed, 135, 139, 150, 272
Yemen, 128, 258, 261; al Qaeda in, 309, 336, 360, 363–365
Yousef, Ramzi, 123

Zadari, Asif Ali, 209
Zaidi, Supna, 349
Zakaria, Fareed, 323
Zakat, 111–115, 117, 174, 250–251, 346
Zaman, Asad, 343
Zawahiri, Ayman al-, 75–76, 136, 178, 335
Zaydan, Dr. Salih, 71
Zia ul-Haq, General, 168, 208